Hunters of the Northern Ice

HUNTERS OF THE NORTHERN ICE

RICHARD K. NELSON

The University of Chicago Press

CHICAGO AND LONDON

International Standard Book Number: 0–226–57175–0 (clothbound)
Library of Congress Catalog Card Number: 78–75136

The University of Chicago Press, Chicago 60637
The University of Chicago Press, Ltd., London

Printed in the United States of America

TO

the people of Wainwright, Alaska,

and to my parents

Contents

PART I
The Setting

PART II

The Biological Environment

Illustrations

A hunter scanning for polar bears
Sharpening the butchering tools
Butchering walrus

Foreword

The Eskimos are a remarkably successful division of mankind. Their ability to adapt to difficult circumstances and to expand is accurately reflected in their geographic distribution. They stretch longitudinally around a large sector of the circumpolar world, and latitudinally from the subarctic into the high Arctic. With their relatives, the Aleuts, they occupy the longest linear distance of any single racial and linguistic group in the world. Although this unique geographic distribution provides objective and conclusive evidence of their ability to expand, rather than simply survive, it does not automatically elucidate the processes of adaptation which are responsible.

For several thousands of years Eskimos have been masters of marine hunting. They used methods that were successful for an astonishing range of sea mammals, from the small ringed seal to the large bowhead whales. Fishing, fowling, and land hunting also were important activities in their hunting system. Beginning in western Alaska, on the coasts of the now submerged Bering Land Bridge some fifteen thousand years ago, the ancestors of the present Eskimos and Aleuts expanded into the Aleutians and from Alaska into Siberia, Canada, and Greenland. The prehistoric record provides evidence that the Eskimos are not newcomers to the Arctic. Present patterns of adaptation have considerable time depth, and there have obviously been enough generations for revolutionary agencies to translate the effects of their behavior and of the environmental stresses of climate, nutrition, and disease into the composition of the Eskimos as we see them today.

In a sense the Eskimos have conducted the crucial experiment in human adaptability. They magnificently illustrate the way in which man, the species, spent 99 percent of his evolutionary history as a hunter, and in doing so prepared himself for the rapid acquisition of civilization at many different places in the world. The peculiar notion that hunting is only a "subsistence technique" rather than a more comprehensive and integrating bio-behavior system with complex physical and intellectual components is still commonly represented in many textbooks. As the reader of this volume will come to appreciate, hunting is a complex activity with many ramifications in childhood training, scanning, stalking, killing, retrieval, and distribution. Without the intellectual challenge of learning animal behavior and anatomy well enough to depend upon the proceeds of hunting for food, clothing, and other fabricational purposes, human beings would not have become human; they would have remained similar to their vegetarian relatives, the gorilla and chimpanzee.

The experiential and performance world in which the Eskimo lives is configured by his habitual activities and by the environmental elements to require a high degree of physical fitness to meet extraordinary peak load demands, and to require a constant monitoring of sensory information. Kayak hunting and ice hunting share the fact that the hunter is operating on a moving surface. Unlike solid land it is a permeable surface through which he may pass rapidly and disastrously. Not only is the surface on which the Eskimo may spend some one-fourth of his life constantly moving, it also lacks the gross complexity of most other geographic zones. The visual cues are small, consisting of subtle changes in the color of the ice, of small patches of snow which reveal wind direction and force, of water texture and slight indications of tidal changes and currents. Even these minimal cues may be obscured by fog, snow, wind, rain, glare, darkness, and low level contrasts that camouflage the animal as well. The anxiety levels generated by this rigorous life have serious implications for the community as a whole.

In general, it is fair to say that the Eskimo must perform in an arena which has many high-level constraints on behavior and which offers little guiding information. Penalties for mistakes are prompt and drastic. Death in cold water is measured in minutes because of the accelerated heat loss in water as compared with air. The Eskimo concern with orientation and sequence, their unusual mechanical abilities, inventiveness, navigational skills, their ethological and anatomical knowledge, and the structure of the language itself, represent an intellectual adaptation with a neurophysiological base and important social and genetic correlates.

The systematic study of hunting and travel imposes unique prerequisites. The observer must be trained by the Eskimos, he must travel with Eskimo hunters and be able to help rather than hinder the efforts of his more knowledgeable Eskimo colleagues. This in turn requires a broad background amenable to Eskimo tuition, in addition to physical agility, endurance, and a substantial sense of humor adequate to withstand and enjoy the joking and ridicule which the Eskimos may use as part of their instructional system. Hunting behavior cannot be studied in the warmth of a kitchen; it must be studied where and when it takes place. Mr. Nelson's previous experience in biological and archeological studies on Kodiak Island and on Anangula and Umnak Island in the Aleutians were a useful part of the background he brought to his Eskimo tutors. It should be noted that the Wainwright Eskimos enjoy a reputation as able hunters and take considerable pride in both their skills and their reputation for those skills. The Eskimos were placed in the position of being authorities in an area in which they were in fact the ultimate authorities. This is the same honest approach employed by an earlier visitor to Wainwright, Knud Rasmussen, who is well remembered.

This is a study of human adaptation to a specific group of animals, birds, and fish in a harsh environment in which an extensive body of techniques and knowledge must be systematically employed. The results of this study range from intensely practical survival information, of use to travelers, downed pilots, stranded seamen, and scientific researchers, to more theoretical human ecological concerns. Throughout Mr. Nelson has maintained the goal of reproducibility so that another person could follow the necessary steps in their proper sequence and thus utilize the information successfully. It is based upon direct observation and actual participation in the activities.

A multidisciplinary investigation of Wainwright has now been launched under the aegis of the International Biological Program. Various studies are being prosecuted on genetics, cardiovascular system, dentition, physiology, nutrition, growth, epidemiology, genealogical matrix, demography, and social culture. Mr. Nelson's study serves as a foundation work for these other studies because of its quality and the natural relations between the data of several different disciplines.

WILLIAM S. LAUGHLIN

Acknowledgments

The research on which this monograph is based was conducted in northern Alaska during the winter of 1964–65 and the summer of 1966. Financial support was provided by the United States Air Force, Arctic Aeromedical Laboratory, at Fort Wainwright, Alaska, under contract number AF 41(609)–2613 and AF(609)–3200. Additional support was given by the Office of Naval Research, Naval Arctic Research Laboratory, at Point Barrow, Alaska.

My major professor, Dr. William S. Laughlin, Department of Anthropology, University of Wisconsin, acted as the Principal Investigator for this research. Dr. Laughlin played a major role in the project, shaping its original design and formulating major aspects of its approach and implementation. I am indebted to him for his enthusiastic support and thoughtful guidance during this study and throughout my university career.

Dr. Frederick A. Milan, formerly Project Officer and Chief, Environmental Protection Section, Arctic Aeromedical Laboratory, United States Air Force, Fort Wainwright, Alaska, initiated the sea-ice study, acted as contract monitor, and gave freely of his assistance.

I should also like to thank the Naval Arctic Research Laboratory and its capable director Dr. Max C. Brewer, for providing facilities and excellent logistic support during the fieldwork.

Mr. and Mrs. G. Ray Bane, Bureau of Indian Affairs teachers at Wainwright for three years, gave invaluable assistance and companionship, and contributed greatly to the smooth beginnings of the study. Fieldwork during the summer of 1966 was conducted in direct collaboration with Mr. Bane, who did a parallel study on Eskimo utilization of inland resources. He gave invaluable assistance by sharing his companionship and exchanging observations throughout this project.

I am grateful to Mr. Kenneth I. Taylor, Department of Anthropology, University of Wisconsin, for his advice and assistance. Mrs. Carol Knott, University of Wisconsin, most capably directed all matters of business and administration, and gave her helpful friendship and advice. My thanks, also, to Mr. H. Cameron Wilson, Department of Botany, University of Utah, who edited part of the manuscript.

My parents, Mr. and Mrs. Robert K. Nelson, gave their continuous, unfailing encouragement during the course of the fieldwork. They also did much of the typing and editing of the manuscript. Through their assistance and support, they have contributed immeasurably to whatever success this fieldwork might have achieved.

To the people of Barrow, Point Hope, and especially Wainwright, Alaska, I feel the deepest debt of obligation and gratitude. Their willingness to share their friendship, knowledge, and way of life has made each visit a most pleasurable one. This book is theirs much more than it is mine.

I would like to extend special thanks to the family of Mr. and Mrs. Waldo Bodfish for their friendship and hospitality. Mr. Bodfish gave generously of his time and his knowledge during many hours over tea in his home. Mr. Wayne Bodfish was an excellent friend and teacher. Homer, Dempsey, David, and Barry Bodfish were good hunting companions and friends.

Mr. and Mrs. Weir Negovanna and Mr. Burrell Negovanna were especially kind and helpful. I would also like to thank Mr. Wesley Ekak, Mr. Alva Nashoalook, Mr. Raymond Aguvluk, Mr. Glenn Shoulda, and Mr. Peter Tagarook, who contributed so much in making my stay in Wainwright an informative and enjoyable one.

In Point Hope, invaluable assistance and hospitality were given by Mr. and Mrs. Antonio Weber. I also wish to thank Mr. and Mrs. Bob Tuckfield of Point Hope and Mr. Peter Sovolik of Barrow.

Orthography

The phonemic system utilized was adapted from that of Mr. D. H. Webster, who conducted extensive research in Wainwright under the auspices of the Summer Institute of Linguistics. Approximate sound values are as follows:

$a = a$ in idea or u in but

$e = e$ in bet

$i = ee$ in feet

$o = o$ in tone

$u = oo$ in tooth

$ch =$ similar to ch in much

$g =$ a voiced spirant (ð)

$\dot{g} =$ a back velar spirant, farther back in the throat than g above (ɤ); sometimes similar to French r

$h =$ similar to German ch in ach

$\underset{.}{k} =$ back velar stop, contrasting to English k (traditionally represented as a q)

$\underset{.}{l} =$ similar to l in million

$ł =$ voiceless l followed by a voiced l

$\tilde{n} =$ similar to n in onion

$ŋ =$ similar to ng in sing

$z, r =$ retroflexed alveolar sibilant

Phonemic values of the letters k, l, m, n, p, s, t, v, w and y are approximately the same as in English. The letters b, c, d, f, q and x are not used.

Introduction

One of my first hunting experiences with the Eskimos took place on the sea ice offshore from Wainwright, Alaska, the settlement where most of this study was conducted. It was early winter. A young Eskimo hunter and I had traveled a long, bone-jarring trail several miles out over the tumbled ocean ice. Now we stood at the edge of a lane of open water. The temperature stood near 30° below zero. The intense cold drew a wispy breath of steam from the water's surface, and a gentle wind blew it perpetually away over the ice, like a thin cirrus cloud. The sun never rose at this time of year, but at midday a flaming orange corona brightened the southern horizon, providing enough light for a few hours' hunting.

We stood at the water's edge for a few minutes, stamping our feet to warm them, staring into the reflected glow of twilight on the rippled water. Suddenly, the Eskimo grabbed his rifle from his sled, dropped to one knee, and started to scratch the ice with a knife he carried in a belt that encircled his parka. I watched him, baffled. "Seal down there!" he hissed softly, pointing into the cloud of steam before us. Squinting into the grayness, I could barely make out a round black silhouette, moving silently in the distance. A moment later it vanished abruptly, like a broken bubble. Instead of giving up, the Eskimo jumped to his feet and ran closer to the ice edge, then quickly squatted on the frosted ice. He began the mysterious rhythmic scratching again. "Watch close-by this time," he said without stopping.

A few minutes later the seal's black head bobbed up in the water not 30 yards away. The Eskimo still scratched the ice, until the animal stared toward us and rose higher in the water, captured by some irresistible curiosity about the noise and about the two figures on the ice. Now the Eskimo lifted his rifle to his shoulder, but as he did so, the seal took fright. With a violent splash it suddenly plunged sidelong into the waters below. Surely now we had lost our chance. The hunter knew better. He held his rifle ready and scratched the ice again. "Very close this time," he muttered softly.

Before its ripple slapped against the ice before us, the seal's head broke surface again, this time only 20 yards away. It stared into the white silence; only a slight motion was visible as the rifle leveled on it. A shot split the air like shattered crystal. Before us in the smoking haze, the low rounded back of the seal settled on the pulsing water, amid a slick of glassy oil spreading from its lacerated blubber.

The Eskimo ran to his sled and returned with a coiled line. Attached to one end was a wooden float with sharpened hooks projecting from it. He drew a length of cord from the coil, spun the float around his head several times, then sent it flying into the hazy air. It splashed into the water well to the left of the floating carcass. He smiled at his own mistake, then quickly hauled the float back, piling the line loosely at his feet. It flew outward again, and this time the line slapped down directly over the lifeless black animal. After drawing the float in until its hooks snubbed the seal's rubbery skin, he gave a single firm tug, snagging the hooks deep into its flesh. Gently and slowly, the hunter pulled his catch toward the edge. In a few minutes he drew the limp seal onto the ice.

He looked at me and a smile flashed across his face as he pointed to his head saying, "You see, Eskimo is a scientist." Over the next year the overwhelming truth of his self-appraisal became ever clearer. Indeed the Eskimo is a scientist, one whose major concern is discovering the secrets of his environment and of the animals that live in it. In this book we will explore the mystique of the Eskimo hunter. We will explore the complicated body of knowledge and technique that lies behind his remarkable adaptation to one of the most unusual and extreme environments on earth—the ice-covered Arctic sea.

By the time we are finished I hope to have shown that there is no mystical inherited "germ" in the Eskimo's mind that allows him to sense the mood of an animal, to anticipate the fickle movements of the ocean ice, or to sense a change in the weather. What may seem unfathomable to us at first is often so only because we lack knowledge and experience. At times the path will be lengthy and complex, but in the end we will have discovered that the hunter's secret is only knowledge and understanding, gained through the legacy of his ancestors, who have hunted the ice for innumerable generations past.

This study is the product of detailed and concentrated research on a very specific kind of environmental adaptation among the Eskimos of northwestern Arctic Alaska. It combines the approach of ethnography with that of ecology and ethology. It is ethnography because it attempts to describe accurately certain aspects of a nonwestern culture. It is ecology in that it examines the relationships between a human population and the environment of which it is a part. And it is ethology in the sense that it focuses on the behavioral aspects of man's adaptation to his surroundings.

In spite of the abundance of literature dealing with the Eskimos, and in spite of the fact that culture change has diminished the amount of traditional knowledge still retained by these people, there is an unlimited amount of data to be gathered which is not yet on any written page. Most available ethnographic materials are quite general and do not delve deeply into any specific area of knowledge.

Modern Eskimo groups retain a substantial body of information relating to their environment, and in many cases they still practice hunting and traveling techniques. Material of this sort is therefore of immediate concern to them, and is still essential to their mode of living. Unlike many aspects of social culture, which are carried on only in the memory of old people, knowledge of the environment which pertains to present day subsistence is still being actively propagated.

The primary aim of this research was to gather information relative to modern and traditional methods of hunting, traveling and survival on the sea ice. The Eskimos have acquired an intimate understanding of their physical surroundings, to which they must respond in order to maintain their existence. Research into such areas of native epistomology can make significant contributions to disciplines outside ethnology, in fields such as geology, botany, marine biology, ethology, psychology, and ecology. This study was originally conceived as an aid to development of survival training programs of the Armed Forces. It therefore constitutes a special kind of applied anthropology. Attempts to amass similar bodies of information through experimentation and primary development by scientists or other outsiders would undoubtedly fall well short of the native tradition.

This study is not complete or exhaustive by any means, but it contains the basic knowledge that is required for safe and successful exploitation of the sea ice. This environmental situation is unique to the polar regions of the world, and is therefore extremely foreign to one who has not previously encountered it. Techniques which are used for hunting and traveling on or among the mobile ice floes are seldom applicable in other environments. Conversely, the methods familiar elsewhere are seldom useful on the sea ice. During a field study focused on actual behavior, one becomes acutely aware of the fact that a residence of many years in any one village would be required in order to do a really "complete" study, and even then the surface would only be scratched. The possibilities for collection of comparative data are literally endless. I feel, however, that much of the basic information contained here should pertain anywhere on the ice-covered oceans of the world.

The initial fieldwork was conducted in the village of Wainwright, Alaska, during the winter of 1964–65. Supplementary research was done during several brief periods spent in Barrow and Point Hope, Alaska. In order to complete the annual cycle, another field study was carried out during the summer of 1966 in Wainwright. A total of twelve months was spent in the field. For a detailed discussion of methodology see Appendix 1.

PART I

The Setting

THE ARCTIC COAST of Alaska includes the long, featureless coastline stretching from Barter Island in the east to Point Hope in the west, with Point Barrow forming the northernmost extension, about midway between the two extremities. From the standpoint of this study the area may be divided into two sections: the eastern, including all the coast east of Barrow as far as Barter Island, and the western, comprising the coast between Barrow and Point Hope. The eastern division is of little importance here, since it includes only one modern settlement, that at the easternmost end, and because the ice conditions more closely resemble those to the east in Canada.

The eastern section of the Arctic Coast is an area of relatively slight ice movement during the winter, the ice lying in great flat immobile plains for many months of the year. These conditions give rise to somewhat different ice-hunting adaptations and require less caution by travelers than in the area west and south of Barrow. The eastern division was very sparsely populated during aboriginal times, with only scattered temporary camp-sites utilized primarily by the people of Barrow (Spencer 1959, p. 17).

In contrast, the region between Point Barrow and Point Hope has a relatively dense population, with four settlements in existence today. Formerly, however, there were small villages and camping sites spaced all along this coastline, including two villages at Point Barrow, and settlements at Atanik, Point Belcher, Wainwright, Icy Cape, Point Lay, Cape Lisburne, and Point Hope. Scattered between these larger settlements were isolated houses or small seasonally used village sites, such as Piŋasuguruk and

Kiḷḷamittaġvik, near Wainwright, and Utoḳḳaḳ, near Icy Cape. In addition to these established habitations there were temporary campsites everywhere along this coast.

Although the ice in the larger bays and indentations along this section of coastline, such as in Peard Bay and the area north of Icy Cape, remains fairly flat and immobile all winter long, most of this entire region has considerable ice movement. One can expect to have leads of water opening periodically during the winter, often quite close to the land. Coincident with this ice movement, and no doubt partly because of it, there is a rich and easily exploited marine resource through the winter. Thus there are settlements concentrated, especially in recent times, around the points and headlands, where ice movement is increased. In these places there is heavy dependence upon the sea for a livelihood. Along with the richness of the sea there are, however, special problems of safety and travel, and among the Eskimos of this region there has developed an elaborate knowledge of the sea-ice environment and methods for its exploitation.

The modern village of Barrow is located at 71°18' north latitude and is the northernmost Eskimo settlement in continental North America. It is situated on the coast several miles south of Point Barrow itself. The hunting economy is today secondary to a rich cash economy made possible by active development of the area by the Office of Naval Research, the Bureau of Indian Affairs, and others. Thus the majority of the 1,200 native residents work a six-day week and hunt only on days off. Those who do hunt on the ice here find a rich resource of seals, and in the spring and fall there is still a fairly active whaling effort. The ice is very mobile due to strong currents, deep water, and the fact that the village is near a point. Thus there are often open leads offshore and the ice here is considered dangerous.

Ninety miles south of Barrow (air distance) is the village of Wainwright, located at 70°40' north latitude, 159°50' west longitude. Wainwright is also situated right along the coast, atop the 20-foot high cliffs behind the beach. There are some three hundred inhabitants in the village, living in about forty-four households. Viewed from the air it is a compact grouping of small frame houses with numerous wooden caches spread about, and an uncommonly large number of tall wooden poles scattered everywhere. On the ground one realizes that these poles are mostly used to support radio antennas, one for every house, and also to string lines or racks for drying clothing and skins.

The houses are mostly one or two rooms crammed full of the necessities of life but containing little else. Normally there is a sleeping room or section, and a room or area in which the stove is situated. The latter area is used for meals and entertaining, and may also serve as a workshop. Some houses are larger, having several rooms and occasionally two stories; others are much smaller and exceedingly crowded. Outside the heated section of the house is the hallway or *kanichak*, which serves as a general storage area for equipment and furs, and is often very long and low, with one or more doors to go through before reaching the entrance to the heated portion of the house. The houses have one or more windows, in varying states of transparency owing to the plastic coverings which are often used to make a double pane.

The Wainwright people are fortunate in having natural outcroppings of coal both inland along the Kuk River and offshore. Most individuals are able to sack their own coal and haul it to the village by dog team or boat from one of three coal mines, or from the nearby beach where it washes up during the fall storms. Coal is burned in stoves for both heating and cooking, although cooking may also be done on gasoline-burning camp stoves.

The presence of coal enables the Wainwright people to save much of the money they earn by summer employment or by the sale of goods such as skins or walrus ivory, or which is given to them in the form of monthly unemployment or welfare checks. They can use the money for purchasing clothing, hunting equipment, and food. They have become heavily dependent upon such goods, which are brought in annually on the Bureau of Indian Affairs (B.I.A.) ship, *Northstar III*, or ordered by mail from outside. They would no longer attempt living without these goods.

In spite of the availability of food at the two local stores, the people still depend upon hunting as their economic mainstay. Their main diet is derived from the surrounding land and sea, and during the colder months they wear parkas, boots, and other items of clothing made from animal skins. Wainwright's geographical location permits exploitation of a very rich land and marine resource, unlike some villages which specialize more in one or the other. During the fall, spring, and summer huge migrations of caribou provide a land resource much larger than most coastal villages are able to exploit. In the sea there are herds of walrus in the summer, seals in the winter and spring, and migrations of waterfowl in the spring and fall. In the rivers and lagoons there is a large exploitable resource of fish. The people are able, therefore, to turn from one resource to another when it is necessary to do so.

Wainwright village is located on a peninsula of land bounded by the Chukchi Sea on one side and by the huge Kuk River on the other. The Kuk, which means "river" in Eskimo, is actually a submerged lagoon which is salt water for about 50 miles inland from the mouth. The river makes a convenient route for travel inland, by boat during the summer and by dog team the rest of the year.

Since Wainwright is not on a point, the ice does not move as easily or as rapidly here as it does at Point Barrow or at Point Hope. During the winter and spring, however, the ice moves whenever there is a fairly strong breeze or when the current is flowing swiftly. Thus the ice opens to form leads periodically, so the hunters can travel out to the edge to hunt seals; and when the ice closes tightly, men go far out from the land in pursuit of polar bears.

The Wainwright people call themselves the Ulġuniġamiut, the people of Ulġunik. They feel most closely related to the people of Barrow—the Utḳeaviŋmiut. Frequently during the summer the men go to Barrow for employment, and during the season of dog sledding they travel north to visit their many relatives. Since the advent of commercial air service on the coast they commute more easily, and the more affluent Barrow people come down to visit Wainwright as well. There is a good deal of village pride and identification, however, and the Wainwright people do not appear to be attracted to the "opportunities" for employment and drink at Barrow in large enough numbers to make inroads into the Wainwright population.

With the people to the south, at Point Lay, 100 miles distant, and at Point Hope, 180 miles away, the Wainwright Eskimos have only sporadic and casual contact. This holds true, also, for the more distant village of Ḳaaḳtoġvik at Barter Island, about 400 air miles away. The Wainwright people have friends and relatives in all of these villages, and visiting both ways is sometimes done, but Wainwright is much more closely linked with Barrow.

A great deal more information could be given regarding the general conditions at Wainwright, where the major portion of this study was conducted. Throughout the text there will be reference to the present-day situation, particularly regarding the economic life and methods of hunting and traveling in use here. The village was selected as the main area in which to conduct this research because it is still heavily dependent upon a hunting economy, is isolated and rather conservative toward cultural change, and offers several other advantages for ethnographic study.

The location is excellent for sea-ice studies, since it possesses the characteristics both of places where the ice seldom moves and of those where the ice is frequently in motion. Therefore, the behavior of sea ice far out on the polar pack as well as within the dangerous areas of ice motion could be observed. Knowledge of both types of conditions is important for exploitation of the sea ice environment.

The village of Point Hope (68°20′ N, 156°47′ W) is approximately the same size as Wainwright, with perhaps 350 inhabitants. It is near the end of a very large spit that juts out approximately 15 miles from the mainland between Cape Lisburne and Cape Thompson. The physiognomy of the village is also very similar to that of Wainwright except that the houses are much more spread out and are aligned along several parallel beach ridges.

The people of Point Hope, the Tikeġaaġmiut, also rely on hunting for their subsistence base, there being little employment within the village other than the sale of native goods and skins. However, they are much more dependent upon the sea and much less upon the land. The Point offers an excellent location for ice hunting, with open leads very close to the village all winter and spring, and an abundance of seals and whales. In the summer and fall, however, when the ice is gone and the game is scarce, many of the men seek employment in larger villages to the south or in Fairbanks. It is therefore a rich, but perhaps a less well-balanced economy than that of Wainwright.

The sea ice around Point Hope is highly mobile and very dangerous. The ice here moves constantly before the force of gale winds and powerful currents. The resultant huge piles of jumbled ice make dog-team travel very difficult, though the distance to the lead is usually short. The Point Hope people are experts in ice lore, perhaps more so than any other north Alaskan settlement, and they are probably more conservative in attitude toward technical and cultural change than the Wainwright Eskimos.

Point Hope maintains closest ties with villages to the south, particularly Kivalina, Noatak, and Kotzebue. The only closely associated settlement to the north is Point Lay, about 90 air miles distant. This village is very small, consisting of only two or three families in 1964 and one in 1966, and is said to be an offshoot population of Point Hope natives who moved north around the turn of the century. The Point Lay people depend mostly upon employment at the nearby military installation for their economy. The village is on a headland but is apparently well enough protected by Cape Lisburne to the south to prevent much ice movement.

CHAPTER 1

Sea Ice: Early Stages of Development

Introduction

THE ESKIMOS have inhabited Arctic coastlines for several thousand years, perfecting an adaptation to one of the earth's unique environments. Within this environment there are two principal divisions, the land and the sea, both of which are the habitat of the Eskimo. On land he has had to learn intimately the behavior of the game he pursues, but there is little need to pay attention to the ground over which he travels. On the frozen surface of the sea ice that covers the ocean for much of the year, there must be a twofold adaptation; not only must the behavior of the game pursued from the ice be understood, but it is equally important to know the behavior of the ice itself.

The resource of the ice-covered sea is much too rich to be ignored, especially in an environment that provides with such frugality. In many parts of the Eskimo domain the sea ice is constantly in motion, sometimes with imperceptible slowness, but always with a hugeness which betrays tremendous power. By contrast, the movement can be almost violently rapid. The sea beneath the ice floes supports an abundance of life in the form of invertebrates, fish, mammals, and (in spring and summer) birds. And only two large predators are able to move over the sea ice in pursuit of this game—the polar bear and man. Of the two, the bear is more at home on the ice, because he rarely foresakes it in favor of the land. Men are only able to hurry out over the ice during its most quiet moods, returning to the safety of land with whatever spoils are taken.

In order to evolve this adaptation, Eskimos have made a ceaseless study of the ice, watching its every move, and experimenting with many different methods of avoiding its dangers. Sea ice is indeed dangerous, mostly because it is continuously subject to the will of the wind and the forces of current. But were it not so, it would not be nearly as productive for predatory man. Regardless of how and why it has been done, the Eskimos have amassed a large body of knowledge of the sea ice which permits them to move in comparative safety over it during their everyday activities. They are experts in ice lore, and we who know little of it can learn from them.

Much of what is learned from one Eskimo group would apply to sea ice wherever it is found, and this covers a huge area of the earth.

The entire area of the Arctic basin together with its seas is about 8,800,000 square km., and the White Sea, with an area of [about] 95,000 square km. can be counted as ice covered in winter. The ice area of the Barents Sea toward the end of the winter is, on the average, ca. 1,000,000 square km. The ice area of the Greenland Sea in April-May reaches 900,000 square km. The total ice area for the whole Arctic Ocean in winter reaches 10,800,000 square km.

By the end of summer, an average of 1,500,000 square km. melts in the Arctic Basin, about 95,000 square km. in the White Sea, and around 250,000 in the Barents. Further, over 1,250,000 square km. of ice is carried off annually from the Arctic Basin into the Greenland Sea, where fundamentally, it melts. Thus, by the end of the polar summer, the ice area of the Arctic Ocean decreases to 8,000,000 square km., due to melting [Zubov n.d., p. 5].

Formation of New Sea Ice

During the late fall the gradual appearance of sea ice is watched with interest by the Eskimos. The ice does not form early, considering the latitude, nor does it form rapidly once it has begun to freeze. Sea ice is seen first at Barrow, the northernmost settlement, where it usually appears in late September or early October. At Point Hope there is no newly formed ice until late October.

In the fall, young ice is erratic in its condition and occurrence, because it is subject to movement by the slightest wind or current. Young ice does not gradually extend out from the shoreline as a large expanse, thickening as the season progresses. Rather, it forms out at sea, far from the sight of shore, and appears whenever an onshore wind or current brings it up to the beach. On cold fall days, ice slush forms along the shore, but does not attain any appreciable thickness because it is usually carried away continuously by the prevailing easterly current and winds.

In 1964 it took over a month after the first appearance of ice slush along the shore before solid young ice was finally carried ashore and grounded, so that it remained until the following spring. On October 13, 1964, the first scattered patches of slush ice, exending out only 15 feet from shore, appeared at Wainwright. The temperature was 15° above zero. Slushy ice appeared along the coast periodically thereafter, spreading in wide patches over all the visible ocean when the wind and current were slight, disappearing whenever they increased enough to carry it away. Slushy ice is easily detected because it dampens the wind ripples, but it is barely visible if there is no wind.

On October 28 a fairly solid cover of pancake ice, consisting of circular pieces of newly formed ice packed together in a wet gray mass, was blown ashore. This ice was carried away the next day by an easterly wind. Slush and pancake ice came ashore again on November 2, gradually thickening to a solid cover of young ice, perhaps a foot thick, over several days' time. This heavier young ice (*sikuliaġezoak*) is white in color, unlike the gray of thinner ice.

The north-flowing current that brought this ice ashore was followed by a heavy east wind and an offshore current, which carried the mobile floes out of sight over the horizon on November 16. On the 19th a south wind began to blow, bringing in first slush ice and pancake ice, and on the 20th a strong southwester piled and grounded heavy young ice. The first ice hunting was done on November 24, 1964.

This is the beginning of the sea-ice year. Because the movements of the Arctic pack are determined by wind and current
more than by temperature, the time of its beginning varies greatly
from year to year. Powerful offshore winds can hold the ice offshore through the month of December, or an early storm from
the sea may pile the ice up to the land in October. In north Alaska
the Eskimos cannot predict when they will begin to hunt on the
ocean ice.

During fall, therefore, extensive fields of thin flat ice do not
develop here, as they do in the protected fjords of Greenland,
for example. The first hunting is done on thick, solid ice, with
little need to move over large thin-ice areas. There is a large salt-
water body in the vicinity of Wainwright, however, where the
ice forms in situ with little or no movement. This is the large Kuk
lagoon. The Kuk is a submerged river outlet which measures 5
miles across and runs about 20 miles inland before narrowing and
gradually becoming fresh. In 1964, ice had formed in this lagoon
by the 20th of September, but it was not safe for travel until two
or three weeks later. Powerful currents flow in and out of the
lagoon, caused by storm tides. When the tide rises preceding an
autumn south wind, the ice cracks and floods around its shores
for some 40 miles upriver from the outlet. Flood water runs out
over the ice and later refreezes, creating an excellent highway
for dog-sled travel.

The tides and flooding breed hazards, because the young ice
may be solid in some areas and weak in others. During the fall
of 1964, for example, the lagoon flooded just before many hunters
traveled inland to hunt caribou. Several sleds and men broke
through the refrozen ice while crossing it or while traveling on it
before it was safe. Dog sleds often begin to sink into this ice while
traveling along on the refrozen flood. Since young salt ice is
flexible, rather than brittle like freshwater ice, it is advisable to
stay on the sled, keep it moving, and "ride out" the thin spots.
If the sled should stop, it would slowly sink through the ice, but
as long as it keeps moving the ice will probably bend but not
break. The Eskimo drivers shout encouragement to their dogs as
the sled rides along in the trough of a moving wave in the supple
ice. Those who travel on this ice before it is very thick test it

with a pick or axe to judge expertly how solid it is. Unlike the ocean ice, lagoon ice cannot be judged for safety simply by color, because it is always turned brown by sediments carried in the water.

Out on the ocean, Eskimos do not take chances by riding or walking on thin ice. Whenever the pack moves enough to open cracks or leads, young ice is formed. Thus, it is likely to occur anyplace and at any time. Throughout the long winter open leads offshore are freezing and refreezing, affording the best opportunity to observe the cycle of new ice formation and the development of young ice. Eskimos say very little regarding the actual formation of sea ice. They do not concern themselves with this as much as with the methods of dealing with newly formed ice and, especially, the characteristics of ice which has become thick enough to support a man. The following notes are given as a brief background which will help in understanding the special characteristics of sea ice which are important to the Eskimo. They are derived largely from a translation of *Arctic Ice*, by Nikolai Zubov, a Russian authority on sea ice.

Ice formation can begin in the sea when temperatures are above 0°C if certain conditions are fulfilled. The sea must be calm and the skies clear, with the sun dropping toward the horizon. This also requires that the surface water layer be thin and sharply differentiated from the layers below, and radiation from the surface must be strong. The first stage in the formation of surface ice is the development of small needle-shaped crystals, which spread and thicken to form a film over the surface of the water. It is this "slush ice" (*uguruġiizak*) that dampens the wind ripples wherever patches of it are formed. In a calm sea, slush ice thickens enough to form an opaque skin of ice called nilas (*saloġok*). Nilas is flexible enough to bend over small waves and swells. When it is broken the pieces gather into clumps. If there is turbulence on the water surface, this new ice forms into disks, 1 to 6 feet across, with raised rims caused by their striking together along the edges (U.S. Navy, Hydrographic Office 1952, p. 21). This condition, called *migalik* in Eskimo, rarely occurs in leads or cracks. It is usually seen only during the fall freeze-up. Snowfall on the sea surface accelerates ice formation by cooling and freshening the water, and providing nuclei for crystallization.

Not all sea ice forms on the surface. Deep ice forms beneath the surface, whenever there is a layer of fresh water below the surface caused by melting of ice floes. This fresh water can freeze, causing ice-under-ice, thickening the melting floes by adding to them from below. A second type is called bottom ice. It forms on the floor of the sea and often rises to the surface. In some years ". . . at the beginning of winter, ships found themselves surrounded by ice which had suddenly risen from the bottom of the sea, this was proved by sand and bottom objects that had floated up with the ice." (Zubov n.d., p. 105.)

Eskimos normally have to cope only with young ice formed on the surface. During the winter ice-hunting season Eskimos along the coast encounter young ice almost every time they travel on the sea ice. There are three places where young ice, called by the general term *sikuliak*, is usually encountered: in cracks, which can occur anywhere; on the "ice apron" which forms along the edge of open leads; and in the open leads themselves.

The Ice Apron

Offshore leads may be several hundred yards to several miles wide, and may remain open for one day to several weeks' time. Along the initial edge of the lead there is usually a sheer wall of ice through which the great crack was rent. The crack does not necessarily follow along smooth ice areas. It may break through rough ice and even large hummocks, unless there are some unusually large expanses of smooth ice paralleling the coast. For the first several days after the lead breaks opens it is difficult to hunt seals from its edge, because a hunter must wait for them in one area rather than traveling along the edge to find the best spots. Almost immediately after the lead opens, however, an apron of ice begins to extend outward from its margins. This is the ice apron, or *ateġineġak*, which serves as a smooth avenue all along the lead edge.

Development of the ice apron is variable, depending on the temperature, current, and location. Sometimes the young ice extends itself outward 20 yards in twenty-four hours, and the thickness along the base of this new development is great enough to support a man or a dog team. This rapid development is especially likely to occur in "bays" along the lead margin, whereas the slowest formation will be near points or "headlands." At other times the ice extends outward very gradually, only a few feet of thin ice forming during a night. This may happen even when the temperatures are well below 0° F.

Current direction is probably the most important determinant of ice-apron development. It carries slush ice away from the up-current edge and deposits it on the down-current edge, where it solidifies and forms an apron or field of young ice. During the cold winter months the far side of a lead is seldom visible because of heavy fog rising from the open water, so this process is usually not observable. Since the Eskimos always hunt on the landward side of the lead in winter, and the lead is held open by an offshore current, this explains the fact that they speak of young ice "coming in" to close the lead. Extensive fields of new ice always grow outward from the down-current side, and when the current changes they are carried landward and close the lead. For example, at Point Hope in mid-May the current flowed away from the landward edge of a lead for several days, with below zero temperatures. Young ice extended approximately 20–25 feet outward in one twenty-four-hour period on the landward side of the lead, while along the seaward margin it spread out perhaps one-half mile.

If the current more or less parallels the lead edge, an ice apron develops more rapidly, and after several days the new ice usually closes over the lead completely. The Eskimos do most of their hunting along leads which run parallel to the coastline, 1 to 5 miles offshore. These leads are held open by offshore wind and current. In spite of this offshore flow, the ice apron usually forms along the landward edge wide enough to travel on within two days. Eskimos drive their dog teams to the margin of the lead, using a trail chopped through the rough ice. Then they follow along its edge on this natural roadway. At first they are careful to keep close to the thick ice at the apron's base. But as the ice thickens and extends up to 50 or 100 yards outward, the hunters travel farther out toward the water's edge to be closer to any seal that might surface.

The thickness of the ice apron is not uniform, but diminishes toward the edge, so a hunter who walks out near the water to retrieve a seal or help another man launch his retrieving boat must know exactly how far out to go before the ice is too thin to support him. There are several ways to judge ice thickness and safety, and there are methods of moving across ice that would normally break under the weight of a man. Young salt ice must be 5 or 6 inches thick before it will support a man or a dog sled with complete safety, but a lesser thickness will usually suffice for short periods of time. We have noted that salt ice will bend; and it will, in fact, soak water up through the cracks that open before giving way beneath a man's weight. Extreme caution must be taken if this happens, however.

Judging Young Ice Thickness

One of the most definitive characteristics of safe versus unsafe ice is its color. Although there are intermediate shades and rare exceptions, unsafe young ice is very dark, usually black. New ice is saturated with water and is sufficiently translucent to reveal the dark color of the sea below. As the ice thickens it begins to rise higher in the water; therefore the color becomes gray (*sikuliak maptizoak*). Once this color transition takes place, the ice is solid enough to support a man or a loaded dog sled. The color distinction is especially important to an Eskimo who is traveling along on a dog sled, because he must decide ahead of time whether to cross an area of young ice or a newly frozen crack. There is no chance to use other methods of testing the ice without stopping or walking ahead for a close check. There are often large fields of young ice along a lead edge, where most of the ice is safe but is punctuated here and there with dark unsafe spots. Such conditions occur especially when young ice drifts in and closes a lead. It is possible even for a fairly inexperienced person to guide a dog team safely between the weak spots and over the narrowest places where unsafe ice must be crossed. With a dog team it is especially easy to move over thin ice because it will bend but not break as the sled glides quickly over. If an Eskimo finds that he has gone out onto weak ice, he will never stop his dogs, but will turn them in a tight corner and return to safer ice without slowing down.

Because the ice within one field is not uniformly thick, one can never plan to encounter ice which is everywhere safe or unsafe. Fortunately the color distinction is nearly 100 percent effective, and the areas of weak and safe ice are usually defined by distinct and abrupt transitions. This phenomenon is especially notable along the ice apron, where there are "lines of equal ice formation" resembling growth rings. These lines represent different stages of ice development, and may be from 1 to 10 feet apart. I do not know why they form, but I have watched an ice apron grow outward for some 25 feet, presumably at a continuous rate, ending up with several of these lines in it.

Somewhere near the water's edge, from 5 to 30 feet away, there is a transition from safe to unsafe ice. This transition is almost always abrupt, and along one of these parallel lines. While he walks along the ice edge the Eskimo usually follows close to this line. In bays the lines are spread widely, and around points they are compressed, so it is necessary to watch fairly carefully and not try to cut across a bay instead of following the lines as they bend inward around the contour of the heavier ice. At points one must walk closer to the heavy ice, always staying inside the safe ice/unsafe ice dividing line. Sometimes the apron fails to develop around points, and it is necessary to move up onto the heavy ice. Lines of equal ice development are important guides for the Eskimo as he walks or rides along this smooth ice bordering leads.

It is worth noting, also, that dogs often shy away from unsafe ice, although not at all infallibly. Their avoidance of thin ice probably relates to its wetness, which chills their feet. Sometimes it is difficult to get the lead dog onto the ice apron or other young ice even though it is quite safe, because its surface is very moist. On the other hand, dogs will sometimes walk right out onto thin black ice if they are not told to turn. The Eskimo who travels on young ice anywhere is continuously alert, and indeed alertness is one of his most exceptionally developed aptitudes. A person who does not watch his step when he is walking can easily blunder onto weak ice without realizing it until the ice begins to bend or break. This is especially likely to happen when he is stalking a seal or a polar bear. While riding a dog sled it is especially easy for one's attention to wander away from the trail ahead. These could be fatal errors, and the Eskimo seldom allows them to happen.

Color is therefore an important and (usually) obvious distinction between safe and unsafe young ice. Fortunately, the new ice does not normally become snow covered because snowfall is slight and infrequent, and because the ice is so moist that snow usually melts fairly rapidly on any questionable surface. As we shall see, however, the color distinction is not infallible, and must often be supplemented by other checks of ice thickness.

A second way to test the ice is with an *unaak* or ice-testing rod. The *unaak* is a pole about 7 feet long and 1 inch in diameter. On one end is a metal rod or spike with a sharpened point, and at the other end is a sharpened hook. The word *unaak* is actually a short form of *unaakpaurak*, "little harpoon," because the implement is actually a highly modified derivative of the aboriginal harpoon. This is the most important piece of equipment carried by a modern sea-ice traveler, and only the rifle is seen with greater frequency in use on the ice.

Usually the pole is round and fairly slender. It is often widest at the prod-end and tapers toward the hook-end. It can be made from any kind of wood. The iron prod is made from a variety of materials, such as screwdriver shafts, pieces of pipe sharpened and flattened at one end, large spikes, and miscellaneous types of iron rod which might be available. This prod is usually inserted into a hole in the end of the pole, and a metal band is fastened around the wood to prevent splitting. At the other end there is a sharp-pointed hook, with a shaft 3 to 10 inches long, also inserted into the pole. The shaft of an *unaak* is sometimes broken or split, but it can be repaired by splicing and binding with wire or thong. In former years the point was made of bone, and at the other end was a leather thong for hanging the pole on the hunter's wrist.

Using an *unaak* for ice testing is as simple as making the color discrimination. The iron prod is given one firm jab into any questionable ice. If it does not go completely through, the ice is safe; but if it breaks through it will not safely hold a man. The *unaak* is carried everywhere by Eskimos whenever they are hunting or walking on the ice. It is thrust into the ice every two or three steps if it is at all questionable. This test is much more reliable than the color distinction, because it is literally infallible and because intermediate coloration does occur. Sometimes weak ice is concealed by storm-blown snow. In these cases the *unaak* is absolutely essential.

Eskimos warn repeatedly that the ice can be dangerous after powerful storms cause heavy drifting. Open holes, cracks, or areas of thin ice sometimes become snow covered during the storm and remain unsafe afterward, covered with insulating drifts. A crack with snow blown over it is called *ḵupaḵ aputilik*. Such covering often happens in the spring, but there is no reason that it could not occur at any time. Several Wainwright Eskimos mentioned that they had fallen through the ice because of this condition. They also said that there may be no ice at all beneath the snow, a condition called *mafshaak*.

During early April of 1964 a heavy south wind raked the Arctic coast all the way from Point Hope to Barrow, causing extensive flooding and cracking of the sea ice. Following this the temperature ranged into the 20's during the day, but sank below zero at night. A week later I found several places where drifts from the storm had covered fairly extensive areas of soft slushy ice. In some cases there was a layer of water several inches deep between the young ice and the snow. There are no surface indications whatever around these areas to warn of the dangerous condition. It was discovered only because dogs and sleds sank deep into the slush. The following day an Eskimo who was running behind his sled fell through in such a place, but fortunately was saved from a deep dunking because he was holding the upstanders of his sled.

Another form of unsafe ice, which is perhaps best discussed here, is called "mush ice," a type of slushy ice formed when the edges of ice floes and cracks grind together. Whenever there is any parallel or shearing movement of great fields of ice, the ice in certain areas is ground and pulverized, sometimes filling the water with deep ice slush. This is called *pogazak*. It later freezes into a solidified mass if temperatures are cold enough. During the winter it often fills a crack completely, and then freezes solidly. This kind of ice is called *iginik*. As long as it is frozen it is not dangerous to the ice traveler. It often forms a trail through rough ice areas, since following cracks is easier than clambering over the hummocks. This solidified mush is very bumpy, however, and it is easy to turn an ankle by walking on it. It is also very abrasive, so it can wear through skin boot soles quickly.

As we shall see later, this slushy ice becomes dangerous in spring and summer because the warmer temperatures allow it to remain unfrozen. Since it tends to thicken and eventually protrudes 6 inches to a foot above the water, it turns fairly white and looks deceptively safe. Quite often, however, its color is noticeably darker than the surrounding solid ice, especially in early spring. There is no color distinction between mush ice that has frozen solid and that which remains unfrozen and soft. In this case the test is the same as is used for any doubtful ice—one thrust of the *unaak*. If it cannot penetrate clear through, the ice is safe for a man's weight. Slushy ice is especially dangerous if a man falls through it, because it bursts instantly and affords no handhold. When a man goes through mush ice, the hole fills up over him because the slush is so unconsolidated.

Moving over Thin Ice

Eskimos are not often forced to walk over dangerously thin ice nowadays, although in the old days men traveled far out onto the ice even when it was in motion. The most probable situations that require a man to walk over young ice occur when: (1) some movement over thin ice is required to retrieve killed seals during daily hunting trips; (2) a hunter is forced to cross an area of weak ice to reach safer ice than he is already on (e.g., when caught on a drifting ice floe); (3) the traveler is not watching where he is walking or riding, and goes out onto thin ice; (4) the ice is snow covered so that its color is not visible; (5) a man is traveling in times of severely limited perception, such as in a windstorm, which an Eskimo will seldom do.

Eskimos may have learned to walk on thin ice by watching polar bears, which are said to be able to move over ice that even the most skillful man cannot walk on. One Eskimo told a story of a white hunter who was searching for polar bears with his airplane. He figured, with disastrous results, that any ice strong enough to hold a bulky polar bear would support his airplane. He attempted to land on black young ice which a bear crossed, and plunged through it. When a bear wishes to move across weak ice, it simply spreads its legs wide, even until its belly touches the surface, and crawls along without stopping. The ice usually does not break under it.

Men walk across thin ice in much the same way, although for them the consequences of falling through are much more serious than for the aquatic bear. The method was demonstrated by several Eskimo men, although none would do so on the thin ice itself, because it is not a common Eskimo philosophy to take chances. In essence it consists of spreading the legs as widely as possible, while still retaining good coordination, and sliding the feet along quickly and evenly without lifting them from the ice. The vital principle is to keep moving and never stop the fast, even pace until safe ice is regained. Learners are advised not to look down, but to keep watching a few feet ahead to avoid a feeling of panic. If one walks out onto thin ice by accident, it is best to spread the legs widely as soon as the ice is felt bending underfoot, turn a tight corner, and move swiftly back toward safety. It would obviously be too dangerous to stop and turn back, hence the idea of turning a corner.

If the ice is too thin to walk over on foot, the polar bear imitation is carried further by getting down on all fours with arms and legs again spread widely. And, this failing, there is no choice but to lie flat on the ice, arms and legs stretched out, and squirm along (Stefansson 1950, p. 366). One Eskimo said that when he was walking over young ice and felt it give beneath one foot, he would throw himself prone, as gently as possible under the circumstances, and roll toward safety. Such methods are strictly for emergencies, because sea ice is so very wet that it would not be worth soaking the clothing if a better means of crossing weak ice could be found.

Regardless of the temperature, young ice always has a wet, salty layer on its surface. Even on ice that is several weeks or months old the snow is somewhat wet near the surface, deriving its moisture from the salt ice beneath it. On new ice the snow is always wet even if it is fairly deep, while on somewhat older ice only the snow near the bottom is wet. To avoid this moisture, the Eskimos seldom sit directly on the snow or ice surface without some kind of protection. This is especially important to men who hunt seals along the lead edge, because the ice apron is usually newly formed and is devoid of snow cover, making it very moist. In old times a flap of loonskin or other waterproof skin was carried by hand or tied around the waist so that whenever a man sat down he was protected from wetness by sitting on the skin. Men today are less careful about this, often sitting down to shoot without any protection for their clothing. Some use pieces of caribou skin, gun cases, or their dog sleds. Moisture that soaks up from young salt ice is called *masallhok.*

There is considerable individual variation in the ability to walk on thin ice. Young hunters, particularly in former times, "followed" the older and especially the more expert hunters out, and learned sea-ice skills by watching and listening to them. Certain men were most expert at walking on young ice, and it was best to learn this skill from them. Today some men are able to walk on young ice fairly well, while others cannot do it at all. One sixty-year-old man, who is an especially good hunter but is 6 feet tall and fairly heavy, said that he can walk on ice about "3 inches" thick, but that some can move over ice "half" that thickness. A twenty-four-year-old man said that he could stay up on "2 inches" of ice, but that a forty-three-year-old man, who was present at the time, could walk on even thinner ice, and his father could do even better than he.

These estimates of ice thickness are probably quite accurate, since they were given by reliable and astute individuals. A man's weight is important, of course, and so is his age. In this case older men are generally better than the younger ones, because they have learned properly and have practiced the skill. The twenty-four-year-old man mentioned above is exceptionally well coordinated and is an excellent hunter, and his skill probably exceeds that of all men his age in Wainwright. Many Eskimos openly admit that they cannot do it well, but most say that their fathers and grandfathers were quite expert at it.

The story is told and retold of an old man from Point Hope who lived at Wainwright, and who was the expert-of-experts at walking on thin ice. They say that this man once shot at a seal that had poked its head up through the young ice to breathe. He missed the seal and wanted to see where his bullet struck the ice, so he walked out to the place where the seal had come up. He could not stop lest he plunge through the flexing ice, so he circled quickly around the hole, checking for bullet marks, and then walked back to solid ice. The new ice was so thin that the front of his foot broke through with every step, and yet he could still stay on top.

There are several implements that are used as an aid for walking on young ice. Modern Eskimos must be able to move out onto the new ice at the fringe of the ice apron, where they launch small skin boats used to retrieve seals. The hunter braces his hands on the rear of his open skin boat (*umiahalurak*) or kayak (*kayak*) and spreads his legs widely. Thus he achieves a tripod effect, by which he can push the boat out onto ice so thin that the boat breaks through and floats in the water as soon as he climbs into it, or even before, depending on how quickly the ice tapers off. A hunter may also stand in his boat near the edge of the ice apron while he retrieves a seal with a snag hook or with the hook on the end of an *unaak*.

In addition to its usefulness as an ice tester, the *unaak* is important for support on weak ice. Along the edge of the ice apron, it is laid flat and one foot is planted on it to spread the hunter's weight more widely while he retrieves a seal. By leaning on it and spreading his legs widely, a man can achieve a tripod effect while he crosses thin ice. Around Bering Strait during the nineteenth century, a stout wooden "ice staff" was equipped with a hoop of antler or bone, like the hoop on the bottom of a modern ski pole. This increased its efficiency as a support by covering a larger area after the point went through the weak ice (Nelson 1899, p. 215).

Stefansson recommends the use of skis or snowshoes for crossing young ice, and believes that skis are best. The Alaskan Eskimos, from Bering Strait north to Point Barrow, traditionally used crude snowshoes for walking on new ice (Nelson 1899, pp. 212–14). The snowshoes were only about 2 feet long, with a rudely constructed oblong frame. The webbing was made with widely-spaced leather thong. By Murdock's time (1881–83) this old type, described earlier by Simpson (1853–55), had been replaced at Barrow by the Indian type. Evidently the use of snowshoes became very popular at Barrow around the turn of the century, but now they have all but disappeared. A few pairs, probably obtained through the National Guard, are seen in Wainwright and Point Hope, but they are rarely if ever used.

At Point Hope the eighty-year-old man, *Tigak*, owns a pair made according to the aboriginal pattern, he got long ago from a Diomede Islander. He uses them for walking on soft spring snow.

Falling through Thin Ice: Emergency Procedures

In spite of the Eskimos' skill in recognizing dangerous ice and in moving over it if necessary, there are accidents every winter in which men fall through the ice. Every man who has done much hunting and traveling on the ice has probably fallen through at least once, but the Eskimos never told of anyone's dying as a consequence. In the past, and to a lesser extent today, Eskimos went out onto the ice prepared for emergencies. They dressed properly and carried whatever gear they would need if they fell through the ice or drifted away on a floe and could not regain the shore. Many of the Eskimos related their own experiences of falling through the ice. Some of these stories, and the lessons to be learned from them, follow:

One Wainwright Eskimo in his forties said he had fallen through the ice three times during the winter, each time on new ice. In the first instance he was crawling out onto thin ice to hook a killed seal with his *unaak*. When he broke through, he was able to "swim" back to solid ice and crawl back up onto it. Van Valin (1944, pp. 203–4) writes of a similar experience when he and his Eskimo companion fell through young ice. In order to reach safety, they had to break their way back through it to the solid ice. They did this by rotating one forearm around the other as they swam.

In another instance the Wainwright man was walking over thin ice and felt himself sinking through. He quickly threw his rifle onto solid ice and managed to swim to safety. This illustrates the importance of throwing the rifle to safe ice whenever such danger threatens. The rifle is the Eskimo's most important tool, and he always has the presence of mind to save it first in an emergency. The third time he fell through, this man was carrying a kayak over young ice, perhaps to the edge of the ice apron, with another man. When he plunged through the ice, he quickly grabbed the kayak and the other man hauled him to safety by pulling on its other end. This suggests the possibility of tying men together with lines when they cross dangerous ice, but the Eskimos never mentioned such a practice.

A young Wainwright Eskimo was once driving his dog team about "6 miles" out on the ocean ice. It was during the spring, at the time when open cracks tend to become covered with drifted snow. His dogs broke through the snow concealing such a crack, but they were able to keep moving and reach the other side, pulling the sled along. The bow of the sled crossed safely, but then the dogs stopped and began to shake off the water. When they did this, the rear part of the sled slipped down into the water. The man was soaked to his armpits, so he turned immediately for shore, running alongside the sled most of the way to keep warm.

Running or walking alongside the sled is frequently mentioned as a way of keeping warm after falling through the ice. Many men, either because they cannot get a change of clothing or because they are close to home, head quickly for the village. One man fell through and had considerable difficulty getting back up onto solid ice, so he became thoroughly soaked. He was able to borrow a pair of dry pants but still had to walk and run "8 miles" to Wainwright.

If there is thin ice all around, or a high steep edge up onto the solid ice, it may be very hard to get back out of the water. The *unaak* is a valuable safety aid in such an emergency. A man can use it to bridge the hole through which he has fallen, to keep from being swept beneath the ice by the current. He can also hook it onto the ice to pull himself up onto thick ice. A second valuable tool is a hunting knife, which ideally is carried on a belt tied outside the parka. It can then be reached easily and used to grip the ice or even to chip hand- or footholds into it.

It is a fortunate man who is near other hunters when he breaks through the ice, because he can depend on them for help if they hear his shouts. The concept of safety in numbers is important in many Eskimo hunting practices on the ice, where men usually stay fairly close together, but far enough apart to have a good chance for game. There is a long-standing tradition of hunting partners, which still exists today, where two men habitually hunt together for mutual protection and assistance.

There are three things that can be done for a man who falls through the ice, after he gets out of the water. First, other men can share their clothing with him, either by lending extra items they might carry for emergencies or by taking off articles which are being worn at the time. Second, they can supply shelter in the form of a windbreak or tent, and perhaps caribou skins, which they may be carrying. Third, and of great importance, one of them may have a gasoline stove, which can be used in the shelter to dry the wet clothing and to rewarm the chilled hunter. Some men, especially those who carry roomy skin boats on their sleds for seal hunting, always take plenty of extra gear (clothing, stove, canvas, etc.), for their own use or to help others in the event of an emergency. The small skin boat itself can be used as a shelter, turned up on its side with caribou skins or canvas hung over the open side.

Kaviḳ once fell through the ice when it was new in the fall. He swam to solid ice and got up onto it, but found that there was no dry snow in which to roll around to blot the moisture from his clothing. Powdery snow, especially at cold temperatures, effectively absorbs water from wet fur, if it can be reached before the moisture freezes. Kaviḳ took his dogs to shore as fast as he could, and found some soft drifts there to roll in, but it did little good because he had already squeezed out as much of the water as he could and the rest was frozen. He was unfortunate to have been alone, because had another man been along they could have divided up that man's clothes and gone home. As it was he had to go back wet and very cold.

Some types of clothing are far better than others in case of immersion in the icy water. A Wainwright Eskimo told how he fell into a crack that was covered by snow and had difficulty getting out because its edges were quite high and steep. Although he was in the water for several minutes, he did not get very wet since he was wearing skin boots, pants, and parka. Unlike cloth, skin is fairly waterproof and, especially if sewn with sinew, allows little water seepage. Clothing made from caribou fur is naturally bouyant as well, and will act as a life preserver.

Cloth, on the other hand, soaks up water quickly, weighing the wearer down. Also, it cannot be dried by rolling in the snow as fur clothing can. Eskimos say that if caribou fur is dried out by rolling in snow, and perhaps squeezing moisture out of the fur by running the hands down through it, there may be no need to go home early from hunting. Skin boots have a drawstring tied around the boot top above the calf. This string normally serves to keep loose snow from entering the boot, but it can also exclude water if the wearer goes through the ice. Extra boots are, however, an important item to carry if extra clothing is taken along on the ice, because if water is squeezed downward out of the clothing, as it should be, the boots may become soaked inside.

Eskimos say that during the fall and winter, the water itself is "warm," but in the spring it is very cold. The relative difference between air and water temperatures at these times could have something to do with this impression. During the spring and summer the best things to do after falling in the water are the obvious ones: immediately take off as much clothing as possible and wring it out thoroughly. If extra clothes are available, hang the wet things in the sun or (preferably) over a stove. They can be worn again before they are completely dry. Cloth, which is usually worn at this time, is fairly easy to wring out and dry. It is always highly advisable to head immediately for a shelter, such as a heated tent or a house, where it is much easier to dry the clothing and to avoid getting chilled.

Kaviḳ once fell through the ice outside the Kuk Inlet in late spring. When he tried to get back up on the ice, holding his shotgun, he was swept beneath the ice by a strong current. He was lucky enough to come up in another hole, where he threw his gun on the ice and was able to clamber to safety. It was not far to the village, so he hurried home to dry off and get warm. During the summer there is no dry snow to absorb the wetness from clothing. Fortunately, it is often fairly warm, and the clothing will not freeze as it does in the winter. Surprisingly, few men seem to fall through during the summer. Those to whom it does happen do not consider the experience to be a serious one, because there is little danger of freezing to death.

CHAPTER 2

Winter Sea Ice

Types of Winter Ice

WINTER ICE includes all types of sea ice which are thick enough to preclude any danger of breakage under the weight of a man or dog sled. In the preceding chapter on young ice, two main types were considered, black young ice and gray young ice. They were distinguished mainly because one is safe and the other is unsafe. Both types share such qualities as wetness of the surface, and they usually are not rafted or hummocked enough to impede travel. Winter ice is also subdivided into two main groupings, winter ice (ice-of-the-year) and polar ice (old ice). While neither type is subject to breakage beneath the weight of a man or sled, both are continually susceptible to movement due to wind and current. Thus, an intimate knowledge of local and seasonal ice conditions, wind and current forecasting, and the dynamics of ice movement must be acquired by the Eskimo ice hunter.

In the Eskimo categorization all sea ice of one season's growth or less is *sikuliak*, or young ice. However, after it exceeds a foot or so in thickness it is called *sikuliaġezoak*, or "thick young ice." Once it is piled or rafted in any way, it is no longer considered young ice. There is apparently no general term equivalent to winter ice or ice-of-the-year, but rather a whole series of terms for particular ice formations, such as piled ice, rafted ice, flat ice, landfast ice, and so on. Old ice, on the other hand, is recognized as a distinctive general type, called *paḳaliaḳ*. But this ice occurs only along the northern portion of northwest Alaska, and is not common except during midwinter. Once the ice is so thick that there is no chance of its breaking beneath a man or loaded sled, Eskimos are no longer much concerned with its age, but rather with its morphology and movement.

Winter ice that is not rafted or piled achieves a thickness of perhaps 10 feet during the cold season, but wherever the ice is disturbed its thickness is increased. It is open to conjecture how great the ice thickness becomes when there are ice piles up to 60 feet high and large areas of hummocks piled 5 to 15 feet above the surface. The ice beneath these piles certainly extends very deep indeed, given the fact that more of it is below the surface than above it. Along the coast between Point Hope and Point Barrow the ice is very mobile. Therefore, it is almost everywhere an expanse of piled and jumbled floes, which consolidates solidly during the entire winter season except for frequent cracking and opening of leads. Only in the deeper bays and indentations or the smaller areas protected by points does the ice remain unmoved all winter. Along the coast from Point Barrow to Barter Island the ice is much more stable, however, making this province more akin to the Canadian Archipelago, where flat ice is also common.

Whether it lies in motionless flat plains or in tumbled ice fields, winter ice is always discernible from polar ice. Polar ice has not melted in the previous summer(s) and is therefore at least one full year old. Winter ice is always much different in appearance, because unlike polar ice it is either very flat or very jagged. Flat winter ice is punctuated only by the minor undulations of snow-drifts, and is always completely snow covered until the spring thaw. Wherever there are ice piles, the relief is extremely rugged because there has been no weathering. Winter ice is broken up into huge chunks of ice piled at random against one another, or it may be crushed into smaller blocks piled high into the air, like boulder-strewn talus. Sometimes layers of winter ice have rafted or slid one on top of the other.

Unlike either flat or piled winter ice, polar ice has gone through a season of weathering in warm summer temperatures, and has developed a more or less gently undulating surface. Hummocks and piles of ice have fused into rounded knolls, and between these scattered knolls there are either flat areas or shallow depressions. Only around the edges of polar ice floes or along cracks through them is there any of the jagged roughness of winter ice, and in such places the differences between the two are also apparent. Whereas winter ice breaks up into small chunks or flat slabs, usually not over 3 or 4 feet thick, polar ice fractures into collossal chunks, some standing like icy monoliths 30 feet above the surrounding ice. And when polar ice cracks it forms yawning fissures 8 to 15 feet deep, much different from winter ice cracks, which freeze over almost level with the surface unless they open through ice piles.

Polar ice also differs from winter ice in that it is not completely snow covered, but has scattered (or sometimes frequent) glare ice areas. Snow does not blow free over the moist surface of salty winter ice, so there are never any bare spots on its level surface until the spring thaw. Even the snow itself seems to have a different texture on polar ice. It is rather hard and crunchy, and often has a crust which is easily broken through to reveal softer snow underneath. This is quite unlike the snow that covers winter ice.

Finally there is the important difference that polar ice is fresh —it does not contain enough salt to be detectable by taste. During the summer thaw, salt percolates downward out of the sea ice, and by the following fall (or usually much earlier) it becomes fresh. Because it is no longer salty and moist, it can be blown clear of snow in places. This change also causes polar ice to become markedly different in color. Winter ice is a grayish or very light turquoise color, and has a milky appearance. Polar ice is a deeper greenish-blue color, or a very dark blue if it is over two seasons old, and has a shiny glare on its surface. It is not moist and sticky for sled runners like ice-of-the-year. And being fresh, polar ice is brittle and splinters, lacking the elasticity and resilience of salt ice.

These distinctions are important to sea-ice travel and survival, because the two kinds of ice have characteristics that make them behave differently under pressure and make one or the other preferable for an ice camp. We will discuss this in detail later. As we noted above, polar ice or *paḳaliaḳ* does not occur all along the Alaskan Arctic coast, not is it present at all seasons. At Point Hope this ice apparently appears sporadically, but a few small pans or floes are seen each winter. At Wainwright, on the other hand, this ice is common every winter. During the 1964–65 season, polar ice appeared here in late February and early March, first as a few scattered pans several hundred square yards in size, later becoming more common and increasing in size to floes up to a mile long. The Eskimos say that polar ice is carried down from the north at this season each year, but in variable amounts.

In 1964–65 the polar ice was exceptionally prevalent, so that beyond 5 or 10 miles offshore it was more common than winter ice. This was said to indicate an unusually solid freeze-up, and was blamed for the small amount of ice movement after the beginning of March. There were few open leads at Wainwright after this time, and those that did open were much farther offshore than is usual.

There are two kinds of ice found in the ocean besides that which is formed directly from the salt water itself. Glacier ice, which forms icebergs, is the most commonly known. Icebergs are not found in this part of the Arctic because there are no glaciers to calve them anywhere along the Alaskan Arctic coast. The other type is fresh ice that freezes in the sea outside the mouths of great rivers such as the Colville or Mackenzie. River ice seems not to occur along the coast between Point Barrow and Point Hope. If it does, it must be quite rare. It is found, however, along the seacoast east of Barrow. This ice is smooth, unlike polar ice, and is blown free of snow in places to expose its brownish coloration. It is quite fresh to the taste. River-produced ice is likely to be found anywhere in the vicinity of the large rivers, but may be moved long distances with the ice pack, as is evidenced by Stefansson's finding it a hundred miles from shore (Stefansson 1922, p. 170).

Landfast Ice

The landfast floe or flaw ice is winter ice that is driven against the coast by a fall or winter gale, causing it to pile so high and so deep that the entire floe becomes anchored solidly to the bottom. The landfast ice becomes an immobile apron of ice extending outward from the coast. Only the ice beyond the flaw or edge of the landfast ice moves with the wind and current. Thus, it is at the flaw that leads usually open up, or somewhat beyond it if some ice fields have been carried landward and fastened themselves solidly to its edge.

Landfast ice is a fundamental aspect of sea-ice exploitation in northwest Alaska, because most hunting and traveling during the fall, winter, and spring are carried out on it. Seldom do hunters venture onto the mobile ice pack beyond its margins. Only when the wind and current hold the sea ice tightly against it will the Eskimos travel far out from the coast. Too many times in the past men have gone beyond the flaw and become trapped on a drifting floe when the wind or current carried the ice away, opening a wide lead which prevented their return to the land. Those who could not find a way to reach the shore faced an ordeal of survival and perhaps eventual death.

The extent of the landfast floe out from shore depends upon the depth of the water and strength of the currents. It also varies seasonally according to the power of the storms that crush it against the coast. Wainwright is located in a shallow bight, and the bottom drops off very gradually. The landfast ice usually extends from one to several miles, building itself outward as the winter progresses. South of Point Hope the flaw ice is not nearly as extensive because the waters are deeper. At Cape Lisburne, near Point Hope, and at Nelson Head, on Banks Island, deep water comes right up to the land so that there is never any landfast ice. In these places the ice can break away right at land's edge, without even an "ice foot" or small projecting ice fringe hugging the cliffs. Generally, however, there is landfast ice extending out one to several miles throughout the Arctic coasts (Stefansson 1950, p. 358). The landfast ice is anchored to fairly great depths everywhere along the northwest Alaskan coast, perhaps down to 60 feet or more. Stefansson records landfast ice extending down 120 feet at Banks Island, where it is initially piled by strong west winds with high tides, and is grounded solidly in spring and summer when there are east and southeast winds with low tides.

The landfast floe is normally composed of winter ice, although polar ice and river ice can be consolidated into it. At Wainwright during the winter of 1964–65, the flaw ice was notably whitish in color and dirty (due to bottom sand or windblown dirt?) compared with the clean turquoise or gray ice which later piled up against it from the pack ice. The crevices and crannies of most winter ice are suffused with a beautiful turquoise hue, but this was not detectable in the landfast ice. The Eskimos never attempted to explain this difference, and it is not known if this is typical of flaw ice near land. If it is, the dirty whitish ice would be an excellent indicator to the ice traveler whether or not he was nearing the coast; however, this might have been just a peculiar occurrence of ice which had accumulated debris from being piled into the bottom.

Until leads have formed and closed several times it is difficult to say just where the ice is grounded and where it is not. The best test of how solidly it is anchored is a powerful gale from a direction which normally would blow the ice away and form a lead. This usually is an offshore wind. Wainwright Eskimos could not say whether or not the ice which came ashore in the fall of 1964 was fast until it had been tested in this way and proved to be grounded. The Eskimos usually do not need to go beyond the edge of landfast ice because leads open up somewhere close to the grounded ice, occasionally right along the seaward flank of the outermost piles that extend to the bottom.

This latter situation is exceptional, however, and usually the lead opens somewhere through ice which is attached to the flaw ice but is not grounded itself. Since this extension of attached floes is usually not held strongly enough to resist breaking away in a storm, especially a south wind with high tide, hunters always watch the current and weather signs closely if they go more than a mile beyond solidly grounded ice. Only when there is an onshore wind that is not likely to shift, and a favorable current, do the hunters go far out onto the pack in search of bears.

Effects of Wind and Current on Ice Movement

Whenever Eskimo hunters travel beyond the landfast ice, they must study the weather, current, and ice condition carefully. They are often able to decide whether or not the ice is absolutely safe for hunting before they venture out from shore. In their prediction of ice conditions and the possibility of ice breakaway, the Eskimos are exceedingly careful. They will not take the least risk of drifting away on the ice and being unable to cross an open crack or lead to return to the land. To the Eskimos nothing justifies taking a chance. The most highly prized game, a large polar bear, would be, and often has been, passed up in order to avoid such a risk.

There is a series of observations that the Eskimo makes as standard procedure before ever going out onto the ocean ice, and several additional ones that he makes while on the ice itself. From this information he can accurately judge the conditions for ice hunting. Since all these observations relate to ice movement, and particularly to movement out beyond the landfast floe, they can be of importance to a man on either side of a lead—to a man who is hunting on the landfast ice or to a man who has been caught on the seaward side of a lead and must survive until it closes.

Around settlements such as Point Barrow and Point Hope the force of current alone can move the ice away from land, opening leads or cracks. In more sheltered places such as Wainwright, where the current is not so strong, the current and wind must usually combine forces in order to move the heavy winter ice. Between November and May wind is the dominating influence upon ice movement along this coast, because it controls the current. Thus the current flows from the north quadrant when there is a north wind, from the east quadrant with an east wind, and so on. In the spring and summer, currents prevail strongly from the south, although they are also influenced somewhat by the wind.

The coastline at Wainwright trends NNE–SSW, and forms a long concave arc from Point Belcher to Icy Cape. Wainwright is 15 miles south of Point Belcher and 50 miles north of Icy Cape, and is located 7 miles inside a straight line drawn between these two points. Because the ice often breaks more or less even with points or headlands, a wind which blows from the NNE, causing ice movements parallel to the shore, theoretically would develop shearing (parallel) movement 7 to 10 miles offshore from Wainwright.

Keeping in mind the trend of the coastline, and assuming that the current is running from the same quadrant as the wind, the following assumptions can be made: A wind from the east northeast, the most common direction of winter storms, blows almost offshore and usually causes the pack to drift seaward, opening cracks and leads parallel to the coast. This is one of the most dangerous winds for ice travel or hunting, because it can easily break the ice away, carrying with it anyone who happens to be out beyond the point of fracture. But for seal hunters this is also the most favorable wind, because it opens a lead near the edge of landfast ice, and when it continues as a light or moderate breeze it keeps the lead open. An east wind will usually do the same thing, but wind from this direction is less common than from the northeast. During the late spring and early summer, when the sea ice moves more readily, fairly gentle east or northeast winds can open the lead. One Eskimo stated that whenever these offshore winds blow during the summer, he will not go out onto the ice without taking along a small skin boat for self-rescue, in case a lead opens between his position and the land.

A moderate southeast wind is usually accompanied by a south (or southwest) current, which holds the pack solidly against the landfast ice; but a powerful southeast gale, especially in the spring, can open wide leads. Southeasters are considered very dangerous for ice travel, and hunters will hurry toward the land whenever the wind picks up from this direction. Eskimos often say that, unlike any other wind, the southeaster can blow away the landfast ice right from the beach, because the accompanying high tides lift the grounded ice piles free of the bottom. Winds from the southeast can also cause ice movement parallel to the shore.

"Onshore" winds, including south, southwest, west, and northwest winds, move the pack shoreward or hold it firmly against the landfast ice in the area around Wainwright. In other areas the conditions are likely to differ. At Icy Cape for example, any wind from the south quadrant will usually move the ice out and open leads offshore. West and southwest winds push the ice solidly in toward the land at Wainwright. When they are strong, the ice heaves, rafts, and piles itself against the immobile landfast floe. These are the winds for polar bear hunters, allowing them to travel with impunity 20 or 30 miles out from land, even if the wind is only a soft breeze. It is preferable that the wind be blowing 10 to 15 m.p.h., however, because a strong wind is too cold and may cause ice piling, and a light wind is more liable to shift to another direction. During the spring and summer, hunters take advantage of onshore winds to wander far afield in search of seals sleeping atop the ice.

If the wind is very light from the west or southwest, a hunter will try to test the current before traveling out far beyond the fast ice, because current often shifts before an approaching wind change. Thus he might find a slow northeast current, and not go beyond safe ice. Should the wind shift while he is far out from landfast ice, he will head for land as quickly as possible, unless he knows that there is a farily strong onshore current. (See below for methods of testing current.)

The wind almost never blows from the northwest during the winter ice hunting season, but there are occasional north winds, which can reach storm velocities. Northerly winds do not open the ice at Wainwright because they are almost parallel to the coast and somewhat onshore. North and east winds also lower the tide, firmly grounding the landfast ice.

There are many differences between sea-ice conditions at Wainwright and those at Point Hope, mostly due to the different geographical situation of the two villages. Unlike Wainwright, Point Hope is located on a long point jutting 15 miles out beyond the surrounding land, which is itself the most seaward end of a huge headland, with Kotzebue Sound to the south, the Chukchi Sea to the west and the Arctic Ocean to the north. Therefore the winds, which blow with greater force here, and the currents, swirling powerfully around the end of this huge obstruction, move the ice more easily and rapidly than at Wainwright. This is manifested in the ability of leads to open right from the beach, carrying away whatever landfast ice there might be.

Point Hope, the long triangular sandspit upon which the village is located, projects westward from the land. It is situated along a stretch of coastline between Cape Thompson to the south and Cape Lisburne to the north. All three of the headlands are characterized by extensive and frequent ice movement.

Because the land around Point Hope faces in three directions instead of one, leads and cracks open up when the wind blows from any quarter except the west. As at Wainwright, the northeast wind is most likely to open the ice. Winter storms frequently blow from this direction, and deep water off the south shore of the spit prevents an extensive grounded floe from developing. East winds have a similar effect, but do not break the ice off so close to the land, and also tend to open the lead off the west end of the spit rather than off the favored south side. A northeaster can open leads less than 400 yards offshore, a situation almost unheard of at Wainwright. Southeast and south winds open leads off the north shore of the spit. Accompanying high tides may lift the landfast ice free so that it is carried away entirely. During April, 1965, a terrific south wind moved the ice out about a dozen feet from the north shore, but it was too heavily grounded to move farther. The same storm created huge ice piles along the south flank of the spit and, although they were not believed to be grounded, these piles were said to be so "heavy" that they prevented leads from opening less than 5 miles offshore. This forced the people to do their spring whaling at a lead west of the point, contrary to their usual practice. As a result they had to go several miles out to reach the lead.

The Point Hope Eskimos are considered fortunate because leads for seal and whale hunting usually open very close to the land, compared with villages to the north and south. Leads also form fairly near the coast at Point Barrow, but the situation is not as good as at Point Hope. By contrast, Wainwright men must travel several miles, sometimes 10 or more, to reach open leads for sealing, and they have been known to do their whaling at leads 20 miles from shore. Sometimes a crew will even travel as far as Icy Cape or north to Point Belcher to take advantage of closer leads which remain open longer and a greater abundance of whales. This habit of traveling far out onto the sea ice sometimes exposes them to a greater risk of being cast adrift, although the ice here moves more sluggishly than that around points. At Point Hope the ice moves easily, but hunters seldom go more than a few miles from land, and usually go less than one mile. In 1965 the Point Hope whalers were disappointed that the lead for whaling was 3 miles offshore. The Wainwright men went out about 12 miles during the same whaling season.

From the "lay of the land" it is possible to predict, even by examining a map, what the ice behavior at any particular locality is likely to be. Winds that blow offshore will open leads parallel to the coast and move the pack out. Winds paralleling the shore carry the ice pack along approximately parallel to shore, and on-shore winds hold the ice onshore or cause it to crush and pile. It is of course necessary to know the peculiarities of each type of wind, the current conditions, the tide, and the conformation of the bottom in order to make effective detailed forecasts regarding the probability of ice movement and lead formation. Wherever Eskimos are settled, they have accumulated a detailed knowledge of these factors for their own region.

The pressure caused by current pushing against the irregular-ities of ice beneath the surface has, as we have noted, an important effect on ice movement. It is capable of aiding the wind or of nullifying its effect, or it can move the ice in the absence of any wind. Whenever there is a current, it affects the motion of pack ice, though it may or may not overrule the force of wind. At Wainwright the people usually blame an onshore current for holding the ice if an offshore gale fails to open any lead. Especially during spring and summer, when the floes do not freeze solidly to the landfast ice, current may be an important determinant of ice movement. Current tends to flow according to a predictable pattern. In the winter it usually runs with the wind and in spring and summer it flows monotonously from the south. However, during wintertime especially, the current cannot always be pre-dicted from the shore, so it is necessary to go out onto the ice and test it.

When a hunter is going out to a lead or far offshore in pursuit of polar bears, he tests the current if he has any doubt about it. When he finds a crack over several inches wide, a hole, or a lead, he tests the current by dropping some light-colored object that will sink slowly in the water. It will sink straight down until it clears the lower edge of the ice, and it will then be swept along by the current. Looking into the clear water, the Eskimo notes the direction in which it is carried, whether it is onshore, offshore, or parallel to the shore. From this he can judge the ice safety. A piece of white seal thong, chewed first to soak it thoroughly, makes a good current tester. Any piece of string or bright cloth, properly soaked so that it will sink, will do. Other objects such as bits of shiny metal, paper, or plastic will also work as long as they do not sink too rapidly.

Usually a hunter does not test the current until he reaches the lead edge. It is simple to check the current flow by throwing chunks of ice in the water and watching their direction of drift, as long as the wind is not so brisk that it overrides the motion of the current. Small pieces of ice that float low in the water are best for this. Of course it is also possible to tell the current direction simply from the movement of the ice floes in or beyond an open lead, so long as the wind is not determining its drift. Thus in one instance the pack ice across a lead was moving directly outward, and on this basis the hunters decided to return to the landfast ice. They feared that several cracks which they had crossed on the way to the lead would open, stranding them on a drifting floe.

One precaution is advised whenever the current is being tested, especially with the method of dropping light-colored objects into a hole or crack. If there is a large hummock nearby the current may be deflected or blocked by the ice protruding down into the water, giving a false indication of prevailing current flow. Whenever he has any doubt, the Eskimo will test the current in a different spot for comparison.

During the late spring and summer months the floes become loose and unconsolidated, consisting of pans and ice-fields of varying sizes. The larger floebergs which project deeply beneath the surface will move with the current. These bergs, called *aulaylik*, will sometimes move contrary to the direction of all other ice pans (*puktaak*), which are carried along with the wind. If there is no wind, all ice moves in the same direction, unless there are reverse current eddies. Under most conditions the Eskimos will watch one or two large floebergs some distance from shore or from the lead edge to discern the current flow. When the observer is on drifting ice himself, it is extremely difficult to test current direction, unless landmarks on the shore are visible. Wind-current relationships can be seen by comparing the movement of large floebergs with that of smaller pans. More will be said about detecting the direction of pack-ice drift in later chapters.

The effect of current on ice movement is greatest around points and forelands, where it flows swiftly and where there is less land-fast ice. Certain general concepts of wind and current effects have been discussed above, but specific forecasts depend upon the conditions at the moment, especially the relative strength of wind and current as well as the particular direction of each. The Eskimos have developed an ability to predict ice movements from their knowledge of the peculiarities of each type of wind and each flow of current, so that for any combination of the two they can make a reliable forecast of ice safety. This knowledge is very subtle and is difficult to acquire, especially without a full understanding of the Eskimo language and many years of actual daily experience with these phenomena.

Wind Forecasting

In order to understand more fully the ways in which Eskimos predict movement and fragmentation of the ocean ice, we might briefly consider their methods of wind forecasting. More than anything else the wind dictates the daily activities of Eskimos in northwest Alaska. During the fall, powerful storms determine when the sea ice is carried ashore and grounded so hunters can move out onto it. In the deep cold of winter, storms or even brisk breezes shut the villagers up inside their houses or in their camps. These storms of the darkest months can open wide leads, providing abundant harvests of seals, or they can close the ice so tightly that even polar bears want for food. In springtime the wind is watched closely, because upon it depends the success of the whaling and the time of annual breakup. And during the summer it strongly influences the movements of the ice pack, which in turn determine the availability of marine birds and mammals.

To the North Alaskan Eskimos, all the weather is controlled by winds. When they forecast the weather, they are forecasting the wind, not the precipitation, temperature, or clouds. These are seen as secondary effects brought about by the wind. Wind is therefore of great importance to the cycle of Eskimo activities, and it is seen as a paramount factor in controlling their environment. For this reason they have developed a rather extensive knowledge and understanding of wind forecasting. Most of these prediction techniques have been used for centuries and require only alert senses for their implementation. A few have been derived from modern technology, such as the use of barometers and radios.

First, we will consider a series of signs which are used as general indications of an approaching storm wind. Following this we will show how these general indicators can be used to forecast the specific wind direction when they occur in particular combinations. In the course of this discussion it will become evident that winter weather in northwest Alaska follows an extremely simple pattern, long spells of uniformly clear skies with light winds, alternating with brief periods of violent wind, snow, and cloudiness. Changes which occur in advance of a storm are often slight, and must be watched for carefully. The Eskimos are attuned to these changes, especially when several of them occur together, and are able to predict the weather with remarkable accuracy.

After one learns to forecast the weather in this way during the winter, it is surprising to find that this simple, predictable pattern does not carry over into the summer. During the warm months, the diagnostic indicators seldom occur simultaneously; instead they seem to operate independently most of the time. Eskimos who foresee the weather with impressive accuracy in the wintertime are unable to do as well through the summer months.

1. Before a storm arrives there is normally a drop in barometric pressure, which begins twelve to twenty-four hours in advance of the storm. In general, a rapid and prolonged drop means a severe storm; a gentle and brief decrease may forecast a small and weak storm, or perhaps no storm will materialize. Conversely, an increase in barometric pressure during a storm usually forecasts the end of that storm, or sometimes a wind shift with or without a decrease. High barometric pressure generally means clear and calm weather; low pressure means windy and often cloudy weather. Changes in barometric pressure are highly reliable weather indicators in the wintertime, but during the summer the barometer often rises and falls in a pattern which is much harder to relate to storms. Eskimos watch the barometer carefully during the winter, but seem to pay little attention to it in the summer.

2. The highest seasonal temperatures nearly always occur before and during storms. During the winter, temperature always reaches its seasonal minimum during clear and calm weather. Warming trends preceding storms tend to be fairly rapid, and sometimes very marked. The temperature often drops as the end of a storm approaches. Often during the winter a glance at the barometer or thermometer is enough to tell exactly what the weather will be, but this does not hold throughout the year. In the summertime, weather indicators must occur in combinations in order to have much meaning. These temperature trends generally hold true in summer, however, and are important whenever they occur along with other storm warnings.

3. At the latitude of Alaska's Arctic coast there is essentially no darkness throughout the summer, because the sun is above the horizon or very near it all the time. During spring and fall there is a period of regular alternation between day and night, and during midwinter the sun never rises above the horizon. Throughout those seasons when there is some period of darkness, the Eskimos watch the stars each night and note how much they "twinkle" or "dance." During clear, calm weather there is only a small amount of twinkle, but for a day or two before a storm wind arrives the stars twinkle noticeably. Before a powerful storm, stars actually appear to "dance" about in the sky. If the sky is clearly visible during a storm the stars can still be seen twinkling, and when this decreases, the storm will probably end within a day. This phenomenon is apparently due to an increase in atmospheric moisture or haze in the air before and during storms.

4. Old timers in the "States" say that a "sun dog" or "moon dog" means that wet weather is on its way. These terms refer to one or two lucent rings that encircle the sun or moon like a giant halo. Usually, though not always, these rings occur before or during a storm, and they are considered important foul-weather warnings by the Eskimos. When they disappear, it usually indicates that the storm will end soon. This phenomenon is undoubtedly related to atmospheric haze. It seems to be uncommon during the summer, and the Eskimos do not consider it a useful weather sign at this time.

5. It is not surprising that haze itself often indicates the ap-

proach of a winter storm, but it is quite difficult to observe directly. It is usually very light, not at all like a fog. It can be perceived as a softening of sharp lines near the horizon, or a disappearance of the horizon altogether. Sharp, clear weather contrasts fairly markedly with this hazy prestorm atmosphere, if one is watching for it. During the summer, when the relative humidity is at its highest levels, little correlation appears to exist between light haziness and windstorms.

Fog, thick haze, and precipitation do tend to occur together at this time. Fog and haze frequently precede the onset of precipitation, which is often accompanied by wind. It is also said that haze and fog which settle above the sea ice in the summertime can be used as an indicator of the continuation or end of wet and rainy weather. If the fog and haze disappear, the weather will clear up, but as long as they remain there will be no change. It is also said that during the winter there is sometimes a low fog on the northern horizon before a strong north wind.

6. Clouds usually move in before a winter storm, and they often appear to originate in the direction from which the wind will blow. This is especially true if they are at a low altitude. When these clouds bring snow, even though it may be calm at the time, they are an especially good storm indicator. On the other hand, snow falling during a storm forecasts its approaching end. It is difficult for a novice to tell when it is snowing if the air is filled with blowing snow picked up from the ground. Yet it is really quite simple to distinguish the two types. Snow which is swept up and blown before the wind (*aġanik*) is granular and almost sandy in appearance. Snow flakes (*kanik, aniu*) which are falling from the clouds are large, geometric, flat, and fragile, tending to stick to the fur or cloth of one's parka rather than bouncing off as blowing snow does. Cloudiness and precipitation do not hold particularly well as wind indicators during the summer, unless they occur in conjunction with other storm signs.

There is one cloud condition, however, which appears to be especially applicable during the warm seasons—an elongation or stretching of the clouds. When long cloud streaks come up over the horizon, they usually forecast a strong wind. The wind will blow out of the direction from which the clouds appeared, which

44

is also parallel to their long axis. There is a much lower elongated cloud that scuds rapidly along, stretched out at right angles to the wind. It may forewarn of increasing wind and precipitation. On one occasion the Eskimos referred to it as a "wind cloud."

7. When there is an open lead offshore and clouds overhead, the clouds above the water reflect its deep black color, and those over pack ice or land are bright white. This "water sky" is important for sea-ice travel, and can also be used to forecast storms during winter and early spring. If the black shade is continuous from high overhead right down to the surface, it is an indicator of stormy weather, undoubtedly caused by haze in the air. But with a lead of the same size, if the water sky hovers as a dark band above the water, with light color beneath it (reflecting the ice across the lead), it forecasts good weather.

8. Ice mirage or "looming" (*iññipḳaḳ*) is a refraction phenomenon which usually appears as a white curtain hanging just along the horizon, resembling low clouds or a fog bank. It occurs almost exclusively during the spring and summer. When a mirage appears only along one part of the horizon, the Eskimos say it indicates that a wind may arise from that direction. When mirages encircle the entire ocean horizon, it usually means that clear and warm weather will continue, with a light easterly wind flow.

9. Tidal changes and current direction are particularly good weather indicators, most accurate during winter. As we have noted, the current shifts largely at the will of the winds in wintertime, but prevails strongly from the south during the summer, regardless of wind. Rising and falling of the tide correlates quite well with wind changes throughout the year. This reliable sign will be considered further below.

10. During the open water season, late summer and early fall, the surf may rise ahead of an approaching windstorm. The Eskimos use this as an indicator both of weather and of the proximity of pack ice. Surf may also decrease before a storm subsides, but the Eskimos never explained this clearly, nor was it observed.

11. Behavior of the wind itself may be used to forecast the continuation or end of a storm, especially when other signs are observed as well. Contrary to what would be expected, storm

winds are said to increase to a peak shortly before they begin to subside. On the other hand, storms often seem to decrease during the evening and night, and increase again the following day. Continuation of a storm can be predicted if the wind periodically increases above its average speed, without corresponding sporadic decreases in its speed. In other words, there are intermittent heavy gusts followed by periods of steady "average" wind. The opposite condition, i.e., periodic lulls, may forecast the storm's subsidence.

12. Several men in Wainwright say that they can forecast storms by the ringing in their ears. One person in particular would mention that a storm was coming if his ears were ringing, and that it would continue or stop depending upon whether his ears were still ringing or had ceased to ring.

13. Dogs apparently have a built-in system for forecasting weather. If they howl persistently during good weather, the Eskimos say that a storm is in the offing, and if they howl during a storm, it will soon subside. During a year spent in Eskimo villages the dogs seemed to howl almost every night and day, but did tend to howl more before winter storms began. It is a certainty that they howled in anticipation of the end of storms. They did not howl at all during very foul weather, for several days at a time if the storm was a long one. But when the storm was about to break, they always seemed to set up their choruses. One can only guess that it relates to barometric pressure changes. Whatever the reason, there is no apparent correlation between dogs howling and wind during the summertime.

14. Seals are also able to sense a coming storm, and by watching their behavior one can reliably predict the weather. If seals in an open lead stay up on the surface looking around or resting for long periods of time and appear to be in no hurry to go anywhere, either the weather will remain good or the wind will calm down. On the other hand, if they rise only briefly in one place and do not appear there again, and if their heads remain low in the water rather than coming up high, it is a forewarning of the beginning or continuation of a storm. This applies during any time of year except when the seals are migrating in early summer.

15. The last general storm forecasting method involves the use

of the radio. At Wainwright and Point Hope people learn about the weather to the north or south by listening to a commercial radio station at Nome and to the daily radio schedule of the B.I.A. school in each village. At Wainwright, for example, the teacher contacts Barrow each day, and weather reports are usually exchanged. On the basis of Barrow's weather, Wainwright people can sometimes forecast what is in store for them. Information on weather to the south is more important because storms which blow from the south apparently sweep northward along the coast in a more cohesive and predictable manner than do the north and east storms. There are also more villages to the south, and a better chance to follow the movement of storm patterns from that direction.

The Eskimo classification of wind and storm systems is based not only on the direction from which the wind blows, but on a series of additional correlated conditions such as temperature, cloudiness, precipitation, current, and tide. Thus the Eskimos group several different wind directions, in practice if not in terminology, into a single class of storm system. For example, what we will call a "south wind" can include winds that blow from the south, southeast, southwest, or north. On the other hand, a particular southwest wind may be considered a south wind or a west wind, depending upon the associated conditions.

The direction from which a storm blows is considered very important, largely because it may determine movements of the sea ice. The general storm type or class, i.e., the associated conditions, is important as well, because conditions other than wind heavily influence Eskimo activities. Along the coast a westerly storm, for example, does not cause poor visibility but is very chilling. An easterly storm (including north, northeast, and east winds) severely restricts visibility but does not prevent return to the village from inland camps, because it blows in the direction of travel. Hunters on the tundra or sea ice must be able to foresee the direction in which an approaching gale will blow, so they can adjust their plans accordingly. As we shall see throughout this study, weather, especially in its violent moods, is a key factor in the life of the Eskimo hunter.

Of all the winds and storms, southerly storms are probably the easiest to forecast throughout the year. These include winds from the southeast and south (ḳyseġeneḳ), and most southwesters (uŋŋalaḳ). It is fortunate that these are easy winds to forecast, because they are probably the wildest and most powerful that sweep this coast, and they can be very dangerous for sea-ice hunters. Storms seem to move up from the south more during the warm months than during midwinter, which is relatively free of them. For travelers a south wind means extremely poor visibility unless the temperature climbs above freezing, softening the snow so that it no longer blows before the wind. This is usually, though not always, a "warm" wind. This decreases the danger of freezing, but the wet snow soaks a man's clothing and the warmth tires his dogs. Southerly storms are apt to rise to heavy velocities very quickly, but can die equally fast. Around Wainwright a south gale usually piles the ocean ice or carries the pack along parallel to store, aided by a strong south current. Sometimes, however, the ice lifted and cracked by accompanying high storm tides will be blown away suddenly by a southeaster. Generally speaking, easterly quadrant winds are more dangerous for ice travel because they blow the pack offshore almost every time they reach storm velocities. What follows is a summary of indicators, some or all of which might occur before and during a southerly storm system.

A storm tide is often the first warning of a southerly wind shift. Tide ranges are very small in this region, varying from 8 to 18 inches. South quadrant winds interrupt the normal tides, bringing with them a tidal swell of up to 5 feet. Storm tides are difficult to detect during the winter, except by cracks in the ice due to lifting, occasionally with water surging out over the surface, and by a strong current flowing from the south. Tide and current changes begin 12 to 48 hours ahead of a storm, their size and strength varying according to the storm's severity. A south current does not always mean that a storm is approaching, because even a moderate southerly wind flow causes a current shift. Tides usually reach their peak at the height of a storm. Current and (especially) tide changes are detectable throughout the year. During the summer, the flow of water in and out of the Kuk Inlet is an excellent indicator of tidal change. A strong inflow means the tide is rising, and a rapid outflow shows that the tide is falling. Water level changes along the ocean and Kuk River beaches also reflect tide shifts.

At Wainwright currents flowing from the south (actually southwest when they follow the coastal trend) often pack the ice inward toward the coast, closing the leads or bringing the drifting floes close to the land. It is sometimes difficult to judge the current direction in summer because eddies and counter-currents occur so frequently along the shore or the edge of a lead. Thus the ice may be moving from the north for the first several hundred yards, but beyond that point be drifting from the south. Surface current may also flow in one direction while subsurface current moves the opposite way. Movement of large floebergs is always the most reliable indicator of current flow.

Many of the weather signs that precede a southerly wind have been listed above. The most definitive of these is temperature, which reaches its seasonal high (fall, winter, and spring) during or before a south wind. But temperature is not always warm throughout a storm. Barometric pressure always falls lowest during or before a south wind. Many Wainwright households have a barometer (*anogasiun*), and its most important function is the prediction of these storms. Eskimos frequently tap the barometer's glass face to see whether the needle is moving up or down, whenever other storm signs are present. This is done especially during the summertime, when barometric pressure is often low, so that slight movements can be important. Sometimes when southerly wind indicators are developing the barometer will reverse itself and begin to rise. If it continues to do so, the wind will probably shift to the west quadrant.

Another definitive sign of an approaching southerly storm is the cloud formation and movement. Systems moving up from the south usually bring overcast skies with snow or rain, the clouds scudding along rapidly toward the north. Certain cloud formations warn of a sudden gale, that may arise very quickly, rather than building up gradually as is usual with a south storm. When there are other signs present, ice hunters watch the southern horizon for the appearance of a deep black cloud. If the sky begins to darken heavily, they get off the ice as fast as they can, because such a cloud warns of a sudden gale.

A very singular phenomenon is the bright red "cloud" on the southern horizon which also forewarns of a gale. On one occasion, south wind indicators slowly developed throughout one day and into the next. Then, when the afternoon sun was still high in the sky, a reddish tinge appeared in the clouds along the south horizon, resembling the glow of sunset. Two hours later the light northerly breeze had changed to a stiff southerly wind, which later mounted to a gale.

Of the winds which blow from the south, the southwester is said to be the most powerful and longest lasting. Southwest winds do not have accompanying conditions which are uniquely their own. They resemble either south winds (warm, cloudy, falling barometer) or west winds (cold, rising barometer, wet in summer or clear in winter). Southeast storms usually resemble south winds, and may be very sudden and powerful. There is one peculiar wind which the Eskimos call by a term meaning "false north wind," because it blows from the north but is associated with southerly wind conditions. According to the native theory there is a southerly circulation aloft which "turns under" somewhere to the north and blows from that direction at the surface. The fact that clouds move directly opposite this wind supports the theory, as do the associated characteristics of falling barometer, high temperature, clouds and snow, and south current. When a "false north wind" blows there is always a good chance that the wind will shift to the south, though this never happened during several such storms at Wainwright during the winter of 1964–65.

Some or all of the southerly wind characteristics may be reversed in anticipation of the storm's end. For example, the tide may begin to fall, temperatures cool off, rain or drizzle (*miñik*) end, skies clear, and so on. These signs are usually noticed easily, but may not occur until just before the wind changes.

Winds from the westerly quadrant, including west (*kanagnak*), northwest, and some southwest winds, blow more or less onshore at Wainwright, piling the ice or holding it tight to the shore. When this occurs in wintertime, the seal hunting is spoiled because the cracks and leads are closed. Conditions are excellent for polar bear hunting or sleeping seal hunting, however, because there is no danger of drifting off un an ice floe. Winds blowing off the ice do not pick up the snow as they do on the tundra, so there is always good visibility on the ice during west winds. This is because of either the stickiness of the snow on salt ice or the obstruction caused by rough ice.

During the winter, westerly winds usually occur following the development of south-wind indicators or after a south wind blows itself out. The Eskimos do not concern themselves much with the westerly gales, because they are usually brief and not very strong. Their direct consequences, during the winter at least, are not particularly important. Frequently, when a south wind seems imminent, the wind shifts clear through the southerly quadrant and into the west. In this case the barometer rises suddenly, temperature falls, and the skies become clear. The west wind usually blows, strongly enough to be extremely chilly, for several days before shifting through the north quadrant into the northeast or east. Sometimes a winter south wind will blow for a day or two and then diminish noticeably. If it switches to the southeast the wind will probably increase again, but if it switches to the west the severe storminess is assumed to be over.

In the summertime westerly winds are accompanied by rising barometric pressure, cool temperatures, clouds and rain, and very high tides. Eskimos waste no time in hauling their boats high up on the beach when the sea wind blows, lest the tide and surf wash them away. The surf builds up only when there is no pack ice offshore, and even then it is not great. Because west winds blow over the moist ocean surface in summer, they bring clouds, rain, and drizzle. Visibility is usually good, however. Onshore winds are usually good for hunting at this season, because they carry the pack ice, with its wealth of game, toward land. Accompanying currents are probably onshore as well. This is especially noted by the presence of long sinuous current lines or *pilaġaġnik* caused by meeting of countercurrents or crosscurrents. When these lines run parallel to shore they are said to indicate an onshore current. "Looming" or mirages on the western horizon are sometimes said to forecast westerly winds.

The last type of storm system includes winds from the east (*kiloaġnak*), northeast (*nigik, nigikpak*), and north (*ikagnak*).

During the winter these storms, which sweep across the great tundra plain, are preceded by many of the same signs as southerly winds. There are some important differences, however. The most definitive signs are falling tide with north or east current, and clouds moving in from the east quadrant. The temperature rises, but not to an unusually high level for that season; the barometer falls, but not too low; haze and overcast appear, but they are not extremely heavy. Unlike the south winds, north or east storms may arise without much warning at all, so it is easy to be caught out on the sea ice when the gale starts blowing. Usually, however, signs are clearly present well in advance of the storm.

Winter storms from the east and north are apparently of longer duration than those from the south or west. It is difficult to forecast the end of such a storm. Although several of the methods listed above are useful, they do not occur near the end of every storm. The more reliable of these are falling snow followed by diminishing winds and perhaps clearing skies, but even these indicators do not occur too often. The dogs howl near the end of almost every storm, and are perhaps the most reliable indicators. Cloud movement contrary to the wind direction, or a similar change in the current, would also indicate the forthcoming end of a storm.

The situation is quite different in summertime, when the pattern of predictability is completely upset. There are a few signs that might be noted, however. A gentle easterly flow brings clear skies at all seasons, but is accompanied by the most intense cold in winter and almost balmy warmth in summer. Stronger winds from the north and east usually bring partly cloudy conditions with good visibility. Barometric pressure does not reliably forecast summer storms from the east, but may anticipate their continuation or end. Decreasing pressure during a storm means that the winds will increase or continue. Fluctuating pressure with a fairly constant average level also forecasts continuation of a storm. Rising pressure indicates that the winds may decrease or change.

Tidal changes are one reliable forewarning of easterly and northeasterly winds. Tides drop to their lowest levels before and during these winds, and rise again in advance of a change. Increasing surf may also forecast the end of these offshore gales. On the other hand, in the spring and early summer a strong current from the west may indicate an approaching easterly wind, especially if other signs accompany it.

"Looming" or *iññipk̲ak̲* is characteristic of sunny, warm, and calm weather. When there is an east wind and "looming" spreads all along the ice horizon, the weather will probably remain warm and pleasant. Usually this means the wind will not change. If the "looming" is only toward the north, the wind may shift to the north.

Cracks and Leads

Several factors other than current and wind are important in forecasting movements of the ice and judging its safety for travel and hunting. Most of these have to do with cracks in the ice, their direction, occurrence, and movement. Cracks may range from an inch to several yards across, but to the Eskimo any crack is a prospective lead—a lead that could trap him on a drifting ice floe from which he might never return. Cracks result from several different forces, the rise and fall of tides, concussion from moving ice, the pressure of wind and current, and perhaps changes in temperature. The cause is important to the Eskimo because it helps him to predict what movement will take place along the line of fracture, but the immediate conditions of wind, tide, current, and ice movement are his greatest concern. Every crack is a line of weakness through the ice, whether it is freshly opened or covered with a week's development of young ice.

The Eskimo is most concerned with a crack or series of cracks if it is fresh, because if so, it is likely that the force which caused the initial movement or opening is still operating on the ice. The frequency of cracks is also considered; the more cracks there are the greater the danger of shifting or extensive ice movement. During the spring and summer there are more open cracks in the sea ice, perhaps simply because those which form are kept open longer by warm temperatures and sunshine. Thus it is impossible to tell if the crack is new, and if the force which opened it is still being exerted on the ice.

When he finds a fresh crack, or in some cases one which may be a few days old, the Eskimo first notes its orientation. If the crack is oriented more or less at a right angle to the coast, it is a sign that the ice is safe for travel and will not easily break away from the landfast floe. But if the fracture runs somewhat parallel to the coastal trend, such as NNE–SSW at Wainwright or NE–SW off the south shore of Point Hope, the ice could easily be carried away by an offshore wind or current. The reasoning is simply that cracks paralleling the shore have severed the bond of the floe ice with the landfast ice, so that the floe is free to move and drift. Thus a hunter never crosses a crack that parallels the coast if there is an offshore breeze or current, or a possibility that one might arise while he is on its seaward side.

Cracks are said to trend in approximately the same direction as the wind (and probably the current) because the ice moves with them, causing shear or parallel movement. It seems logical, therefore, that the wind or current which produces cracks does not always cause them to widen, but may initiate shear movement instead. It is sometimes possible to predict a wind change by observing the trend of the cracks. This is probably due to the current changing in anticipation of a wind shift. Thus an approaching north wind would cause cracks to form in a north-south direction, and might induce shear movement along them. A northeast wind or current which arises after such cracks are formed can easily widen the cracks and create offshore leads.

The "behavior" of cracks is a good indicator that movement or opening may be imminent. Eskimos regard motion of cracks as very serious, and are easily discouraged from traveling farther if there is evidence of pressure being exerted on the ice. When a crack is likely to start moving, it is not quiet but pulsates or shifts slightly as a warning that force is being applied to the pack. A crack that has a thin but complete cover of ice is probably "dead"; but if the young ice that has formed in it has a small line of open water down the middle, the crack is still moving, though it may be too slow and slight to be seen. Gradual motion in an open crack can be detected by jamming a stick of the right length between the two sides. If the ice moves, the stick may fall, break, or move to a different angle because of shear action. Shear (parallel) movement is also indicated by places where the snow or ice juts out on one side of the crack and has a corresponding indentation on the opposite side. If the protrusion and concavity are not directly across from each other and the crack is fresh, shear motion has taken place recently.

But cracks do not always move slowly. Their pulsating may be a quick jiggling, and parallel movements may be a series of rapid jerks. Pulsating is sometimes caused by piling of the ice somewhere in the distance, or it may indicate that pressure is being exerted to widen the crack. In this case, current and wind direction must be considered before crossing to the crack's seaward side. Cracks that show any motion whatever are very important, because they could begin large-scale movement at any time. Sometimes they close with such rapidity that water is forced up out of them in a spray. They can open equally fast.

Generally, the Eskimos pay much less attention to cracks during the summer, unless they are moving, because there are so many of them and there is no way of telling their age. Hunters also do not travel as far out from the coast, and therefore take fewer risks. Cracked areas should be avoided, because they indicate weakness in the ice. Eskimos never camp near any sort of crack, because the ice can begin to move or crush at any time.

In former times the Eskimos routinely crossed moving cracks as long as the movement paralleled the shore and the landfast ice. Thornton (1931) describes the Bering Strait Eskimos' method of continuously walking against the current while they hunted, in order to remain close to the spot where they crossed onto the drifting pack. Modern Eskimos with highly efficient hunting methods using rifles and large mobile dog teams need not take such risks, and rarely cross over a crack onto moving ice. If they ever go across a crack that might be dangerous they are certain to carry a small skin boat with which they can return to safe ice, and to keep a constant watch for signs of the ice opening behind them.

There are several methods an Eskimo can use for crossing a crack or lead that opens between him and the landfast ice. The most basic and least advisable method is simply to swim across. This is done only as a desperate measure and when the lane has not opened very wide. Nuliak said that he had crossed cracks several times by this method, once swimming two cracks before he reached safe ice. In this case his five dogs swam across behind him and he rode his sled back to Wainwright, which was many miles away when this occurred.

The story is told of another Wainwright Eskimo who was caught on the wrong side of a crack near the Kuk River inlet. He took his *manak*, a snag hook for game retrieval which has a long line attached to it, and threw it to the other side, catching it on some projecting ice. He attached another line to his waist, and tied it to the lead dog of his team. Using the *manak* line, he pulled himself across the lane in the water, and once across he pulled his dogs and sled to the safe side with the other line. Sled dogs are usually very reluctant to enter the water, and can be forced into it only if a line is used in this way. Since a dog team is an exceedingly valuable possession, a man would hesitate to leave it behind even under these circumstances.

The fact that men are willing to swim across leads illustrates how deeply they fear being forced to spend a period of days or weeks out on the drift ice. Fortunately, they seldom must resort to this undesirable method of reaching safety. One man told a story of his own experience, which illustrates a commonly mentioned technique of crossing open water. He first warned that a man should never cross any fresh crack that runs parallel to the shore, because "If you do, you are giving your life away." Once he went far out from Wainwright on the ice, and made the mistake of crossing such a crack on the way out. As he returned toward shore, he found a new crack, at a right angle to the coast. Taking this as a warning, he started to run, but he did not reach the first crack until it had opened so wide that he could not jump over it. He looked up and down the crack quickly, because speed was essential, and spotted a small piece of ice less than 2 feet in diameter. He picked it up out of the water, threw his rifle and hunting bag across, and then tossed the ice chunk to the middle of the crack. Keeping his *unaak* (ice-testing pole) as a balancing rod, he jumped across the crack, using the chunk for a stepping stone in the middle. That piece of ice saved his life, he said, because the lead opened very wide and did not close again for two weeks.

If larger cakes are available, the hunter uses them as a boat for himself and even for his dog team. He may find a piece floating loose in the water, or he can chop one free from the ice along the edge. He can paddle the ice pan across with his *unaaḳ* or the stock of his rifle, or he can throw his snag hook over and catch it on the ice to pull himself across by its line. If the pan is too small to hold man and dogs together, he fastens a line to the lead dog and pulls them from the opposite side.

Some hunters always carry with them a small skin boat which they use to retrieve seals they have shot in the open lead. These small open boats and kayaks are carried on the dog sled, so that they are always handy for use. If a man finds himself on the far side of a lead, he can always cross it in his boat, unless the water is very rough. The kayak has the disadvantage that two or more hunters cannot always get into it. The open skin boat is poor in rough water, but can hold several men or one man with several of his dogs and most of his equipment. This is one reason these open skin boats have become so popular in northwest Alaska. Several times whaling crews from Wainwright have been caught on the far side of leads, and the men have always returned to safety by using the large skin *umiaḳs* which they always have in whaling camps for chasing whales.

There are also ways of crossing cracks without even leaving the solid ice, excluding the method of waiting for the lead to close in due time. The first of these involves a simple knowledge of the dynamics of crack and lead formation. Eskimos state that leads generally open first from the direction of the current or wind, and the opening slowly progresses down current. Therefore, if an Eskimo comes to a crack which has opened behind him, he will immediately toss a piece of ice into the water to see the direction of current flow. Then he will go quickly as possible down current. When he does this, he hopes to reach a place where the crack has not yet widened enough to prevent his crossing it. Thus, if the current (or wind) is from the north, he will go south, or vice versa.

There is a second advantage in traveling down current or downwind in such an emergency, when it occurs along a coast with a headland to the north or south. Ice that moves parallel to the coast off Wainwright, for example, will often remain in contact with landfast ice, even piling, at Icy Cape to the south or at Atanik (or Point Belcher) to the north. If a lead opens and the pack is drifting southward, a man who is trapped on it will probably travel in the direction of movement, hoping to reach landfast ice near Icy Cape. A man set adrift at Barrow would not travel north because there is no land in that direction, but he might escape if he reached Point Franklin, the first headland south of Barrow.

Another way of crossing leads is finding an ice bridge, i.e., a place where there is still contact across a lead by a solid ice pan or peninsula. Quite often heavy points of ice (*nuwuk*) jut out into a lead, and drifting ice will contact them first when it comes in, last when it moves out. A Wainwright hunter narrowly escaped from a drifting floe this way on February 6, 1965. The weather conditions, with a northeasterly breeze at about 10 m.p.h., did not forewarn of ice breakup, but a rising tide had cracked the ice parallel to the shore. This man was the only hunter to go out, because the others were afraid of the ice conditions.

He found an open lead several miles offshore, where he waited for seals to come up. After a short time he had a "feeling" that he should head for the grounded ice. As he approached the edge of the landfast ice, where there had been a lead less than a week earlier, he came to a crack that was widening rapidly. When he crossed this crack it was only about 2 feet wide, but soon after he passed over, it was several yards across. He thought that he now had reached ice that was firmly attached to the landfast floe, but soon he came to a small lead that he could not cross. He was in a bad position, caught between two opening cracks.

The floe was drifting outward, but also parallel to the edge of grounded ice, so he stopped and listened carefully, hoping to detect the sound of ice piling and crumbling against the landfast ice. He was lucky. Toward the south he heard the distinctive noise of piling ice. He turned his team as quickly as possible in the direction of the squeaking and crumbling noises. Soon he reached a very long point of solidly grounded heavy ice, still in contact with the drifting pack. This point was visible a long way off, and would have undoubtedly seemed a logical place for the last contact to take place. He crossed to the fast ice just before the two sides separated. Had he not been alert and moved quickly he might have been adrift until the lead closed.

In this case the ice that broke away was a large section between the flaw ice and an open lead beyond its edge. This happens fairly often, and is called *tuwayagaatigut siku*. The extent of the ice which remains attached when a lead opens varies according to the strength of the wind and current, the tide, thickness of the ice, and existence of cracks or weak areas. The original lead may open right along the landfast ice, it may leave ice in bays or areas protected by projecting points, or it may open beyond several miles of floe extending far outward from the solidly grounded ice. These large expanses of ice which are not grounded are the most susceptible to breakage.

When a lead opens, it is not usually a single fracturing of the ice, which opens wider and wider until a broad lane exists. The cracking is much more complex, and the opening may increase in size as new fields and pans, separated from the flaw ice by cracks, drift out into the lead. Before a lead opens, extensive fracturing often interlaces an area several miles wide. Gradually certain of these cracks widen to form a complex of lanes or leads. If the wind or current lasts several days, this fragmented ice area is gradually cleared out, the pans and floes accumulating along the seaward margin of the lead, and the landward edge becoming a clean break without loose pans along it. If a storm passes quickly, however, fresh cracks which have not yet been subjected to enough force to open them remain along the landward edge. This creates a dangerous field of loose, unconnected ice floes, which can drift out into the lead at any time.

Eskimos are especially cautious of this situation, in which they can easily be stranded on a drifting floe while they are waiting for seals along a newly formed lead. The complex fragmentation involved in lead formation explains why multiple crossings may be necessary in order to reach safe ice.

In some cases the loose floes that are left along the flaw ice margins are carried away later by the current, which may flow swiftly for several days after a storm subsides. Even a light wind can eventually widen the cracks following a storm. Because of the danger of being carried away on these loose ice fields, Eskimos seldom go to the lead edge immediately after a heavy blow, even though there are usually many seals at such a time. It is also said that the ice can break loose when cracks suddenly form after the storm wind dies. Leads develop swells in them during a storm, which continue after the wind subsides. These swells can crack the ice and allow it to drift away during the day following a storm.

There is another way that fields of ice are broken away from the lead edge, which can happen after a storm or any time that rapid ice movement parallels the lead. During a severe gale the pack can be moving up to 2 m.p.h., and when such tremendous masses of ice are involved, the potential impact force exceeds the imagination. Ice movement usually continues for a couple of days after a gale subsides. If there is any contact between projecting areas of landfast ice and the drifting pack, cracks running for miles may be rent in both ice fields. As a result, some of the immobile ice may be broken loose and set into motion with the pack.

Usually this involves rather small points or projections of ice, not over a square mile in area. If there is any chance of impact with the moving floes, such dangerous areas are avoided by Eskimo hunters. If cracks are present already, even if they are covered by young ice, they create an even more dangerous situation. At Point Barrow in February, 1965, there was a large crack covered with ice thick enough to hold a man. It had moved several feet at least once, however, as revealed by the fact that the young ice covering it was rafted, one layer having moved and overlapped the other. This crack ran for miles parallel to the coast, about one-half mile shoreward from an open lead. Hunters would not cross this old crack to reach the lead, fearing that a moving ice floe would contact this ice and carry it away. Ice which is moving north or south off the end of Point Hope can break away sections of ice paralleling the north or south shore. If the ice is drifting rapidly, hunters are cautious about going to a lead north or south of the point (depending on which direction it is moving) lest they be stranded on a floe which is knocked loose in this way.

The force of this impact was demonstrated at Wainwright, where there were several large cracks through the landfast floe over 10 miles shoreward from an offshore lead. These cracks, up to 5 feet wide, were said to have been caused by impact of heavy "mother ice" (*aakaŋa siku*) somewhere out along the lead. There had been no wind, tide, or strong current to cause these cracks. Eskimos often say that ocean ice moving someplace "far away" can crack and open the ice simply by its impact and pressure.

Usually the impact which breaks fields of ice away is ponderously slow, and does not cause a heavy jolt or make a loud noise. Thus it is difficult to detect ice breakaway of any sort. Sometimes there is a slight concussion, but it is not likely to be felt. Ice movement is usually almost silent, especially if the ice is opening or there is momentary contact between landfast ice and the pack drifting parallel to its edge. One of the loudest sounds, a sporadic squeaking or "budging" noise, is caused by young ice being rafted or crushed. This sound probably carries for a quarter or half mile, and is unmistakable when heard. There is also a hissing sound in some cases of shearing movement or slight piling. Only when the ice is really piling actively is the noise loud and rumbling. This sound is sometimes almost thunderous, and can be heard over a half mile away if it is not obliterated by a buffeting gale. When the piles grow to great heights, huge boulders of ice tumble and slide down their flanks, sounding like a giant bowling ball slamming through the pins. On a calm day, with a strong current pushing a huge floe majestically along a lead, this sound is strikingly powerful and curiously out of place.

There are several methods of detecting whether or not one is on moving ice. If the current suddenly appears to stop flowing, chances are that the floe is now moving along with it. Eskimos sometimes watch the relative positions of conspicuous ice piles, and should they change, it means that one body of ice is in motion relative to the other. Thus a hunter will watch the ice toward the village for any change, and will also note his position relative to landmarks on shore. These techniques will be explained more fully when we discuss summer ice.

One very clever method used today involves placing a compass on the ice in a set position, so that any ice movement will cause a slight change of the needle from the position where it was set. One day at Point Hope there was a fairly brisk southeast wind giving rise to some concern among the men in whaling camps that the ice might break away. In one camp a compass was set up to detect ice motion. First a small wooden stool was placed carefully and solidly on the ice, and around its windward side three snow-blocks were set to protect it from jiggling or movement by the wind. A compass was placed on the stool with its needle set pre-cisely north and south, and for a while there were two compasses to insure absolute accuracy. Every five to fifteen minutes a man would check the compass to see if the needle had shifted from its exact setting. When a crack opens, there is always some rotary motion, which would be recorded by the compass needle.

Eskimos sometimes have a chance to warn each other if the ice breaks away. If a man notices that a crack is beginning to open, so that anyone across it would be in danger, he shoots his rifle three times in rapid succession. This is a signal of long standing on the Arctic Coast to warn of ice breakaway. All hunters im-mediately head for land when it is heard, and they wait along the safe side of the dangerous crack or new lead to see that no man is caught on its far side. If anyone gets caught, they rescue him with a small skin boat, or they bring a large boat from shore to conduct a rescue operation. If a man finds himself trapped by a lead, he gives the same signal as a call for help, and marks his posi-tion by putting some cloth on his *unaak* pole and waving it. The use of rifle signals and *umiaks* (large skin boats) with outboard engines for rescue in modern times is one reason so few men drift away now compared with former years. At Wainwright, when several whaling crews were set adrift without knowing it, they were warned by an airplane which flew out from the village and dropped a note. Usually there is no chance to give a warning this way, but there are numerous instances of airplane rescues from drifting floes.

Piling Ice and Rough Ice

The dangers of sea-ice hunting have to do mostly with being cast adrift. But occasionally during normal travel or hunting activities, and certainly when a person becomes stranded on an ice floe, there is the danger of actively piling and rafting ice.

Almost everywhere over the thousands of square miles of sea ice in the polar oceans there are evidences of ice piling, in the form of ridges, hummocks, and huge piles of broken ice. The problem of dealing with rough ice and ice which is actively piling is therefore almost universal except in the most protected areas of bays and fjords. It is hardly necessary to say that crushing ice is dangerous, mostly because of the huge tumbling chunks of ice and the possibility of slipping into a crevice and having it crush together. The physical problems of crossing actively piling ridges are so great as to render it nearly impossible, unless the piling is very slow. Dogs are so frightened by it that they are very reluctant to approach such areas.

Even going too close to piling ice, whether it is a small heap of young ice or a huge mountain of heavy polar ice, is extremely dangerous, because the surrounding flat ice can break, sink, or heave without warning. When ice piles up, its sheer weight causes downward buckling of the ice around it, which in turn causes flooding. This flooding will soon be covered with young ice, but the thin ice is not black like ice in the ocean itself. The whitish-blue color of the ice below is transmitted through this thin ice or slush, making it look deceptively safe; so it is easy to walk onto it and break through into the water underneath. These areas also become covered by drifting snow; so any questionable ice around fresh piles or downward bucklings must be avoided.

When ice is piling and being forced together by great pressure, Eskimos say that it is best to avoid flat winter ice, especially if it is rather young. Once ice piles become solidified, a couple of days after formation, they are the safest place on the ocean ice. Flat winter ice can crack, raft, and pile suddenly, even before a man can escape. It is not unusual to see a flat area where the ice almost began to pile but did not quite break, leaving a series of rippling undulations or wrinkles in its surface.

Once ice piling has ceased and the topography has solidified, the ever-present problem of traveling through the jumbled and jagged landscape remains. Along this coast the ice moves so frequently that long-distance travel is done only on the ice near shore, unlike those areas of northeast Alaska or the Canadian Archipelago where great flat expanses of ice offer an ideal highway for travel from place to place. Most of the ice-covered sea presents this barrier, as witnessed by the reports of many explorers who have attempted to travel on it. Some of the recent attempts to reach the north pole over the ice have been stopped short by its incredible roughness.

Anyone who has experienced a long day's travel by dog team through mile after mile of chaotically jumbled ice will not soon forget it, even long after the bruises have healed. Between the scattered pans of unbroken winter ice and the relatively flat polar ice, it is as though the horizontal dimension no longer exists. True, the huge piles can be avoided, but there is no trail which avoids the smaller jumbles of ice. One is continually being hauled abruptly to the top of 3- or 4-foot chunks, only to have the sled pulled off sideways, tipped, hung, twisted, jammed, pinched, or simply crashed straight off an abrupt drop, with the driver stumbling behind or clinging to the upstanders. The driver's arms and legs become rubbery-tired and tempers flare. The dog lines constantly snag on small pinnacles of ice, and the dogs run ahead as soon as the tangle is released, pulling the sled, driverless, over whatever lies ahead. It seems as though the sure-footed dogs take sadistic pleasure in reserving their bursts of speed for the roughest ice or for the times when their master stumbles into a crevice but does not release his grip on the sled stands. Up once again, he looks ahead to a seemingly insurmountable pile of boulders, and shortly is pulled and pummeled through it. It seems that each pile must be the last, and yet there is always another. And at least once on every trip across the floes, the sled slips down the face of an ice pile only to crash directly into a low flat wall of ice, which the dogs are agile enough to jump up onto but which the sled runners cannot ride over.

Indeed, even the dogs are stiff and bruised the day following such an excursion, but the Eskimos are so accustomed to it that it is scarcely worthy of comment. Occasionally an Eskimo will fall or in some way injure himself, but this is not common, because he usually stays on the sled as much as possible to avoid slipping on the ice. Ankles, legs, and ribs are the most likely places to be injured during dog team or foot travel through rough ice. Persons who have weak ankles susceptible to sprains are perhaps least suited for this. Only one injury was noted during this study, a severe leg bruise sustained by a man running to catch his sled. However, every man falls on rough ice once or twice every time he travels through it for any distance.

Certain individuals are much better at traveling through rough ice than are others. For the most part this is the result of skillful reconnoitering. The expert traveler constantly stops his team and goes to the top of high ice piles to pick the smoothest trail, and once he has decided he makes long detours and follows a winding path. On one occasion I traveled with two other teams for some 15 miles through very rough ice, and observed firsthand the difference in skills of two drivers. One man felt that he could do best by traveling a more or less straight line without stopping to reconnoiter. The other stopped every few hundred yards to find a smooth trail, and then wound in and out of the ice until he was forced to stop again. The latter individual was continuously far ahead of the former, and returned to the village with all his equipment in good condition. The man who followed a straight trail returned several hours later with a badly broken sled and, undoubtedly, a very tired back. In rough-ice travel it is also best to stop frequently to avoid excessive perspiration.

Another problem with rough ice is the condition of the snow, which accumulates in deep soft piles in areas of sharp relief. These drifts are especially dangerous, because they conceal holes and crevices into which a leg might slip or a man might fall. Drifts also tend to extend over the edges of abrupt drop-offs, so it is best to stay well back from any edge. At times the fluffy whiteness of this snow, especially in whiteout conditions, obliterates the sharp features of the ice landscape, so that travel is very risky. Even sunglasses do little to relieve the strain of such conditions, where concentrated effort is needed to keep a good line of travel. Regardless of the conditions, an Eskimo is seldom deterred as long as there is no danger of drifting away or being seriously injured. Eskimos are most perseverant in their traveling and hunting. No expense of physical labor or time will deter an excellent hunter from reaching his objective or putting forth his best effort to get game. And yet a good hunter rarely expends his energy if he feels there is no chance of success; for instance, he does not shoot a seal if it probably cannot be retrieved. Attitudes such as these, or deviations from them, can strike the outsider as rather irrational or even foolish. Sometimes, however, it is difficult to understand behavior when its context is not fully comprehended.

The tundra is seldom completely snow covered except after a rare windless snowfall. Both the sea ice and the land are usually covered with snow ranging in depth to 30 feet, depending on where the wind sweeps the surface clear and where great drifts are deposited. Drifts can also be a great aid to ice travel, where they smooth over the rough and jagged ice piles with a hard-packed snow surface.

The rare deep snowfall raises real havoc with any sort of travel until the wind can harden it. At Point Hope there was a heavy snowfall in early May, 1964, which covered the land and ice with 3 feet of soft thick snow. During the time before a storm hardened the snow, travel by dog team was almost impossible and walking was worse. The fact that such snowfalls are rare, and that Arctic snows are usually packed into a pavement-like surface, makes these regions the best on earth for dog-team travel. The modern Eskimo with his large dog team is seldom forced to walk alongside his sled, as the inland inhabitants usually must do even with the largest and strongest dogs. In short, the winter snow surface in the Arctic offers excellent conditions for foot and dog travel except in places where the sea ice surface is piled and heaped so that it is almost impassable by any mode of travel.

Occasionally an ice traveler is fortunate enough to find huge areas of flat ice, ḳaiaḳsuaḳpok, that are oriented in the direction he wishes to travel. And when the ice is rough everywhere, there are sometimes small leads or cracks which have frozen over solidly enough to support a man or a dog team. These cracks form a perfectly flat trail cutting through even the roughest ice, so they are sought out by Eskimo travelers. They also attract seals because the thin ice allows them to scratch breathing holes most easily. In midwinter, at 30° or 40° below zero, a lead freezes over solidly enough for travel in a day or so. In spring (e.g., April) it may be frozen for a week and have ice 6 to 10 inches thick but still remain unsafe, because young ice formed at higher temperatures is not as strong as that which develops in extreme cold (Stefansson

1950, p. 355). Most of the cracks formed near the landfast ice by a particular wind tend to run the same direction. Far out at sea, however, beyond the area where drifting floes and grounded ice meet, cracks are probably oriented more randomly.

The Eskimos usually chop and smooth a trail through the rough ice from the village to the edge of landfast ice. The trail runs from 1 to 15 miles, depending on the year. It is chopped beyond the flaw only during whaling season, when large skin boats must be hauled out to the lead. For winter sealing the trail is a convenience, and it becomes essential whenever large numbers of seals are taken, because the weight of a heavy load will break the sled on rough ice. Th trail is leveled with axes and picks. Several men can chop a half-mile trail in three hours, if the ice is not too rough, but in some places it takes an hour to make 50 yards of trail smooth enough for the passage of loaded sleds. Care is taken to make the trail through the smoothest areas, in order to minimize labor expenditure. As a result it follows a serpentine route.

There are general patterns of ice piling along the northwest Alaskan coast; so in a given area the Eskimos can always predict that the ice will be smooth or rough. Around Wainwright there is fairly active ice piling, but there is usually enough flat ice near shore to permit easy travel. An "ice foot," produced by splashing and freezing of water on the shore in fall, often forms along the beach. It forms a smooth, clear "road" in early winter, but is soon deeply covered by drifted snow.

North of Wainwright, around Point Belcher and the abandoned village of Atanik, the ice piles heavily due to powerful currents, deep water, and seaward projection of the land. Dog mushing is seldom possible on the ice here, but just to the north the sheltered ice of Peard Bay lies flat and undisturbed, providing excellent dog travel during the ice season. In the opposite direction, beginning about 15 miles south of Wainwright and stretching to Icy Cape, the ice is also flat, because it is protected by the Cape and the shoals offshore. All along this coast, long ice ridges pile up like huge windrows, paralleling the coast and the edge of landfast ice. Smaller ice pilings, more or less randomly oriented, are produced by crushing around the edges of circular ice pans. Viewed from the air, the ocean ice is an endless series of small pancake flats, each encircled by the walls of its own crumbled edges. The largest pilings, parallel ridges that may stretch for miles, mark the edges of former leads and shear cracks, disrupting this circular pattern.

Murdoch (1892, pp. 31–32) summarized the conditions of ice movement and piling at Point Barrow:

> Outside of the land-floe the ice is a broken pack, consisting of hummocks of fragmentary old and new ice, interspersed with com-paratively level fields of the fomer. During the early part of the winter this pack is most of the time in motion, sometimes moving northeastward with the prevailing current and grinding along the edge of the barrier, sometimes moving off to sea before an off-shore wind . . . and again coming in with greater or less violence against the edges of this new ice, crushing and crumpling it up against the barrier. . . .
>
> The westerly gales of later winter, however, bring in great quan-tities of ice, which, pressing against the land-floe, are pushed up into hummocks and ground firmly in deeper water, thus increasing the breadth of the fixed land-floe until the line of separation between the land-floe and the moving pack is 4 or 5 or sometimes even 8 miles from land. The hummocks of the land-floe show a tendency to arrange themselves in lines parallel to the shore, and if pressure has not been too great there are often fields of ice of the season not over 4 feet thick between the ranges of hummocks, as was the case in the winter of 1881–82. In the following year, however, the pressure was so great that there were no such fields, and even the level ice inside the barrier was crushed into hummocks in many places. . . .

CHAPTER 3

Sea Ice: Early Summer Conditions

Snow and Water on Sea Ice

URING the course of winter, there is a considerable accumulation of snow on the sea ice. Where the ice is flat, the snow is more or less uniform in depth. Where the ice is thrust up into ridges, however, snow accumulates in the lee of each ice pile, forming an alluvium of long, tapering drifts that may be many feet deep. And within the jumbled hummocks themselves, snow gradually fills each crevice and hollow. Throughout the winter it becomes progressively easier to travel over the ocean ice as it is smoothed off in this manner, and as the snow becomes wind-packed until it is pavement-hard.

The months from December to April are nearly free from thaw, and, in fact, the temperature seldom climbs above 0° F. Warm spells are not considered a blessing at this time of year, because the snow becomes soft and sticky, creating poor conditions for dog mushing. The wetness eventually permeates everything and later freezes solid when temperatures plunge to more seasonal levels. By the end of April daytime temperatures are always above zero, and thawing takes place even if the temperature does not exceed the freezing point.

With the warmer temperatures and bright sunshine of spring, the snow really begins to thaw. The rate of melting is very rapid by late May and early June. Snowdrifts become a quagmire, no longer strong enough to support a man or a dog sled without allowing it to sink deeply. Beneath the snow surface, water and slush begin to accumulate. Then the water puddles appear. At first they are small and widely scattered, but they grow rapidly as the drifts melt away. Travel over the ocean ice becomes increasingly tedious, because it is difficult to avoid the soft snow and the network of puddles that covers the surface.

In previous times the northwest Alaskan Eskimos used snowshoes for walking over the soft snow and decaying ice of spring. But the present-day Eskimos prefer to wear rubber hipboots when they must walk on the ice, and use dog teams as much as possible in order to evade the problems of foot travel. Hipboots are so high that a man seldom steps into a drift or puddle which goes over the top. But it is best to avoid snowdrifts and snow-filled hollows entirely if possible. In late spring the snow waits like quicksand for something to step into it. So the dogs flounder and the sled sinks, often forcing the Eskimo to wade clumsily behind the sled, pushing it to help the dogs. He stands on the sled whenever it passes over deep snow, if he can, because neither the dogs nor the sled sink as deeply as a man. On foot it is best to walk around drifts or spots where the snow is deep.

It may be difficult for the inexperienced person to understand the fact that the snow and the ice often look so much alike than an ice traveler may not know whether his next step will be onto a hard ice surface or a deep soft pocket of snow. There are two ways to judge the difference between snow and ice surfaces. First, snow is generally darker in color and more granular in texture than ice. The difference is not readily noticed until a person has acquired some experience, so a beginner will certainly make mistakes in judgment. It is especially hard to distinguish the two when it is very bright and one is wearing sunglasses; and the difficulty seems to increase owing to eye strain after several hours' walking. But

70

it is sometimes possible to make good progress without relying on this method.

The second technique is much slower, but also less fallible. An iron-tipped pole or *unaaḳ*, normally used for judging ice thickness, is carried by hunters whenever they travel on the sea ice. In order to tell whether the surface ahead is snow or ice, the Eskimo simply pokes it with the point of his *unaaḳ*. If the surface is snow, a single firm thrust will test its consistency and depth. Occasionally, this probing shows that the drift is hollow underneath or conceals a deep subnivean puddle, or perhaps even a small stream which has cut its way under the snow. In doubtful areas it is best to use the *unaaḳ* as a walking staff, jabbing the surface ahead every two or three steps. This can become slow and tedious after a while, however, so it is best to combine it with visual techniques.

It is much simpler to traverse such areas by dog team, but by no means does this compare with the ease of winter dog mushing. The dogs quickly become tired and overheated from wading through tacky drifts and dragging the sled with its rider over steep ridges and through deep ponds. Eskimos try to steer around the largest drifts, if possible, and to watch closely ahead for the least difficult trail. Before deep puddles and rivulets form it is best to follow smooth ice, but once there is considerable water it is sometimes necessary to travel on rougher ice. In the latter case it is often easiest to follow along the edges of hummocks and ridges, where there is likely to be less standing water. But this is also where drifts often extend across the line of travel, so that the sled is constantly dragged up and over steep banks of snow. This is hard work for dogs and drivers alike, because a man often has to assist his dogs in pulling the sled over the drifts.

By early June there is already a considerable amount of water on the sea ice. During cold weather the puddles and ponds may freeze over with a skin of ice. It is usually impossible to tell at a glance if this ice is thick enough to hold a man, since it is identical in color to the surrounding ice. The *unaaḳ* is effective for judging the existence and safety of such ice. It is not really dangerous because the underlying water is only knee deep at the most. As

71

the month progresses the size of puddles increases, and they are connected by flowing streams of water that erode little valleys into the ice everywhere. These streams become larger and deeper, and may eventually eat holes through the ice so that water can swirl into the ocean below. The sea ice beneath these ponds and streams gives them an uncommonly beautiful turquoise hue, which is light in color where the water is shallow and appears darker in the deep places.

This dark color is the first thing to be noted when deciding whether to wade or drive a team across a puddle. Color can be seen from 5 or 10 yards away, but it is often difficult to make an exact judgment of water depth until the edge is reached. For dog-team travel, quick decisions must be made before the lead dog reaches the water. This requires some experience. Those who travel on foot move much slower and are therefore less likely to make errors in judgment. It is especially easy to be misled in places where mud or dirt has fouled the ice, making the color darker than it would normally be in a puddle of similar depth. This can occur where dirt has blown out onto the ice, or where bottom debris has been picked up by deeply piled ice. Fortunately, there seems to be no condition that makes the water seem shallower than it actually is.

Some Eskimos use short rubber or sealskin boots for travel at this time of year, but as the season progresses almost every man wears hipboots. Even when the water is not deep enough to go over the top of low boots, some is always splashed onto a man's legs, eventually soaking them thoroughly.

In addition to good boots, the *unaak* is essential for walking on water-covered ice. There are three reasons why it is very helpful under these conditions: First, it is almost impossible at times to maintain one's balance on the slippery, uneven ice that forms the bottom of water puddles and streamlets. An *unaak*, or any kind of substantial pole, helps to prevent slipping and to regain balance if footing is lost. Second, the *unaak* is used to test the depth of water before stepping into it. Often it is difficult to estimate the depth of a puddle if it is surrounded by a ledge 1 or 2 feet high, or the water may be so dirty that its depth cannot be seen clearly. Thirdly, the iron prod of an *unaak* is useful for testing the hardness and safety of the underlying ice. If it cannot be punched through the ice with one thrust the ice is safe enough to hold a man.

The little rivulets which flow across the ice must drain somewhere, so in many places there are holes going completely through the ice. These holes, which greatly increase in number by late June, must be watched for and avoided. They are not difficult to see as long as the water is clear, because they are deep black and contrast sharply with the bright blue of solid ice. Drain holes are usually surrounded by safe ice right to their edges. Many began as breathing holes made by seals during the winter.

Hunters are always careful not to walk right to the edge of puddles or ponds where there is a little wall above the water rather than a slope down to its edge. Such walls are often eroded by the warm water, forming a thin shelf of ice projecting 6 inches to 2 feet over the surface of ponds. This overhang may give way beneath the weight of a man, plunging him into the water. Ice ledges are also found along the edges of open leads, where they are very dangerous to hunters. All suspected edges are tested first by jabbing them firmly with an *unaak*.

Water on the ice is a still greater problem, although a less dangerous one, for the dog-team driver. In the first place, dogs will go to great lengths to avoid wading through any sort of water. Of course, the icy water must be an important factor in this aversion, but perhaps the sharp-pointed needles of ice that often cover the ice surface under water are more important. These little bladelets of ice rasp the dogs' feet until they get very sore; they can even wear through the tough bearded-sealskin boot soles in a fairly short time.

Dogs begin to get sore feet during the early spring thaws. The ice and snow become very abrasive, and after a while they wear away the pads of the dogs' feet, causing tenderness. Eventually, the dogs begin to limp, their feet leave blood marks on the snow, and they are no longer able to pull. This problem becomes acute by early summer, when nearly every team has some lame dogs. The Eskimos try to save their dogs' feet by traveling during the warmest part of the day, when the ice surface does not cause abrasion and cutting; but underwater ice seems to remain the same at all times. Even polar bears make long detours to avoid wading in puddles on the ice, probably because of the ice needles (Degerbøl and Freuchen 1935, p. 112).

Because of their incredible aversion to walking through water, some dogs devise various maneuvers and tactics to evade or postpone the inevitable wetting. They will haul back at the water's edge until their neck line jerks them bodily toward it, and then they spring madly into midair with eyes half-closed and head high, hoping to reach the other side unmoistened, even though it may be 30 yards across. And when they land in the water, they pull frantically for the nearest dry shore, whether it is straight ahead or in a direction quite different from that in which the rest of the team is traveling. These pathetic creatures wear themselves out with their acrobatics, but they never seem to change even though they are punished for their hesitation.

The Eskimo tries to use a lead dog that willingly enters water on command. The dogs that follow immediately behind the leader should also be unafraid of water. The misfits are placed toward the rear of the team, where their behavior does the least damage and where persuasion and punishment are most easily handed out. It takes a well-trained team for summer travel, for it is at this time that discipline and training pay the highest dividends.

Dog sledding is always enjoyable, but even the greatest enthusiast will find that his ardor wanes after a few hours of splashing his way across the summer ice. Not only do the dogs get soaked, but so does the sled and its contents, as well as the driver. Some of the little rivulets are narrow enough for the sled to span them, but wide enough that the stern plunges down into the water as it passes over, unless the driver jumps off and wades across. But many puddles are so wide that the sled must either slide or float across, with the dogs straining ahead toward the far side. There are occasional ponds with straight, sheer walls surrounding them, low enough so that the dogs can jump up onto the dry ice, but high enough so that the sled jams solidly against them. Then, with the dogs straining forward, the driver must simultaneously pull the sled back and lift it up until it can ride onto the ice again.

Examples of the trials of summer dog sledding could be multiplied ad infinitum. In short, it is a relief to all concerned when it is no longer possible to travel on the ice. The season of soft snow and deep water on the sea ice passes quickly for the Eskimos. In the first place, the water reaches a maximum point and then quite suddenly seems to disappear, swirling downward through the growing number of drain holes. After this time sledding improves and travel is somewhat easier. By no means does the water vanish entirely, however. There is water on the ocean ice throughout the summer.

Dog mushing usually ends in June, because it becomes impossible to reach the ice from the land. Along shore the ice thaws quickly, due to runoff and heat radiation from the land. Thus, the shore ice is treacherous and water covered quite early in the season. If the landfast floe is not carried away by wind and current, a narrow lead of open water, 10 to 50 yards across, forms along the coast. This effectively bars travel by dog team, even though the ice farther out is still safe. Sometimes, under these conditions, Eskimos take their skin boats across the shore lead and pull them over the landfast ice to the open lead farther out, where they hunt for seals and walrus. Dogs are apparently not taken onto the ice in this way.

Rotten Ice

During the warm spring and summer months, sea ice becomes increasingly mobile, which causes more fracturing and grinding. At the same time, young ice no longer consolidates the fractured ice floes, because cracks and leads do not freeze over. Wherever ice movement has taken place, the traveler must be certain to watch every step closely and to plan his route of travel well ahead of his present position, lest he walk onto rotten or slushy ice. He must be able to recognize such unsafe areas by their appearance and to move over them with the aid of his *unaak*.

During the late spring and early summer the first rotten ice (*auŋazuk*) and slushy ice (*pogzak*) appear. At this time they are closely associated with areas where the ice has been grinding. Such unsafe ice is often recognizable because it is darker than the surrounding thick ice; sometimes it is quite black. For example, a traveler may encounter areas of unconsolidated ice consisting of many flat pans of ice pressed edge to edge, like pieces of a puzzle not yet fitted together. The numerous spaces between these pans may be filled with slush, rotten ice, smaller chunks of safe ice, or open water.

Moving across these areas is tricky and hazardous. The small solid chunks that lie amid the slush or rotten ice between larger pans look like good stepping stones. Indeed they can be used in this way, but extreme caution and some practice beforehand are helpful. Some will sink easily or tip over when a man steps on them, which can cause a dunking. So if they are used, they must be tested first by pushing them down forcefully with an *unaak* to see if they are bouyant. If they are too small to support a man, but have almost sufficient bouyancy, they can be used as stepping stones by jumping quickly from one to the next. This is often done by sea-ice hunters, who use their *unaaks* to test and to balance as they move across.

Rotten ice is not always easy to recognize, however, because the color distinction may not be evident. For example, mush ice, formed by heavy floes grinding together, sometimes becomes thick and accumulates high enough above the water surface that it is no longer saturated. This ice turns white as the water drains from it, and at times it cannot be distinguished visually from solid ice. Rotten ice can also be fairly light in color, or it may be concealed by a layer of snow.

Whenever the safety of ice is in question, as in these cases, Eskimos test it with their *unaaks*. In the spring and summer, doubtful ice must be tested before every step. A Point Hope Eskimo said that when men became "lazy" and do not use their *unaaks* continuously, they are toying with danger. Sometimes the *unaak* will unexpectedly plunge through 1 or 2 feet of white slush into the water below. The next step might have been fatal. Eskimos always watch the configuration and color of the ice very carefully. Generally speaking, they watch for dark coloration and use the *unaak* whenever the ice is at all questionable.

The bottoms of puddles and rivulets are usually quite solid, but during the summer some of them become soft and unsafe.

In other cases the bottom may be perforated with small holes going clear through the ice, while the ice surrounding these holes is firm enough to hold a man. It may even be possible to step right on these holes as long as they are too small to admit a man's foot. In a situation like this the sound of the *unaak* when it strikes the ice is a good indicator of safety. When it is dangerous, the *unaak* strikes with a soft muffled thud. This is very different in sound and feeling from the crisp hard sensation when the ice is solid and firm.

By the month of June there are soft spots in the ice caused by the warm air above and warm water below. These places occur unexpectedly, because they can be anywhere, whether or not the ice has been grinding. This again requires constant and acute alertness to the condition of one's surroundings. The Eskimo is highly alert at all times when he moves over the ocean ice, and this quality is one essential prerequisite for safe travel in this environment.

The most rapid melting apparently occurs underneath the ice, where warm swift currents eat it steadily away. This can erode the ice until it becomes very thin, even though it looks normal and solid on the surface. During June, warm temperatures and sunshine melt the hummocked ice somewhat, but it is actually reduced very little this way. Even much of the drifted snow remains. Therefore, it seems necessary to explain the existence of thin ice by melting from below rather than from above. Also, along the edges of open leads and ponds one can see that the ice is being heavily eroded. Constant streams of tiny bubbles rising to the surface indicate that air is being released as the ice dwindles below.

By far the most dangerous places for thin and rotten ice are areas offshore from the mouths of large rivers, such as the Kuk River near Wainwright. Early in June a powerful current sweeps out from the mouth of this river, rapidly cutting away at the ice for a mile or two offshore. Ice in and around the river's outlet is entirely gone by early June, but offshore it remains intact for a much longer time. Puddles filled with dark muddy water instead of the usual clear turquoise-shaded ponds are the first indication that the ice is weakening. This brownish coloration is caused by silty river water seeping into the puddles through holes in the underlying ice. Dark-colored puddles are carefully avoided during travel, because the water is so murky that one cannot see the size of the holes, and there is always a chance that the ice is very rotten underneath.

The Wainwright Eskimos must pass the mouth of the Kuk River whenever they travel south by dog team. As the season progresses they move farther and farther out from the coast in their attempts to avoid thin ice. The safest places to travel on such rotten ice are near the edges of ice ridges, or, if necessary, right along the tops. Thus, Eskimo travelers stay on or near the piled ice whenever the surrounding flats appear dangerously thin.

Another dangerous area in early summer is a narrow strip of ice paralleling the beach. This strip thaws quickly and, as we noted above, it forms an open shore lead between the land and the more solid ice beyond. In 1966 the conditions at Wainwright were ideal for its formation. A strip of flat winter ice about 100 yards wide skirted the coast. Because it was considerably thinner than the ice farther out, it melted quickly. By mid-June it was noticeably darker than the rest of the sea ice. The Eskimos stated at that time that once the ice began to change color, it would rot very fast. A week later there was an open shore lead 5 or 10 yards wide along the shore in front of Wainwright, which effectively prevented dog sleds from getting out onto the ice. By the first week in July the entire area, extending outward to the first piled ice, was filled with black rotten ice and water. The ice quickly fragmented and began to drift with the current.

Several Eskimos using an *umiak* picked their way through the fragmented ice to reach open areas north of the village, where they could hunt seals. In places where rotten ice was lying in solid "floes," it was very difficult to move the boat along. Often they had to drag the boat over ice pans or push the pans apart to open a trail of water between them. This was an excellent chance to learn the methods of walking on very rotten ice. It was surprising to find that some pans were completely black and rotten, thoroughly saturated with water, and yet would hold a man's weight. There was a percentage risk involved, however, because one pan that looked exactly like the rest might suddenly break in half or disintegrate when someone stood on it. Ice that was white on the surface was always quite safe.

The Eskimos would always test dark ice before standing on it. Sometimes they did this by keeping one foot in the boat while they stamped the ice firmly with the other foot. If it felt solid and did not break or bend, they would step out onto it. They would also thrust an *unaak* or paddle solidly into the surface to test its strength. To use this method each hunter relied heavily on a "feeling" he had as to whether the pan would support him. As long as he could keep one hand on the boat there was no great need for caution. Occasionally the ice would split or sink when a man jumped onto it, but he easily pulled himself back into the boat. But when an Eskimo jumped from one drifting piece to another, without the boat close at hand for safety, he would reach over and jab each pan with his *unaak* beforehand. On this very rotten ice each man was careful to avoid stepping into puddles, because they often had little or no bottom ice left.

The essential facts that an Eskimo must know to move over rotten ice are more or less the same as those needed for young ice during the winter. First, the color must be watched closely and dark ice considered dangerous. Dirt, dust, or debris on the ice can make safe ice appear rotten. The Eskimo hunter is also alert for light-colored slush or snow-covered ice, which may be too weak to support a man. Doubtful ice must be given the "one thrust test" with an *unaak* or a similar implement. Whenever there is any chance of encountering thin ice, it is a good idea to use the *unaak* as a walking staff, habitually punching the ice ahead.

If a man finds himself out on dangerous ice, he again proceeds much as he would on newly-formed ice. He spreads his legs apart, the distance depending on the thinness of the ice, and steps or shuffles gently along. If the ice is too weak for walking, he must crawl on hands and knees, or even flat on his stomach. Van Valin (1944, p. 206) describes several cases where men had walked onto thin ice and escaped by rolling to safety. This allows faster moving, but soaks a man's clothing. Some Eskimos are better than others at moving over rotten ice or jumping from pan to pan. Both skills require certain athletic aptitudes and quick judgment, as well as a good measure of self-confidence.

There are several dangers of summer ice associated with thawing. We noted briefly above that the edges of water puddles, rivulets, or open leads sometimes have overhanging shelves of ice which may break under a man's weight. This is especially true along open leads or at the edge of drifting floes, where the ice is undercut by warm currents and wave action. An ice overhang (*kaŋattaak̲*) may extend for several feet over the water. Sometimes it is very thick and will easily support a man, but sometimes it is thin and weak. Therefore, whenever an Eskimo walks near an edge that might be undercut in this way, he gives it a firm jab with the point of his *unaak̲*. If the point goes through this ice, or if it sounds hollow, he will be very leery about going any closer to the edge.

Seabirds that have been killed will sometimes drift underneath this overhang before the hunter can retrieve them. Then he will usually try to chop the weakest part of the ice away, so that he can lie prone and peer beneath the ledge to find his game. He may also place his *unaak̲* on the ice parallel to the water's edge, so that he can lean on it and spread his weight over a larger area, decreasing the chance of ice breakage.

Overhanging ice is also dangerous during *umiak̲* travel, when boats are frequently landed on ice pans or floe edges. The steersman usually watches the edge as he lands the boat, avoiding areas where there is a large overhang. If one is present, however, the first man to leave the boat stamps it with one foot to test it before stepping out. Eskimos generally avoid stepping onto the very edge of the ice under any conditions. They usually jump 2 or 3 feet from it when they leave the boat.

A similar shelf often projects outward from the ice edge beneath the water. This extension, called *itcheak̲*, occurs more frequently and is always larger than the overhang above the surface. It is easily seen, ghostly white or turquoise ice sloping downward, often with holes eroded through it by the warm ocean water. The *itcheak̲* is a safety factor along ice edges, because it can prevent a serious dunking if a man slips or falls from the ice above. Ice overhangs do not occur in the winter, because the ice edge is not eroded by the current or waves. Instead, an ice apron forms quickly along newly formed leads.

Another danger of summer ice is caused by sudden surfacing

of ice chunks that have been buried in the ocean bottom by piling. Hunters are occasionally startled by the explosive surfacing close by of a large piece of ice (sometimes many feet across). This ice, called *alliviñek*, may rise with enough force to break the ice along a lead edge. Eskimos also warn that pieces of ice that rise under a boat can damage its bottom. In one case during 1966 a large wooden launch was lifted by the impact of such a collision, and the men feared that it might be tipped over or staved in. Skin boats are considerably more resilient than wooden boats, and probably can withstand a greater impact without damage.

Piled Ice

During the winter, hummocks are a great inconvenience to travel over the ocean ice. Yet they are the safest places to escape the dangers of cracking or grinding ice, and they are good elevations from which to scan for game or open water. In the summertime this situation is considerably altered, because the stability of ice piles is greatly diminished.

Actively piling ice is extremely dangerous, and must be avoided at any time of the year. Throughout the winter months, however, a new hummock becomes a solidified mass within a few hours or days after its formation. During the summer months a new ice pile never becomes a single unified mass of ice. It remains a jumble of ice blocks, which by their own weight and friction against one another stay piled together. Sea water, which covers blocks of piling ice, no longer freezes to cement them together. Thus, newly formed ice piles remain quite unstable. It is not unusual, therefore, for an entire pile of ice to suddenly disintegrate and go crashing down into the water below.

The dangers of this situation are obvious. An Eskimo hunter does not climb up onto a fresh ice pile to scan for game, nor does he use these hummocks for an emergency ice camp. But ice piles which remain from the preceding winter are safe throughout the summer for such scanning, camping, or for traveling the "high ground" to avoid thin ice or water.

It is very important for the Eskimo to be able to distinguish between old ice piles, formed during the winter, and fresh piles, formed in late spring or summer. Fortunately, it is quite simple to tell the difference. Old ice piles are obviously weathered and have been rounded off by the summer warmth. They are likely to have deep snowdrifts in some of their hollows, and along their flanks. Fresh ice piles consist of many distinct geometric boulders of ice with large hollows, sharply squared edges, and little or no snow drifted in or around them. During the summer of 1966, especially near the edge of landfast ice, fresh ice piles were often quite dirty, unlike those formed during the preceding winter. This could have been caused by dirt blown from the land, brought up from the bottom while the ice was piling, or picked up from the silty Kuk River water.

The threat of ice piles disintegrating is greatest when the sea ice is moving or when the pressure of wind or current is being exerted on it. Sometimes this motion or pressure is very difficult to perceive. The first signs are usually an intermittent subtle creaking, cracking, and budging sound in the ice. These creaking noises are sometimes spaced minutes apart, and they are often barely audible above the sounds of the wind. But they are important signs to watch for, especially in the summer, when the ice can move very suddenly. Piling and moving are often quite slow, however, so that one must watch carefully for several minutes before the pieces of ice can be seen moving. Also, movements are intermittent; one cannot judge on the basis of several minutes' observation whether a pile has ceased to move.

One of the greatest dangers of being caught on or near a hummock when it disintegrates is that it so frequently occurs without warning. The ice may only move a half inch, but that is enough to send the giant pieces tumbling back into the water below. This happens so suddenly that a man could never hope to escape, and would very likely be crushed to death or drowned. Regardless of how solid summer-formed hummocks may look, Eskimo hunters will not climb onto them, and they avoid crossing over them whenever possible. There are usually plenty of solid winter piles around for scanning places, and easy alternate routes can be found for bypassing recently piled ice.

CHAPTER 4

Movements and Fragmentation of Summer Ice

Landfast Ice

A s WE HAVE SEEN, the Eskimos possess a great knowledge of the causes and characteristics of ice mobility, which they must call upon each time they travel on foot or by dog team over the ocean ice. They must know the extent of the grounded floe and of the ice fields which are solidly attached to it. They must know how much current and wind would be necessary to break this ice away and set it adrift with the pack. During the summer they also know under what conditions the landfast ice itself could be carried away. This coastal ice cannot remain through an entire summer, but the Eskimos travel on it for as long as is possible without taking undue risks. When it has finally gone, the Eskimos' maritime activities are greatly altered.

During late spring and early summer, the landfast ice decreases steadily in extent. Large pieces are broken away from its seaward edge by the movement of the pack. Piles of ice become less solidly anchored to the bottom as they are eroded by the current. Finally they are lifted free by a high tide and drift away to join the mobile floes. The loss of anchoring ice piles allows further fragmentation, and the outer limit of grounded ice moves closer and closer to the shore. The edge of landfast ice may be easy to identify when the pack is pressed firmly up against it. There is usually fresh piling here, but even more notable are evidences of parallel (or shear) movements. These consist of a series of cracks, or windrows of slushy ice produced by the grinding of ice edges, all of which are parallel to the trend of the coast. This is a zone of considerable danger, because the ice here is often weakened or rotten, and because this is the place where leads and cracks are most likely to open. Eskimos are very cautious about going out beyond this point, which they call the "old edge."

At the same time that the landfast floe is breaking away along its outer edges, the landward margin is thawing and opening as well. After a shore lead forms, the landfast ice can become an isolated strip of ice running parallel to the coast, with open water on both sides. It may disappear very slowly, finally being reduced to a series of large grounded ice islands with little or no ice between. This occurred during the summer of 1964, when several huge mountains of ice remained offshore from Wainwright until the end of July. And in 1966, numerous grounded piles within a quarter mile of the beach remained until July 20. According to the Wainwright people, the main body of landfast ice normally breaks up sometime in June.

During some years the flaw ice does not disintegrate slowly, but is carried away suddenly by high tides accompanied by an offshore wind. Thus, dog-team and foot travel on the sea ice may end very early, with a correspondingly early beginning of ice hunting with skin boats. The people usually hope that landfast ice will remain through most of June, because there are seals around as long as the ice remains. But they hope that it will depart early enough to allow easy access to the unconsolidated ice floes of summer as soon as the bearded seals (*Erignathus barbatus*) and walrus (*Odobenus rosmarus*) appear in their annual northward movement. Conditions are ideal when an isolated coastal strip of landfast ice remains, with open water on both sides and lanes cutting through it. The grounded ice keeps water open for boat travel and seal hunting near the village, and also permits easy passage by boat to the scattered ice floes farther out.

Thus, landfast ice is of fundamental importance in Eskimo sea ice activity throughout much of the year. Once it is gone there is no longer a dependable "road" out onto the ice and to the open leads where most sealing is done. "Leads" then consist of open water between the land and the ice pack, which may be many miles out to sea, so that little or no marine hunting can be done without the use of boats. Methods of hunting are much different, therefore, once the landfast floe is gone and summer ice conditions prevail.

Summer Lead Formation

Before moving on to discuss the unconsolidated summer ice floes, let us backtrack a moment to consider the effects of wind, current, and ice piles on the formation of open leads in spring and early summer. Similar forces cause ice movement throughout the year, but because the ice fractures easily and is less firmly grounded during the warm season, it moves more readily at this time. Thus, the chances of cracks and leads opening, and the consequent dangers of drifting away on a floe which has broken away, are increased.

Yet for the Eskimo hunter the danger of sea-ice activity is probably lessened. This is largely because men do not often travel out to open leads to hunt, preferring to stalk seals that are basking on top of the ice not far offshore. Even if they do hunt at leads, they usually find open water much closer to shore than during the winter. This means that it is not necessary to travel as far out from the coast, and as a consequence there is less danger of drifting away. Therefore, Eskimos appear to be less concerned with factors causing ice movement and lead formation at this time of year.

Current is more important as a factor in ice movement during the warm months than at any other season. This is the only time, in the vicinity of Wainwright, when current regularly moves the ice without the aid of wind. In summertime, the entire pack may slowly and silently move away from the landfast ice, even though the winds are calm. This condition is intensified around points and headlands, where currents flow swiftly through the deep offshore waters. The influence of wind is always mediated by current, especially during the summer months. The Wainwright hunters are always more concerned with the wind than with all other factors combined, but when the ice does not behave as it should under particular wind conditions, a contrary flow of current is usually blamed.

An ice hunter should be able to judge the relative forces of current and wind in order to predict which will prevail in setting the ice into motion. This is very difficult to do with a high degree of accuracy, even for a highly experienced Eskimo. The hunter will most likely be able to judge that the ice is "probably safe" or "possibly dangerous," and when the latter condition is present he stays off the ice if he can. He predicts this only in terms of probabilities, rarely in terms of certainties.

Except that the ice moves and cracks more readily during the spring and summer, general conditions of lead formation are identical to those of the winter months. The force and direction of winds and currents, the influence of cracks, and the power of impacting floes, which we outlined in some detail earlier, remain the same until the landfast ice is gone. But the effect of ice piles on ice movement and lead formation becomes particularly evident as the summer thaw progresses.

As we mentioned above, grounded ice can slow down or prevent the opening of leads, and is important in determining the extent of the landfast floe. During the winter months, Eskimos have a good idea which ice piles offshore from the village are grounded. On the basis of this knowledge, plus observation of the positions of open leads, they generally know where the edge of the landfast floe is located. As the winter progresses, continued piling extends its margins further seaward.

When spring arrives the Eskimos watch ice movement and the location of leads, in order to mark the landward progression of the flaw edge. On this basis they can estimate which ice piles are still grounded firmly and constitute the outer fringe of landfast ice. They are quite reluctant to go beyond this point under most conditions, much more so than during winter. In the large expanses of flat ice south of Wainwright there are few piles to anchor the ice, so greater caution must be observed when hunting in this region. The ice here is notorious for drifting away right from the beach, as happened during early July of 1966. North of the village the ice usually moves and piles a great deal. There is less probability of a break in the landfast floe here, although currents are stronger and water is deeper.

Ice can be grounded far offshore in this area. On one occasion several hunting crews from Wainwright landed on a grounded floe about 5 miles from shore. This happened during the month of July, 1966, while the Eskimos were hunting bearded seals with skin boats. There was an extremely powerful current from the south, and the men decided to use this stationary ice to avoid being carried far to the north while they stopped to have tea (G. R. Bane, personal communication). Boat crews often use grounded ice as a hunting station. Thus, when seals are moving in one direction, they will continually pass by the place where the hunters are waiting for them.

Hummocks which remain in the fast ice all winter are often used as landmarks, because their shape and position become generally known during the course of hunting activities. They may also be used as points of orientation during conversations between hunters—to point out the location of open water or an especially good hunting spot. Finally, ice piles are places of safety, which a man will attempt to reach whenever dangerous ice conditions arise.

Ice piles and ridges greatly influence the time when the "seasons" change in the Eskimo year, because they may determine when the landfast floe breaks away, which in turn has much effect on the beginning of hunting with skin boats. This marks a complete change in the pattern of sea-ice exploitation. It is the end of the long season of open lead hunting, when there is little need for concern about the dangers of ice fracture and driftaway. Now the open water permits the use of boats rather than dogs for transportation from the shore to the ice and among the drifting floes themselves. The sea-ice environment is drastically altered.

Unconsolidated Summer Floes

Until the time of "breakup," sea-ice conditions are basically similar to those of midwinter. After this time the ice is no longer a single mobile mass, but a scattered conglomerate of millions of ice pans, floes, and floebergs of every conceivable size and shape. There is no way to move from one piece of ice to the next except by boat or by waiting for their edges to bump and grind together. Summer floes are constantly in motion; not the slow, creaking, intermittent movements of winter ice, but continuous fluid drifting at the slightest will of the wind and current. So the Eskimos must use different means of predicting the movements of the ice, concerned not with the presence or absence of open water, but with the occurrence of the ice pack itself. They have devised many techniques of dealing with the physical and biological aspects of this enviroment, some used in the course of routine daily activities and others reserved for emergency situations. Let us first discuss the characteristics of the summer ice itself.

Scattered amid the summer pack ice are huge solid floes, some measuring several miles in diameter. These larger floes, and even rather small ice pans, usually have on them areas of flat ice and hummocks. Some of the ice piles are old, while others are freshly formed and therefore dangerous. There are water streams and ponds, snowdrifts and slush, rotten ice, ice overhangs, and cracks —all of which are dealt with in the same ways we discussed earlier. So the surface of this ice is in many ways very similar to the unbroken surface of early summer ice, with the important exception of size and stability.

In the beginning of summer the pack is heavily fractured, especially along its margins, but the floes and pans drift along closely together. A boat can be taken into the edges of the ice, but there is not enough open water to allow passage far into the pack itself. But with the season's progression, floes become increasingly fragmented; large ice fields are uncommon, while small pans, blocks, and floebergs proliferate. The ice becomes broken and scattered. In many areas there is more water than ice, especially along the expanding margins of the pack.

In northwest Alaska the north quadrant winds are especially effective in scattering the ice, because they blow in opposition to the prevailing current. Large floes and floebergs (*aulaylik*) are carried toward the north by the current, while smaller ice pans (*puktaak*) move south before the wind. According to the Eskimos, the net result of this opposite movement is loosening and scattering of the pack. Wind and current running together may tend to pack the ice somewhat more closely, but this would be most likely to occur when a westerly wind pushes the ice ashore and packs it solidly together.

The Wainwright Eskimos are deeply concerned with general movements of the ice pack, because its presence in the area for the entire summer means great abundance of marine animals. Early disappearance of the ice, on the other hand, means poor hunting and can spell eventual starvation for the dogs, which are usually fed walrus meat and blubber through the winter. Around the end of June and beginning of July, the Eskimos hope for strong offshore winds, which carry the pack far out toward the horizon. This allows the sea mammals to move north in the open water, and when the ice drifts landward again, it will bring them in with it. Along with this hope for open water there is, as we have indicated, an abiding fear that prolonged offshore winds will hold the ice far from land, while the current carries it north away from Wainwright. Fortunately, this very seldom occurs before the people succeed in taking many walruses and bearded seals.

Once the ice breaks up into somewhat unconsolidated floes, probably beginning in early summer, it is carried more or less constantly north by the steady and powerful south current. There is only one way this northward movement can be slowed, and that is when a brisk westerly wind packs the ice tightly against the shore. During middle and late summer, even a north or northeast wind does not halt this northward progression, according to the Eskimos.

When the ice cannot be seen from shore, its position is reported by pilots and passengers of the frequent airplane flights to Wainwright. The land rises only 20 to 40 feet above sea level here, so it is impossible to see the ice far offshore unless there are clouds to reflect its brightness. Airplane passengers are able to see much farther offshore, and they usually watch the ice conditions and look for game as they fly south from Barrow.

The people are most concerned, however, about the position of the pack's southward margin, which moves steadily northward during the summertime. Its position is reported first by radio, from places south along the coast. In this way the Wainwright

Eskimos learn of the departure of ice from Point Hope and Point Lay. At the same time, its progression is watched during airplane flights between Wainwright and Point Lay. This is an especially valuable source of information on the approaching margin of the polar ice pack. Finally, as open water moves to within 50 miles of the village, hunting crews returning from excursions to the south report their ice observations.

From this knowledge the Eskimos can predict how long the ice will remain in the area, and adjust the intensity of their hunting accordingly. If, for example, the end of the ice is reported to be passing Point Lay, people at Wainwright can expect ice hunting to continue for a couple of weeks or more, depending on wind conditions. If the wind blows from the south, the pack could more north quite rapidly. Hunters intensify their activities if the ice will be gone in the near future, unless they already have a good supply of walrus and bearded seal cached away.

The date of final ice departure is highly variable. In some years, as we noted, it is gone before much summer hunting can be done. In other years the ice remains throughout most of the summer. During such times, as happened in 1964 and 1965, the men stop marine hunting altogether, and will pass by herds of walrus without bothering to hunt them. On the average, the pack seems to remain through July, departing sometime in August. In 1964 the ice left near the end of August, and in 1965 it left during the first week of September. The summer of 1966 was not as good as could be hoped for, because the pack was gone by the first of August. There is always the hope that it will return in late August or early September. When this happens there is excellent walrus and seal hunting.

The ice departs somewhat earlier to the south, the date depending upon the latitude. At Point Hope the ice usually breaks up sometime in June, and it may remain through that month, sometimes into July. If south winds blow steadily, some ice packs against the south flank of the spit and remains there until the wind changes. North winds hold the ice offshore and allow the current to carry it northward (Van Stone 1962, p. 59). At Point Lay the coastline is similar to that at Wainwright, and presumably the ice conditions are generally comparable.

Point Barrow is considerably more fortunate with regard to the length of the ice season. Because it is farther north and remains cooler during the summer, thaw and breakup proceed more slowly. It is also on the margin of the Beaufort Sea, where an extensive pack is almost always present close offshore. Thus, sea ice is frequently held close to Barrow all summer. When the east wind blows, the ice does not disappear as it does at Wainwright, because it is constanty replenished by the limitless pack to the east. Winter leads are usually narrower here than at places to the south, because ice moves around the point and into the open water, filling it almost as rapidly as the ice drifts away toward the west.

Effects of Wind and Current on Summer Pack Ice

One of the most important differences between summer and winter ice movement is the greater role played by current and the correspondingly lesser role of wind during the warm months. As we discuss these factors, it is essential to bear in mind that what is said here may have only a local application, and that ice conditions at every coastal locality will be somewhat different. Therefore, the situation at Wainwright corresponds for the most part to Point Lay, only 100 miles away and along a similar coastline. But at Barrow, conditions are so different that we can make only basic comparisons; and we can say much less about ice movement at more distant stations, such as Barter Island, Pond Inlet, or Thule. But with a certain amount of background knowledge of the local weather and currents, the same basic principles probably apply throughout the ice-covered coasts of the Arctic.

During the summer at Wainwright, when there is little or no wind, the prevailing south current brings the ice pack toward shore. When this happens a shore lead is usually held open by large floebergs which become grounded several hundred yards offshore and prevent the ice from moving closer to the land. There may also be remnants of landfast ice which block the onshore advance of pack ice. Smaller pans often move into this shore lead and drift along in it. Again, local geography is an important factor when considering the effect of current. North of Icy Cape or Point Hope, for example, the southerly current tends to carry the ice offshore rather than onshore. But once the pack moves north beyond all the coastal settlements except Barrow, there is little chance that it will return for some time. A north wind alone cannot carry the ice southward against the prevailing current. During the winter such a wind would be accompanied by a current from the same direction, and the ice would drift rapidly southward. The fact that current does not change with the wind is very important for understanding summer ice movements.

One other current phenomenon is said by the Eskimos to affect ice conditions. Wherever two opposing or different currents meet, sinuous lines of ripples or wavelets form on the ocean surface. These lines, called *pilaġaġnik̲*, usually cause only slight roughness, but occassionaly disturb the surface enough to make it bad going for boats. According to the Eskimos, current eddies which cause *pilaġaġnik̲* are able to hold the ice offshore even though the current may flow toward the land (G. R. Bane, personal communication). Current lines are said to be fronts along which the currents turn under at their point of meeting. They appear to run at right angles to the coast most commonly.

Except for the differences caused by prevailing current, essentially the same principles govern summer ice movement as were discussed with regard to lead formation. The most common winds that push the ice offshore are from the northeast and east, although north and southeast winds can have the same effect. "Onshore" winds, blowing from the south and west quadrants, nearly always carry the pack shoreward. Unless the onshore wind blows quite briskly, there is normally enough open water for hunting by boat.

Offshore winds of 15 to 25 m.p.h. can blow the ice out of sight over the horizon in the summertime, but how long this will take depends on the current. In one case, with a brisk northeast or east wind, the pack may gradually recede over a 3- or 4-day period, until it disappears from sight. And when the wind dies it will drift right back to the coast. In another case, a wind of the same strength may blow the ice quickly out to sea, aided by a following current. When the wind and current prevail strongly from the southwest or west, a huge stationary ice field packs ashore at

Wainwright. Farther out at sea, beyond the margins of the bight in which the village is situated, the floes drift northward.

If an Eskimo is caught out on the pack ice in summer, he knows that it will be in almost constant motion unless a strong west wind packs it in against the land. In this case he would see that the ice was crowding closer and closer together until it became possible to walk over it, most open water having disappeared. Then he would hurry toward the land, hoping to reach shore or at least find grounded ice before the wind shifted.

With any other wind the ice will move. It is often extremely difficult to tell if an ice floe is in motion unless some nearby stationary landmark, such as a grounded ice pile or the seacoast, is visible. Difficulty is most likely to occur when a man is on a large floe or ice field. On one occasion, for example, several Eskimos were hunting seals about a mile offshore on a very large floe. After four hours of hunting one man noticed that this floe had drifted several miles northward, as shown by their position relative to landmarks on the visible shore. This man was the only member of the group who had been aware that the ice was moving.

At times one can feel a sort of motion in the ice as it drifts slowly along. This feeling cannot be described, except that it seems to be less a horizontal movement than an imperceptibly slight up and down motion. It also imparts a sensation of the hugeness of the drifting ice. Even though it seems to occur whenever one is on a moving floe, one always feels that the motion is imagined. It can only be compared to riding very slowly in a huge ship on a calm sea.

On large floes such as this another way to detect movement is to watch floating chunks of ice, a foot or so in diameter, to see if they move relative to the floe edge. If no wind is pushing them along, but they move by fairly fast, the floe may be grounded. However, if they appear to be standing still and one is certain that there is some current, then the floe must be drifting along at the same rate as the ice chunks. Large pans of ice often move at a different speed from that of the floe or ice field, and are therefore less reliable than small ones as indicators.

Small ice floes, 50 yards in diameter or even considerably larger, are apt to revolve constantly. Hunters on such floes must watch their bearings at all times or they will become utterly confused. If a man gets too engrossed in his work while butchering walrus, for example, he may look up to find that without his moving his feet the land has "moved" clear around to another direction. And if little pieces of ice are watched in the water, they may seem to be passing quickly by, when their apparent motion is actually caused by the pan's rotation. If the ice is rotating, it must also be moving with the current, and one should not be fooled into thinking it is standing still.

Another way to detect movement is to drop a weighted line down until it touches bottom, and feel the vibration caused by the weight's being dragged along. Sometimes it is difficult to tell when the weight hits bottom because the current is strong enough to keep pulling out line. Thus, the line must be held with just enough tension to keep the sinker on bottom without releasing more line. An Eskimo can use his *niksik*, or weighted snag hook, for this purpose. Ice movement is rarely tested in this way, because Eskimos usually know if the ice is moving without using this method.

If an Eskimo is trapped on drifting ice at any time of year, he tries to keep track of his position if he possibly can. He may be able to walk over the ice in order to stay parallel with the village (in the winter), or he will at least know in which direction he is drifting and where the land is. As we have noted, this may be complicated by steady rotation of the ice. Knowing the sun's position at various times of the day is essential, unless the man is carrying a compass. But once he is far from the coast it is extremely difficult to determine the direction of drift. There is an overwhelming probability that movement will be toward the north at this season, and if the wind blows offshore it will be simultaneously toward the west. An Eskimo would watch wind speed and current flow carefully in order to estimate the distance and direction traveled. It is very helpful to have a watch so more accurate estimates can be made.

Methods of Detecting Pack Ice Offshore

Once the ice is carried out of sight over the horizon, Wainwright Eskimos attempt to discern how far it has gone, in order to help predict its return. This is especially true if it seems possible that the pack has moved well to the north and may not return until fall or winter. Once the pack has gone far out of sight the Eskimos watch each day for signs of ice in the distance, hoping that it will come back. In late August and September the pack usually begins to drift southward again. According to the old timers this return is caused by pressure of the *aakaŋa siku* or "mother ice," which modern Eskimos interpret to mean the polar ice pack to the north.

The Eskimos use several methods to detect the presence of pack ice offshore. Some of these same methods were probably used by ships' captains of the last century who first visited these areas. The first and most obvious sign is sighting the ice itself. Sea ice shines brilliant white on the horizon when skies are clear, standing out sharply against the black ocean waters and blue sky. But sighting a few pieces of floe ice is not a definite sign that the pack lies just beyond. In the first place, there always seem to be "stragglers" of ice trailing along well apart from the main body of ice; and sometimes there are small floes consisting of many pieces of ice, which are separated from the pack.

These ice floes often have been stranded in shallow water and left behind when the pack moved away. It will be recalled that near Wainwright heavy piles may remain long after the other ice departs, then finally drift away alone. In 1966 this included one floe about a half mile long which grounded solidly on the beach north of the village. Many large pans also become stranded on the shoals off Icy Cape, and break away singly or in large groups from time to time after the ice recedes beyond that point. These little floes, which may stretch for miles, sometimes fool the Wainwright Eskimos into thinking that the ice pack is coming ashore. Thus, actual sighting of ice is not always as reliable an indicator of the pack as might be expected.

Perhaps a better sign is the reflection of ice in the clouds. We have mentioned the phenomenon of water sky, where the dark reflection of open leads is mirrored in an overcast sky. Similarly, when most of the sky is tinted dark by the open ocean, ice which is near the horizon reflects as a bright whitish color or "ice blink." Thus the entire sky might be dark or gray except for a light strip running along the horizon. The height to which this reflection extends in the sky depends on the distance to the ice and the altitude of the clouds. The closer the ice the higher overhead its color will extend. But it also moves higher if the clouds are at greater altitude. Refraction (*iññipḳaḳ*) may also reveal the presence of ice which is over the horizon. A very dark, water-colored refraction bulging above the horizon means that there is no ice in the vicinity. But if it appears as a foglike curtain draped along the horizon, there is ice in the direction from which it appears.

Refraction is easily confused with fog, which frequently occurs over the ocean in summer. Fog is often associated with the summer ice, and it can be used as an indicator of the pack's proximity. When the ice is far in the distance, fog may appear as a low strip along the horizon. Its color depends on the angle of the sun. It usually appears dark when the sun shines directly onto it, but it is white where the sun shines through it. Fog is not a particularly good indicator, however, judging from the number of times it appears when the ice is nowhere in the vicinity. It seems to be most common when there is ice around.

Surf is another indicator of the presence or absence of ice offshore. Until the ice moves completely north of Wainwright there is hardly any surf. The ice might be somewhere offshore when a westerly gale arises, but there is not enough open water to allow any but small waves to build up. When there is no wind, the water is perfectly flat, so that a child could stand with his toes an inch from the ocean's edge and never get them wet. As soon as the ice is gone, however, there is nearly always some surf coming in. When the wind blows from the west or northwest in late summer, Eskimos watch the surf to see if it begins to diminish in size. If it does so without a decrease in wind, it is a good sign of ice approaching the land.

Even if all visible signs are absent, the Wainwright Eskimos sometimes know where they can go to find ice. As long as the pack has not receded to the north, there are certain places where ice is usually nearby, even if it has drifted out beyond the horizon off Wainwright. Usually they travel north, to the area around Point Belcher or the old village of Ataniḳ, about 20 miles up the coast, if they want to find ice. If they do not find it there, they continue traveling, sometimes as far as the Seahorse Islands. The ice blows several miles out from Wainwright before the power of the north-flowing current overcomes the pressure of wind. Near promontories, such as those mentioned above, the main current flows closer to the land, so the pack is carried along nearer to the shore. The same thing happens south of the village, toward Icy Cape. But the Eskimos prefer not to travel in that direction late in the season because the ice is likely to have receded north of there.

The hunters do not travel to these distant points unless they are in dire need of game and there seems to be little chance that the ice will reappear at Wainwright. It is a long trip, and it is always a gamble. When they go north it means traveling home, heavily loaded, against the current. An *umiak* does not hold a large enough load to justify such a trip unless it is quite essential. If some indicators, such as "ice blink," are visible toward the north, or if airplane passengers report ice in that direction, the men will undertake such a journey. Even a radio report that the ice has come ashore at Barrow would indicate under certain conditions that ice is present near the Seahorse Islands. Hunters are more willing to make these trips during the fall whaling season, when the stakes are much greater and they do not depend on finding ice in order to hunt.

CHAPTER 5

Emergency Conditions and Drift Ice Survival

Effects of Storms on Activity and Navigation

IN THIS CHAPTER we will discuss some of the emergency procedures developed by Eskimos in response to the kind of unexpected and highly dangerous situations in which they sometimes find themselves. This body of knowledge and techniques is as essential to Eskimo life as that which they utilize during their everyday activities, though they are forced to rely upon it much less frequently. It is a difficult sort of information to collect, because most of it must be gathered by word of mouth rather than through actual practice and observation. In some respects it is unfortunate that the ethnographer is seldom exposed to emergency conditions with his Eskimo companions, because these situations bring out some crucial aspects of their environmental adaptation and demonstrate most clearly the kind of intimacy which these people have established with their surroundings. After looking at some of the Eskimos' responses to storm conditions we will discuss the problem of drift-ice survival, certainly one of the most rigorous tests to which a human being can be subjected.

We have seen that wind is one of the most important elements of the Eskimo environment, and that it, above all else, dictates their routine of daily activities. According to Boas (1964, p. 19) the Central Eskimos must sometimes endure winter starvation, not owing to scarcity of game but because the fierce winter gales prohibit hunting for days or weeks at a time. By the same token, in Wainwright the only times people run out of coal, ice for drinking water, or meat are periods of severe storminess. Even when the temperature sinks to 40° and 50° below zero, as long as the wind is light, men are able to travel by dog team to get coal, to hunt on the ice, or to travel far inland checking their traps. By contrast, during a severe January storm the following notes were written:

> This storm has completely stopped all activity and has kept most people inside of their houses. It is the worst storm that I have ever seen, and is powerful enough to make walking outside difficult and uncomfortable. The blowing snow cakes itself into the fur of mukluks and parka ruffs, so that they are soaking wet after you go inside. The snow makes it very difficult to face the wind. More so than any storm so far, this storm literally takes your breath away when you face it.

The most obvious problem created by storms is the cold, since in this region the subzero temperatures can be whipped by the wind to a temperature equivalent lower than the coldest levels ever recorded in the inland areas of the northern hemisphere. (See Appendix 3 for climatic data.) But only in extreme cases, such as minus 30° with a 25 m.p.h. wind, will the cold alone prevent travel by these hardy people. They are likely to go out under such harsh conditions as this if they can travel with the wind, which is least uncomfortable for man and dog alike. Dogs have a strong distaste for pulling into a wind, and often will veer constantly to one side or the other if not watched and guided closely. Whenever a man decides to travel in very cold weather, he is certain to take a trip which is upwind on the way out and downwind on the way home, so that late in the day he has the easiest travel.

During powerful winter storms the visibility is often reduced to a few yards by wind-blown snow. The condition of visibility is often sufficient in itself to clinch the decision to stay home, to turn back before reaching a destination, or to stop and set up an emergency camp to wait out a storm. The Eskimo is usually quite particular about not traveling when blowing snow obscures visibility, because this is when he is most likely to become lost. No man wants to face these dangerous conditions with only a poor emergency shelter to protect him from the frigid gale. The Eskimo who becomes lost, *tammnak*, faces not only immediate personal danger, but humiliating social ridicule as well. Both provide a strong impetus for watching the signs of navigation closely. Hunters, especially the younger men who are learning the skills, are subjected to merciless ridicule and degradation if they become lost or, worse, if they do so repeatedly.

The best friends of a poor navigator or a man who loses his way in a storm are his dogs. A lead dog is praised if it is good at find- ing its way home in bad weather. If a man has a young or inept lead dog, he will replace it with an older one that "likes to go home" whenever he feels that he might become lost. In most in- stances the dogs will seek out dog trails that lead in the right di- rection, but if necessary they can probably guide themselves without this aid. When an Eskimo wants his dogs to take him home, he sits quietly on the sled and gives them no orders, lest he turn them in the wrong direction and confuse the leader. Even though they swing away from the proper direction from time to time, they always seem to get back on course by themselves.

Stefansson (1950, pp. 340–46) has pointed out that dogs are not reliable guides unless they are living in a village where they are familiar with the trails. Although there is undoubtedly some truth in this statement, there are many cases which show that dogs are often quite good at finding even a temporary camp. Some Eskimos have fallen from their dog sleds and lost their teams, but the dogs returned on their own to a temporary campsite where they had stayed the night before. An actual instance of a similar happening was this one from my own field notes:

> We had used most of the short light of day running a long trap line north of our camp. Shortly after we started back, my team dropped a mile or two behind Titalik and his son, who were riding on one sled. To my surprise the moon disappeared in a full

eclipse as the last daylight faded. As a consequence, it became pitch dark; almost nothing was visible, and navigation for me was impossible. I did as I had been told, keeping quiet and letting the leader find the trail. He did so with his usual infallibility, despite the fact that the snow was so hard that there was usually no visible trail, and we were in an area where I had never driven him before. The leader went right into camp and laid down at his spot in the dog line.

In spite of the fact that dogs appear to be reliable in their home area, Stefansson's warnings about their use as navigators in strange areas are undobutedly well founded. A traveler who is caught in a storm and is uncertain of his directions will always do best to follow the Eskimo axiom: When in doubt, stop and wait for the weather to clear, then continue to the destination. Kusik̇ described his own experience, when he was caught by bad weather and stayed in a small snow shelter for four days before it cleared enough for him to travel safely home. Stefansson (1950) describes an old Eskimo woman who spent seventy hours in a blizzard that arose when she was only half a mile from home. She sat out in the open, her mittens beneath her and arms inside her parka, alternately sleeping and getting up to walk around when she became chilled. The logic behind doing this, even if one has only a few hundred yards to go, is based on the fact that it is too easy to become hopelessly lost and exhausted, and then when the weather clears to be unable to reorient and find home.

Stefansson (1950, p. 445) suggests four rules to follow while waiting for the visibility to clear: (1) Keep still, and move around just enough to stay warm. (2) Do not overexert or in any way allow the clothing to become damp. (3) Sleep as much as possible. (4) At 10° below or colder, build a snowhouse or snow shelter of some sort. As we will see later, these rules are followed by men who drift away on the ice while they wait for a chance to get back to shore.

There are other methods of finding the way to a campsite or village in stormy weather besides depending on dogs. Most important of these to the Eskimo is memorizing every landmark on the terrain surrounding his village or camp, and closely observing the features of land and ice over which he travels for the first time. In this way he will recognize features when he comes onto them in a storm, and he will know in which direction to travel and how much time should elapse before he reaches his destination.

On the flat and monotonous tundra or the jumbled piles of sea ice the smallest unique features become important landmarks— an upturned rock, a cut in the river bank, an unusually large or strangely shaped ice pile. The Eskimos are extraordinarily skillful at observing such landmarks and remembering their spatial relationships. A very important and easily recognized type of landmark is a linear feature, such as a long ice ridge, the recognizable features of an old lead edge, the ocean beach, or cliffs paralleling the ocean or a river. For example, in order to find Wainwright in a storm, a traveler should head toward the beach either north or south of the village, but never straight toward where the village should be. When he hits the beach he will turn toward the south, if he has been heading somewhat north of Wainwright. If he traveled straight toward the village and missed it, he would not know which direction to go to find it. This method can also be used to find a camp near a long ridge on the ocean ice.

On one long dog-team trip it was demonstrated just how much the Eskimos depend on knowledge of the landscape for navigation. Between Wainwright and the first camp, at a shelter cabin about 40 miles away, my Eskimo traveling companion demonstrated an amazing knowledge of the landscape. He had often trapped and hunted in this region and had traveled to the cabin several times. He was able to keep a true line of travel through what appeared to be a featureless landscape, and found shallow steam valleys infallibly when there seemed to be no indication whatever where they would be. He also knew the location of fox holes completely "in the middle of nowhere," in spite of the fact that they were not visible from over a hundred yards away.

On the second day of travel we came to an area where he had never been with a dog team, and it became clear that his ability to navigate had been due to knowledge of the landscape. In this region he knew only what he had seen while traveling along the coast by boat or had heard from other men. He could not tell how far it was to our destination, and he knew little of the landscape even though there were cliffs, hills, and buildings, much more prominant landmarks than those along the first day's route. On the first day he was able to predict at noon that we would reach the cabin at four o'clock, and was exactly correct; but on the second day he did not know whether we would arrive at our destination at five o'clock or midnight.

Stefansson's conclusion that the white man is superior to Eskimos in ability to find his way probably relates to the kind of contact he most frequently had with them. The Eskimo relies on a mental map which he has composed through his own experiences and travels. A white man cannot hope to equal him on his own ground without many years' experience. But in completely unfamiliar territory, the nonnative may be more adept at carefully timing himself as he travels, and keeping a close record of changes in direction. A good part of Stefansson's experience with Eskimos was probably on terrain that they had never seen before, where a white man might indeed excel in certain navigational skills.

On familiar terrain, or in traveling out from a camp and returning later, the modern Eskimo usually keeps track of the time that passes. In this way he can tell if he has passed by the village or camp in a storm. If a certain hill or ice pile is half an hour out from the village, after forty-five minutes' travel the destination has probably been bypassed.

Most Eskimos own watches, which they keep set carefully to the correct time by listening to radios. In fact, their concern with keeping their watches set to the exact minute seems rather unusual in view of the overall context and situation. One explanation for this is their concern for time as a factor in navigation. Aboriginally, they did not use measures of distance, such as feet or miles, but must have relied on time as a unit of distance. Today they are inept at measuring distances, but are expert in dealing with time. A similar observation was made by Jenness in 1913 regarding their use of time as a measure of distance. At that time, which was also the period when Stefansson was conducting his explorations, the Eskimos owned watches but did not use them extensively (Jenness 1961, pp. 69–70, 108).

Eskimos today, as in the past, sometimes mark the trail at important places or turns. In former times men occasionally shot more caribou or seals than they could haul back home alone on foot. They would leave trail markers along the way, such as pillars of snow with willow twigs stuck in them to point the proper direction, and would mark the game itself, so their wives could go out with the dogs and bring it home. Near a trapping camp north of Wainwright several empty oil drums were placed along the trail to aid in locating the camp in stormy weather. Long sticks can also be placed in the snow leaning toward the correct direction, as guides to a particular spot.

The wind itself can be used as an aid to navigation along the northwest coast of Alaska. Easterly and northeasterly winds are very constant in this region, especially during the cold months. Under conditions of poor visibility the wind can be a guide, if it is watched closely to be sure that it is not changing direction. In a northeast wind, for example, a traveler who is headed homeward down the middle of the featureless Kuk River lagoon tries to keep going at exactly a right angle to the wind.

As long as the wind and its relation to the snowdrifts is watched, there is no danger of being thrown off course by a gradual wind shift. Snowdrifts themselves are like the needle of a compass, especially in these regions of consistent prevailing winds. To anyone who flies over the sea ice or tundra in an airplane, or moves slowly over it on a dog sled, the east-west orientation of the thin elongated drifts is obvious. The snow, wisping along before the wind, forms drifts elongated parallel to the wind direction.

Realizing in which direction the drifts trend, the problem is knowing from which direction the wind blew that formed them. The solution is not difficult. First, the wind deposits snow on the lee side of any obstruction, whether it is a marble-sized lump of snow or a mountainous ice pile. In flat areas the surface of the snow is usually studded everywhere with small lumps of snow less than two inches high, behind which there is a small "tail" of snow that tapers to a point several inches behind the lump. This little tail was left there because it was on the lee side, the tail pointing downwind and the flat end forming the upwind side. The tail usually points southwest or west in this area. Snow also accumulates on the lee flank of hummocks, often in deep soft drifts called *mauya*. The windward side is always blown free of all loose snow, leaving bare ice or hard packed snow (*sillek*). On mobile ocean ice this pattern is always liable to disruption, because the floes may rotate so that their drifts become disoriented from the prevailing wind.

Large snowdrifts formed without any obstruction are shaped exactly the opposite way, tending to have a long tapered windward end, both in cross section and top view, and a more steep and abrupt leeward end. This type of drift is called *kaiuhulak*. Its usual shape can be disrupted easily, however, by wind eroding the drift's windward face. It is important to watch for drifts with one end carved away, with a blunt eroded face upwind and a more gently tapering slope to leeward.

In this region there are, of course, drifts shaped by winds that blow contrary to the usual east-west axis. Most important are the powerful south winds, which occur sporadically throughout the year. The drifts formed by south winds can be distinguished from those of northeast winds because they are stout and lumpy, being produced at warmer temperatures than the long and slender northeast wind drifts.

Navigation is a much smaller problem during the summer than at any other season. Visibility is not diminished by storm winds, because there is no snow to be blown before the wind. Game animals remain active regardless of wind, and the boats can move in the lee of the shore or through the ice floes, so Eskimos are usually able to hunt and travel even when storm winds are blowing.

However, wind is occasionally strong enough during the summertime to prevent most outdoor activities, especially when it is accompanied by rain and sleet. For example, in late June, 1966, a storm hit an Eskimo camp on the beach 20 miles south of Wainwright. In the afternoon a gale arose from the south, reaching estimated velocities of 60 to 70 m.p.h. Blowing sand was so thick along the strand that it was difficult to face the wind at all. In this same area a man was once caught about a mile north of camp when a south wind came up. He was forced to walk all the way to Wainwright rather than return that mile facing the wind. During the 1966 storm the ice began to warp and pile ominously close to the beach, forcing one man to move his tent because he feared that it might be crushed beneath the ice if it began piling upon onto shore.

On another occasion a large number of Eskimos were hunting

at an open lead during a fairly strong windstorm accompanied by driving snow and sleet. Seals were unusually abundant, so the hunters remained on the ice all night, exposed to the weather without shelter of any sort. Although the temperature was in the upper 20's, I will remember this as my coldest experience in the Arctic. Some of the men had come out from the village the same evening and were dressed in heavy flight pants and parkas. Others had been camped to the south for several days and were dressed for warmer weather. These men became deeply chilled. Although this situation was exceptional, Arctic summers can produce very foul weather, and the Eskimos must occasionally endure considerable discomfort.

Protection from Cold Injury

In the preceding section we discussed various procedures by which the Eskimo protects himself from unnecessary exposure to dangerous weather conditions. If he is to live successfully in this environment, however, a man cannot escape frequent exposure to deep cold and biting winds. Since no suit of clothing is perfect, he must devise certain behavioral adaptations to protect his body from the cold his clothing admits. There are procedures which are followed during normal daily activities outside. In such routine situations they provide comfort and safety. In an emergency they could provide the margin between life and death.

Eskimos have a hard time protecting certain parts of their bodies from cold injury. During travel in extremely cold weather the most difficult part of the body to keep warm is the exposed surface of the face. In the winter of 1964–65 several men were frostbitten over fairly large areas of their cheeks, noses, and chins. Small nips, resulting in blisters or sores, were quite commonly seen, especially on certain individuals who appeared to be more susceptible. Several men in Wainwright were apt to become chilled more easily than the others, but no mention was made of tendency toward frostbite.

It is especially difficult to protect the face from a cold breeze when a man is on foot, because he cannot turn his face away from the wind while walking against it. Driving a dog sled is much more comfortable because the rider simply turns his face to the side or stands sideways on the sled to escape the wind. Occasionally Eskimo men become frostbitten while chasing game such as caribou with a dog team, because they have to watch the trail ahead and their hands are occupied with setting the snow hooks and holding their rifles.

Eskimos typically warm their faces with their hands, pulling one hand out of its mitten or glove and holding it briefly over the cold parts. Usually it is possible to feel a sharp stinging sensation in the flesh before it gets cold enough to be frostbitten. When this happens, a warm hand is quickly placed over the chilled flesh. Hunting partners watch each other's faces if the weather is cold, and if white spots appear in the flesh a warning is given by the other man.

Eskimos do not warm their hands or face with their warm breath. Inexperienced persons tend to believe that breathing into a glove to warm the inside, or onto a part of the clothing while holding it against the face, will satisfactorily warm the flesh. At moderate temperatures, perhaps above zero, this may be done without harm; but when the temperature is low, vapor from the breath does more to chill the flesh than to warm it.

Occasionally a man will hold his fur mitten or parka ruff over his face to protect it from chill and to rewarm his skin. An Eskimo once said that it is sometimes not harmful to breathe through the nose into caribou fur, but one should not breathe through the mouth or into cloth or poor types of fur. However, absolute safety is insured by using a bare hand. The brief period that a hand is exposed for rewarming chilled flesh is not enough to endanger the hand itself. When caribou mittens are used, there is so little heat loss inside that the hand is immediately rewarmed.

A favorite method of preventing frostbite, which is frequently used when the face becomes very chilled, is wiping mucus from the nose over the affected areas. This may seem to be of questionable validity, but it hardly seems possible that a pragmatic people such as the Eskimos could be mistaken about something so important and ever present in their daily life as frostbite. Several individuals were seen using the technique on various occasions, certainly without ill effect. It was reported that a white man who was resident in Wainwright for several years often used the technique, because he was quite susceptible to frostbite.

Considering the amount of time they spend outside in severe weather, Eskimos have remarkably little difficulty with freezing or frostbite. Their hands are evidently seldom frostbitten. When a man's hands become chilled, he holds them inside his parka hood, pulls them inside through his sleeves, or holds them against the flesh of his lower abdomen. If they become very cold, he may place his fingers inside his mouth. Eskimo footgear is so effective as protection from the cold that cases of frozen feet seem to be almost nonexistent. During the winter of 1964–65 the only case of frozen feet at Wainwright was a white man who was wearing military-issued rubber footgear, while a white companion using native boots felt little discomfort.

If a person's feet become very cold, the Eskimo remedy is to hold them against someone's bare stomach. This method is also used to thaw feet that have become frozen. When blisters form on frostbitten skin, they are left alone as long as the individual is away from home, but upon returning he will puncture them at the edges to drain them. Brower (1963, p. 99) mentions that he once froze his feet and could not walk, so an Eskimo fashioned for him a pair of "sandals" that were cut so that his blistered heels did not touch the ground when he walked. During this study no reports were heard of adults ever suffering serious frostbite, although in the past adolescents and children have become lost and have frozen to death.

Besides protecting their flesh from freezing, Eskimos must know how to keep comfortably warm in bitterly cold weather, when even the best skin clothing will not suffice alone. Physical exertion is the most common way of generating enough warmth to remain active outside for long periods of time. For example, it is fairly common to see a man run alongside his sled while he travels by dog team. Sitting on a dog sled hour after hour is very conducive to chilling, so these periods of exercise are a necessary way of restoring warmth. Several Eskimos told of being caught in a storm when improperly dressed or of falling through young ice and soaking their clothing. In most cases they were close to the village and headed for home, running alongside their teams to keep warm.

During winter sealing, which often requires a long wait at the edge of an open lead, the hunter's hands and feet become cold rather quickly. He will often stamp his feet or do a kind of native dance step while he watches for seals. And even more commonly men are seen clapping their hands together or slapping them against their sides. Young men sometimes play jumping games in order to keep warm.

As long as the men are close to the village, there is no real danger of overexertion, and it is of little consequence if their clothing is dampened by perspiration. In any survival situation care must be taken to avoid this, because perspiration robs the clothing of some of its insulating qualities. If an Eskimo is forced to remain outside without a shelter or sleeping bag, he will find a sheltered spot and sit it out, sleeping as much as possible and walking around to generate warmth as often as he becomes chilled. In this way he stays warm without overexerting. Sitting it out is safer that groping through a storm or traveling when directions are lost, which only amounts to a senseless waste of energy.

We mentioned earlier that Eskimos may become deeply chilled during summer hunting activities. This is particularly true during lengthy boat trips, when they must sit for hours exposed to the wind and spray. As they travel, winter or summer, the hunters make frequent stops for warm tea, and to move around and perhaps do some strenuous work that will restore warmth. Frequently, they will run around a little as soon as the boat is landed on an ice floe; or they may decide that some job must be done, such as unloading the boat and spilling out the water that has accumulated inside. Men cannot rewarm themselves constantly when they travel by boat, as they can by running alongside their dog sleds at other times of the year.

During the warm months it is as easy to become overheated as it is to become chilled. Thus, when an Eskimo is butchering walrus, hauling meat from the ice or tundra to the boat, dragging a seal home across the ice, or paddling an *umiak* through thick ice floes, he frequently has to remove one or two layers of clothing. This is why it is important to wear a light parka with other clothing underneath rather than a single heavy parka. Otherwise it is too easy to perspire heavily while exercising, and then become chilled afterward. A man tries to maintain a certain level of warmth, whether he is active or inactive. He can do this only by adding or shedding layers of clothing.

Drift Ice Encampments

If an Eskimo is trapped on the drifting ice floes, his most immediate problem is finding heavy ice that he can be sure will not break up underneath him. This is not as easy as it might seem, even in the middle of winter, because the awesome power of the drifting pack can crush or fracture almost any ice. Heavy ice means, first of all, thick ice. The thicker it is the less apt it is to crack or pile when subjected to pressure. Sea ice is obviously thickest in places where it has been piled into ridges and hummocks, increasing its vertical dimension to 30 to 50 feet or more. Even the largest ice piles, once movement has ceased, will freeze and solidify into a unified mass. The geometric ice boulders that make up a hummock do not pile loosely, but are firmly fixed, as long as temperatures are below freezing. Thus, whenever the Eskimos camp on sea ice, they look for the largest pile and camp next to it or on it.

When a hummock is chosen as a camping spot, the size of its base and amount of flat ice surrounding it are taken into consideration. If there is only a little flat ice around the pile, and if the smaller windrows of piled ice which surround every ice pan are close to the pile, it is not as good for a camp as if there were more "room" around it. This is because the margins of each pan or flat area grind away when there is ice movement, especially during the spring thaw. Stefansson (1950, pp. 363–64) warns that a crack or grinding area several hundred yards from a camp can eat away at the ice very rapidly, especially if the floe on which one is camped is not as thick as the one it is grinding against. The greatest danger, he states, is when the lines of motion of one's own floe and of the adjacent floe intersect at a small angle, such as 10° to 30°. Actively piling ice should never be approached closely, or ignored if it is close to a camp.

Ice ridges, piles, or large hummocks are convenient camping places in the winter, because a small shelter can be made among the crevices or caves, as long as the pile is solidly consolidated (i.e., is not freshly formed or in the process of thawing). The ice making up the formation should be fairly heavy, around 1½ to 3 feet thick, for greatest safety. This heavy ice forms crannies large enough to shelter one or several men. According to an old custom a man did not lie down in his shelter, even if he had enough skins to do so. Instead, the shelter was made with a snowblock seat, and the man sat upright. One man said that it is "bad luck" to lie down. Sitting might also decrease heat loss and prevent the survivor from sleeping so soundly that he fails to notice changes in ice or weather conditions.

Polar ice, or *pakaliak*, ice that is over a year old and has become fresh, is not a reliable place to camp on the sea ice. At first glance it seems that it would be quite safe, because of its thickness and because it usually appears to be less crushed than the surrounding winter ice. But this ice is not as thick as heavily piled winter ice. It is also brittle, and fractures more easily than the resilient salt ice of high piles and ridges. And it melts more rapidly in spring and summer, making it less reliable over a period of time because it deteriorates and honeycombs.

These Eskimo statements are supported by a note from Freuchen and Solomonsen (1958, p. 225) that walruses will never climb up onto fresh ice pans because ". . . they know that these might crack and break into small pieces, while salt ice is tough, and even if warmed it will only melt." Exception to this idea was taken by one of the most experienced Arctic pilots in the world, who has flown over and landed on sea ice around much of the Arctic Basin. He stated that he never had noticed that polar ice melts faster than salt ice, nor did he think that it would crack more easily. In his opinion polar ice is the best place for a sea-ice encampment.

The Eskimos, however, have the benefit of accumulated objective observation of sea ice over innumerable generations. One who lives closely with Eskimos finds that even those statements which seem utterly incredible at first almost always turn out to be correct. These people are extremely pragmatic and competent in such matters as survival. On the basis of familiarity with the

Eskimos and their knowledge of the ocean ice, it would seem foolhardy to reject their statements on such an important point as this.

If an Eskimo drifts off on the ice in late spring or early summer, before much fragmentation of floes has taken place, he follows approximately the same procedure to find safe ice as that followed in winter. He is especially careful to camp well away from lead edges, because of their increased tendency to fracture and disintegrate. Although he tries to camp on heavily piled ice, he carefully avoids newly formed hummocks. Only ice piles that remain from winter are safe at this time.

As the ice pack becomes less and less consolidated the problems of finding safe ice for a camp are greatly increased. During this study an attempt was made to learn as much as possible about this subject, to get an idea of what would be the most suitable kind of ice formation. But in spite of these efforts, and in spite of repeated observations of the kind of ice pans Eskimos choose as landing places during boat travel, it is always difficult to say whether a given piece of ice is absolutely safe. The Eskimos are much more definite about the sort of ice pans that should never be chosen. The picture will be clearest if we begin with these negative situations.

To an inexperienced individual, it might seem logical to choose the largest floeberg or iceberg that can be reached as a drift ice encampment. During the winter the highest pile may be the safest one, but this does not hold true in summer. It is well known from the literature that floebergs and icebergs tend to get topheavy and suddenly overturn without warning. Therefore, mountainous floating ice piles and floebergs are eliminated as safe ice for a camp, or even for a brief stop. Wainwright Eskimos never stop on or near one of these piles of ice, except in the few cases where they are solidly grounded near shore and there is no chance of their upsetting. Glacially derived icebergs are never found along the north Alaskan coast, but are considered dangerous in areas where they do occur.

Not only are top-heavy floebergs dangerous because of their tendency to roll over, but a much greater danger arises from the fact that many of them are composed of freshly piled or conglomerated ice so that they can break up suddenly. During summer ice hunting it is very common to hear frequent intermittent rumbling caused by disintegrating floebergs, especially when the water is rough or the current is swift. They are seldom seen rolling over, except while they are actually breaking up.

The method of telling if a floeberg is made of freshly piled and uncongealed ice is almost exactly the same as that which was discussed above regarding ice piles on early summer ice. Agglomerations of ice chunks which are clearly separate from each other, with many geometric shapes and sharp angles, are signs of danger. Often these ice formations look as solid as a pile of boulders, and equally as often they seem to be held together by some mystic force, like the balanced rock formations of the American southwest. There is no way of predicting when any of these floebergs will suddenly let loose. In a matter of seconds they can become half their original size or disintegrate suddenly into a mass of floating brash. Anyone who has seen the quiet calm of the northern ocean split by the thunderous avalanching of a giant berg would certainly be reluctant to climb onto one.

From what we have said thus far it may seem that a drift ice survivor would seek out the smoothest ice pan that he could find and use it for an encampment. This is not true either. Ice which has not piled at all during the winter and is only a single layer in thickness breaks up more readily than any other kind of sea ice, and can melt with unbelievable rapidity. During late June and early July a large flat area next to the beach at Wainwright fairly disappeared in less than a week. What had been solid ice with scattered holes and rivulets became a mass of drifting ice cakes not capable of holding a man or allowing any kind of safe crossing whatever. In the open sea this mass of ice would have distintegrated literally overnight.

What remains as a safe camping place, therefore, is some sort of combination of piled and flat ice characteristics—the solidity of piled ice and the stability of flat ice. The ideal place for a camp on summer pack ice is a fairly large pan, at least 100 square yards in size. It should be formed of ice that has been piled somewhat during the previous winter, so it is thicker than a single layer of winter ice. Large pans are best because they do not grind as rapidly as small ones, but a huge ice field is not necessarily good if it is flat and therefore subject to easy breakage. It is hard to tell where a large floe might crack, and if there are ice piles on it, they might tend to overturn once they broke free of the surrounding ice.

The horizontal surface, however, should greatly exceed the vertical dimension; in other words, the cake should be much longer and wider than it is high. The surface should resemble that which we described for ice piles formed during the preceding winter. It should be irregular or undulating (but not as smooth as polar ice would be), with a relief of 5 to 20 feet above sea level. Thus, it should appear somewhat shiplike in profile, but more round than elongated. Because they are formed around ice ridges, there is a tendency for floebergs and pans to be longer than they are wide.

During summer ice hunting the Eskimos frequently pull their boats up onto ice pans to scan the surrounding area for game. In actual practice, almost every conceivable size and shape of ice is used except that which is freshly piled or top-heavy. If they are looking for game, there must be a fairly high ice pile. These heavier ice cakes are usually the type that would seem most appropriate for encampments.

When the hunters stop for tea breaks or for open water sealing from the ice edge, however, they choose a different sort of ice. In this case they look for flat winter ice which is still quite solid, and which has places where the ice dips low to meet the water. The low spots are convenient for landing and launching an *umiak* without having to lift and drag it. On flat ice it is easy to pull the boat onto the ice so the hunters can reach it without having to climb inside, and there is also plenty of room to walk around to get warm. Low ice seems to be best for shooting seals in the water, perhaps only because the people are most accustomed to shooting from just above the water level.

The Eskimos need not exercise the kind of caution during normal hunting that they would if they were forced to stay on a single ice pan for a long time. The boat is always handy if the ice begins to crack, and they can easily move around until they find just the kind of ice they want. Before they stop they take some time to look for suitable ice, and one or two approaches are often made at places that are subsequently rejected because they are too rotten or too wet. High ice pans are less likely to be approached when there is a strong wind or current than when it is quiet, because of the increased possibility that they will overturn.

Drift ice camps should be placed on the most solid-looking part of the ice pan or floe, and never close to the edge if it can be avoided. Edges are usually the weakest part of the ice, most subject to grinding and most likely to break off and float away. In at least one recorded incident, however, this breakage along an ice edge was responsible for saving human lives. In July, 1897, a group of seamen and ship's passengers were beset in the pack near Icy Cape. After abandoning ship they walked to the edge of the pack ice. They had no boat, but found that large ice pans were breaking loose from the pack and drifting toward land. Sixteen people boarded one of these floes as it broke away. After a day or two they were rescued by a ship that passed close by. This group owed its survival to Charles Brower, a trader who had learned sea-ice techniques from the Eskimos.

Emergency Camps

Eskimos have devised some excellent means of providing themselves with shelter when they are camped away from the village. These shelters are made partly from items that are carried along on the dog sled, partly from materials that are available on the spot. But if a hunter drifts away on the ice or is caught in a storm without the tent and stove that he usually carries for camping, he must improvise a shelter from the snow and ice, and he must find a way to keep his shelter warm inside.

For certain kinds of winter camping, the northwest Alaskan Eskimos use square snowblock houses with a cloth tent inside. These shelters, which will be described later, are not used in emergency situations involving one or two men. In this situation a small temporary shelter is constructed. An emergency camp described by Titalik consists of a hole dug into the snow just large enough for a man to sit in. Blocks of snow taken from the hole are placed around it to make a wall and roof, and the man drapes his cloth parka cover over the door opening. Once he is inside, his mittens are placed beneath him on the snowblock bench to prevent heat loss and melting of the snow. He pulls his arms inside his parka and folds them across his chest to help keep warm.

Kaviḳ was once out on the tundra alone and became lost in a heavy fog. He built a snowblock shelter with a roof and a bench of snow inside. On top of the seat he made a cushion of reindeer moss and sat down on it. He sat in that shelter, which had an open side facing downwind, for four days. Each day he would get up and walk around a little, trying to find a landmark to orient himself, and then he would trace his own trail back to the shelter. He had no food and the only water was that which he melted by putting snow in a tin can held against his body. Melting water instead of eating snow is an important principle that will be considered further below.

It is worth reiterating that because of the danger of heat loss and of dampening the clothing, Eskimos are always careful not to sit directly on cold surfaces such as snow or ice. They always place something between their bodies and the subsurface. It might be suggested for such emergency shelters that a cloth or pad of some sort be placed under the feet as well, as is done for the long cold waits at seal breathing holes.

It is also essential to provide insulation beneath a sleeping bag, and the universal practice of northwest Alaskans is to use a caribou skin. In an emergency a man may be caught without any sleeping bag whatever, but if he can kill a polar bear or a large caribou it will provide a skin with which to improvise one. In this case he must be sure to lay the skin beneath himself as well as on top, but in so doing must not place the ends of the skin under his body. Fresh skin will freeze solid during the night, and although it still retains the body heat of the man inside, it will also trap him securely unless the opening is on the side or top where it can be forced apart.

A man should never have to rely solely on a sleeping bag for shelter in the Arctic winter, because normally there is plenty of snow with which at least a windbreak can be built. In one case a man said that he and his wife slept for three consecutive nights on their dog sled, covering themselves with the sled canvas, because they had no sleeping bags. Situations like this are unusual, and it is seldom necessary to endure such discomfort.

During the summer shelters are less important, because weather conditions are much less harsh; but the Eskimos use tents for overnight camping, usually on the beach near the ocean's edge rather than on the sea ice itself. Shelters consisting simply of a windbreak are most often set up for the purpose of brewing tea while hunting at open leads or during temporary halts in boat travel. A simple windbreak could be used in an emergency situation if nothing else were available.

The most typical windbreak is made by standing several wooden poles (usually ice-testing rods, or *unaaks*) on the ice and draping a large piece of canvas over them so the pressure of the wind holds it in place. For whaling the poles are set up in a row along the windward side of a snowblock bench or dog sled on which the men sit. A smaller type is set up to protect the stove while brewing tea on the ice during open-lead sealing or walrus hunting. This consists of a tripod made with wooden poles, resembling half of an Indian teepee. The stove is placed in the lee of this structure so that the man who brews tea can work out of the wind, and hunters can crouch behind it while they warm their hands over the flame.

Occasionally the *umiak* is turned up on its gunwale and supported in this position by poles, forming a very good windbreak. This is rarely done, but would serve as an emergency procedure to shelter exposed persons or to protect a tent from a gale. Tents are occasionally set up on the ice for wind shelters. This is done during a tea break, or to facilitate drying an article of clothing that has become wet.

By early summer there are few snowdrifts remaining which are a suitable source for snowblocks. Summer temperatures would quickly melt a snow structure even if one were built. Ice blocks could be used to make a wall, or the natural protection of an ice pile could be sought as a refuge from a gale. The Eskimos make little mention of emergency shelters that can be constructed from materials immediately available on the summer ice. In this sense the provisions of the environment are meager compared to the winter. Thus it is fortunate that the need for shelter is much less acute.

In former years the Eskimos made tents from seal or caribou skin, but by the 1880's canvas had come into use (Murdoch 1892, p. 84). If enough animals were available, their skins could be used to make an emergency shelter. Another kind of waterproof material was made in aboriginal times from intestines of the bearded seal or walrus. After removal, the intestines were emptied, inflated with air, and hung up to dry. The resultant material was cut into strips and sewed together to form a solid piece. It could be used to cover a shelter or it could be made into a raincoat.

Protection from moisture is perhaps the most important consideration for an Eskimo hunter in summer. The temperature and wind appear to have less effect on his behavior and activities. Natural shelter is very difficult to find or construct on summer ice, so a tent is an important piece of equipment. Protection from cold and moisture of the ice itself must be considered, because a good sleeping bag can become useless very quickly if it is soaked with water from beneath.

Although today's Eskimos use manufactured gasoline-burning stoves during normal hunting activities, they know how to provide themselves with heat and light if they are caught without a stove. The characteristic Eskimo stone lamp is well known, and since it is no longer used in this region it will not be discussed in detail here. But certain principles of these oil lamps are important to survival practices that are still used. In aboriginal times each house and camp was provided with a stone lamp, called *nanik* or *tuuaniktak*. This consisted of a shallow bowl containing rendered-out seal oil (*ohuzok*). Along one edge or across the middle there was a wick made from powdered moss, crumbled decayed wood, willow fuzz, ivory shavings, or other fine material. When lit and trimmed properly, the oil-soaked material gave off a soft light and sufficient heat for warming the house or boiling water.

To keep the lamp burning for a long time, a slab of seal or polar bear fat was hung on a hook almost over the flame. As the oil became low, more wick was exposed and the flame heightened, trying more oil from the fat. This, in turn, raised the oil level, submerging some of the wick and lowering the flame, so the oil dripped more slowly. This self-regulating lamp would burn for six to eight hours with no tending if set up properly (Stefansson 1950, p. 217).

Stone lamps disappeared following early contacts with whalers and other outsiders, but knowledge of their use is carried on by today's hunters, since an improvised lamp can provide heat and light in emergency situations. One such lamp which was made as a demonstration required only four elementary materials: (1) a container—preferably flat and saucer-like, but anything from a tin cup to a piece of aluminum foil will work; (2) a wick, which can be made from cloth, rope, sawdust, crushed tobacco, or any similar material; (3) seal oil, or perhaps other types of oil—even peanut butter will do; (4) something with which to light the flame.

This kind of lamp can be made from a jar cover and a small piece of cloth. The cover is filled with seal oil and the cloth is laid flat in the oil, with one end turned up along the lip of the cover. This exposed edge is lit and begins to burn with a quiet yellow flame. The flame is controlled by simply moving the wick higher or lower, exactly the same as is done with the wick of a kerosene lamp. With seal oil it is even more critical that the flame be kept low, lest it produce a heavy, black, sooty smoke.

These lamps have a fairly hot and bright flame, so a good-sized lamp could be used for making water from snow and for cooking. They are very simple to make, being almost identical in principle to a kerosene lamp. They are easily supplied with oil, since one seal can produce from 10 to 100 pounds of blubber. Aside from these good qualities, however, they are difficult to light initially, since the gentle flame is so easily affected by air movement. It is also difficult to keep the wick burning at the proper level to avoid heavy smoke. Even if it is done correctly, the burning oil always gives off a powerful odor.

Seal-oil lamps can be improvised in many styles. If one is made from a tin can or jar, a slit can be punched along the top to admit a wick that hangs down into the oil. If no top is available one can be made from a piece of cardboard or metal, folded in half and placed over the can by cutting slits that slide down over its edges. The cardboard or tin sits like a peaked roof over the container, with a slot cut along the fold. The wick slips up through this opening.

Seal oil is usually extracted from blubber by cutting it into strips which are placed in a jar or can, or inside a sealskin *pok*, and allowing the oil to render out slowly. There are two ways to make seal oil quickly, as one must do in an emergency situation. First, the oil drips from blubber when it is placed near a fire. The Point Hope people use this method when they burn blubber in their stoves, throwing it in on top of a wood fire. Second, oil can be made by pounding blubber with a hammer or mallet. This kind of oil is called *ḳaavaḳsiñeḳ*. This method would probably be most convenient for a camper, as long as he has something with which to pound and collect the oil.

Because fire is so important in the Arctic, modern Eskimos always carry matches wherever they travel. This is especially true on the sea ice, where a hunter may not require matches unless he is caught on a drifting floe and must provide himself with a fire. Under survival conditions, matches are split lengthwise to make them last longer. Eskimos favor wooden matches, probably because they light anywhere (Eskimos always seem to light them with their thumbnails), and they burn better and longer in the wind. Some Eskimos also use cigarette lighters.

Fires can also be started by striking metal against stone to create a spark. This was demonstrated by striking a file against an old cherty artifact. On top of the stone, right at the edge, a dime-sized piece of willow fuzz that had been rubbed in soot was held. The edge of the stone was struck briskly with the file so that the resultant sparks shot into the fuzz. Eventually it was ignited, and the glowing fibers were used to light a larger flame. The old techniques of fire making such as this or the use of fire drills have been forgotten by all except the older men, and even they are seldom without matches.

Procurement of Fresh Water

Another major problem of ice survival is the procurement of drinking water. For the Eskimo, or anyone with a basic knowledge of the techniques used to obtain water, this is actually no problem at all. First, there are two facts of vital importance: (1) snow is not a source of drinking water if it is to be eaten; and (2) salt-water ice cannot be used for drinking. These restrictions seem formidable on the sea ice, but there remain several easy methods of getting water.

Most important, there are simple techniques for melting snow. It must be melted, because eating snow usually induces greater thirst, and may eventually cause weakness. When snow is taken from winter ice, especially young ice, it must be scraped from the top layers, not from deep down near the salty, moist ice surface. If there is an ice crust on the snow, this is an ideal source of water. The ice crust is fresh, easily melted, and can even be eaten safely. The best snow to melt for water is granular snow, such as is often found beneath the surface of drifts. This grainy snow has a much higher water content than very fluffy snow, while hard-packed snow from the upper surface of drifts is intermediate in value.

An old Eskimo method of melting water from snow utilized a little pouch or bag made from the skin of a seal flipper. The pouch not only held water but also served as a melting apparatus. Snow was put into the bag in the morning, and the bag was carried inside the man's clothing next to his skin, where body heat melted the snow. After drinking from it, he put more snow inside to replace what had been used.

Another method utilized the stomach of a freshly killed caribou. The outside of the stomach was cleaned well, and then it was turned inside out and filled with snow. This done, it was put back into the body cavity of the dead caribou, where the heat still retained melted the snow.

Seal blubber can be burned to melt snow or ice for fresh water. After a seal is skinned, its hide, with blubber attached, is placed in a depression in the snow. Snowblocks are set up around it. Wick material is put in the fat and oil, and then it is lit. Heat from the fire melts the snowblocks, and water collects in the solid ground or ice depression underneath. On fresh ice, such as polar ice, pieces of blubber with wick material (e.g., cloth) are burned right on the ice itself. One or several channels are chipped in the ice, radiating out from the fire, so that the water will collect in several deeper cavities along these troughs. Water is taken from a cavity at the end of each trough, farthest from the fire. The holes nearest the flame collect water that is tainted from the fire and has a bad taste.

In modern times a gasoline stove is carried out onto the ice, or hot tea is taken along in a thermos bottle. Fresh snow or ice is used to make water in pots over the stove. Sometimes good ice is carried along from the village. When snow is melted in this way, surprisingly large quantities are needed to make a little water. This requires considerable heat, and therefore uses a lot of gasoline. Eskimos usually keep stuffing the pot with snow until it soaks and melts enough to fill it with slush, and then they leave it until it boils. Out in the open, the stove is shut off immediately when the water begins to boil. Inside a tent, however, the stove is left on to provide warmth.

Polar ice, which is easily identified by its dark blue or almost black coloration and its brittleness, is a good source of fresh water. There are other sources as well. In the first place, salt ice begins to freshen shortly after the spring thaw starts, after perhaps a week or ten days of above-freezing weather. Freshening results from downward percolation of the salt, so it is best to look for fresh ice near the top of a hummock. Ice changes color as the salt filters out, losing its light green or turquoise hue in favor of a bluish or whitish cast. In early spring the Eskimos find fresh ice only at the tops of high ice piles, but as the season progresses, lower hummocks and isolated ice chunks become fresh. They may also make fresh ice by standing a rectangular piece in the sun and allowing it to freshen for a few days.

By late June or thereafter, any hummock that formed during the preceding winter will have fresh ice around most of its surface. Wainwright Eskimos sometimes obtain drinking water for their homes by filling large buckets with ice and slushy water from the floes offshore. They prefer to use water puddles rather than solid ice when they do this. Occasionally, chunks of ice that float up onto the beach are picked up for drinking water. These pieces are thoroughly saturated with salt picked up from the sea water, so they must be left outside for a couple of days while the salt drains from them.

One more source of fresh water on spring and summer ice is small crystal-clear icicles that hang from beneath chunks of piled ice. These icicles are generally derived from water that drips from the melting snow and ice. In the winter, icicles are formed by sea water's draining from chunks of ice after they are pushed up from the water during piling. These salty icicles are hazy or opaque, like the winter ice itself, while the fresh icicles are always clear. If a man does not wish to prepare water or drink from a puddle, he can suck or eat icicles. Although there is no harm in doing so, the Eskimos seldom eat ice. They prefer water or hot tea, which warms them as well as quenches their thirst.

Drift Ice Experiences

The techniques of drift-ice survival are best illustrated by recounting actual experiences of Eskimo hunters who became trapped on the ocean ice and were unable, for varying lengths of time, to reach the land. In contemporary times there are very few of these accidents compared to the precontact period. In 1890 the Cape Prince of Wales Eskimos could recall the names of at least sixteen men who had been set adrift within the previous ten years and had never been seen again. During the winter of that same year there were two drift-ice accidents, though neither resulted in a fatality. Today, at Wainwright there are probably few active ice hunters who have not come close to drifting away, but most of them were either rescued immediately or managed to find a way across a crack or lead in time to avoid becoming stranded.

Kavik said that fewer men are cast adrift now because they are very careful, and should danger arise they will probably be warned by somebody's shooting his rifle three times as a danger signal. Also, if anyone is caught on a drifting floe, motor-driven boats will most likely come to his aid. Sitkok, a Point Hope Eskimo, feels that the fact that men no longer have to stay out on the ice at night, as they used to do for seal netting, is the most important reason so few of them drift away nowadays. Other important factors include the decrease in general hunting activity, lack of necessity to "take chances" or to travel far out onto the ice on foot to get game, and use of small skin boats for seal hunting, which can also be used to cross open water.

The most expert hunters are often the most active, and are therefore most frequently exposed to the risk of drifting off on the ice. These men are usually the most cautious, alert, and intelligent, however, so they are less likely to make mistakes. Several of the most successful hunters at Wainwright and Point Hope have never been stranded on drifting ice. They have been trapped briefly but were able to return almost immediately to the landfast ice. Kusik drifted away only once, and was rescued, along with many other hunters, by an *umiak* taken out from the village by men who reached them in time.

Igruk and Kaviizak, both successful old hunters, had never drifted away, because they said they had always "watched carefully." Sitkok had many close calls, but always managed to reach safe ice by crossing a crack on a bridge of ice or by running downcurrent until he found a place where the crack was still narrow. When these men were in their prime, they were all considered excellent hunters.

It is an important fact that Eskimos are extremely cautious people, who do not face dangers that can possibly be avoided. Thus they do not risk traveling out onto the ice when they can foresee any chance of drifting away. In modern times, when efficient hunting techniques and technology produce more game per unit of expended time and energy, there is little need to take risks. The possibility of shooting a few seals, or even killing a huge whale, does not justify taking any chance of facing death or undergoing severe deprivation.

During this study, many Eskimos told how they had been caught on the far side of a widening crack or lead. In most of these accounts, the men escaped by successfully crossing the open water in boats, on ice rafts, or by some other method. For example, three men escaped from the ice in a small boat when they were caught on a drifting floe near Wainwright in 1964. In this instance the ice was cracked by a tidal wave resulting from the Good Friday earthquake which occurred near Anchorage. Fracturing loosened the ice, and a large floe was carried away by an offshore current, even though there was little or no wind.

Several years ago at Wainwright, twenty-two men, eight dog teams, and three *umiaks* were set adrift on the ice about 15 miles offshore. The ice was cracked by a high tide preceding a south wind. When the wind began to blow from the southeast, the ice broke away. The men were unaware of their plight until a missionary stationed at the village flew out with an airplane and dropped them a note. They began pulling the boats shoreward, through rough ice and across several open leads, the last one about a mile wide. This lead had to be crossed many times to get all the men and their gear. It took thirteen hours from the time they realized they were adrift to get all men and equipment to safety.

Another time, five men and their whaling *umiak* were set adrift south of Wainwright, also by a wind from the south quadrant. These men pulled their boat all night long, and finally stopped to camp when they thought they had reached landfast ice. A short while later they realized that they were still adrift. They had set a compass on the ice, and noticed that the needle was slowly shifting as a shoreward crack widened more rapidly to the south than to the north. They broke camp hastily and headed for shore, leaving much of their heavy gear behind. When they reached the lead, they were able to cross it to safety. Regardless of the size of a party it is best for all the men to stay together, not only because this allows for mutual aid and the guidance of older and more experienced men, but also because once two parties separate on the sea ice, fracturing of the floes may prevent them from reuniting.

It is more common for two or three men, sometimes one alone, to drift away. Many years ago two men who were netting seals at night were set adrift on the ice from Point Barrow when a northeast wind came up. They had with them a dog team, a Primus (kerosene) stove, and a kayak, but no tent. When they discovered that they were adrift, they could have crossed to safety in the kayak, but they did not want to lose their dogs. So they stayed out on the ice, using the seals they had taken in their nets for food, eating the meat raw so the kerosene was burned only to make drinking water. Having no sleeping bags, they "sat down" to sleep, perhaps using the sealskins for protection from the cold snow beneath them (the informant was not clear about this). In about two weeks they reached shore at Ataniḳ, 70 miles south of Barrow. Their dog team was sighted by a Wainwright man who was hunting for polar bears on the young ice that was drifting in and closing over the lead. In most places it was thick enough to walk on, so he immediately began looking for places where the thin ice had rafted and found an area solid enough for them to cross to safe landfast ice, after two weeks of drifting.

Another man told of drifting out on the ice with two other hunters and three dog teams, when a heavy storm broke the ice away. They wisely remained well away from the lead edge where the ice breaks into smaller and smaller pans. They made their way out to the heavy ice, which does not break easily and is protected from the swell. Since they had planned to be out for only one night, they quickly ran out of gasoline, but they burned seal oil and ate the food they had carried along. After four days the fragmented floes were frozen together, the weather having calmed, and the men made their way back to shore. According to Stefansson (1943) the zone of greatest motion, and consequent breakage of floes, is within some 50 miles of shore. Beyond this distance the ice fractures less because there is less contact with the shore and the grounded ice. Drift-ice survivors often move seaward away from the land and the lead. Although they probably do not go out more than 15 or 20 miles, they find heavier ice and get well away from the swells that build up in wide leads.

Another problem is getting back across a lead that closes by freezing over with young ice rather than by the heavy ice's moving in to meet the landfast floe. Near Kotzebue two men once drifted away and were unable to regain the land for "about a month." They tried repeatedly to cross the lead but were thwarted when the wind or current would reopen the ice before it froze over solidly. These men stayed alive by hunting seals in the open water, heating their shelters with seal oil. They finally crossed on the young ice and landed at Kivalina. Men are not always lucky enough to find seals, as these two did. They may be forced to eat whatever skin or leather they have, such as thongs made of sealskin. In other instances they have been forced to live without any food, which probably accounts for the numerous records of men drifting away and never being heard from again.

A Barrow man said that he was caught out on the ice alone, but was only forced to stay on it overnight. He had followed a polar bear far out onto the ice and shot it before dark, but the ice began to crack and move so much that he decided to stay in one place until it stopped. His father had often told him that whenever the ice traps a man, he should wait until it is really safe before he moves. Attempting to escape immediately increases the chance of falling through thin ice or being injured while trying to cross piling ice.

The same man gave two other accounts that illustrate some important principles of drift-ice survival. Putu was born in north Alaska near the mouth of the Colville River. The first incident took place in this region, probably near Barter Island. He was out on a seal-hunting excursion with several other men. The weather was perfect, with no wind at all, good skies, and no current changes to create ice disturbance. Putu was just setting up to make tea and take a break when he heard a rumbling sound seaward from him. Listening in the direction of the roaring, he detected the grinding and tumbling sounds of ice breaking up; yet the winds were calm. Suddenly he saw a great heaving of the distant ice—an undulating wave, bursting the ice into huge oscillating blocks. He threw his gear onto the sled and tried to flee from the onrushing wave, but he had hardly moved before it overtook him. Wave after wave passed, while the other men made their way over the ice to him. They headed immediately outward together, toward heavy ice, where they could camp on a solid place that could not be broken up. They moved as quickly as possible, so that they could find a good camping spot before the hundreds of cracks opened too wide for travel.

Two inexperienced young men who were along foolishly wanted to head for the edge of the lead that had opened behind them, thinking they would await the first chance to reach land. They stayed on the heavy ice, however, held back by the elder hunters, or they would surely have been drowned. Through the whole night the waves came. The young men became seasick and frightened, but still they all remained on the solid ice. After four days the cakes froze together. With an older man leading, the group carefully picked its way toward the shoreward edge of the ice, where they found a lead about 10 miles wide between them and the shore. Here at the edge they camped, posting a constant watch, as they had on each previous night. The following day, under a favorable breeze, the pack began drifting landward. They all moved to a place where the ice projected farthest toward the land, and were able to escape as soon as first contact was made. During five days on the ice, they had eaten food from their supplies and several seals they had killed. When they reached their village, they found that the waves had broken the ice all the way up to the shore. Putu thought that the waves must have been produced by an earthquake.

On another occasion, Putu took his aged father out onto the ice with him to hunt seals at an open lead. They met two old men and two boys on the ice, and hunted with them all day in good weather. When evening came, Putu went to shore, but the rest stayed out on the ice to net seals. He took his dog team, leaving another team and a sled behind. The next morning he got up early and prepared to go out to the lead with another man. As they got ready, the gut-skin window in the roof of their sod house began to flap, as a strong wind suddenly arose. A minute later it was torn completely off. They tried to go outside but were literally knocked down by the wind, so they could do nothing but wait for the gale to subside. They waited inside all day and night, and in the morning the wind had gone down. They could see that the ice had broken away and blown completely out of sight. The temperature was bitterly cold.

Putu traveled all over the coast, trying to find out if his father had come into a village, but he had no luck for perhaps a week or more. Then he heard that his father and another man had come ashore and were in a village. He went there immediately and found them in good condition, but they said that one more man was out on the ice. That man had been left behind because his legs and pelvis were crushed when he tried to cross an actively growing ice pile with the dog team and sled. His foot was pinned and a large block of ice had tumbled onto him. The others were able to save some dogs and to pull him from beneath the blocks of ice. Then they headed out for heavy ice to make a camp and build a snowhouse. The two boys later took a dog and attempted to reach shore. Both were found later, lying in the snow frozen to death. They had apparently become lost and exhausted without any food. The three older men remained in the snowhouse, but were also without food. As soon as the wind carried the ice back to land, the two able-bodied men walked to shore, leaving the injured man in the snow shelter. Putu took one of the survivors with him and they returned to the shelter, where they found the injured man alive after five days alone, without food or any source of heat. His life was saved.

These two stories vividly illustrate the necessity of remaining in one place until the storm subsides and the ice solidifies. They also demonstrate the value of heading for heavy ice to make camp. Both of these incidents occurred during the early twentieth century, before the Eskimos had given up wearing all-skin clothing. They carefully followed the tradition of carrying the proper gear with them in case of emergency, regardless of how long they planned to stay out. Certainly the most cautious of the contemporary Eskimo ice hunters are the old men. Whenever they go out, they wear the best clothing they have and carry extra items of equipment that they would need only in an emergency. "The ice is like a mean dog," said one Eskimo, "he always waits for you to stop watching him and then he tries to get you."

Although many modern Eskimos advise going onto the ice prepared for any emergency, in actual practice few of them ever do. A notable exception is Sitkok, a Point Hope man who is an expert sea-ice hunter. When he goes out hunting seals or polar bears, no matter how close to shore the lead may be or how safe the conditions appear, he normally carries a full complement of emergency provisions: on the dog sled he carries his *umiahalurak*, or small open skin boat, so he can cross a lead if necessary. Over his shoulder or in his "sled bag" he has a wolf-skin ammunition pouch, which measures 1½ feet long and 1 foot high. In this pouch he carries seven boxes of shells for his .243 caliber rifle and four boxes for his .222 caliber rifle. He always takes both rifles along. In the skin boat he places a gasoline stove small enough to fit into a two-pound coffee can, plenty of fuel, extra lighter fluid, cigarettes, snuff, a compass and a canvas tarpaulin. The sled has a caribou skin on it, to pad the boat bottom and to serve as an emergency sleeping mattress. The tarp can be used to make a small tent, which can be heated by the stove while snow is melted for water. He usually carries a small amount of food along as well.

If he drifts off on the ice, Sitk̦ok̦ says, he will try to find a solid place to camp, where there is good snow for a shelter. He will stay away from the lead edge, hunting seals at cracks or holes in the ice. Then he will wait for the ice to close, keeping watch on the wind, current, and stars, so he can move enough to stay parallel with the village in case he gets a chance to cross to safety. Old timers who drifted off hunted seals at their breathing holes, but often had to go without food or eat their seal-hide harpoon line. A drift-ice survivor can tell when he has reached landfast ice. Young ice that has formed in the lead will probably be moving onshore when he crosses it. When this young ice reaches solid ice, it rafts downward beneath the immobile ice edge, which it probably would not do if it were hitting against another drifting floe.

In spite of the fact that the ice moves and cracks more easily in the summertime, it seems that hunters rarely become trapped on the seaward side of an opening lead during this season. Although travel on the ice is quite dangerous, the kinds of activities the Eskimos conduct at this time compensate for whatever risks might be present. In the first place, because they are hunting for sleeping seals and spend little time out by the open lead, they do not travel so far from the land. This also means that it is usually unnecessary to reach or pass the edge of the landfast floe, especially since many of the men hunt in areas where the ice does not move readily. When they do travel some distance out on the ice, they are extremely conscious of the risks involved, and will head toward the shore at the least indication of danger. In fact, when conditions are at all unfavorable, Eskimos do not venture out onto the ice, but occupy themselves with other activities instead. When it is close to breakup, they are even wary of traveling on the ice near shore.

If a man is caught on drifting ice, he stands a good chance of being rescued immediately. During the spring and summer, leads are usually close to the land; so by firing three shots in quick succession, a stranded hunter can signal the nearby hunters or the villagers that he is in trouble. At this time of year, boats with outboard engines are often kept on the beach, where they are left after whaling season ends. Thus, rescue parties can be on the move almost immediately. This is in sharp contrast to the winter season, when boats are not so easily available. After a fairly short haul over the ice, a boat can be launched and on its way to the other side of the lead. There is also no thick steam fog rising from open water to block visibility, and the sun is always present to provide good light. Thus men on the ice can be seen from a considerable distance.

A Wainwright Eskimo told how he and another man were set adrift briefly when part of the landfast ice was swept out by a sudden south wind. They had gone far out from the shore to avoid rotten ice outside the Kuk Inlet. As they moved through the rough ice, headed toward Wainwright, they realized that a lead was opening landward of their position. They went along the edge of this lead until they were straight out from the village, and then began to yell for help until the people saw them and came with boats. One of the men had a flare which he waved in order to be more easily seen.

Once the landfast ice gets very rotten there is little chance of being trapped on a drifting floe, because nearly all sea-ice activities are conducted with large skin boats. There is a possibility that a boat might somehow be damaged beyond repair, although this never seems to happen. But boats are sometimes trapped when the ice closes around them and then drifts out to sea. Strong offshore winds can also make the seas too rough for boats to leave the safety of the pack and return to land. These situations are most likely to occur during walrus hunting. There are ways of dealing with either problem, however, so the boats are seldom trapped amid the summer floes. This will be discussed further in the chapter on walrus hunting.

An opposite situation frequently happens during the summer, when the ice can move out from the beach, stranding dog-team travelers on the shore far from home. This forces them to undertake a tedious journey over the bare tundra or to wait for a boat to come after them. On the other hand, hunters who travel by boat may become stranded ashore when a strong west wind forces the ice solidly against the land, so that no open water remains.

The Eskimos say that summer is the worst time to drift away on the pack ice, although this is hardly what one would expect at first glance. The weather is warm, and game is so abundant that it would be difficult to starve. But the ice itself is most dangerous at this time, because it is continually melting and breaking into smaller pieces. This makes it very difficult to find a floe or pan that is certain not to break up or roll over in the water. During the fall, by contrast, ice is forming all the time and the floes are consolidating. A man caught on drifting ice need not worry that a pan will get smaller at this time, more likely it will increase in size by freezing together with other ice.

A summer drift-ice survivor also cannot move over the ice easily to choose the best place for a campsite. He might be able to move from cake to cake, provided the pack is jammed close enough together. Of course, the greatest amount of contact between pans takes place in early summer, and scattering increases as the season progresses. As we have seen, the amount of scattering depends on several variables, such as wind, current, and the proximity of land or heavy pack ice. In general, it seems that the more space there is between ice floes, the greater the danger to persons who are caught out on the pack.

CHAPTER 6

Astronomical Phenomena

Sunlight and Darkness

THE ACTIVITIES of Eskimos are profoundly influenced by the period of daylight and darkness. In this respect the Arctic is a region of great extremes. At Point Barrow there are seventy-two days in midwinter when the sun does not rise above the horizon, and a similar period of continuous sunshine in the summer. But the period of light sufficient for travel and hunting is of much greater significance than the position of the sun above the horizon.

In 1964 the sun rose at Wainwright for the last time on November 21. The sky was very clear, so the sun was visible during the fifteen or twenty minutes that it was above the horizon. The sun may be seen for several days after it has actually set for the last time, because atmospheric refraction sometimes projects the sun's image higher than it actually is. The sun was not seen again until January 24, 1965. It was probably above the horizon several days earlier, but storm-blown snow reduced the visibility and obscured the sun.

This brings us to the important factors influencing the period of light sufficient for travel. Throughout the winter there is always fair illumination during some part of the day, even though the sun never rises above the horizon. On December 21, 1964, the shortest day of the year, dim twilight lasted from 11:00 A.M.

until about 2:30 P.M. Although the sun is well below the horizon, clear air and bright snow help to create fair light outdoors. As mentioned above, however, the presence of clouds, blowing snow, or fog diminishes the length and brightness of daylight. If skies are overcast the period of light sufficient for travel is cut down by two or three hours, and is almost nonexistent during the very darkest time of the year.

Eskimos are very particular about traveling when it is light outside, because they regard night travel as highly unadvisable. They always plan to travel so they can camp or be home well before dark, and they prefer to camp too early rather than wait until nightfall is approaching. This practice holds true in ice hunting, although seal hunters often wait at the lead edge until dusk, because it is supposedly a good time for hunting. It is unusual for a hunter to go out on the ice late in the afternoon, however, lest he be forced to return after dark. Those who travel after dark are "crazy people."

Some night travel cannot be avoided, however. During the very brief days of midwinter there is not enough time to hunt without departing before daybreak and, often, returning long after darkness has fallen. Seal hunters are especially inclined to leave the village in time to reach the edge of open water before the first light of dawn. They often have to wait awhile before it is light enough to take the first shot. It is the ebbing light of late afternoon and early evening that sends them hurrying home, and few men will tarry at the lead edge after it begins to darken. Of course there is little need to remain there late, because hunting requires even more light than traveling.

It sometimes appears to the outsider that Eskimos could just as well do their traveling to and from hunting or trapping camps during the brightly moonlit nights. This is almost never done, no matter how bright it may be outside, and the occasional non-native who does it is considered either foolish or brave. This attitude was never explained further than to say that night travel is dangerous, and it is just as easy to wait for daylight. The danger of being caught in a storm is probably one reason for this reluctance.

In springtime the sun returns and the land lies brilliant white in the lengthening days. The intense light greatly facilitates hunting and provides long daylight hours for travel. This is the season when Eskimos have always traveled to visit neighboring villages. From Wainwright, dog mushers make the 100-mile trip to Barrow, camping once midway or occasionally traveling nonstop if there is twenty-four hour daylight. At Point Hope many visitors come by dog team, *umiak,* or airplane from Kivalina, Noatak, and Kotzebue for the whaling season. Spring weather is usually ideal for travel along the sea ice, beach, or tundra.

Twenty-four hour sunshine begins in mid-May at Wainwright, and lasts until early August. The period of continuous daylight sufficient for hunting and traveling lasts appreciably longer, however, because the sun's trajectory is so low that it does not go far beneath the horizon. About a month before the sun stops setting there is continuous brightness, except when the weather is cloudy. And a month after it begins to set in late summer, the Eskimos start using gasoline lanterns to light the interior of their houses. Their day-night activity schedule becomes more and more rigorously defined near each equinox.

During the summer months the modern Eskimos regulate their activities somewhat according to clock time. This is particularly reinforced by the fact that the native store, post office, and church follow daily time schedules. There are other considerations, such as improved visibility when the sun is high and the night fog dissipates. Also, dog-team travel in early summer should be done when the warm sun at its zenith prevents sharp spicules of slush from freezing and cutting the dogs' feet.

But for many reasons someone is always active at almost every hour of the day and "night." This is especially true among the adolescent children and the hunters. The children simply choose not to maintain regular hours. Hunters dictate their activities mostly according to the presence of game or the distance they have traveled during the day. Generally, hunters try to leave the village sometime in the morning and return by midnight. But nothing actually regulates when they will return except hunger or the urge to go home.

Moonlight

During the late fall and the dark months of winter, the moon is present for about two weeks of each month. Because it is an important source of light at this time, its arrival is anxiously awaited. The moon first appears as a thin sliver low in the afternoon sky, and for several days it rises only briefly and does not cast appreciable light. But it is soon circling around the horizon twenty-four hours each day, and at the same time it becomes full.

When the moon is present and the skies are clear, there is no darkness, because bright moonlight is reflected by the snow. The land glows in twilight all night long. At such times it is possible to read outside at any hour, and people could hunt seals very easily. Travel by moonlight is no more difficult than travel in the evening. Throughout the winter this periodic moonlight can be an aid to navigation and travel. Early in spring its effect decreases, until the moon's presence is no longer noticed.

Stars and Aurora

There are times during the winter when the moon is not present. After ten or twelve days it begins to wane and grow "lazy," sinking lower on the horizon each night. Soon there is no moonlight, and the land is plunged into complete darkness for many hours each day. At this time, especially if there are clouds in the sky, there are almost no visible landmarks, except those markers along the trail that can be seen with a flashlight. It is even difficult to walk at such times, because the irregularities of the ground, snow, and ice are invisible in the blackness.

If a man is forced to travel under these conditions, he must depend upon feeling the snowdrifts and allowing his dogs to find the trail, but he can also use his knowledge of the stars and aurora to guide him. Eskimos say that in former years men who were cast away on drifting ice floes could guide themselves home by using the stars. Nowadays Eskimos depend less on the stars for navigation, because fewer of them travel at night or drift off on the ice. Thus there has been a decline in such skills.

The big dipper (*Ursa Major*) is most frequently mentioned with regard to star navigation. It is an excellent "compass" because the time of day can be told from it. By memorizing the angle of the constellation (i.e., the "handle") to the horizon at various times of the day, and its position in the sky at certain times, a man can get his bearings from it. For example, if the "handle" parallels the horizon at 6:00 P.M., and the constellation is known to be always in the west at that time, directions can be derived from this observation.

Contemporary Eskimos own watches and are able to use them for navigation. Thus the position of a star, a constellation, the sun, or the moon at a particular time of day can be learned and used for direction-finding. In the summer this is particularly easy because the sun, circling continuously above the horizon, is always present as an aid to navigation. For example, the sun is in the northwest during the late evening. Therefore, in order to head toward the coast from out at sea (i.e., to travel east), the sun should be somewhere astern and toward the left of the boat. Many Eskimos also own compasses, which they call *taaktoksiun* (*taaktok* = fog, *siun* = instrument for). The compass was never used during this study except as an indicator of ice breakup (discussed above), and the Eskimos apparently seldom resort to its use in navigation.

There is one recent introduction which has had a very important effect on Eskimo methods of navigation—the electric light. Near Wainwright, Barrow, and Point Lay there are lights not only from the houses and buildings, but also from high towers at the Dew Line sites. Many of the stories that Eskimos tell about being caught in storms or becoming lost eventually relate the sighting of a Dew Line beacon which guided the way home. Others tell of being lost because they were unable to locate this landmark, or of going so far from the village that it was no longer visible. These towers and lights are probably visible for 20 miles, especially at night, and stories are told of unusual atmospheric refraction's making the light at Icy Cape visible from Wainwright, 50 miles away.

Many of the houses in northwest Alaskan villages now have

electric lights, and all of them have at least bright gasoline lanterns. These lights always mark the village from far away on a clear night, especially from out on the sea ice with Wainwright. Several houses have "yard" lights or lights up on towers, which are an even greater aid to navigation. This differs greatly from precontact times, when there was no light to mark the location of a village except a faint glow through the gut-skin windows in the house roofs. This helps to explain the loss of native skills in navigation by heavenly bodies. It would be difficult for today's Eskimos to do without these landmarks, especially the high towers and beacons of the Dew Line stations which are spaced every 50 miles along the coast.

The only other means of navigation to be dealt with here is the aurora borealis. Several Eskimos mentioned, when asked, that the northern lights are sometimes used for navigation, because they are always oriented in bands running from east to west across the sky. Throughout the entire winter, notes were kept on the auroral orientation, usually observed around midnight. The results of this check show a monotonous regularity at this hour; the east-west orientation occurred in nearly 100 per cent of the observations, whenever there were long cohesive bands. There is also a characteristic curvature of the bands, such that their ends bend toward the north. It is therefore possible to get oriented by observing the luminescent auroral bands. It is worth noting, also, that the more spectacular displays of aurora produce enough light to aid the traveler in picking out landmarks if there is no moonlight.

PART II

The Biological Environment

URING the sunless months of Arctic winter, gale winds tear the ebbing warmth from the land and bury it beneath shifting dunes of blown snow. The ocean is covered by a congealing pavement of ice, its tumbled vastness betraying no whisper of life. But underneath, the waters of this ice-covered coastal slope are rich with living things. Currents flowing deep below the surface carry with them millions of tiny benthonic organisms, the basis of a long chain of biological interrelationships. Larger invertebrates and fish, living always in the silent depths, feed upon the drifting clouds of krill. They, in turn, fall prey to the larger animals that must rise to the surface to breathe.

Seals that live always among the drifting floes gnaw holes through the ice to reach the air above, or rise in the steaming leads. On the surface of the ocean ice, polar bears quietly stalk the seals and follow drifting scents to carrion encased in the frozen pack. White foxes, whose tiny tracks so often follow in the bear's trail, feed on the scraps it leaves behind. And competing with the polar bear for food, or hunting the bear itself, is the Eskimo.

The winter ice provides with great frugality for the Eskimo hunter. He can move out over the ice only when the breeze is light and the floes lie still. And when the mauve grayness of day fades, he must hurry toward the safety of land, hauling with him whatever spoils he has taken. A man on the winter ice walks the thin line between danger and safety, pursued by the predatory darkness and cold just as he pursues the animals of the sea below.

In its time the sun returns, followed by the northward rush of spring. Now the hunter leads a richer life. Seals, attracted by the sun's warmth, crawl out atop the ice to bask and sleep, and perhaps to die beneath the bear's crushing paw or the Eskimo's shattering bullet. Spring and summer are marked by a steady passage of the ice and its animals toward the north. As powerful currents sweep the ice northward, they carry with them the animals of the sea—whales, seals, and walruses in abundance. Winds blowing from the south give speed to the flight of migrating birds and waterfowl, which pass by in an endless succession of flocks, winging just above the ice surface. But the opening of the sea ice must precede them all, for only after it breaks apart are the animals able to reach the life of the waters, on which they feed, while they can rest and sleep on the shifting floes. And when the last ice moves north beyond the horizon, the plentitude of animal life moves with it. The open waters behind are silent and lifeless, except for the small creatures that live beneath their surface.

For the Eskimo, summer is a time of ceaseless activity, but this is the kind of work he loves and enjoys. So long as the ice remains the hunting never ends, with the sun circling above the horizon, providing freedom from the darkness and cold of winter. There is no greater pleasure than to spend the days traveling among the ice floes and across the tundra, where there are animals everywhere—some to hunt and some just to watch—filling the land with life. Every day there is ceaseless coming and going of boat crews, and crowds line the edges of the ocean bank, watching the crews as they return with their game, and listening to stories of the hunt. The animals have come back, and no one stops to think of cold and hunger now.

But everyone knows the fickle habits of the ice and of the animals. They are here today in abundance, but they may be gone tomorrow. The lessons of lean years bear upon the Eskimos, for they know that the land and sea do not always provide in excess of present need. So they hunt until sleep catches them, and then they hunt again.

We have seen that the Eskimo has a great knowledge and understanding of the physical properties of the sea-ice environment. He must know the ice in order to move safely over its surface or to hunt among the mobile floes. But equally, he must know the habits of the animals upon which his life may depend—when they arrive or depart, where they feed and sleep, when and where they give birth to their offspring, and what habits they have that make them vulnerable to a hunter. Only one who lives with these people can begin to appreciate the depth of their understanding and knowledge of the animals they hunt. This knowledge is based upon the accumulation of several thousand years of observation of the behavior of game and of experimentation with methods of exploiting these behavioral characteristics.

The availability of game determines where the Eskimo will live. But the techniques of exploiting the game, as well as its actual presence, determine its availability. We must, therefore, consider what changes have taken place in the methods of exploitation during the recent past in order to understand the changes in total Eskimo ecology which have occurred during the same period. Eskimo economy has undergone a tremendous change since the introduction of certain methods of procuring game, such as hunting with firearms. These changes have greatly altered the way in which the Eskimo goes after food, the degree of dependence on particular conditions of weather and ice for hunting, and the overall productivity of the search for food.

Let us now consider, one by one, the resources of the sea-ice environment, the methods of exploiting them, their productivity and efficiency, and their effect on the movements and the total ecology of northwest Alaskan Eskimos. We are studying a special kind of animal behavior and ecology: This includes, first, interactions of the behavioral patterns of two species; man and the animals on which he preys. And, second, some consideration must be given to the ecological relationships between all species in this marine environment, especially as they affect the human economy. These patterns change considerably with the seasons, especially because the composition of the fauna is quite different, but also due to alternations in the behavior of those species which remain here throughout the year.

This is largely a descriptive account of hunting behavior and of the methods for dealing with each particular aspect of the sea-ice environment. Conclusions or generalizations regarding the significance of a particular factor or phenomenon to the total ecology, past or present, are made theoretically and not on the basis of quantification or intensive specific study.

CHAPTER 7

Invertebrates and Fishes

Invertebrates

INVERTEBRATES and fish constitute a part of the basis of the food chain upon which these coastal Eskimos depend for a livelihood. It is only in this sense that either plays an important role in the provision of resources that these people derive from the sea, because they make little effort to exploit them directly. Thus they are of little concern to us here, and will be given only brief consideration.

Marine invertebrates are rarely seen in northwest Alaska at any time of year. There is no intertidal fauna to speak of, and invertebrates that live on the ocean bottom are found only when they are cast up onto the beach by the surf. The sole exceptions are small crabs which are sometimes trapped by Eskimos at the edges of open leads. Crab fishing is still done today during the spring, from late February or early March until almost the end of whaling season. They are caught by sinking a small wire grid through a hole or from the lead edge. The grid is baited with a seal head, seal meat, or blubber. It is left on the bottom for "ten or twenty minutes," according to Van Stone (1962), who saw it done at Point Hope. The grid is then pulled to the surface by a long line attached to it, often bringing with it a dozen or more crabs that were feeding on the bait.

Of the invertebrates that swim freely in the ocean, only certain crustaceans are said to be used for food. These are small "shrimp," which can be netted through openings in the ice or along cracks, where they sometimes occur in abundance. During the fall they are also found, drifting in the water along shore. Netting is usually done during the spring whaling season, when the shrimp are larger and more abundant. They are said to be used for "soup." In the fall of 1963 a tremendous storm washed long windrows of shrimp onto the strand. The local B.I.A. school teacher, and perhaps some of the Eskimos, gathered them in buckets and bags in such quantities that they were used for dog food through much of the winter. In the course of this fieldwork no use of shrimp was seen at Wainwright or Point Hope.

These little creatures, which the Eskimos often refer to as "whale food," are obviously important as food for many kinds of marine animals. Seal stomachs are sometimes crammed full of them. When the shrimp come up into puddles on the ice surface in the springtime, birds gather in large flocks to feed on them. Puddles on flat ice right next to shore sometimes swarm with these animals (measuring perhaps 1 to 3 inches in length). They lie on the bottom like a residue until something disturbs them. At this time the Eskimos make no effort to collect them, and they seldom comment on them unless asked.

They have some effect on hunting at this time, however, because large numbers of Sabine's gulls (*Xema sabini*), glaucous gulls (*Larus hyperboreus*), and a few jaegers (*Stercorarius*) are attracted by them. These birds are occasionally shot with .22 rifles and used for dog food. Both the shrimp and the birds could, however, provide important sources of food in case of an emergency. In one famous instance, members of the Greely Expedition in 1884 were saved from starvation by shrimp netted in tide cracks (Todd 1961, p. 239).

Fish

Fishing is a very important activity of the Wainwright people during the months of September and October, but it is carried out 40 miles or more inland up the Kuk River. Once in a while, nets are set along the shores of the Kuk River near Wainwright, where the water is highly saline. Also, during late summer (August) nets are occasionally put out along the ocean beach, after the ice is gone. Fish taken in these nets include some kinds of salmonids, a few cottids, and some small flatfish.

The Wainwright people do not fish at all with hooks during the summer, though they say that there are fish around to be caught. The presence of fish in the ocean far from shore in summertime is indicated by the abundance of fish-eating birds such as loons (*Gavia*). However, there is so much other game at this season that Eskimos do not try to catch fish.

The only significant fishing done on the sea ice is for tomcod, or *ikaluġak*, (*Boreogadus saida*). Eskimos in many of the villages along Alaska's Arctic coasts hook tomcod during the winter. This activity has become less and less important, however, and has disappeared at Wainwright, where there is a richer fish resource taken from the Kuk River. Active tomcod fishing continues today in Point Hope between January and March. I unfortunately had no chance to observe cod fishing firsthand, so the following descriptions derive largely from the literature.

The tomcod is apparently a migratory species, so it is available only at certain times of the year. At Barrow, cod do not begin to run until the beginning of February, but they remain until the ice is rotten in spring (Murdoch 1892, p. 282). Cod fishing is done close to the beach, which may be simply for convenience or because the fish run close to shore in the shallow water. At Wainwright it was sometimes said that seals were feeding on cod near ice piles a couple of miles offshore, which indicates that they may be found quite far out.

Tomcod tend to congregate in the lee of large hummocks of ice, where there is little current. Thus they change their position according to the direction the current flows. The fisherman will chop his holes through the ice on different sides of an ice pile depending on the current. According to Murdoch (1892) the Barrow natives prefer to fish in flat places with hummocks surrounding them. A hole about 1 foot in diameter is chopped through the ice with a heavy ice chisel made of a wooden pole with an iron point (formerly bone or ivory). Floating ice debris is cleaned out with a scoop (*ilaun*) consisting of a wooden handle 2 to 4 feet long, with a webbed scoop fastened to one end. The scoop has a rim about 8 inches in diameter, made from caribou hoof or horn, with a mesh of baleen strips. Modern Eskimos some-times use a metal rim and wide-meshed wire screen for their *ilaun*.

A cod fishing rig described by Murdoch (1892, p. 282) consists of a line 10 to 15 fathoms long, with a stick attached to one end and an ivory or metal "sinker" at the other. This "sinker" has four hooks, which are made from two pieces of iron passed through it at right angles and bent to form the correct shape. In modern times the Eskimos use manufactured triple hooks, but the old type may also be retained.

The line is dropped down to about a foot off the bottom. There it is jigged up and down to attract the fish, which are snagged when they approach the jerking hooks too closely. When one of the little fish is hooked, it is reeled up by winding the line sev-eral times between the fishing rod and the handle of the ice scoop or another slender stick carried for the purpose. Around Bering Strait the Eskimos have basically the same methods, but place a windbreak made from "grass mats" around them. In that region the daily fish take is listed as ten to forty pounds, ranging up to two hundred pounds (Nelson 1899, pp. 175–76).

Other fish, undoubtedly some kinds of sculpin (*Cottidae*) are taken at the same time. Most of the fishing is done by women, children, and old men, who go out daily in groups of five or six. The hunters fish only when there is nothing else to do. This is, therefore, one of the few resources which can be exploited by the nonhunting segments of the population.

At Wainwright, winter fishing is also done for smelt, or *ilhoġanik*, (*Osmerus dentex*). This remains an important activity today, especially for women and old men. Smelt begin to run up into the Kuk lagoon near the village sometime in January, and they remain through March. However, the availability of these small fish varies markedly according to the current. There is also considerable fluctuation in their abundance from year to year.

The method of fishing is similar to that used for tomcod. A hole is first chopped through the ice, preferably in a crack where the ice is thinnest. The hole is made with a *tuakpok*, a wooden pole with an iron point. The pole usually has a bulbous enlarge-ment near the lower end, which makes it heavier and therefore a better chopper. Once the hole is made, through ice up to 5 feet thick, the man, woman, or child sits on his sled or stands and jigs for fish. Because it is done in the coldest part of the year, the warmest clothing is worn, layer upon layer of it. A snowblock windbreak is often used as well.

The fishing pole is about 2 feet long. Attached to the pole are 6 or 7 feet of line, made nowadays from monofilament bought at the store. At the end of the line is a sinker made from a walrus tooth, sometimes with a piece of lead set into it to increase its weight. A hole is drilled through the lower end of this sinker, and a thin strand of baleen is placed through it. The baleen acts as a springy crosspiece, and suspended from each end of it by a 6-inch long piece of line or gull wing tendon is a hook. Another hook usually hangs straight down from the bottom of the sinker, also on a piece of gull wing tendon. The hooks are slender, curved pieces of ivory, dog tooth, metal, or plastic. A hole is drilled at one end for the line and a sharp metal barb is set out from the other end. Often a piece of red wool or plastic is set onto the base of the barb. These hooks are jigged up and down until a fish is felt on one of them. It is pulled up by winding the line once over the left sleeve and once over the end of the pole.

There are many subtle influences of the current which must be taken into account when fishing for smelt, because they move in schools following the direction of the current. Most important, the rising tide before and during a south wind brings them into the lagoon in large numbers. Very good catches, up to three hundred and four hundred fish, are taken on the best days, while on poor days people may not catch a single fish. Sculpins are usually caught at the same time. During October through December these less favored fish, called *kanaiok*, may be specifically fished for. In 1964–65 the fishing was unusually poor, but groups of people were out fishing almost every day when the weather was good during February and March. Smelt fishing is never done on the ocean ice.

CHAPTER 8

Birds

Introduction

BIRDS that are of economic importance to the Eskimo are most abundant during late spring and early summer, when they pass by on their northward migration. But birds, in general, are prolific throughout the summer, until the sea ice is gone. Large flocks pass by on their way south in the fall, but they are not systematically hunted. Because birds are the most common and conspicuous animals here, the Eskimos are very interested in them, even in the ones they do not hunt. Each species has a name, and many of its peculiarities and behavioral traits are known. Eskimo hunters are experts at identifying birds by their color, behavior, and call, even from long distances, and they delight in being able to name each species that is seen. Even the young boys at Wainwright are able to name many species of birds and distinguish between closely similar species.

One of the favorite pastimes of hunters when they are riding in a boat or waiting for game is attracting birds by imitating certain of their calls. Whatever kinds of birds are nearby—ducks, loons, gulls, terns, or jaegers—someone will probably mimic them with his voice or by whistling. They say this is usually done to make the birds fly closer so that someone can get a shot at them, but in actuality it seems to be done for the enjoyment and diversion it provides. Sometimes these calls work very well, but equally often they have no visible effect.

The Eskimos classify almost every species of bird in the same way that ornithologists do, and every hunter can give the Eskimo name for most of them. Older men seem better able to do this, while the younger and more active hunters group certain closely related species under a single term. In most cases they consider the differences between these similar species to be significant and can distinguish them from some distance away, but normally they do not bother to do so. It was very difficult to learn from them the specific names of these similar species, and in some instances it was impossible to do so. In a couple of cases the Eskimo classificatory system may differ significantly from the Linnean system. The older men, who would have been able to give the name with certainty, were seldom actively hunting, so it was usually not possible to acquire their assistance.

In general, traits used for distinguishing species are the same as those found in bird guides, such as Peterson's *A Field Guide to the Western Birds* (1961). But there are some instances in which the Eskimos become confused by a book such as this, which omits some characteristics they might consider significant and stresses others which are unimportant to them. In one case, my informants and I were never able to resolve the differences between the native classification of several species of gulls and that of the ornithologists.

The following is a list of species observed during the summer of 1966 in the Wainwright area, including some which are said to be found there by the Eskimos but were not seen during this study. This list includes only species which occur on or near the sea ice.

Species	Eskimo Name
common loon (*Gavia immer*)	tulik
Arctic loon (*G. arctica*)	ḳahraoḳ
red-throated loon (*G. stellata*)	ḳahraoḳ
double-crested cormorant (*Phalacrocorax auritus*)	?
snow goose (*Chen hyperborea*)	kaŋoḳ
black brant (*Branta nigricans*)	neġliḳ, neġlinaġaḳ
white-fronted goose (*Anser albifrons*)	neġlivailuk
pintail (*Anas acuta*)	kurugaḳ
old squaw (*Clangula hyemalis*)	ahaaliḳ

Species (Cont.)	Eskimo Name
Stellar's eider (*Polysticta stelleri*)	iginikkauk̦tuk̦
common eider (*Somateria mollissima*)	amaulik
king eider (*S. spectabilis*)	k̦iŋalik
spectacled eider (*S. fischeri*)	k̦avaasuk
red-breasted merganser (*Mergus serrator*)	akpahraoyuak̦
rock ptarmigan (*Lagopus mutus*)	k̦azagik̦
red phalarope (*Phalaropus fulicarius*)	auhuroak̦
northern phalarope (*Lobipes lobatus*)	auhuroak̦
pomarine jaeger (*Stercorarius pomarinus*)	isuŋŋak̦
parasitic jaeger (*S. parasiticus*)	isuŋŋak̦
long-tailed jaeger (*S. longicaudus*)	isuŋŋak̦, isuŋŋag̊loak̦
glaucous gull (*Larus hyperboreus*)	nauyak̦
mew gull (*L. canus*)	k̦ag̊mag̊loak̦
black-legged kittywake (*Rissa tridactyla*)	teketeg̊aak̦
ivory gull (*Pagophila eburnea*)	nauyavaak̦
Sabine's gull (*Xema sabini*)	ik̦edagig̊yaak̦
Arctic tern (*Sterna paradisaea*)	mitk̦utaillak̦
thick-billed murre (*Uria lomvia*)	akpa
black guillemot (*Cepphus grylle*)	iŋag̊ik̦
crested auklet (*Aethia cristatella*)	igzuk
tufted puffin (*Lunda cirrhata*)	k̦ilaŋŋak̦

In the following sections, comments will be made as to the occurrence and abundance of all these species and their economic importance to the Eskimos. Many are not hunted at all, because they are too rare or because they have no value as food. Only a small minority assume any importance at all in the native economy, but we mention the others because they might be of value in emergency situations or be of purely scientific interest.

Waterfowl

Ducks and geese are the only kinds of birds that are of genuine economic importance to the Wainwright Eskimos. They are not only the most easily available, but are also the most highly preferred type of fowl. Caribou meat is the staple food here, and waterfowl is the only other hunted meat that forms a part of the people's normal daily fare. During the spring and fall a considerable effort is put into waterfowl hunting. The birds are stored by freezing them in underground ice cellars, to be used during the periods when they are not easily available. In spite of intensive waterfowl hunting, the actual volume of meat is miniscule compared to that of caribou or sea mammals (the latter used mainly for dog food). For this reason the supply of ducks and geese usually runs low after summer's end. In the fall and winter they are saved for special meals and holiday feasts.

Four species of eider ducks are found along the coastal waters near Wainwright. The common eider (*Somateria mollissima*), which the Eskimos call *amaulik* or *mitiḳ*, is the most numerous. The king eider (*S. spectabilis*) is probably second in abundance, followed by the spectacled eider (*S. fischeri*) and Stellar's eider (*Polysticta stellari*). The eiders are called by the collective term *ḳaugaḳ*.

Sometime during the month of May, ducks begin to pass Wainwright on their spring migration. Their northward flights may occur early or late, depending upon several conditions. First of all, they cannot precede the open water. When leads open toward the north, they are able to move. This point is brought out clearly when an onshore wind closes the ice during June. As long as conditions do not change there is a steady stream of ducks (as well as gulls, terns, and other seabirds) flying back toward the south in search of water.

Winds also influence their migration, because ducks prefer to fly with a tailwind. Before and during south winds the spring sky is studded with flocks of ducks winging along just above the piled ice. They do not follow this general pattern of movement with favorable winds infallibly, however. On some days in late May or early June there may be no ducks flying when there is a fresh southerly breeze. The next day, with identical conditions, they may be everywhere. And sometimes the winds are calm or from a somewhat contrary direction, but for some reason the ducks are flying north. When these migration days occur, and there may not be many, the Eskimos hunt continuously. They know that the ducks are difficult to predict, and each man wants to get as many as possible while he can.

Through the month of July and into early August, only scattered groups of eiders are seen during sea-ice hunting. They have moved onto their breeding grounds, widely scattered across the tundra, and will not concentrate again until the fall migration begins. This usually occurs sometime in late August or September, although it may begin earlier. After the ice recedes north of Wainwright, very few waterfowl are seen. They apparently prefer to remain in the vicinity of sea ice until they begin their southward flights.

The earliest waterfowl hunting is carried on during the whaling season, when ducks and geese are sometimes migrating in great numbers along the open leads. Many are shot from the ice as they fly overhead, or from boats cruising the lead. In the latter case, tremendous flocks of waterfowl may be found swimming in the lead. They are approached by the outboard motor-powered boats and shot at with shotguns when they begin to take flight. At times these flocks are so huge that the air almost roars with the sound of their wingbeats as they rise in alarm. When there is a lull in the whaling, men will go out in the lead and sit quietly in their boats, waiting for birds to fly overhead. These are effective methods of hunting. Of those which are shot few will be lost, because they are easily picked up with the boat, and wounded ones cannot escape. On a good day over fifty birds can be shot, but these are divided among all the crew members.

During summer *umiak* hunting among the scattered ice floes, waterfowl are sometimes hunted, if they are seen in large enough flocks. However, those that are shot are strictly coincidental to the main objective of sea-mammal hunting. Shotguns are usually carried along in the boats, in case of an exceptional abundance of birds, but they are rarely used. Instead, smaller .22 caliber rifles are used for potshots at flying or swimming birds.

The most important waterfowl hunting is done from the beach or out on the sea ice during the latter part of May and in early June. Migrating ducks and geese may fly far out over the ice floes, but they often tend to follow the coast. Duck hunting is especially good at Point Hope, because it is at the end of a long sandspit that projects out from the coast. The point intersects the migratory path, turning the ducks westward along its south shore. The people here are able to hunt from the edges of the spit, practically from their doorsteps. Wainwright is less favored as a waterfowl hunting place, because it is not on a point or head-land of any sort. In this region, better places can be found by camping away from the village. For this reason some of the men (as well as women and older children) move to beach camps north or south of the village, where there is less competition from others, less chance of having the ducks frightened before they can be shot at, and more ducks flying over the land or along the ice just offshore.

Also, people who camp on the beach reap additional advantages for waterfowl hunting. First, some flocks of ducks, as well as geese, fly right along the beach rather than out along the sea ice. Second, from a tent it is easy to hear the birds as they approach and to get outside in time to shoot them as they pass. In fact, men or families camping on the beach usually have someone watching outside to warn the others well ahead of the birds' arrival. This is done especially when the migration is heavy.

There are certain places on the land or ice where ducks seem to pass most frequently, and the hunters try to find one of these spots. If it is on land, they will probably build a blind of some sort, using wood or some other shoreline debris, or a snowblock wall. On the sea ice there are plenty of ready-made blinds in the form of ice piles and ridges. Good hunting spots may be known from previous successes, or they may be places where ducks are seen passing on the particular day. Ducks are said to fly more during the "night," when the sun is low, than during the warm part of the day.

On the sea ice small open areas or leads are especially good hunting places. For example, during June, 1966, there was a small open pond along the edge of landfast ice off Wainwright, elon-gated in their direction of flight. The ducks would occasionally fly close by, and would change course in order to fly over the opening. As they did so, they flew very low and presented excellent close shots from the side, where the hunter sat very still but in plain view.

Usually the hunter attempts to hide himself from the ducks' view by sitting behind a pile of ice where the birds often fly to one side of his position. He can walk around while he waits, but he must always be alert so he sees or hears them in time to hide. If he is in the open he must remain perfectly still (preferably wearing a white "snowshirt" for concealment), hoping that the ducks will fly close without noticing him.

Each flock numbers fifteen to seventy-five ducks, and on a good day a flock passes by every five to fifteen minutes in the best places. When it is not too windy, ducks fly very low, 5 to 25 yards up, and they stay in a tight formation. It is necessary to watch closely in the direction from which they will come, because they are very difficult to see until they are nearby. Eiders utter low, abrupt quacks and groans as they fly, which the Eskimos imitate by saying "ḳau, ḳau, ḳau. . . ." This calling is sometimes heard before the birds are seen, and hunters may answer in order to bring them closer. Sometimes a flock of ducks will circle back to investigate this sound.

A hunter can get more than one duck, and up to ten, with a single shot from his 12- or 16-gauge shotgun. Usually he waits to fire until the birds are passing to the side or overhead, or are a little beyond his position. In this way there is the greatest chance of breaking wings. Head-on shots are said to be the least effective for downing several with one or two shots. When they hunt close to the village, as they do at Point Hope, each hunter is spaced 50 to 200 yards away from the others. When many people are shooting, a man is lucky if several flocks fly close enough for a good shot during a day's waiting. At Point Hope the hunters are aligned with the ducks' direction of flight, along the beach, but at Wainwright they usually spread out across the line of flight over the offshore ice.

After the Eskimo shoots into a flock, he watches carefully for wounded birds that fall to the ice. As soon as the flock disappears, he chases down the wounded ones. They are usually killed by grabbing them behind the head and spinning them around just off the ground to wring their necks. On one occasion an Eskimo killed a wounded duck by piercing its heart and lungs with the quill of a feather pulled from its wing. After probing in, out, and around with the quill, he put the duck on the ice, where it died soon afterward without evidencing any pain.

When wounded ducks land in open water, they are difficult to retrieve. There is no point in chasing them with a boat (such as the little open retrieval boat), because they can dive and elude capture almost indefinitely. The hunter usually kills them first with a .22 rifle, then retrieves them. Wounded eider ducks are very hard to shoot, because they swim very low in the water and dive often. They even hide underneath the ice overhangs along the edge of a pond or crack, hoping to escape detection.

After they have been killed, it is easiest to wait for floating birds to drift to the ice edge. Sometimes, however, there is no wind or current, so they may be hooked with a snag hook (*manak*), consisting of a wood float with hooks on it which is attached to a long line. The float is tossed over the bird and pulled in until the hooks catch onto it, then it can be dragged in toward the hunter.

A more efficient way to retrieve birds is to carry a small open boat (*umiahalurak*). In this case the man simply rows out and picks them up by hand. They are left inside the boat and the boat tied onto the dog sled to be carried home. If no boat is used, the ducks must be loaded directly on the sled. They are rather difficult to fasten unless they are tied together. This is done by binding them with a cord around their necks, in bunches of five. These bunches are easy to handle and load securely.

Duck hunting, on land or sea ice, can be quite productive for the man who is patient enough to wait hours for flocks to pass over within shotgun range. In a twelve-hour day a hunter might shoot only three or four birds, or he could get ten to twenty or more. Again, we should mention that waterfowl are never wasted or used for dog food, because they are highly esteemed by the Eskimos. During a lean year, a good catch of waterfowl could provide the margin between an adequate food supply and hunger, so it is little wonder that waterfowl hunting is considered an important occupation.

The diet of the Eskimo, both the foods eaten and their method of preparation, differs greatly from that of the white man with whom he has contact in modern times. Matters relating to food have, in fact, created some stress between members of the two cultures. These dietary differences persist today, even among groups which are highly acculturated and have been brought into a cash economy. An Eskimo once told me that his people simply could not live on a steady diet of the white man's food. At first glance it seemed that he might have made this statement only to support his wish to hunt, even though he was earning a steady income. But on second thought, the overwhelming truth of his statement is readily apparent if we simply reverse the roles, placing the outsider in a position of having to live entirely on the aboriginal Eskimo diet. It would be very difficult, as I learned from personal experience and observation of others, for the white man to make such a shift in his own diet. And it is at least as difficult for the Eskimo to live entirely on the white man's food. It is because of this need for their own foods that the Barrow Eskimos, who rarely hunt, are willing to pay incredibly high sums of money to other natives who will sell caribou meat to them.

Before the introduction of firearms, ducks were taken with bolas (*killamittaun*) as they flew low over the ice or points of land that projected into their line of flight. This device consisted of six or seven weights made from bone, ivory, or walrus teeth, each on a string of braided sinew about 30 inches long. The strings were tied to a tuft of about nine wing quills bound together. These quills were doubled over, with the strings held securely in the folds. The *killamittaun* was carried by putting its lines together in a series of slip knots, which prevented them from tangling. Then they were placed in a pouch that could be hung around a person's neck.

When ducks came into sight, the hunter grasped the tuft of quills in his right hand, the weights in his left, and with a quick pull straightened the strings. He whirled them overhead once or twice and then flipped them into the air ahead of the oncoming ducks. As the weights flew, they spread apart, covering a circular area 4 or 5 feet in diameter. If any part of the bolas struck a bird the rest of the weights would wrap around it and send it plummeting helplessly to the ground. These bolas were said to have an effective range of 30 to 40 yards. Each man, woman, and child carried several with him during the seasonal waterfowl migrations (Murdoch 1892, p. 244; Nelson 1899, p. 134).

The method of using a *killamittaun* was similar in many ways to that which is now used for shotgun hunting. The techniques of concealment and waiting were essentially identical. It was necessary to be more selective in choosing a spot for waiting, to make sure that the ducks would fly as close as possible to the hunter. For example, a favored place was at the end of a long flat ice area, where a man could sit behind a hummock and watch the ducks coming toward him. They would fly very low over the flat ice, and as they rose to clear the hummock it was easy to get a close shot at them.

As with shotgun hunting, it was best to get a side shot as they flew past. In this situation this was not to increase the chance of breaking their wings but to reduce the impact of the strike, which might otherwise break the bolas strings. Also, the learner was advised to aim for one bird, and not the entire flock. This principle is still used today, because the Eskimos feel that by aiming at one duck (or caribou) their chances for a hit are increased. A Wainwright man who is in his seventies said that he learned to use the *killamittaun* before he knew how to shoot a shotgun. The transition to waterfowl hunting with guns must have been fairly recent, therefore, and the change must have been simplified by the similarities of the old and new methods.

One of the most ingenious procedures was the capture of ducks without any tools at all except the voice. When there was a very heavy fog, the ducks became so saturated with moisture that flying was a strenuous effort. The Eskimos would go out onto the ice in the line of flight and await the ducks' approach, always forewarned by their constant calling. Men waited in concealment until the ducks were almost upon them, and at the perfect moment they would jump up and shout. The ducks would try to bank and turn suddenly, but were so heavy with moisture or frost that they fell to the ice and were caught by hand. The Eskimos no longer use this technique.

Ducks were also netted during their low flight over the sea ice. This activity was often conducted cooperatively. Nets made of sinew were laid out on the ice in areas where ducks were especially likely to fly low, such as along the margins of bays in a lead edge or places where they flew over ice ridges and would not see the net until it was too late to rise over it. The net was fastened between two poles or ice piles, but would be laid on the ice until the ducks were at just the correct distance from it. Then one or two men would suddenly pull the net up by ropes strung over the tops of the supports. One man could tie his net to an ice pile and then pull it from the other end. Ducks that hit the net and fell to the ice had to be caught quickly, before they flew away.

The last of the prerifle methods of capturing ducks was snaring. A pole was laid in the water or held above the ice edge at an open spot. Spaced along it were a series of slip-knot snares made of baleen. Ducks came in along the ice or up onto it to rest in small bays or ponds, and as they swam along, their feet or necks became entangled in the snares. The pole was somehow tethered to the ice, or in freshwater places was anchored to the bottom, but it was evidently arranged so the snares would stay parallel to the water surface. Snares were also used to catch ducks by the neck on the ice itself, but informants' descriptions were unclear. A snare described by E. W. Nelson (1899) for the Bering Strait area was evidently set above the water and snared ducks by the neck.

The old squaw duck (*Clangula hyemalis*) is one of the most abundant and "personable" animals in the Arctic. The Eskimos call it *ahaalik*, a name that imitates its ceaselessly uttered call. This little duck not only makes itself conspicuous with its noisy vocalization, but also by the sheer weight of its numbers. Old squaws arrive early in the spring, and remain until fall. They are found everywhere, on the open ocean, among the ice floes, and on tundra lakes and rivers.

Old squaw ducks are most abundant during the spring and fall, in their migratory concentrations. For example, in early June, 1966, several miles from Wainwright they swarmed in countless profusion on the waters of an open lead. Before reaching the lead's edge, from up to a mile away, their great noisy gatherings could be heard, a ceaseless clangor of sonorous calls. The only familiar sound that compares to it is a turkey farm, where the gobbling of thousands of birds blends together from the distance. One is immediately struck by the multitude that must be present to create this uproar. As one arrives at the lead edge, the call "a-haa-lik" can be discerned, repeated monotonously until it becomes nerve wracking.

On this occasion thousands of ducks were scattered along the edges of the lead and in its ice-strewn waters. As several groups flew overhead, the Eskimos began shooting at them with shotguns. Perhaps because of the frightening noise of the guns, the air was suddenly filled with wheeling flocks of ducks. They passed overhead in wave after wave as the men continued shooting, until the sky everywhere was filled with ducks. When they finally began to diminish, the hunters stopped their shooting to pick up the surprisingly small number of birds that had been shot in those moments of chaos.

Besides being small, old squaws fly very fast and usually quite high. This makes them very difficult to shoot unless they are swimming in the water. Eskimos do not shoot at them in the course of eider-duck hunting unless a large flock flies very close by so there is a good chance of getting several with one shot. They do not taste especially good, though people will eat them. Eskimos would rather save their shots for the easier-to-hit and tastier eiders or geese. Old squaws are also very hardy birds, so they are difficult to catch when wounded. After falling into the water, they constantly dive, hide along the ice edge, or swim amid the labyrinth of ice fragments so they will not be seen.

Old squaw ducks are also shot at with .22 rifles during *umiak* hunting, but very few are ever hit. Hunters often imitate their singular call to bring them closer, but almost invariably they fly past unharmed. In the fall men will sometimes take boats out into the open ocean to pursue great flocks of old squaw resting and feeding in the offshore waters.

Several kinds of geese are hunted on or near the sea ice, the most common being the black brant (*Branta nigricans*), which is called *neglik̇* or *neglinaġak̇*. The white-fronted goose or *neġli-*

vailuk (*Anser albifrons*) and snow goose or *kaŋok* (*Chen hyperborea*) also occur here. Geese are generally less abundant than ducks.

In the month of June, geese are hunted as they migrate northward. The technique is almost identical to that used for duck shooting, but while ducks prefer to fly with a tailwind, geese fly against the wind. They are not fast fliers, particularly into a headwind, so they make a fairly easy, large target. Movements of geese are sporadic, tending to occur when winds are from the north or northwest during early summer. At this time most of them are shot in hunting camps along the beach.

Flocks of geese can be seen from quite a distance, which enables hunters to run for their blinds or to hiding places on the ice. Previously killed birds are sometimes placed near the blind, their heads propped up by sticks to make lifelike decoys. One Eskimo stated that if a man is walking along in plain sight and a flock of geese approaches, it is best to continue as if he has not noticed them. If this is done, they are less apt to become frightened. When they fly overhead, he raises his shotgun quickly and shoots. Generally, men try to conceal themselves and remain very still when geese are approaching.

Geese are seldom hunted from the sea ice unless it is coincident to some other activity. The really fruitful hunting is done inland, or along the beach south of Wainwright in the fall. Near Icy Cape in early August and September there is a tremendous migratory concentration of brants. In the past, men have shot up to four hundred in a week there. A Wainwright Eskimo said he once shot twenty-nine brants with two blasts of his 12-gauge shotgun, and on the same trip he carried two boatloads of them back to the village. When geese are running in large numbers, the upper arms of some men become entirely black and blue from shooting.

Waterfowl are not cleaned or protected from warmth after they are shot. They may be left outside for several days, then tossed into the ice cellar, where they keep indefinitely. The viscera and feathers are not removed until the birds are ready to be eaten. Geese are in a position similar to ducks in the Eskimo economy. They are perhaps more highly esteemed as food for humans, and all that are taken will be consumed sometime during the year. The people apparently do not eat waterfowl uncooked, and usually make it into a delicious stew.

Loons

Three species of loons occur here during the summer, the common loon (*Gavia immer*), red-throated loon (*G. stellata*) and Arctic loon (*G. arctica*). The common loon is not often seen on or over the ocean, seeming to prefer the area around the Kuk Inlet above all other places. Fish, apparently of a type preferred by these birds, are said to be abundant in this narrow inlet. The other two species are usually seen around the ocean and up the Kuk River. Of these two, the Arctic loon is far more common. Both are called by the same word, *ḳaḥroaḳ*, although the Eskimos are aware of the differences between them.

Loons arrive here in late spring, when there is plenty of open water. While the sea ice is present, they are very common, often congregating in small flocks. Once the ice is gone, all three species are still seen, but they are not as common.

Loons are not valued as food, except by the old people. They are usually given to the dogs. It is a bit surprising in view of this that some effort goes into shooting them. Most of them are taken during spring and early summer duck hunting on the land or sea ice. They are shot as they fly overhead, just as ducks would be. Common loons are very large birds indeed, so the Eskimos always try to shoot them if possible. The other two species are smaller, and are not sought as ambitiously.

Loons can be attracted by imitating their calls. This is sometimes done while hunting birds from a blind of some sort, and very frequently during hunting or traveling by boat. Small flocks of red-throated or Arctic loons are seen almost constantly during *umiaḳ* hunting in July, and they are not much afraid of the boat. Thus, younger men enjoy shooting at them as they fly overhead nearby or swim in the water. From a moving boat, with a .22 rifle, it is something of a feat to hit even as large and slow a bird as this, and success is not common.

Even if one is shot, it is usually only wounded rather than killed outright. This results in a long chase, in which the bird continually dives, to surface again in some improbable place. Wounded loons are seldom caught unless they are badly injured. The Eskimos warn that the common loon can be very dangerous in such a situation, because it attacks with its sharp-pointed beak. Tradition has it that kayakers have been killed by such attacks. At any rate, shooting them with small rifles during the middle or late summer is not a very profitable occupation.

Loons could be a valuable source of food for a drift-ice survivor. They are quite large, and with some patience can be shot as they swim close to a lead edge. By concealing oneself behind an ice pile, it is possible to get a close shot at them, although they are extremely wary. Loons also have a warm and moisture-proof skin, which can be used as a seat on wet surfaces.

Gulls, Terns, and Jaegers

Seagulls are very common during the spring, summer, and fall, but they are of minor importance to the Wainwright Eskimos. The most conspicuous and abundant is the glaucous gull (*Larus hyperboreus*), which is called *nauyak*. Glaucous gulls do not gather in large flocks or concentrations, but they are encountered everywhere, resting and feeding on the water, sitting on the ice, or circling overhead. These birds are actively hunted only during the fall, from late September through October, as they ride the winds southward along the ocean cliffs. They are more concentrated at this time than during the spring and summer. Men station themselves along the beach and shoot the low-flying gulls with shotguns. Gulls can be attracted as they pass by if the hunter leaves his first-killed in plain sight on the beach. The others will slow down to investigate it, and make easier targets as they wheel and pirouette overhead.

During the course of spring and summer sea-ice hunting Eskimos often take potshots at gulls with .22 caliber rifles, but they rarely hit one. At Point Hope during the whaling season gulls were seen in abundance, but people rarely shot them even for dog food, in spite of the fact that they had little to feed their teams. Seagulls are attracted toward people, hoping to scavenge some food or offal that is left behind. For example, when someone shoots a seal in open water, they are quickly drawn to the radiating cloud of blood on the water's surface. They swoop down repeatedly in attempts to find a bit of meat amid the blood. Gulls can be attracted by tossing bits of meat, blubber, or even a dead gull into the water or onto the ice.

Their habit of gulping down scraps sometimes leads to their demise. Eskimos may place a sharpened stick or fish hook with a line attached inside a wad of meat. The gull swallows the meat and, as it flies off, the stick or hook catches in its throat and the Eskimo pulls it down. A Wainwright man had taken gulls by baiting a fishing line and dragging it behind the boat as he traveled. When a bird swallowed the bait, he reeled it in like a fish.

Seagulls are used for dog food or given to older people who enjoy eating them. Their wing tendons are used in the manufacture of fishing gear. These large, slow, and rather fearless birds could be a good source of emergency food, especially since they can be captured without wasting ammunition. Young glaucous gulls (*nauyagvaak̦*) are probably better tasting than adults, and are easier to kill because they are less cautious.

The kittywake (*Rissa tridactyla*) and mew gull (*Larus canus*) are similar species that occur commonly in northwest Alaska during the summer. They seem to be most abundant in middle and late summer, after the ice has broken up into drifting floes. Seagulls are among the few kinds of birds that are commonly seen after the ice is gone entirely.

Methods of attracting and killing these birds are identical to those discussed above for the glaucous gull. Eskimos frequently imitate the calls of kittywakes and mew gulls as they fly past in flocks of varying size. Although the mimic sometimes works, the hunters seldom bother to shoot at them. Mew gulls are referred to as "walrus birds," because they are said to frequent areas where walruses are sleeping on ice pans. Although the Eskimos never mentioned it specifically, they might be used as an aid to locating walrus herds.

Another common gull of the summertime is Sabine's gull (*Xema sabini*), which appears in June (or perhaps earlier) and remains after the ice is gone. These birds are occasionally shot when they congregate around puddles on the sea ice in early June, or when they fly overhead during *umiak* hunting. They are smaller than the previously mentioned seagulls, however, and are of little value as human or dog food.

Two other species of gull occur in this region, Ross' gull (*Rhodostethia rosea*) and the ivory gull (*Pagophila eburnea*). Neither species is commonly sighted here at any time of year, although many ivory gulls were seen off Point Hope in May, 1965. The local Eskimos are fairly familiar with the ivory gull, which evidently prefers the waters far offshore and remains through the winter. Ross' gull is a rare and little-known bird, which is said to occur around Wainwright, probably in the spring and fall.

The Arctic tern (*Sterna paradisaea*) is very common in this region throughout the summer. These birds are always seen fluttering overhead during ice-hunting activities. The Eskimos sometimes imitate their flight call. They are seldom shot at and literally never hit, because they are small and have an erratic flight pattern. They would be of value only as emergency food. In former years, but apparently not today, tern eggs were collected and used as food.

Three species of jaegers are found in this region—the pomarine jaeger (*Stercorarius pomarinus*), parasitic jaeger (*S. parasiticus*), and the long-tailed jaeger (*S. longicaudus*). All three are called *isuŋŋak*, although there seem to be individual names for each species which are rarely used. These are fairly large and conspicuous birds, which are seen throughout the summer over the ocean, along the reaches of the Kuk River, and over the tundra.

Jaegers are easy to approach while they fly overhead or rest on the ice. This makes them fairly good targets for .22 caliber rifles or shotguns, but the Eskimos seldom bother to shoot them. When they are killed, it is done less for meat than for spite. These birds are genuinely disliked, because of their habit of chasing other birds until they disgorge their food, which the jaegers swoop down on and pick up in midair or from the ice. Eskimos say that jaegers are "no good" because they steal food.

Jaegers can sometimes be attracted by imitating their call or throwing pieces of meat in the water. Their susceptibility to this kind of lure would make them a potential food supply for men set adrift on the ice.

Gulls, terns, and jaegers do not form a significant part of the native economy in northwest Alaska. But these birds are considered an excellent source of food for emergency situations, because they are common; they are fairly large sized, fly slowly, and come close to humans, which makes them easy targets, and most of them can be caught with a baited hook.

Shorebirds

Several species of shorebirds are seen flying over the sea ice during the warm months, but of these only the phalaropes actually land on the ice or water. Species which commonly occur on the beaches or tundra bordering the ocean include the following:

Species	*Eskimo Name*
black-bellied plover (*Squatarola squatarola*)	tuligak
American golden plover (*Pluvialis dominica*)	tuḷigaaluk
dunlin (*Erolia alpina*)	iḷiaḵtalik
pectoral sandpiper (*E. melanotos*)	nuvakroaluk
least sandpiper (*E. minutilla*)	alavloġauraḵ

None of these species is likely to be hunted by the Eskimos under any conditions, especially during sea-ice hunting when they are only seen as they fly quickly past. An ice hunter could bag a few with a shotgun as they flew by, if he had any reason to do so. There are two species of shorebirds that live almost entirely on the sea, the red phalarope (*Phalaropus fulicarius*) and northern phalarope (*Lobipes lobatus*). Both are usually called by the same Eskimo term (*auhuroaḵ*), though the northern phalarope is also known by a separate name.

In early June hundreds of little flocks of red phalaropes gather in and around puddles which are scattered along the sea ice close to shore. They tend to be as fearless as they are prolific, and if a man walks slowly he can approach them to within ten feet.

Although these little birds are said to make delicious soup, Eskimos rarely shoot them.

During the months of August and September red phalaropes seem to disappear, but they are replaced by abundant flocks of northern phalaropes. These sociable birds spend most of their time swimming and dipping amid the turbulent waters of the ocean surf. Innumerable flocks, numbering one or two hundred birds each, are strung out all along the coast. When the breakers are too heavy, most of them fly across to the Kuk River or perhaps farther out to sea. When they are abundant, Eskimo children spend hours stalking them along the beach, trying to walk close enough to hit one with a rock, which they either toss by hand or shoot with a slingshot. When they are frightened, the entire flock flies up and alights a short distance away. Then the stalk begins anew.

In general, shorebirds have little significance in the economy of today's Eskimos. Few of them wander out over the ocean ice, as they prefer to remain on the swampy tundra where they breed in summertime. There is one other species of bird that normally lives on the tundra but sometimes flies out onto the sea ice—the ptarmigan (*Lagopus mutus*). Especially during the spring and summer, ptarmigans land on the ice up to a mile or so offshore, leaving willow leaves and tracks among the rough ice as evidence of their presence. Eskimos hunt ptarmigan on the land whenever they have a chance, but they do not bother to look for them on the ice.

Alcids

The only Alcid that is regularly hunted by the Wainwright Eskimos is the thick-billed murre, or *akpa*, (*Uria lomvia*). At Point Hope the murres arrive early in May, and from that time clear through the summer they are seen continuously, flying back and forth from their nesting colonies at Cape Thompson and Cape Lisburne. They constantly fly north or south over Point Hope spit, their flight direction depending upon the wind. They have a habit of flying against the wind, so their movements can be forecast on a given day according to its direction. At Wainwright they arrive somewhat later in May and become prolific in June, when they gather in large flocks on the water or winging overhead.

Unlike the eider ducks, they seldom fly low, staying from 50 to several hundred yards up. This, and their habit of flying side by side in lines that may string out over a quarter mile long, makes them very difficult to hunt when they are on the wing. The only way to shoot them would be with a light rifle, and then it would take quite a marksman to get any. Men in whaling camps sometimes shoot low-flying murres as they sweep along over the open water before landing. They are usually heard before they are seen because their wings whistle loudly.

Murres do not seem much afraid of man. During the whaling season, there are always a few in sight, swimming along in the open water, diving to feed on small fish or plankton. By stalking or simply waiting for a group to swim close, hunters can pick them off one by one with .22 rifles. They can also be approached rather closely by boats, which is done through the summer months. When there are ducks or seals around, the Eskimos do not bother to hunt murres, but sometimes, especially when they are very abundant, they are shot for dog food.

Although murres do not seem particularly intelligent, they are very hardy and can escape by diving repeatedly, even if badly wounded. Sometimes they are shot with .22 rifles while Eskimos are traveling by boat. This is not done systematically, however, because a murre is difficult to hit from a moving boat, and too much trouble is involved to make the endeavor worthwhile.

At the sound of a gunshot, they dive and attempt to swim some distance away, but they do not go far, and they soon return if it remains quiet. In open holes there is no place to go, so they can be shot at again and again when they surface, until the remainder fly away. When murres are abundant and can be shot easily, the Eskimos may put a real effort into hunting them, even though they are not considered especially tasty.

As July passes they seem to be less common around Wainwright, although a fair number remain in the open ocean through the entire summer. They apparently do not breed anywhere be-

tween Icy Cape and Point Barrow, although there could be a few
nesting places on high beach cliffs north of Point Franklin.

Along this coast, at least in the region between Wainwright and
Barrow, and perhaps farther south, one species of bird is seen in
open leads during midwinter. This is the black guillemot or *iŋagik*
(*Cepphus grylle*). Guillemots are resident in the far north
throughout the year but are most common in the winter. Somehow they manage to find open water through the coldest months.
By no means are they seen every time the lead opens up, although
some may be spotted during any part of the winter. Wainwright
Eskimos do not hunt them today, but know how to get them if
they want or need to.

During the winter, black guillemots are not much afraid of
man, and, in fact, seem to be attracted to him. This makes them
an easy target for a rifle. Guillemots are best hunted with a .22
caliber rifle; because they are small and usually occur singly or
in pairs, there is little need for a shotgun to hunt them. Their
white winter plumage makes them very conspicuous against the
black water. If a hunter waits patiently along the ice apron, he can
probably shoot them from 20 to 30 yards or less. Retrieving the
birds once they are shot is a problem if they are along an area of
thin ice so that they cannot be picked up by hand. In many cases
the wind or current carries the bird away from the ice, so that a
small retrieval boat or snag hook has to be used. Like many other
birds, they can be attracted in the summertime by imitating their
shrill wheezing call.

In former times guillemots were caught in nets placed along
the lead edge below the water surface. The birds were attracted
toward men moving along the lead, or they could be brought
close by throwing a piece of ice into the water. Once they were
over the net the hunter frightened them suddenly, so they would
dive into the net below and entangle themselves in it. Actual
methods of setting the net, and its dimension and weave, were
not described by the informant.

CHAPTER 9

Arctic Fox

(Alopex lagopus)

Feeding Habits

THE ARCTIC FOX (*pisukkaak*) is commonly found out on the ocean ice. It is a small animal, ermine-white during the winter but drab brown during summer. The fox ranges over the tundra in summertime, feeding on berries and whatever animal food it can find—lemmings, birds, eggs, nestlings, and carrion. When winter arrives, it usually forsakes the land and roams far out over the moving ice. It is believed to owe much of its ability to live on the sea ice to the polar bear, upon which it depends for part of its food. It is improbable, however, that the fox lives entirely on the remains of seals left behind by the bear, which usually eats only the skin and blubber and leaves the rest. Foxes are gifted with a remarkable ability to smell out food far beneath the snow surface. This can be meat which they cached on land during the summer, or something that died or was killed and became buried. Because of this ability they are able to find walrus and whale carcasses that have been entombed in the pack ice, and they dig out these carcasses or wait for a polar bear to do the work so they can eat after the bear leaves.

Eskimos have learned to watch for places where foxes urinate on the snow, because this sometimes marks the location of meat or carrion buried under the snow. Caribou that are shot in the fall and later become covered with hard snow may be located by looking over the area for places where foxes have urinated. Kaviḳ once caught a fox in a trap after the animal had dug down through several feet of drifted snow to get at it. Men who become lost on drifting ice could perhaps follow the fox and bear tracks to find dead seals, walruses, or whales.

Because Arctic foxes live as scavengers on land and on the sea ice, they are able to withstand long periods without food. One Eskimo reported that he had seen two instances in which a live fox was caught in a trap when he first saw it, and he found the same animal still living when he passed by a week later. In each case he knew that it was the same fox and that the trap had not been checked or emptied.

There is one danger from foxes, and it is not an uncommon one. During this study, both at Wainwright and at Point Hope, rabid foxes were killed after they entered the village. In two cases they had even gone into the hallways of houses. On the sea ice, rabid foxes will occasionally walk right up to a man. Sometimes they have to be beaten away with a stick or rifle. The Eskimos call such rabid animals *malukalayrak*, and although they fear them, they still skin animals that are killed and are obviously rabid.

Pitfalls and Snares

Before the white man's coming, foxes were used only casually by most Eskimo groups, but the animals soon assumed great importance once the fur trade opened up. There was enough use for their pelts and meat, however, that several methods of trapping foxes were devised during aboriginal times. The Arctic fox is not endowed with the cleverness of the red fox, and is much easier to trap. The old-time methods have all been given up in favor of modern steel traps, which are evidently more efficient. One of these old methods is the pitfall or *ḳazagisaaḳ*, of which two types are described:

The first kind of pitfall consists of a hole dug into the snow. The hole is too deep for a fox to jump out of, and its sides are iced so the animal cannot dig out. Sharp pieces of antler are placed vertically at the bottom to impale the fox when it falls in. The top of the hole is covered by a thin slab of snow, by willow sticks protruding from the sides with snow covering them, or by flexible pieces of baleen covered with snow. Baleen is ideal because thin slats can be stuck out from the sides, and they will bend downward to drop the fox into the pit, springing back into position afterward. Usually a sort of "drift fence" of snowblocks is set up to guide the animals toward the trap. Bait is placed on the far (upwind) side of the trap so the fox will walk onto the opening in order to reach it.

Van Valin (1944, pp. 105–6) describes a variant type that is made in the sea ice. It consists of a hole chipped 5 or 6 feet deep and 3 or 4 feet in diameter in the heavy offshore ice. Around its opening there are protruding slats of baleen with their points radiating toward the center like the spokes of a wheel. The whalebone is covered with snow, and bits of meat are scattered around the area. Several foxes may fall into such a trap between checkings.

Another pitfall trap that is familiar from the literature is the tower or well trap. On land, the tower trap is built of rocks, piled up to form a high (often over 6 feet) conical structure which is hollow inside and open at the top. A putrid seal or other smelly bait is laid in the bottom and some rocks are removed to open a hole in the base. This is left open for a while to allow the foxes to come and feed "free," but then it is closed up after they get used to jumping in through the top and escaping out the bottom (Degerbøl and Freuchen 1935, p. 132).

Similar traps can be made from snow or ice blocks. A "box" or tower is constructed with an open top. Baleen slats covered with snow are stuck out from the edges of the opening. A snow ramp leads up to the top, and bait is placed on the far side. The fox falls inside when he tries to step across on the flexible baleen, which snaps back into position to catch another fox if one should come along. The tower must, of course, be high enough so that a fox cannot spring to the top and escape.

Another type of trap is made with a roofed "box" of ice blocks. Two round holes are made in each side and one in each end, each large enough to admit a fox. Bait is placed inside and the trap is left unset, so that the animals get used to reaching inside it to get food. When the Eskimo finds many tracks around it, he sets the trap by fitting nooses into grooves around the inside of each opening. Each noose encircles a hole, so that when a fox enters, the noose surrounds its body. The noose line goes up through another hole at the top. A trigger mechanism is made whereby the fox, putting its head inside or tugging at the bait, releases a weight attached to the end of the noose. The weight falls, and with the line threaded over a "pulley" of ice, snaps the loop part of the noose tight enough to hold or strangle the fox. The most likely disadvantage of this trap is that it is probably as hard to construct as it is to describe. It has been many years since devices like this were made by northwest Alaskan Eskimos.

Winter Camping

With the introduction of steel traps and fur trade, the Arctic fox assumed a much more important role in the Eskimo economy than it ever had during aboriginal times. Modern fox trappers must tend long trap lines that run many miles away from the village. As a result, the most important time for winter camping nowadays is fox-trapping season, which runs from December 1 through April 15. During this time men spend periods of one to fourteen days away from the village, generally using one "permanent" camp for the entire season. Since these camps are used a great deal, often by several men, every attempt is made to have them as comfortable and as warm as possible.

Some trappers set up their camps inside wooden frame buildings or abandoned sod houses along the coast or inland. Many of these, such as the old shelter cabins along the coast, are in poor condition, so it is necessary to use a tent inside them. This is still more substantial and roomier than snow shelters, and there is no problem with melting, so these wooden structures are preferred.

During the 1964–65 season, one man and his son used an abandoned sod *iglu* at the village site of Atanik̦, on the coast about 20 miles north of Wainwright. This *iglu* had been the home of the man's father many years earlier, and it was still in excellent condition. The internal dimensions of the house itself were about

10 × 12 feet, with a roof about 5½ feet high. The walls, built of vertically placed logs, slanted gently inward, and the roof was slightly gabled. Entry was made through a long (8-foot) passageway that was about 4 feet high and flat-roofed. The entire house was covered with sod and, during the winter, nearly buried by snow.

A tent was pitched inside this structure. It nearly filled the interior, but left enough space around the edges for extra food, gear, and clothing. In this space the temperature remained below freezing, while inside the tent a camp stove kept the temperature in the 60's or 70's. Arranged inside the tent were caribou skin mattresses, and, around the edges, the camp stove, "grub box," dog-food container, and miscellaneous gear. Clothing was piled along the back end, to be used for a pillow at night and as a back rest for sitting.

These two men owned a single sleeping bag, but did not use it. They slept instead with light jackets on or over them, leaving all their clothing on, and burning the camp stove at night. This was done because their dog food was piled outside the house, which in this particular area might easily attract a polar bear. If the dogs started barking the men could run out quickly, grabbing one of the rifles left in the passageway, in case the dogs had seen a polar bear.

Pogazak set up his trapping camp, along with two other men, at a spot 20 miles inland from Wainwright. Since there were no buildings or old sod houses at this location, they constructed a *killegun*, a square snowblock shelter with a canvas roof, inside which a tent was pitched. The *killegun* was built by constructing four snowblock walls around the square hole from which the blocks were taken. The blocks were cut out with an ordinary hand saw and removed with a shovel. This left a hole about 2½ to 3 feet deep, surrounded by a wall made from several tiers of blocks, about 3 feet high, for an inside height of 6 feet. The floor was about 8 × 10 feet, leaving some extra room around the 7 × 7-foot tent.

Across the tops of the end walls a ridgepole was laid to support the gabled canvas roof. The roof was weighted down around its edges by blocks of snow. Caribou skins and other items for hunting and trapping were also laid atop the roof. The entry was at one end, made by cutting a step down to the floor level from the outside and then making a small opening. During one storm an extra canvas-covered "hallway" was made outside this opening so that the door would be at a right angle to the wind instead of facing into it.

The tent was pitched inside this shelter after all the spaces in the outside walls were chinked with snow. The side ropes of the tent were tied to stakes put into the snow walls. Around the space in front of the tent some items such as dog food, gasoline, and extra food were placed, much the same as in the camp previously described. Inside the tent, "grub boxes," the camp stove, clothing, and caribou skins were kept. The skin mattress is an essential for all camping among the Eskimos, and they seldom travel without one on the sled to use in case of emergency and to pad whatever gear is carried. Caribou hide is an excellent insulation when placed beneath a sleeping bag. One or two skins, placed hair side up, are all that is needed for each camp.

Most Eskimos own down sleeping bags, which they normally use whenever they camp. Aboriginal sleeping bags were made of caribou hide, and this was replaced by reindeer hide during the period of reindeer herding in north Alaska. Reindeer was preferable because it had thicker fur. These sleeping bags were made by simply sewing two skins together with the fur inside. Though they were warmer than the down used today, they were very bulky. Nowadays men usually wear most of their clothing inside their sleeping bags, removing only boots, parkas, and heavy outer pants. This is done mostly for the convenience of getting out quickly in the morning, or of being prepared for any situation, such as a dog fight that might arise outside.

Sleeping bags were used in the camp described above, but during the waking hours the tent was heated to an uncomfortably high temperature by the camp stove and gasoline lantern. With the outside temperature a very stormy $-18°$ F, the temperature inside the tent was $105°$ 4 feet above the floor and $85°$ 2 feet above the floor. This certainly demonstrates the efficiency of such double shelters. It is little wonder that in all winter camping the *killegun* is used if no wooden structure is available.

The "typical" dome-shaped Eskimo snowhouse has never been used in the western portion of northwest Alaska, although it was sometimes used in the areas close to Demarcation Point on the Canadian Border. Igruk, an old Wainwright man, had lived in them as a boy near Herschel Island, but said that they were not used very much. Preference was given in all of northwest Alaska to the *killegun*, or to the *anegiuchak*, which was a square snowhouse as described above but with a gabled snowblock roof.

The *anegiuchak* was not seen in use during 1964–65, but was described by Brower (1963, p. 21) as a rectangular snowblock house with an entrance in the middle and sleeping areas at each end. The small space between the sleeping areas was reserved for the stone lamp, which supplied heat and light. Blocks of snow were also taken from the hole and set up around it, slanted somewhat inward. The roof blocks were set atop the walls, meeting in the middle to form a gabled roof. Snow was shoveled over the entire house, and then a door was cut down to the level of the floor. In this case the door was closed with a block of snow, but in a similar house described by a Wainwright Eskimo, the sunken door (*kattak*) was covered by a grizzly bear or caribou skin.

In modern times, temporary shelters are heated by efficient gasoline stoves and lanterns. Kerosene lamps and Primus stoves have undoubtedly been owned by Eskimos along the coast since the time of the first whalers. Although still used today by some individuals, there have largely disappeared in favor of pressure-gas Coleman stoves and lanterns. Only within the last ten years or so have privately owned electric generators supplied power to some households in Wainwright. In Point Hope a village generator has become operative. Electricity is not important for camping and traveling, where gas-burning stoves and lamps are used.

Every hunter owns a camp stove (*siohuzok*) and many of them own two, three, or four. A stove is carried by at least one man in every hunting party, even if the trip is expected to last only a day and no camping is involved. There are two reasons why a stove and plenty of gas are carried. First, the Eskimos never go for more than a few hours without a tea break. Sometimes a thermos bottle is taken along, but more often the tea is brewed on the spot with a stove. Second, it is usually carried in case of emergency, such as drifting off on the ice or being stopped along the trail by a sudden storm.

The Coleman stoves are two-burner types, fairly bulky but easily carried on a sled. A 2- to 5-gallon gasoline can is taken on all trips longer than one day. White gas bought at the native store is undoubtedly one of the largest expenses for most families. A single-mantle Coleman lantern is also carried with the sled load for all winter camping, but is more difficult to pack because it is more fragile. Extra mantles are always required on each trip, since they break on the rough trail. Many Eskimos do not replace the glass globe once is has broken, but wrap the lamp in cardboard whenever it is carried on the sled.

Gas lanterns are considered essential nowadays, and candles are almost never used. One man was forced to return to Wainwright from his trapping camp because his gas lamp was malfunctioning. He had candles along, but did not care to camp without bright light inside or outside, since this was the darkest part of winter. The gas lantern is very bright, and is sometimes left outside so that a passerby can locate the camp in the darkness. Inside a well-built camp, lanterns throw off a surprisingly large amount of heat, and are often left on all night to supply warmth for the tent.

The gasoline stove is the primary heat source for an Eskimo camp. It is carried more for this purpose than for cooking. Since much of the meat is eaten raw, the main cooking function of the stove is heating water for tea or coffee. As soon as any camp is set up, the stove is lit immediately and the men crawl inside to enjoy its warmth. If there is work to be done outside, such as skinning game or feeding the dogs, they leave the stove burning, usually with water on top for tea. Thus warm shelter and refreshment await their return. Tents may be set up along the trail for a tea break if it is stormy, or out on the ice in the afternoon, so the hunters can go inside, remove their parkas, and warm up.

Since he must remain outside for many hours each day, these breaks and warm camps appear to help the hunter resist the cold more easily, psychologically if not physiologically. This is why houses and camps are heated to high temperatures, and why so much effort is made to provide comfort even for the shortest tea break.

According to the Eskimos, food, especially certain types, will help to maintain bodily warmth during camping, hunting, and traveling, or under emergency conditions. They say that only Eskimo foods, called *nekepiak* (*neke* = meat, *piak* = genuine), are really helpful for this purpose, and certain types are the best. Most preferred by the Wainwright people is *kwak* or frozen meat, especially caribou, eaten with seal oil (*ohuzok*).

The idea that meat with fat or oil will warm the body is held very strongly, and this is a common food on the trail or in camp. Other meats eaten raw are frozen fish, walrus, and seal, the latter two being rather uncommon. Fat or oil is not normally eaten alone. Meat is dipped into it or else small chunks of fat are sliced off with a knife and eaten along with the meat. Oil is taken alone only as a cure for sickness, such as a stomach ailment, or in case of food deprivation. In the latter case a piece of fat is stuck on the end of a stick and held over a fire, and as the oil renders out it is licked off.

Consistent with the idea that raw meat and blubber help to maintain body warmth, food for the dogs is adjusted according to the weather. In warm periods dogs are likely to be fed a variety of foods, but when the temperature drops far below zero and the wind blows, dogs are fed only what is considered to be the best food available. Usually this is *kauk*, walrus hide with a thick layer of blubber attached. This must be thawed during cold weather, both for the sake of providing more warmth for the dogs—so they will not have to thaw it in the mouth and stomach —and to soften it enough so that it can be chewed.

Seal blubber, cut into 3- to 4-inch strips, is said to be the best food for keeping the dogs warm through the long winter nights. It is not used if the dogs will do much pulling the next day, how-ever, because they will run slowly or even become sick. Seal meat with some blubber atttached makes an excellent dog food for cold weather, supplying warmth and energy even though small amounts are used.

The tendency is to feed dogs plenty of food, up to 4 and 5 pounds per dog each day, if the weather is extremely severe.

They must lie outside on the snow in all weather, and during years when food runs low, dogs will freeze to death due to insufficient feeding. Perhaps it is also true that people eat more during outdoor activities in cold weather. There are few overweight Eskimo men, though they do appear to consume a great deal of food.

Seal meat is not important at Wainwright except for dog food, but at Point Hope it must be a significant part of the diet. In addition, whale meat is very important at Point Hope, but is seldom available at Wainwright, where whales are rarely taken. In both places walrus meat is apparently not favored. Polar bear meat, usually prepared by boiling, is considered delicious, though its availability has dropped off considerably because of the decrease of bears in recent years.

There are two common methods of preparing food in camp: either it is boiled or it is eaten raw. At Wainwright caribou is the staple meat in camp and at home. It is frequently boiled and made into a "soup," with rice and condiments added. It is much preferred if it is fresh. When caribou are killed, the tongues and hearts are removed. As soon as a camp is set up, they are boiled together in a large pot for fifteen to thirty minutes. Boiling is the easiest way to cook for a group, because it requires a minimum of space, effort, and utensils. Tongues are considered the greatest delicacy from the caribou. They are boiled whole, unlike hearts, which are cut into strips. After cooking, they are pulled from the pot on the end of a knife, and each man cuts off sections from his own piece, dips them in seal oil, and eats them enthusiastically.

If there is no chance to eat caribou immediately after it is killed, it is eaten raw and frozen. Fish are easily carried, and are occasionally taken along on hunting trips. Ice hunters sometimes carry some frozen meat, perhaps as an emergency supply in case they drift away. Walrus *kauk* is carried for dog trips of over one day's duration, but is seldom included in the camp diet.

Tea, coffee, bread, butter, and jelly are the important camp foods besides meat. At every stop and many times each day in camp, tea is prepared and bread is eaten in large quantities. In fact, bread may be the staple food for days at a time, as long as it holds out. "Bread" includes homemade bread, biscuits, or "hardtack." Each hunter usually carries a small flour sack full of bread, which is eaten frozen along the trail or thawed after reaching camp.

Coffee is usually prepared first in the morning, and tea is made later to fill the thermos jug, if one is carried. Although it is inconsistent with the idea that good meals stimulate warmth, the morning meal is light in camp, usually including only coffee and a little bread. In fact, the Eskimos frequently state that the fathers of the older men only drank water in the morning and did not eat until the day's end. This was done because "eating makes you hungry." But if they did eat at all, they always had raw meat because it stayed with them best. To some extent this is still practiced. Men also say that cigarettes help to dull their hunger, and almost all of them smoke, with the exception of a few who have recovered from tuberculosis or whose religious beliefs prohibit smoking.

Modern Fox Trapping

Before the fur trade became available to north Alaskan Eskimos, little effort was made to catch foxes, which offered little meat and only a fragile hide. After the beginning of fur trade and the introduction of steel traps, they began to devote great amounts of time and energy to pursuit of the fox. Some men left the village for weeks at a time to run traplines that stretched over 100 miles and took a week to travel end to end. Nowadays the fox pelt has decreased in value and the longest traplines run 50 miles. Men seldom leave the village for more than a week at a time for trapping. The best trappers alive today are sixty years old or over and are no longer active.

There has never been much fox trapping on the sea ice even though foxes often abound there, because the ice "steals" too many traps by drifting away with them. At Point Barrow in March, 1965, there were fox tracks in incredible abundance just offshore. For several miles there was always at least one set of tracks in sight, and many of the ice piles were dotted with footprints going in every direction. However, few trappers are willing to walk through the rough ice to check their traps, or to risk losing them if an offshore gale breaks the ice away.

Traps are often set near the carcasses of caribou killed in the fall or winter, because they are visited regularly by foxes. They may be set next to old walrus or whale carcasses along the coast, or by any small mound of earth or prominent mark such as an old caribou antler, where the foxes stop to urinate. If a trap is set on a mound of earth, the snow is scraped away to make a conspicuous dark spot that will attract foxes.

Traps set near dead animals are put on the west side, because foxes usually approach from downwind and will step on the trap before reaching the meat. The fact that winds prevail from the east makes it easy to predict the direction from which they will approach, because they pick up the scent from downwind. Little caution is necessary while walking around setting traps, except that the Eskimo does not step downwind of the set. In addition to using old carcasses for bait, a trapper may carry some frozen stomach contents of caribou, and perhaps some meat. The frozen guts are easily carried and can be chopped off with a large knife. The bait is scattered just upwind (east or northeast) of the set so that the fox, reaching for it, will step on the pan of the trap. Baited sets are usually placed on or near some conspicuous landmark, such as a mound.

The trap itself is put into a little excavation or depression, approximately the same outline as the trap, which is cut into the snow. The trap is opened and set into this hole, and then a chunk of snow a bit larger than the excavation and two or three inches thick is placed over the top. Snow is pushed in around the edges of the slab where it rests on the surface, to plug all holes. Then with the large knife (*saviraaktuun*) the block is shaved thinner and thinner, until it is very delicate and about level with the surrounding snow. The trapper must be very careful not to break through this thin cover, especially as he smooths the area with his knife or with a furry mitten. The top of the snow packed over and around the set will be covered by a little drift if it slopes to leeward, or will be eaten away by the wind if it slopes to windward. Thus, it must be kept perfectly level. Each trap is held in place by a chain, which the trapper loops around a stick several inches long and buries in the snow beneath the set. If he packs the snow tightly, it will harden solidly enough for the chain to hold a fox. The chain may also be frozen into a freshly killed caribou which is to be left on the tundra.

Usually several traps are set in a particular place, so the trapper can check more than one trap at each stop. Every trapper has his own camp from which he travels by dog team in various directions setting traps, making each trapline long enough to occupy one winter day checking and returning to camp. Traps are also set along the route between camp and the village. Some men use the village as their base camp so that they can go out to check their traps and return home the same day.

The legal trapping season, which lasts through the midwinter period, is rigidly adhered to. Some men start out very early in the morning of the first day and pull out their traps on the very last day. Their willingness to follow regulated seasons in this instance contrasts markedly with their attitude toward seasons on other game. This probably derives from the fact that fox trapping was never important in their economy aboriginally, and the white man introduced trapping seasons along with the rest of the fox-trapping complex. The season's opening on December 1 marks the beginning of winter for the Eskimos, and the end on April 15 means the beginning of spring and preparation for whaling. After trapping is over the hunters hope for warm weather to bring the seals up on top of the ice and for open leads to hurry the whales' arrival.

Today, foxes are taken exclusively for their fur. The Eskimos make little use of the fox pelt themselves, except that occasionally the tail is used as a cold-protector around the neck and chin. In the old days, when food became scarce, they would use a fox tail to soak up the blood of any animal that was killed, bringing it home frozen in the fur to add to the broth.

Pelts to be sold are prepared by "casing out" the skin, i.e., turning it inside out and removing it entirely. To do this four incisions are made along the insides of the legs, so the skin can be removed from them. Using a small knife, the trapper next cuts away the skin around the lips. The skin is then peeled back over the head, turning it inside out, cutting it free very carefully as it is removed. Once the pelt is off there are no holes in it except the natural orifices and the leg cuts. The pelt is then placed, inside out, on a stretching frame, and is dried for several days inside the house. When this is finished, the fur is cleaned with flour and is combed. It is then sold to the native store.

Fox carcasses are apparently discarded, although they are often piled neatly beside houses in the village. Some are occasionally eaten, but only if they are fat. Preparation is by boiling for one to several hours, and they are evidently not eaten raw. Foxes have often been the salvation of stranded and shipwrecked men in the Arctic. They are said to be quite palatable.

CHAPTER 10

Polar Bear

(Thalarctos maritimus)

Occurrence

THE POLAR BEAR (*nanuk*) derives all its food from the sea, and is seldom found far from the drifting sea ice. These giant animals, which are frequently 10 feet in length and weigh 700 to 1,000 pounds, live all over the ice-covered Arctic seas below 75° north (except in North Greenland, where they reach 80° north). They prefer regions of greatest ice movement, and therefore are more or less absent from areas such as the sheltered sounds and inlets of the Canadian Archipelago and are most abundant in areas like northwest Alaska.

Polar bears are usually seen in this part of the Arctic only during the fall, winter, and spring. Within this period they apparently undergo three migratory movements north or south along the coast. The first takes place in December, when the bears move northward, often following the edge of the landfast ice. At this time in 1964 several bears were sighted from the village itself, and many trails passing toward the north were found farther out from shore. In February the bears apparently move south in a rather small migration. And during March they are again moving northward in what is often the largest movement and the best time for bear hunting. Eskimos say that during the migrations bears tend to follow each other's trails, so hunters will sometimes wait near a trail if they find one. They actually do most of their moving at night, sleeping during the day, which makes them more difficult to encounter.

The occurrence of polar bears is also influenced by local ice conditions. They are especially likely to be seen just after a lead closes, because they are often near the edge of an open lead and cross over onto the landfast ice as the two sides come close together. When there has been a west wind, or for some reason the ice has not moved enough to open cracks, the people start watching for bears coming up close to the village, especially at night. When there is no open water, hungry bears are attracted by the smell of meat in the Eskimos' caches. A fair number of bears have been killed when they came right in among the houses of Wainwright, arousing the dogs to a great commotion that warned the Eskimos of their presence. During the fall polar bears come ashore so regularly around Ataniḳ, 20 miles north of Wainwright, that men go up there and leave walrus meat outside the old sod houses to attract them. They camp there for several days or a week, hoping to get one.

Bears become uncommon after March, although they are occasionally shot during the whaling season (late April, May, and early June). They are rarely sighted during the summer, especially after the ice breaks up into unconsolidated floes. Although they wander close to shore on occasion, the polar bears' real home is out on the pack far from land. This is especially so during the warm months. Eskimos say that in early summer, for example, the best place to look for bears is around the Seahorse Islands, where the main pack drifts closest to shore. Along straight or indented coasts, one must travel far out from the land in order to find them.

In some parts of the Arctic these animals forsake their normal habitat in favor of the land during the summertime. They live by scavenging on dead animals that are washed onto the beach, or forage on vegetable food or organisms that live along the ocean beaches. In autumn they return to the ice (Degerbøl and Freuchen 1935, p. 114). It is not surprising that polar bears try to move onto the main pack or even live on land for the summer, because the ocean ice becomes so fragmented that they have to swim constantly from one floe to another in search of food. They are occasionally encountered in such broken ice fields, however. Some of the Wainwright Eskimos have shot them while hunting walrus.

Feeding Habits

It is remarkable that the polar bear has been able to perfect an adaptation to the sea-ice environment. Certainly this is one of the most unusual habitats in which a terrestrial mammal has been able to live. One of the most interesting aspects of this adaptation is the polar bears' ability to locate and kill the animals on which they prey. Seals, which they kill by very ingenious methods, appear to be the most important element in their diet. They also eat frozen carcasses of whales or walrus, which they find in the pack ice or washed up along the coast. Because they sometimes depend upon this kind of food, they have developed an acute sense of smell. The Eskimos say that they can detect a dead whale from "50 miles" away. On occasion bears have crossed leads so wide that the opposite side was not visible because they smelled a whale that the Eskimos were butchering.

Polar bears often catch seals by waiting for them at their breathing holes, small openings through the ice where seals come periodically for air. Seals are extremely cautious when they come to these holes, and the bear has evolved elaborate behavior patterns in order to succeed in hunting them. If polar bears could not catch seals at breathing holes, they probably could not survive through periods of midwinter when there is no open water.

The first thing a seal does when it comes to breathe is take a quick sniff of the air to detect danger. Thus, the bear must not station itself upwind of the hole. Eskimos say that they sit or lie on the ice at a right angle to the wind, and they may have to wait all day before a seal comes. One man also stated that they will lie facing the east in a southerly wind and the west in a northerly wind.

If the breathing hole is in thin young ice, the bear simply waits until the seal comes and then smashes the surrounding ice with its front paws, simultaneously crushing the seal's skull. If the ice is thicker, the bear excavates the ice all around the hole, weaken-

ing it sufficiently so that it can carry out the same method of killing. It always fills the excavated area with snow so that when the
seal swims up underneath, it cannot detect any change. Also, in
thick ice the bear may dig a hole through the ice some distance
from the breathing hole and wait there until it hears the sound of
the seal's breathing. Then it slips silently through the hole and
catches the seal by swimming up from beneath. Many Eskimos
have found places where the bears have used these methods. For
example, one man related that during the early spring of 1966 he
followed the tracks of a female and cub bear far to the south
along the coast, almost to Icy Cape. These bears had wandered
all over the flat ice fields, and at every breathing hole they had
waited for a seal. But they had been unsuccessful each time, in
spite of the fact that they waited at so many holes that the Eskimo
said he wished he had kept count of the number.

Wherever there is open water, the polar bear can capture seals
when they come to the surface to breathe. They make a hole
through the ice as described above, somewhere near the water's
edge. The hole may be through ice up to 2 feet thick. The bear
conceals its excavation either by leaving a thin layer of ice in the
bottom or by covering the opening with its forelegs. When a seal
surfaces in the open water, the bear slips quietly into the water
through the hole and attempts to catch the seal by swimming up
under water. Sometimes there is no need for such elaborate preparation. The bear just waits somewhere along the edge for a seal
to come up close enough to slip into the water after it. An old
Wainwright man has watched bears attempting to catch seals this
way, but he never saw an actual kill. When they fail to catch their
prey, they usually crawl back up on the ice and wait for another
seal to appear. Sometimes a seal breaks the surface within reach,
and it is killed with a single swat of the bear's paw. During summertime, seals habitually rise in cracks and small holes, where they
can be caught rather easily by a bear waiting along the edge.

Seals also sleep at the surface of the water, especially during
warm spring and summer weather. When they are alseep, their
bodies move rhythmically back and forth and their noses point
skyward. They are often seen this way, especially in open leads
and large bodies of open water, and they can be approached quite

closely because they sleep soundly. Bears take advantage of this behavior to stalk or swim close enough to a seal to kill it.

Ringed seals (*Phoca hispida*) and bearded seals (*Erignathus barbata*) also habitually sleep on the surface of the ice during the warm months. Sleeping seals must form a large part of the polar bears' summer diet. Before the ice breaks up, while large ice fields still remain, they stalk carefully until they are close enough to sprint across the ice and slam the seal dead with a paw before it escapes through its hole into the water below. Eskimos often mention the bear's ability to conceal its dark nose by covering it with a paw or with its tongue in order to escape detection. The famous Arctic explorer and author, Peter Freuchen, reports having seen this himself. This same author states that there are too many accounts of polar bears holding up a piece of ice to conceal their noses to doubt that it is actually done.

The fact that Eskimos and polar bears use almost identical methods for hunting seals atop the ice and, to some extent, at breathing holes is more than a coincidence. It could be the result of "parallel invention." But since the bears presumably took to the ocean ice well before the Eskimos did, it does not seem improbable that the Eskimos learned certain of their seal-hunting techniques by watching them.

Seals also sleep on small ice pans or on the ice along a lead edge. When a bear spots them, it swims toward where they are sleeping, and at some distance from the ice edge it dives beneath the surface. It swims along under the water, resurfaces right next to the ice, and springs up onto it, cutting off the seals' escape into the water. Bearded seals must be especially easy to hunt on the ice, because they sleep soundly and are less apt to be frightened away. They also tend to lie atop very small pans of ice, where a bear can swim right up to them and jump onto the ice before they can get away.

When they catch a seal, polar bears eat only the skin and blubber, unless they are very hungry. Kavik said that twice he had found a polar bear sleeping right beside the carcass of a bearded seal that it had killed. When he inspected the remains, he found that the skin had been removed by cutting around the flippers and head, and then pulling the skin off by turning it inside out, without making a single tear. The blubber was then stripped off the skin and carcass, without damaging either the hide or the meat to which it had been attached. Eskimos are very unlikely to be mistaken about information such as this, since they place a high value on objective observation of the game animals they hunt.

Polar bears enjoy a fairly easy existence during the summer months, because plenty of food is available to them. Not only are there more animals around, but their habits make them more susceptible to predation. Seals are certainly easier to catch during this season. There are also many speculations in the literature as to the polar bear's ability to kill walrus. Certainly, judging by the behavior of walruses toward man in northwest Alaska, a bear would have little trouble approaching these huge animals closely when they are lying atop drifting ice pans. According to Freuchen and Solomonsen (1958, p. 216) ". . . it is generally accepted that no animal at sea can overcome the walrus. Occasionally we have seen a dead bear found close to the edge of the ice or an ice hummock with gaping puncture wounds. Probably he tried to snatch a pup away from a mother walrus, and the fight that resulted ended with the long and powerful tusks piercing the bear's ribs. There was rarely much blood at such scenes, indicating that the bear's claws had not been able to cut through the thick hide of the walrus."

This last statement seems a bit doubtful to say the least, in view of the fact that bears tear apart the carcasses of dead walruses along the beaches in northwest Alaska. This they do in spite of the fact that the heavy skin is frozen solid and is so tough that it cannot be butchered with a sharp axe. They are so powerful that they can lift and carry in their jaws pieces of frozen walrus that weigh hundreds of pounds. I have seen these carcasses, with most of the meat removed by bears through the course of winter. It seems that both claws and teeth are used in the process of tearing them apart. Any beast that has the power to do this is strong enough to injure a live walrus. In fact, bears are said to be able to "case out" walruses from their skins in much the same way that they do with seals. It is quite possible, however, that when they attack live walruses, they only go after the young ones.

Some Wainwright Eskimos once saw a bear try to get a baby

walrus from a herd that was sleeping on an ice pan. A group of men were butchering some walruses when they saw the bear some distance away, swimming up to the herd on a nearby floe. The bear got up onto the ice and tried to attack a pup, but the adults would not let it approach closely. Kavik, who described the happening, said that they saw the bear pick up a chunk (or several chunks) of ice with both paws, stand up on its hind legs, and throw it at the walruses in a vain attempt to move the large ones away from the infant. Even the smallest walrus could provide quite a repast for a polar bear, since they weigh several hundred pounds by July. Walrus hunting by bears is often said to involve hurling pieces of ice or rock. Most authors have questioned whether this occurs, however, apparently doubting that the hunters are able to view their own surroundings objectively. Yet it is worth re-iterating that Eskimos are highly reliable observers of animal behavior, and many of their least believable statements have been proved to me by personal observation.

Bears probably do not depend on walrus as an important ele-ment of their summer diet, because they must find plenty of easier game at this time of year. They are likely to succeed in killing these huge beasts only when one or two (perhaps an adult with a pup) can be found, separated from larger herds. They probably would be more tempted to pursue walrus during the winter months, when it is much harder to catch a wary seal, but walruses are rare during the cold months.

Tracking

Because bear tracks are usually the only indication by which the Eskimo hunter knows that a bear has been in the vicinity, he must learn to recognize the information in them. An account of a polar bear hunt will illustrate these methods: We walked out from Wainwright before there was much light on December 10, hoping to find a bear before the morning twilight became very bright. When we reached the edge of the landfast ice, we stepped right into a bear trail, which excited Kuvlu and caused him to scan eagerly in the direction that the tracks led. Seeing nothing, he knelt over the trail, pulled off his glove, and felt the snow between the sole pad and the depression of the toes, where there was a little bit of raised snow. The snow was somewhat hardened, he explained, which meant that the bear had passed several hours before. If it was very soft the bear would not be far ahead. Had there been frost crystals (*kanik*) and considerable hardness, there would be little point in following the trail, because it would be at least a day old. We decided to follow it.

Our pace was very brisk, but the hope of finding the bear seemed to make it easy. We occasionally glanced behind us in case another bear should be following in the tracks of the first. A small pile of excrement was an important sign; frozen fairly solid, it indicated again several hours since the animal had passed. Kuvlu became less certain about following the tracks, especially since we were now quite far out and on relatively young ice. He pointed out that the bear, being a fast walker, was probably too far offshore to be pursued on foot. A mile farther on, we climbed a pile of ice about 25 feet high and spent a long time scanning in all directions with binoculars. To the south, he said, there would be more tracks, perhaps fresher ones than what we were following.

We headed south. Our movement paralleled the coast, because we had already gone out for several miles. Kuvlu led along the smooth ice. There were great flat expanses this early in the season, but never did he go more than a few yards away from rough ice ridges and hummocks which paralleled our direction of travel. There were three reasons for doing this: (1) polar bears follow the edges of rough ice and seldom move out onto large flat areas; (2) when the hunter is close enough to rough ice, he can hide quickly and avoid frightening the bear; (3) if the young ice begins to move, the flat areas are most dangerous because they break and pile suddenly.

About a mile farther on we began to find cracks with one day's ice cover on them. Kuvlu said that this would be a good area for bears because one might have killed a seal and remained nearby to sleep off its meal. We crossed three more bear trails, one of which he said was that of the same bear we had followed on the way out, and other two made by another single bear. Both animals were apparently following a rather zigzag trail. Perhaps they had smelled the village and investigated, then moved out again.

From their tracks the Eskimo was able to estimate that the bears were 8 or 9 feet long, about average size. In both cases the depression of the pad of the foot, excluding the toes, was the length of an outstretched hand from middle finger to thumb, or about 9½ inches long and 7 inches wide. When the bear was running, it left a long drag mark with its heels. When it was walking at a leisurely pace, the distance between hind footprints was equal to a long stride of a man, a little less than a yard in length.

While he walked, the Eskimo hunter continually scanned and watched for signs of the game he was pursuing. In this case, early in the winter, the bear's coat would be a dull white or yellowish color, but later on it would be a brighter white, even to the point of appearing to shine. He explained that bears are not always seen walking, but may instead be resting. They often do this in a large depression dug into a snowdrift in the rough ice, raising their heads to look around occasionally. They also may be seen lying astride high pinnacles of ice.

As the brief day began to fade, the northeast wind picked up slightly and began to move and shift the ice. We hurried back to the landfast ice, fearing that the ice would break away and strand us. On the way in, we followed a bear trail to within a quarter mile of the village. The curious animal had finally stopped and risen up on its hind legs before sensing danger and running back out toward the ocean. Kuvlu noted from the tracks exactly what each bear had been doing, and, with intense concentration, inferred the behavior of the animal. Each place where it had licked the snow or sniffed it, where it had stopped to look around, where it had urinated, or had quickened its pace, deserved a closer look and a comment. In this way the Eskimo learns to understand his prey.

When he returns to the village from any type of hunting or traveling, the Eskimo tells the others what he has seen. If he has observed some peculiarity of the behavior of an animal, the others will hear of it and in this way enrich their own knowledge. And, of more immediate importance, the report of each hunter as to the presence of game or game signs will affect the hunting activities of the others. Each day or evening the men gather at the native store or the small "coffee shop" and exchange this type of information. These gathering places, therefore, serve important

THE BIOLOGICAL ENVIRONMENT

social and economic functions. If one man has seen a bear, it is likely that many will go out to search for bears the following day.

In a similar way the presence of regular mail flights between the large and small villages has affected the efficiency of hunting, because the pilot always reports whatever game he spots on the way. On November 10, 1964, my field notes from Wainwright recorded the following: "The pilot reported seeing two polar bears near Franklin Point on the beach, and fresh tracks on this side of Peard Bay. He also reported a large herd of caribou moving north between Wainwright and Icy Cape, with the closest ones near Kiḷḷamittaġvik (12 miles south)." A day or two later one man headed north to look for bears, and several others went south after caribou. Success of polar bear hunting has been drastically reduced in recent years, perhaps due to the rise of airplane hunting by wealthy outsiders, which, if nothing else, keeps the bears far out on the pack ice. The Eskimos no longer go out every day looking for bears, especially not on foot as they used to. This also decreases their success.

It is quite difficult to track polar bears during the late spring and summer, even if the hunter dares to follow them far from the land at this dangerous season. In the first place, there is considerably less snow; much of the ice is hard and white on the surface. The remaining snow usually melts so rapidly that tracks disappear soon after they are made, and there is little way of estimating their freshness. In some parts of the Arctic, ravens (*Corvus corax*) are used as guides in the search for bears. Whenever they are seen flying out over the ice, it is likely that a bear can be found by following their flight, because they habitually feed on the remains of animals which are killed and partially eaten by bears (Degerbøl and Freuchen 1935, p. 112).

Stalking and Attracting

Eskimos say that the best way to hunt bears is on foot. This way there are no dogs to frighten them and a hunter can stalk ahead of the bear and wait for a close shot. The best bear hunters also know how to attract their game, so that they do not have to walk so far to get it. There are two methods of attracting bears. One of these consists of using seal blood or blubber. When the men shoot seals and drag them up onto the ice, a trail of blood freezes on the surface. This is one means of bringing in bears, though it is not done intentionally. The hunters always watch closely for bears wherever they know there is seal blood. Occasionally a hunter will purposely drag a seal home on the ice, behind his dog sled, so that it leaves a trail which a bear might follow close to the village. Men may also leave pieces of blubber out along the lead edge before they go home. This is especially effective if there is an offshore breeze to carry the scent outward over the ice. One old man said that some bears, especially very hungry ones, are also attracted by the noise of seal hunters shooting.

Another method of attracting bears takes advantage of their stalking behavior. Igruk explained that he once was walking across a large area of flat young ice when he spotted a polar bear some distance away. He did not have a white parka cover on, so there was no chance of stalking the animal without being seen. He decided that his only chance was to lie on the ice and "play seal," hoping that the bear would be fooled and try to stalk him. Shortly it began to walk toward him, so Igruk alternately lifted his head and dropped it again as a seal does. The bear was fooled. Each time Igruk looked around the bear stopped crawling toward him, but when Igruk "slept" it moved closer. Finally it came within range and was killed with one shot.

Another old man said that his father taught him to use the same method to get a bear that cannot be shot because it is across a lead and could not be recovered. If a hunter spots the bear before it sees him, he removes his white parka cover (because seals are not white) and starts "playing seal." If the bear sees this it may slip into the water on the opposite side, hoping to catch a meal. Then the hunter jumps up, hides in some rough ice, and waits for the bear to come up onto the ice on his side of the lead. Finding nothing, the bear searches around, and when it comes close, the hunter shoots it.

Normally an Eskimo will be near rough ice and in a position to stalk a bear, as long as the animal does not see him first. A bear will usually run away if it sees a man. Hunters normally carry or wear white parka covers during winter ice hunting. Thus, if a bear is spotted, it can be approached without its detecting the hunter. The first thing that an Eskimo will do is watch it to see in which direction it is moving and how often it looks around, so he can get ahead and wait for it without being seen. He also tries to stay on its seaward side in case the bear senses danger and flees, because polar bears always try to escape toward the ocean. As soon as he feels that he is right in the bear's line of travel, the Eskimo hides in rough ice and awaits its arrival, hoping for a side shot from the closest possible range.

The polar bear will usually run if it happens to see its pursuer, or if it is shot at and missed or wounded. If this happens, the Eskimo will run after it. A bear is slower than a man on flat ice, but much faster on rough ice. Many stories are told of catching up to bears, wounded or healthy, and killing them. But it is always noted that if a bear reaches hummocky ice, no man can keep up with it. If the animal becomes spooked but has not sensed the man well, it is best to wait in concealment before setting off in pursuit. When this happens, a bear will often go only a short distance, stop to look around, and then go back to its business.

Polar bear hunting is usually done during the day, when there is good visibility. Only when bears walk up close to the village or into a camp are they hunted after dark. On New Year's Eve, 1964, two Eskimos heard a dog barking out on the ice at Wainwright. They figured that a bear had come close and the dog had chased out after it. One of them went out onto the ice with a rifle and flashlight to look for it and found tracks but no bear.

A Barrow native told of spotting a bear that was waiting at a seal hole in the middle of some flat ice. He could not stalk it so he waited in some rough ice. All through the dim early spring night the bear stood there, alternately lifting one foot after the other and placing it slowly and silently back down. Finally it gave up and shuffled off. The Eskimo ran up ahead of it and shot it from 20 feet as it passed by his concealed position.

Very frequently a hunter will have his dogs and must be careful to keep them quiet. Men hope to encounter bears when they are on foot so that they do not have this problem, or else to be traveling with a partner so that one of them can stay behind to watch and quiet the dogs while the other stalks the game. If they plan to travel far out from the land, which they do when a west wind blows, two men will go out with their dog teams. They try to spot a bear when they stop to scan (*nesisaaktok*) with binoculars. Occasionally, Eskimos see a bear on flat ice and are able to run it down with their dog team before it reaches rough ice.

In the eastern Arctic, and occasionally in northwest Alaska, bears are brought to bay by dogs that are set loose from the team to chase them down (see Nelson 1899, p. 121). Several of the older men at Wainwright had owned dogs which they used for this purpose. Igruk once had two dogs that he had trained to chase and detain bears when he let them loose from the team after an animal was in plain sight. His father once used them when he shot two bears north of Icy Cape, where he was hunting sea gulls. He spotted a female bear offshore with a yearling cub. First he stopped and tried to find a round stone to use for a slug. Finding none small enough, he even tried to shove his ivory pipe stem down the barrel, but to no avail. Finally he took all of his shells and opened them, putting the shot from several shells into each of six that he chose to use.

Then he released two dogs. They caught up to the bears, harassed them, and eventually brought them to bay. After he caught up, he waited for the proper moment, shot the large female once, and ran back away from it immediately. Advancing again, he shot it once more, and it fell mortally wounded. Then he pursued the yearling, which had run some distance away and was being harassed by a dog. This one he killed with a single blast.

In late April, 1966, a Wainwright Eskimo and his companion went out on the ice to hunt seals. When they were about half a mile offshore, they saw two sets of polar bear tracks. They had passed this spot two days before and there were no tracks, so they decided to try to catch up with the animals. After some time they sighted a female with her cub ahead, but the bears had already seen the men and dogs approaching. They started shuffling away, following the edge of some young ice which they did not want to cross because it was too thin.

Since the bears were already alerted, the only chance of catching them was by chasing them with the dog team. The bears set off on a run, but the dogs had to be coaxed and whipped to make them run quickly, because they had not seen the animals. When they saw that they could not close the gap, the men set a dog loose, but because it did not see the bears, the dog would wait for the team. Finally it saw them and sprinted off in pursuit.

Since the Alaskan Eskimos do not regularly use their dogs in this way, they are not trained to chase bears as the Canadian dogs are. However, they do know how to chase caribou, which is similar. Although this dog had never been turned loose to chase game, nor had this sort of contact with bears, it began to bite them on the rump, causing the bears to stop and turn. Finally the bears decided to try crossing the young ice, but the dog followed and eventually harassed the female until she sat down to protect her hind quarters from the attacks. When either she or her cub tried to move away, the dog would give chase and force a halt. This continued briefly, until the men arrived. They could not walk out onto the thin ice, so it was necessary to shoot the animals from solid ice.

The female fell through the ice when she was hit, but the ice supported the smaller cub. The men were forced to use their boat to reach the dead animals, breaking the ice in front of them as they moved ahead. Fortunately, the ice where the bears had fallen was solid enough to walk on, and after chopping many holes through it, they found the female. Usually bears sink when shot, but this one was very fat and remained afloat. Before the bears were towed to solid ice and skinned, the men permitted the female dog to "fight" a dead bear (bite at it and try to tear it), so that the next time it was released it would know what to do.

Probably the most productive type of bear hunting is done in the fall, from late October until around Thanksgiving. At this time Eskimos camp near places where bears come onto the beach to feed on stranded walrus and whale carcasses. This is the only time that congregations of several adult bears are occasionally encountered. The method of hunting is easy, because the bears may be seen right in or near a camp. They can also be attracted by walrus meat carried for dog food and left outside.

The old man, Igruk, has probably killed more bears than any

man in Wainwright, and certainly holds the record for the most killed single-handedly at one time. Many years ago he was driving his team along the coast near the Seashore Islands. He left his team and walked over the ice to one of the low sandy islands. As he approached it, he saw two bears through his telescope. When he sneaked closer, he saw not two but fourteen bears, gathered around a dead walrus. He killed eight of these with seven shots, shooting two cubs at once. The others he left alone because they were on thin ice, and he feared losing them.

Kaviḳ noted that when animals gather in large numbers like this, they tend to lose their fear of man and can be approached closely. He once encountered about thirty-five bears feeding on a floating whale carcass. He and his companions in an *umiaḳ* shot thirteen of them. These bears did not flee until shot at, and after the shooting stopped, they came back again.

There is a method of killing polar bears with a rifle-set. This technique was formerly used, but is outlawed today. The rifle was set into a hollow or snowbank, attached to a baited line. When a bear reached its head in and pulled the bait, the rifle fired. This method is never used today, but might be resorted to by a drift-ice survivor who was facing starvation.

Eskimos do not bother to watch for bears when they hunt in boats amid the summer pack ice. Their lack of expectation reflects the rarity of bears at this time of year. Murdoch, who visited Barrow in the 1880's, stated that ". . . umiaks when walrus hunting sometimes meet with bears among the loose ice. If the bear is caught in the water, there is very little difficulty in paddling up close enough to him to shoot him." (Murdoch 1892, p. 263) These summer kills are very rare today, but polar bears can certainly turn up at any time and at any place.

When they are caught in open water or on ice pans, it is easy to shoot them. They apparently do not swim very fast and can be approached very closely before being shot, and then harpooned to prevent them from sinking. Likewise, on a small pan of ice the bear would have no hope of escape, and could be shot from the boat. On a larger ice field, or where the pans are jammed together, a bear could easily escape by running away in the rough or rotten ice.

Behavior toward Man

The polar bear is one of the few animals on earth that will stalk a man under normal circumstances, but the accounts of this and the explanations for it vary considerably. According to Degerbøl and Freuchen (1935, pp. 110–11), a bear is usually more curious than belligerent, and stories of bears attacking people are probably often the result of curiosity's leading the bears to investigate what they see. Sometimes, however, a bear will risk anything in order to get food, and may even attack a man. Or the bear may be an old male which is accustomed to having everything flee from it. It has never had a reason to fear anything, so it will walk right up to whatever it finds interesting.

On this subject, the works of Stefansson (1921, 1943, 1950) are probably the most authoritative accounts, written by an experienced sea-ice traveler who encountered many bears himself and had chances to observe their behavior in uninhabited regions. He emphasizes more the "hunter becomes the hunted" aspects, but is careful to point out that it is not sheer meanness that provokes the polar bear to hunt man, but the fact that he is only accustomed to having seals, foxes, or birds around. Smelling seals in a camp or seeing something moving across the ice, the bear walks right up to it or flattens down to begin a stalk, assuming that whatever is out on the ice must be a seal (Stefansson 1921, pp. 155–56).

Stefansson's experiences are based primarily on areas far from any human habitation. One might expect that the behavior of polar bears along a relatively populous coastline, such as northwest Alaska, would be appreciably different. This, indeed, is what we find. Polar bears seldom actually stalk a man in this region and, unless they are starving, will cautiously avoid contact with humans. Bears are still a source of danger to the Eskimo hunter, however, because they will charge if they are wounded but not disabled. For this reason, hunters usually try to get as close as possible to the animal before shooting, to assure that they hit a vital spot. It is possible to get the best target by waiting until the bear has reached the most favorable position and then making a noise. Then it will stop, so that the best steady aim can be taken and the chance of a poor shot minimized.

Eskimos also will not shoot a bear which has just come out of the water onto the ice, because they say that the bullets will not penetrate its wet fur. They wait until the bear rolls in the snow to dry itself. Otherwise it is necessary to make a perfect shot in the eyes, ears, or anus. One man supported that statement with a case from his own experience, when he and three companions tried to shoot a bear that had just climbed out of the water. It took about fifteen shots, he recalled, until one man hit it in the anus and another killed it with a shot in the ear. They found that their bullets had penetrated only about a "half-inch" beneath the skin. Another man, who is very intelligent and reliable, said that after his shots failed to wound a wet bear, he found the rifle slugs lying on the snow where the bear had been hit. None of them penetrated its fur. Another man killed the animal after it dried off in the snow.

Eskimos say that there are three vital spots to shoot a bear: neck, shoulder, and heart. The heart shot is used especially when a man has only a light rifle (e.g. .22 or .222 caliber) which would not shatter neck vertebrae or shoulder bones. For the best heart shot, the hunter waits until the animal moves its leg forward, stretching the skin just behind it. He shoots right behind the leg, where this skin tightens. Although this shot is deadly, the bear usually makes a bursting run before it drops. With a caribou this run presents no danger, but a bear is likely to charge in the direction of the report, which is a great threat to the hunter. Thus, it is not very safe to shoot a bear this way with a light rifle; but an Eskimo will not allow one of these most prized animals to pass unpursued as long as he has some kind of firearm. It is interesting that Stefansson insisted that his men use heart shots.

There is an instance of an Eskimo who unexpectedly came face to face with a polar bear and shot it in the heart with his .22 caliber rifle. His perfect shot killed it after only a short run. The Eskimos believe that polar bears are left-handed, and that if a hunter is charged, he should wait until the bear is very close and then run to its right side. The left paw is so quick that it is harder to avoid a mauling from that side. When a bear charges, the hunter should wait until its head is up and then shoot it in the neck. If it does not lift its head, he should shoot for its hind quarters, which causes the bear to turn and bite the wound, exposing its neck for a good side shot. Eskimos usually wait for the best possible shot, with dogged patience, even if a bear is charging toward them.

The neck is said to be the most vulnerable spot on a bear. It is a difficult shot to make, however, because it is easy to shoot too low and miss the bone. The safest shot is probably the shoulder, where it is very easy to disable the animal by shattering its bones. Once it can no longer walk, it is a safe, sure kill. The Eskimos say: "When you shoot an animal, think about the bones and organs inside." They do not aim at an animal's skin, but beneath it, visualizing its anatomy as if they were shooting at an X ray. If a bear stands up on its hind legs, the hunter shoots for the base of its neck.

In prerifle days, bears were killed with lances, but this was given up because of the danger involved. One very old man, Takumik, is said to have killed a bear with a knife when it stood up on its hind legs. This feat proved him one of the greatest of the old-time hunters. Female bears with cubs are especially dangerous. If one were to be shot, the adult would be killed first. A she-bear will certainly charge if its cubs are shot.

Not all wounded bears charge. In fact, the percentage that do is probably quite small. In December of 1964 a Wainwright Eskimo shot a bear twice, and lost it when it ran off in the darkness. On the other hand, a young man took a long shot at three bears just offshore from Wainwright, wounding one, and was chased back to shore before the bear gave up and ran away. In this instance the man shot from too great a distance, and when the bear charged, his gun jammed. Fortunately, he was close to the village. The fact that bears will sometimes stop charging and turn away is established by another incident several years previous when a man got up and ran toward a charging wounded bear, causing it to stop and turn the other way.

Nonwounded bears are generally quite timid. Whether they see a man from a distance or are suddenly confronted, they nearly always run away. Well-fed bears are particularly unlikely to bother with man, because they are afraid or because humans are regarded as a second-rate meal. In northwest Alaska, many stories of polar bears attacking or stalking men relate to the fact that the animals were thin and hungry. Even then they are probably only after seals or other meat that is being carried on a sled or stored in a camp. Bears often follow sled tracks, but they may simply indicate their preference for walking a "beaten path" rather than searching for an easy meal.

Bears are therefore most likely to approach humans during periods, usually in midwinter, when food becomes scarce. In the spring and summer months, when there is an abundance of food, they would be least dangerous to man. For example, in some parts of the Arctic, old people are left alone to guard meat caches because ". . . during the summer no bear would attack a human being" (Degerbøl and Freuchen 1935, p. 225). The following cases of bears approaching men represent marked exceptions to the usual behavior of these animals in northwest Alaska. However, the Eskimo traveling on sea ice must be prepared for such an eventuality.

Men who have caught seals and are dragging them home on foot are especially wary of hungry bears. This is particularly true during the dim hours of early morning or early evening. If a man is trudging home with his load dragging on the ice behind him, and he feels a pull on the line, he slips its strap off his chest and grabs his rifle in case it is a bear tugging on the seal. Brower (1963, p. 247) describes an actual case of this at Barrow, where the man had no time to grab his rifle so he thrust the sharp pick of his harpoon into the bear's brain, killing it. Another man, who still lives at Barrow, was bothered by two bears as he tied seals onto his sled. He was evidently in considerable danger, but managed to get his rifle out in time to kill both of them from very close range.

In a few cases bears have come into whaling camps in daylight with men walking around in plain sight. These were always starving bears. For example, an old man who was walking along on the ice was chased by a very skinny bear. He dropped it with a single shot when it was just 20 feet away. Only one other instance was recorded of a bear walking up to a man when there was no meat around. In this case the man was setting traps and carried only a knife. When this brave fellow noticed the bear coming up on him, he turned around and walked toward it with his knife drawn, telling it to go away or he would cut it up. The bear retreated, but followed again, each time being confronted in the same way. The man finally made it safely to Barrow village.

It appears that confronting bears in this way will usually scare them off, if one must resort to this. E. W. Nelson (1899, p. 120) records a case where a man was approached by a bear. The man lay down on the ice in hopes that the animal would not notice him. The bear walked up and took a sniff, but hearing the man's partner, ran over and attacked him. The partner was later found dead and partially eaten.

There are few instances in the literature of men actually being killed by polar bears. Only one informant at Wainwright mentioned a case where a man had been hurt by a bear, while others could not recall any. Perhaps a classic tale of confronting a bear is the one told by Akpa of Wainwright:

> Once, within remembered times, a woman was walking south along the beach across the inlet from Wainwright. She was going to a place to collect beach coal. She noticed a polar bear walking toward her, and finally as it came nearer, she stopped. She did not run, because she had been warned that if a person did this, the bear would give chase, "play" with him, and probably kill him. She held her ground as the bear came nearer, and when it finally came right to her and opened its mouth to bite, she used her only defense—her mittens. She jammed her hand down the bear's throat as far as she could, and pulled it out before the animal bit down, leaving the furry mitten in its throat. The bear immediately began to choke, forgetting about her in its efforts to breathe. Finally it lost its strength and suffocated.

Although polar bear meat is considered delicious, it is never eaten raw, because it carries many parasites. The polar bear's liver is never eaten or fed to dogs, because it sometimes causes vitamin A poisoning, which results in severe illness or death. If a bear is shot too far out on the ice to bring in the meat, the hide is folded into a small bundle and pulled to shore. Polar bear skins are stretched to the greatest possible dimension, cleaned, and sold to outside buyers. As long as the hunter has his dog team he will take as much meat as possible, perhaps going back a second time to bring all of it home. There is no question, however, that the hunt for bears has become more a cash occupation than a means of obtaining food.

CHAPTER 11

White Whale

(Delphinapterus leucas)

Open Lead Hunting

HE WHITE WHALE or beluga (*sissuak̲*) migrates northward in the spring, usually passing Wainwright during the whaling season. Belugas arrive ahead of the
large whales, first appearing sometime in March, but
the largest numbers occur during the month of May.
From this time on, through the entire summer, they occur sporadically. They are not large animals, running from 12 to 15
feet in length and weighing about 1,000 pounds. Although they
are small in comparison to the huge baleen whales, they may travel
in herds of great size. During their principal northward migration
in spring, they may be in sight almost constantly for a week.
According to Degerbøl and Freuchen (1935, p. 265), some whites
and Eskimos with long experience in the north have said that
the white whale is the most abundant mammal in the Arctic
regions.

The principal hunting time for white whales is during spring
whaling, when they are shot from the ice edge. As these whales
move along in a lead the noise of their breathing is heard far
ahead of their appearance. The short but very strong puffs cannot
be mistaken for any other sound and resemble only the much
longer and deeper breathing of the large whales. Eskimos in
whaling camps listen for their blowing, and when it is heard they

run for the high ice pile lookouts trying to spot the herd as it comes closer. Belugas are easily recognized by their bright white or gray bodies rolling over in the black water, periodically appearing to breathe a few times, then disappearing for several minutes as they swim along beneath the surface.

If belugas appear in the lead close by, the hunters station themselves close to the water's edge, preferably among some piled ice so they won't be seen. Belugas have a whistling call that warns of danger. When it is given, all of them in an area will dive and resurface far up the lead or in another hole. This is why they are shot from the ice edge during spring whaling, rather than pursued with boats. They can detect any foreign sound in the water, such as paddling or running an outboard engine, and sometimes even hear the noise of feet moving around on the ice. If they do, the warning call is given, and they are gone.

Another thing that makes the beluga a difficult animal to hunt is that it is a fast swimmer and presents only a small target for a few seconds at a time. Hunters hope for a head-on shot, because then they do not have to move their rifles while they aim, but they usually must settle for a side shot. They watch closely for the animal's light torpedo form gliding just underwater, indicating that it will soon break the surface. When it does, they shoot immediately, aiming for the head. It is possible to shoot for its back, also, but this shot only wounds the animal.

Added to the difficulty of shooting a white whale is the fact that it usually sinks immediately when killed. Some of them will float, especially in the early spring. The gray ones, which are said to be the young, will float more often than the white ones. Females, especially those which are carrying young, will float more frequently than other adults. There is no way to identify them from the surface, however. The best chance is probably to shoot for the gray ones and hope that they will float. When they do, it is simple to retrieve them with a boat or a floating snag hook (*manak*). If they sink, they are probably lost, but men will sometimes spend several hours attempting to snag them with a *niksik*, or sinking retrieval hook. (Use of snag hooks will be discussed in the chapters on seal hunting.)

206

Suagssat

Herds of belugas are occasionally trapped by moving and closing of the ice and cannot find enough open water to breathe. In northwest Alaska this happens when the ice moves in to cover a lead, and perhaps occasionally when open water freezes over. Unlike the large whales, belugas cannot break through the ice to breathe, and are therefore caught in a desperate struggle to find open spots in which to get air. At such times there may be hundreds of them crowding and literally fighting to reach the open spaces. Northwest Alaskan Eskimos call this phenomenon *imayguraat;* the better-known Greenlandic term is *suagssat.*

This happens fairly often in the eastern Arctic, but is reported to have happened only once in recent years at Wainwright, and once near Barrow. Pogazak and two companions discovered an *imayguraat* about 15 miles south of Wainwright. It was April, when the first herds were arriving. They were guided to it by the frantic hissing and blowing of hundreds of the whales at some holes along the edge of a closing lead. They shot seven belugas and retrieved them, then headed toward Wainwright to tell the rest of the men.

Hunters from the village eagerly headed south. Pogazak said that he heard the noise while he was still far off, and soon he saw their churning bodies in a large hole. As soon as everybody arrived, they began to shoot. Pogazak and some others found smaller holes and waited there. He waited until a gray-colored whale surfaced and shot it, hoping to kill one that would float. He cut a hole in its flipper and fastened it to the ice so it would not be lost. Then he killed another. In all, they shot and retrieved about thirty. Most were retrieved with snag hooks if they floated, and then tied to the edge to be pulled up later. The ice finally opened up, allowing the rest to escape. It took many trips over the next few days to haul the meat back to Wainwright. Unfortunately for the Eskimos, this happens so infrequently that it does not add significantly to their overall economy.

Umiak *Hunting*

At any time during the summer, whether or not there is sea ice in the vicinity, herds of white whales may pass along within sight of the coast. Eskimos always keep a watchful eye out for them, because they may be able to kill many animals from such herds.

One August morning in 1966, a large school of white whales was spotted in the ocean offshore from Wainwright. The wind was a brisk 15 to 20 m.p.h. from the north, flecking the ocean surface with whitecaps. The whales were not seen until they were directly offshore from the village, because their white bodies flashed as they rolled over on the surface to breathe, resembling the bright crests of the waves. If the waters were fairly calm, a beluga herd could be spotted while still far off.

Because the whales were already passing by, the Eskimos very quickly ran for their rifles, and in about fifteen minutes six skin boats loaded with men were off in pursuit. The boats moved out together, hoping to circle ahead of the whales. Once they shoved off, the crew members had a difficult time seeing where the belugas had gone, because they were easily lost among the whitecaps. They had begun to disappear as soon as the first outboard motor was started, apparently because the water-transmitted noise frightened them. It was impossible for the Eskimos to do more than guess where the animals had gone. They said that if there had been Arctic terns (*Sterna paradisaea*) around, they might have been able to follow the herd, because terns sometimes fly along with belugas, feeding on what they leave behind.

The boats moved northward parallel to the shore for about a quarter mile, and then turned out to sea. The Eskimos hoped to head the whales off and drive them toward land. However, most of the animals were about a half mile offshore when first sighted, and as the boats began moving out, the whales fled seaward. Although one or two boats went over 2 miles from the coast, they could not go far enough out in the rough sea to turn them landward.

Some whales surfaced quite close to Eskimo boats. When this happened, the boat was immediately turned in their direction in an attempt to get close enough for a shot. When these whales came to the surface, they would usually take a breath, then submerge and resurface a few seconds later to breathe again. This was repeated several times before they dove for a long period without surfacing. Thus, the Eskimos knew that when a group was sighted, they would submerge and reappear repeatedly several times. But in this case only a few boats got close enough for this kind of pursuit, and no hunter was able to get a shot at them. The seas were choppy enough to make aiming a rifle nearly impossible, even if a close shot had presented itself.

There are other reasons why this hunt was entirely unsuccessful. Usually, when a school of white whales is seen, Eskimos do not chase them with motor-powered boats. They prefer to use an ingenious technique of driving or herding the entire school toward land, which can be done without setting foot in a boat. Several of the older men said that the impetuous young men had gone out in boats, forgetting that belugas can be herded by shooting bullets into the water ahead of them and beyond their seaward flanks. The sensitive animals are frightened by the sound of bullets striking the water, so they head for shore. Each time the whales appear on the surface, men on land shoot volleys of bullets again, until they are finally close to shore. At this time, boats are set out to shoot and harpoon the confused animals. They may even be shot from the beach.

Ikolivsaak told of one time many years ago when a large school of belugas was driven to shore in this way, but because the crews were not well organized they only succeeded in killing six animals. A white trader who lived in Wainwright called a meeting after this happened, and the men decided on a hunting plan which they used the next time whales appeared. The first shots were fired by the man who lived in the northernmost house, the location most likely to be ahead of the herd. A man on the south end of the village shot a few minutes later, so that his bullets would land behind them. This caused the animals to bunch up into a close group, as shown by a violent swirling and rippling in the offshore waters. Then these two men, plus another who was near the middle of the village, all began to shoot on the far side of the herd, driving it toward shore. They waited until the whales crossed a long submerged sandbar offshore from the village. Knowing that once they had crossed the sandbar they usually would not cross back in order to reach the open sea, the crews shoved off in pursuit. This time they killed sixteen belugas.

When the belugas have been driven this close to the land, there is no harm in using outboard motors, because they are "trapped" and do not escape over the sandbar. But boats may also be paddled out or allowed to drift with the wind in order to frighten the whales as little as possible. After missing the entire herd during August, 1966, the men decided to follow a similar plan if another group should be sighted.

Shooting belugas from a boat is done in much the same way as shooting them from the sea ice. This means that one must shoot as soon as the whale's head breaks the surface, while it is still coming up. If this is done, it will float, at least briefly, after it is killed. But if the shot is late, so that the whale is on its way down when hit, it simply continues to glide downward and cannot be retrieved. The beluga is very easily killed, more so than any animal of comparable size (Degerbøl and Freuchen 1935, p. 268), but one must be an excellent shot in order to hit it properly.

In the recent past, Wainwright Eskimos harpooned belugas before shooting them. In this case they also drove them toward shore; or if the approaching animals were spotted some time before they arrived at Wainwright, the men would go out in boats and wait for them to appear. When the water was clear, their white forms could be seen beneath the surface, and they were harpooned when they swam close to the boats.

Seal or walrus harpoons have been used for beluga hunting, but for a live animal they would not hold as well as the large whaling toggle iron. On a good hit, toggle irons have gone clear through a white whale's body, or have killed it instantly. However, if it was not killed or badly wounded, it would take off with great speed after it was struck. It was allowed to tow the boat, to which the harpoon line was tethered, until it broke surface and could be shot. Van Valin (1944, pp. 180–82) described a hunt at

Wainwright in which a man killed a beluga by jumping onto it from a boat and stabbing it to death with his knife.

Once a Wainwright Eskimo went out in his kayak among the larger skin-covered *umiaks* that were chasing belugas. He was almost drowned when one of the whales is said to have come up in front of the kayak, grabbed the bow in its mouth and tipped it over. An *umiak* crew which happened to be nearby rescued him. Men who had seen this advised against chasing them with kayaks; however, these little boats have been used traditionally throughout much of the Eskimo domain for hunting narwhal and white whale with harpoons.

Beluga hunts usually end when the herd crosses over the sandbar and escapes out to sea. Eskimos say that, having become disorganized and scattered, they will go to the vicinity of a large pan or floe of ice to regroup. For this reason, and because they like to feed near ice floes (if any are present), these are the best places to wait for belugas when some are known to be in the area.

There have been rare occasions when a man on the shore without a boat has been able to herd belugas in so close that he was able to shoot them. Kavik, a man in his sixties, did this successfully near the place called Mitliktaġvik, 20 miles south of Wainwright. He was then a young man, working as a reindeer herder. After returning to camp from the herd, he saw belugas a short distance offshore. He had only five shells with him, and the first shot to the far side was enough to turn the herd toward shore. Two more shots were used to hit the water behind them as they appeared, heading landward. When they reached the beach, the ones behind kept crowding those in front toward the shore, so some of them came almost to the water's edge. With the two shells remaining, Kavik killed two belugas, and could have gotten more had he not been out of ammunition.

In this case the whales must have been swimming fairly close to the land, as they apparently do sometimes. Around the village of Wainwright they are said to have done this frequently during former years, but now they always stay well offshore. The people blame this on the accumulation of garbage, barrels, and junk that litters the ocean bottom in front of the village. Also, there are engines running almost constantly (e.g., the native store generator), which may produce enough noise or vibration to frighten them away. One advantage of the aboriginal villages for hunting was that their small size, lack of noise, and sod-covered houses made them so inconspicuous that game animals, such as walrus, seals, or caribou would come very close to the settlement without fear. For example, the older people tell of shooting caribou on the beach not 30 yards from their houses, while in recent years they rarely come within a mile.

Eskimos do not attempt to herd white whales unless they are on land, because they say it cannot be done successfully from the sea ice. When there is ice around, bullets landing nearby only force them under and around ice floes, where they "hide." When they are pursued or frightened, they will even swim up onto the narrow underwater ledges that extend outward from the margins of ice floes.

Belugas are occasionally found in the mouth of the Kuk River, and sometimes farther up into the main body of the river itself. They may be attracted there by fish. In the eastern Arctic, for example, they regularly swim up certain rivers in order to feed on salmon (Degerbøl and Freuchen 1935, p. 269). If the Eskimos can catch a herd of white whales in the narrow Kuk Inlet, or if they can drive them into it, they usually kill a good number.

Whenever the Wainwright people talk about hunting white whales in the Kuk River, they invariably tell about the time when they killed some three hundred from a single herd. It happened during the summer about twenty years ago. A large herd of white whales was sighted by some men returning to the village from the south. These men managed to get in front of them with their boats and drive the entire herd into the inlet. Once inside, they were driven into a small deep bay along its north side. Then they were kept in a tight herd and prevented from escaping to the sea by running a motorized boat back and forth across the outlet and by firing bullets into the water ahead of the animals, if they started moving around.

The hunting method was basically the same as that described above. They were either shot when they surfaced near the boat or shore, or harpooned first and then shot. While the killing went on, and after it was over, carcasses were dragged up on the grassy tundra and butchered. The entire village, including old people and children, turned out to help. Every family received a large share from the kill, and many did not finish eating the prized skin and meat for two years.

Hunts like this may happen once in a lifetime. The Wainwright Eskimos usually get some white whales each year, but the take may vary from less than five up to a hundred or more. They cannot count on this as a reliable food resource, and only hope for it as a windfall that gives an added boost to their economy.

Spring Whaling

The Eskimos relish no food more than *maktak*, the black skin of baleen whales (*ahgavik*). These monsters, reaching up to 60 feet in length and averaging a ton per foot, can provide a prodigious amount of food for men and dogs, especially if the season is a good one. At Barrow, ten whales were taken during the fall of 1964, and three more the following spring. People filled their underground storage cellars to capacity and had to pile whale meat and *maktak* outside their houses. But there are also years when only one whale is taken at Barrow, and divided among well over a thousand people this does not go very far. At Point Hope in modern times one to five whales are taken each spring, the only whaling season. And at Wainwright whaling is becoming a lost art. With only token efforts put forth each spring and fall, there have been few whales taken in the past fifteen or twenty years. One was killed in the spring of 1966, the first in five or six years. The following discussion is based largely on observations made at Point Hope in 1965.

Whaling demands a great effort and expenditure of time and wealth on the part of every person in the village. In order for whaling to be highly effective, the entire spring season, April through June, must be devoted to the maintenance of whaling camps. Even when no whales are taken there will probably be a fair harvest of seals, waterfowl, some belugas, and perhaps a few walruses. But if there is no whale by June, the season is considered a failure; and that it is, because the expenditure far exceeds the yield if no whale is taken. One is naturally impressed by the fact that 60 tons of whale may be taken in an afternoon. More often, however, it is a small whale, divided among many. The resource is potentially great, but it is sporadic in comparison to "everyday" game such as seal, caribou, walrus, and waterfowl. How significant whaling is or has been in the total economic picture is open to question, especially in modern times when it is degenerating even in its greatest stronghold at Point Hope. Whaling involves hard work and long cold nights for the crews, expense and effort with the hope of prestige for the *umailik*, or crew captain.

A thorough discussion of whaling is beyond anything but a book-sized monograph and several years' study, which it deserves and almost demands, lest it be lost from memory without extensive documentation. It is outside the scope of this study to give anything but a brief, general description.

Whaling begins at Point Hope sometime in the latter part of April, depending upon the condition of the lead and the time of the first whales' arrival. At Wainwright whales are seen in late April at the earliest, but usually not until early May. The large whales are able to break through fairly thick ice to breathe, and are therefore not in danger of drowning if there is no open water. There are several "runs" of whales, separated by brief lulls. Whalers therefore experience periods of continuous activity and alertness (perhaps a week long) interspersed with periods when few whales are seen. At Point Hope there are three main runs, the last one usually finishing early in June, just before the crews come in for good.

Whaling activity is dependent upon the condition of the ice and weather. At Wainwright the whaling is not good, because leads do not open as readily here as they do around points, and because the village is in a bight so the whales usually stay far offshore. Whaling is excellent at Point Hope, because the animals usually pass very close to the land, and during the spring there is nearly always an open lead. The lead preferred for whaling at Point Hope is one that parallels the south shore of the spit, held open by winds from the north or east. As at Wainwright, south or west winds close the lead and temporarily halt the whaling. Strong winds from any quarter also force the crews to the land, hauling their boats and equipment, wary of the ice breaking away and unable to chase whales in the rough water. Nothing is left on the ice at such times lest it be carried away and lost on the trackless floes.

Narrow leads, such as those caused by wind blowing parallel to the coastline, are best for whale hunting. This condition forces the whales into fairly narrow areas so the whalers can approach them more easily. Whaling camps are reached by trails chopped through the rough areas so that the *umiaks*, which are lashed on heavy sleds (*ḳamoti*) towed by men and dogs, can be hauled easily. The boats are set right at the edge of the lead, spaced 5 to 50 yards apart, in ramps chopped almost to water level. The bow of each boat hangs over the water, so that it can be quickly and silently slipped into the water when a whale surfaces nearby. In 1965 there were two main camps along the lead at Point Hope, with six boats in one and five in the other.

Near the boats there are windbreaks made with snowblocks or pieces of canvas. Behind the windbreaks are "benches" made from the large boat-hauling sledges with caribou skins on them for warmth and softness. Nearby ice piles are used as observation points where men watch for whales or for changes in the ice conditions. Behind the ice edge there must be a flat area large enough for the camp of each crew, for the dog teams used for transportation to and from the village, and for butchering whatever game is taken.

Each crew has its own tent, which is used as a resting place and "cook shack." The tent is larger and higher than those used for winter camping, measuring about 10 feet square and 6 feet high. The floor has only a canvas over it, if it has that. Snow or ice blocks are used as anchors for the side ropes, and to weight down the lower edges of each wall. No effort is made to protect the tent with snowblock walls, nor is there a tarp thrown over the roof, so the tent is always rather chilly inside. Whaling camps are actually not designed for warmth and comfort, and the men do not use sleeping bags except as a sort of blanket.

Most of the tents in Point Hope whaling camps are warmed by

blubber-burning stoves. These stoves vary somewhat, but most are a homemade metal "box" divided into a burning compartment and a baking compartment, placed up on metal legs. To burn seal oil, chunks of raw blubber (*mitahinagaḳ*) which are kept frozen outside the tent (to prevent loss of oil) are thrown into the stove "as is." In the village, chunks of wood or coal are usually placed inside first and the fat thrown in after they are burning, but on the ice, blubber is used alone. Once lit, it burns very rapidly, with a characteristic sputtering and an even more characteristic black smelly smoke. Most of the smoke leaves the tent through the stovepipe, and the stove heats the tent cleanly. Seal-oil stoves are not used much for cooking in whaling camps, although they are used for this purpose in the homes at Point Hope. Whalers usually prefer gas-burning camp stoves for cooking. Women and young boys cook the food and take care of menial tasks for each crew.

Point Hope Eskimos rely heavily on seal blubber to heat their homes, or else on coal or oil purchased from the store. Some people use wood for heat, both at Point Hope and at Wainwright, but only in combination with other kinds of fuel. Wood, which must be gathered along the beach or bought from "outside," is too valuable to use as a principal heat source. Most of the people at Wainwright gather native coal for fuel.

In former times there were many restrictions during whaling, allowing no use of tents, no cooking, no changes of clothing, and so on. The hunters were then forced to wear their warmest clothing. These restrictions on comfort and leisure also kept the men in their camps and away from the village, and made for greater alertness and organization. In modern times this discipline has broken down somewhat. There is still little use of sleeping bags, although a man may pull one over him as he catches some sleep in the tent or behind a windbreak. They often go back and forth to the village, though somebody always remains to watch for whales day and night. Some other restrictions, such as maintenance of silence when whales are in the area, are still observed to some extent.

During the long chilly night watches it is mostly the younger men, under thirty, who stay awake. They spend much of their time standing around watching the ice and water, walking to keep warm, and occasionally conversing. When murres swim close by they shoot at them with light rifles. Periodically each man sits or sprawls on one of the benches to rest or sleep, but the cold has him up shortly, walking, stamping his feet, or clapping his hands to warm up again. The sun's early morning warmth, after these cold nights, is welcomed.

The quiet of a night watch, or the leisurely activities of daytime, are broken instantly when a whale is sighted or heard. Everyone stops what he is doing, runs to the lead edge and onto high places, straining to spot the rolling back of a whale or watching the activities of another crew which has gone out in pursuit of a whale. If the whale is seen far from a crew that set out after it and closer to another crew not yet in the water, or if an unpursued whale rises close to a camp, the men run for their boats. With an ordered efficiency the boats are manned and launched so rapidly that anyone who delays a moment will be left behind on the ice to watch. There is no shouting, no commotion, as the crews come running in answer to hushed commands and hand signals.

The only men who are absolutely essential in order to chase a whale are the harpooner, stationed in the bow with a darting gun at his right side, and the helmsman, who sits high in the stern and guides the boat. Thus it would be possible for two men to kill a whale if it surfaced close to them. But usually four to six paddlers are seated along the gunwales, stroking hard and yet as quietly as they can. Of these, the only one with a special task is the man right behind the harpooner, who tosses out the sealskin float (*pok*), which is attached to the harpoon line, if the harpoon is thrown.

Whales are pursued generally, but not necessarily, from behind. When a crew closes in on a whale that has surfaced to breathe, they have from five to thirty seconds to get within harpooning distance before the whale submerges and swims on ahead. It may rise again in a few seconds, unless it has filled its lungs. In the latter case it remains submerged for several minutes. The crew paddles swiftly up along the whale's left side, so the harpooner can plunge the toggle iron into a vital spot with his right hand. If the whale surfaces in an open hole in the ice, it remains more or less stationary while it breathes. But in a lead with open water ahead, the whale simply rolls and blows several times in succession as it swims, like a huge porpoise. Occasionally a whale will break the surface without blowing, showing its back above water only once and not coming up in that area again. After a whale dives the men usually remain in their boat in the lead or next to the edge for five to fifteen minutes, awaiting a possible reappearance.

Whales are harpooned with a darting gun, consisting of a metal toggling harpoon with line and float attached, and an explosive "bomb." When the harpoon is driven into a whale, the bomb is shot into the animal by a triggering mechanism. It explodes deep inside. An extra darting gun is usually carried in the bow of the boat, but without the harpoon portion attached. Thus a wounded whale can be "bombed" a second time by the same crew. Several bombs may be needed to kill a whale. Before darting guns were introduced, only the toggling harpoon was used, and a wounded whale was dispatched with lances. At Barrow during the fall of 1964 a whale was taken with the harpoon alone by a man from Wainwright. This man said later tthat he had listened carefully to the old man, Takumiķ, a great whaler, who had taught him the correct places to wound a whale mortally.

Once a whale is killed, its huge carcass is towed by paddled *umiaķs* to the edge of the ice, then pulled up on it with a block and tackle. The whale may be flensed as it is hauled up or, if it is a small one, it may be pulled entirely onto the ice. It may take over twenty-four hours to butcher the monster, and another day to haul all the meat and *maktak* to shore. When a whale is killed, the entire area around the camps is covered with meat and blubber, divided and sorted according to the shares for each crew.

Old whaling boat captains are proud of the number of whales they have taken. At Point Hope one old man said that he had killed twenty-three in his lifetime, and Takumiķ, who died at Wainwright in 1965, had taken seventeen. Each man had aided in the killing of many more.

Fall whaling, done at Wainwright, Barrow, and Barter Island, uses most of these techniques, but is carried on in the open sea with little regard for the presence or absence of ice. I unfortunately had no opportunity to accompany a crew on this type of whaling. In villages other than Point Hope whales are first shot with a "bomb" from a shoulder gun. After this they are approached and harpooned with a darting gun in order to secure them with a line. Crews traveling singly or in pairs make excursions 20 to 40 miles north of Wainwright to pursue whales as they pass close to the land on their way south in the fall. Wainwright whalers are rarely successful at this time, while at Barrow this is the most productive whaling season today.

CHAPTER 12

Harbor Seal

(Phoca vitulina)

Occurrence

THE HARBOR SEAL or spotted seal (*ḳasegiaḳ*) is widely distributed along the coasts of North America and Greenland. It is primarily a boreal and low Arctic species, however, and only in west Alaska, Greenland, and northeast Canada is it found north of the Arctic Circle (Weyer 1962, p. 32). Within most of its range the harbor seal is nonmigratory, but where it extends well into the north (at least in Alaska) there is a seasonal north-south movement, to avoid areas of solid ice cover.

Freuchen and Solomonsen state, for example, that harbor seals are "almost resident" everywhere within their range, and that they appear to be ". . . sedentary in their home waters. . . ." But these authors are aware that along the Labrador coast harbor seals apparently move south into the Gulf of Saint Lawrence when sea ice begins to form (Freuchen and Solomonsen 1958, pp. 38, 56, 176). Whether or not such a movement is to be called a migration is purely a matter of definition. For our purposes this term will be used to refer to the seasonal movements of harbor seals, as well as those of ringed and bearded seals.

Harbor seals do not arrive in the vicinity of Wainwright until late July, and they are not common until late August or early September. The Eskimos do not know where they come from, except that it is somewhere to the south. The closest place where this species remains through the winter is Cape Lisburne (about 200 miles south), where there is apparently enough open water to allow these seals to live even though they do not make breathing holes. It seems highly probable that the large numbers of harbor seals which are found near Wainwright in early fall must come from broad areas farther south than Cape Lisburne.

Harbor seals do not avoid the sea ice entirely, but they are seldom found on or around it. Sometimes they crawl up onto drifting ice pans to bask and sleep, often in small groups. But they migrate north when the sea is largely or entirely open. Eskimos who are hunting walruses or seals amid the summer pack ice occasionally shoot a harbor seal.

They do not come north, however, to remain in the open ocean, but to enter several large brackish lagoons with their broad sandbars. By far the greatest numbers flock into the extensive Kasegaluk Lagoon north of Icy Cape (about 50 miles south of Wainwright). Although they are found everywhere in the lagoon, their most preferred spots are Avak̞ Inlet and Avak̞ River, where they bask in great herds on the sandbars and feed in the protected waters. According to the native accounts there must be thousands of harbor seals in this area during fall.

In addition, a smaller concentration is said to occur north of Wainwright, in Kugrua Bay and Kugrua River (actually Kugroak̞, but misspelled on maps). The seals reach this place in early August. A few are also found in the Kuk River, especially near its mouth or around some sandbars in the mouth of the Mikigealik River. In all these rivers, they may swim clear to the upper reaches where the waters are narrow and fresh. Harbor seals evidently feed heavily on fish. There are large migrations of fish into the rivers at this time of year, which may explain their presence.

Hunting with Boats

Harbor seals are hunted with several kinds of boats, including wooden launches, skin-covered *umiaks*, kayaks, and small retrieval boats. Most commonly, however, the *umiak* is used, because with it the Eskimos can travel long distances as well as hunt effectively. Harbor seals are shot from boats when they are in the water and also while they bask atop sandbars or ice pans.

During *umiak* hunting in the ocean, boats are used to pursue seals swimming in the open water between ice floes. Because they are curious, some will not dive when the motor-powered boat turns toward them; instead they stay on the surface and watch, or submerge briefly and resurface almost immediately. Occasionally, one of these animals will be a harbor seal.

Harbor seals in the water generally resemble ringed seals (*P. hispida*) in that they have a fairly small head and narrow snout. Their skull is wider and more globular, however, and they have a more pointed nose. They are said to be considerably larger as well. Harbor seals are more easily frightened than ringed or bearded seals. For example, one was seen in mid-July by a group of Eskimos hunting from the edge of an ice floe. Like a ringed seal, it was attracted by scratching the ice, but it would come no closer than about 100 yards away. Ringed seals can usually be attracted to within 10 to 50 yards.

In the ocean or in lagoons, harbor seals are shot from boats. When they use an *umiak*, the Eskimos bear down on the seal, trying to get as close to it as possible before shooting. It will start to sink immediately when shot, so the bow man grabs a harpoon quickly after he shoots. As the boat passes the sinking carcass, he throws the harpoon into it, holding the line securely so the animal will not be lost. (More will be said about retrieval in the chapters on seal hunting below.)

Essentially the same method is used when harbor seals are hunted from smaller boats, such as the kayak. However, when the small retrieval boats are used, the Eskimos warn that harbor seals which are only wounded will sometimes regain consciousness and attack the boat or its occupant. One man said that he had hunted them with his kayak as a young man and had never been attacked. After shooting one, he would fasten it alongside the boat and begin to stalk another. In this way he had gotten up to four before returning to his camp (near Avak Inlet).

Another man related that he had once been attacked by a harbor seal he had shot from shore. After wounding the animal, he rowed out in his small *umiahalurak* (a miniature *umiak*) and harpooned it. The seal regained consciousness and attacked his boat, biting at the gunwale and threatening to upset the small craft. An old man on the shore told him to cut the harpoon line, but he decided to try for the shore. Each time the seal ran to the end of the line it would turn and come up to attack the boat. The hunter would fend it off, attempting to stun it with a stick. Finally he got to shore and killed it. Thus, harbor seal hunters are always advised to carry a rifle in their retrieval boats in case such an emergency arises.

A surer method of shooting harbor seals from boats is to approach herds that are lying atop an ice cake or (more commonly) a sandbar. When a herd is sighted, the boats approach it slowly and quietly until they are within shooting range. Then every man takes aim and attempts to shoot a seal. After the first volley the entire herd swarms into the water, usually before there is time for a second shot.

After the seals have reached the water, however, they surface again, so the hunters begin shooting whenever a head breaks the surface. At times there are so many that each man will aim his rifle in one direction and wait for a seal to surface near where his gun is pointed. There may be enough around so that he does not have to move to one side or the other to shoot, and thus he avoids frightening them away by unnecessary movements. This method may also be used from the shore, shooting at seals as they pass. Again, the rifle should be kept at one's shoulder so that as little movement as possible will be made.

The behavior of harbor seals is very different from that of the other kinds of seals found here. They are present in larger aggregations, but they cannot be shot or approached as easily. Whereas ringed and bearded seals are curious and sometimes foolish in their attitude toward man, harbor seals are apparently very clever and wary. This is also the only kind of seal in north Alaska that is aggressive toward man. In fact, it is said that the walrus, killer whale, and harbor seal are the three kinds of animals which are most dangerous to man and should be treated most respectfully.

Hunting from Land

We have already mentioned that harbor seals can be hunted by waiting along the beach for them to swim by. The method is similar to hunting ringed or bearded seals from the ice edge, except that this species is much more wary of movement or approach by a human being. Also, harbor seals will not resurface nearby after they have been shot at, unlike the other seals. Thus, the Eskimos consider them a difficult animal to hunt.

On Saint Lawrence Island the Eskimos hunt for harbor seals when they come into the lagoon near Sivokak during the fall. The men construct blinds out of wood, stones, and whale ribs, which they place 10 or 15 yards above the water line. They are strung out for about a mile along the lagoon's edge. Hunters enter their blinds early in the morning and shoot seals that are feeding in the shallows near shore. Kills are retrieved with snag hooks similar to the Wainwright Eskimos' *niksik* (Hughes 1960, p. 109).

Hunters from Wainwright often shoot harbor seals which are basking and sleeping atop sandbars. This is done especially around Icy Cape, where the largest numbers are found. The best place is the outermost point of Avak̦ Inlet, which has an extensive sandbar. Other bars farther inside the inlet and near Ak̦oliakatat Pass are also frequented by seals. If the tide is high, they are driven away by submergence of the sandbars. This is also true on the sandbars in Kugroak̦ River north of Wainwright, where smaller herds of seals are found.

When harbor seals are stalked on foot, the hunter must approach them carefully, using much the same method as that followed in sleeping-seal hunting on the sea ice. Some of the sandbars are separated from the land, and must be reached by boat. Others extend outward from shore, so they can be reached on foot. A hunter can crawl toward harbor seals in plain sight, as long as he moves slowly and with patience. On Kodiak Island, in southwestern Alaska, I have approached harbor seals to within

5 or 10 feet by crawling toward them while imitating their movements and sounds.

An Eskimo said that in the old days, rather than crawling unconcealed toward harbor seals, the hunters would push an inflated sealskin (*pok*) ahead of them like a shield. This enabled them to get close enough to kill seals with a heavy club. A solid hit on the head would kill them instantly, without making enough noise to scare the rest into the water. Thus a man could crawl from one animal to the next, killing several before the herd took fright.

Seals have been killed in a similar way within more recent times. Ikolivsaak said that he and several other men were once approaching a sandbar with a group of seals on it. They noticed one lone seal lying a considerable distance from the others. When they got close to this young seal, they were surprised to see it crawl fearlessly toward them. Ikolivsaak ran up and kicked it in the jaw to stun it, then picked it up by the hind flippers, swung it over his shoulders, and slammed it sharply onto the ground. To be sure of killing it he broke its neck by bending its head down onto its chest.

This done, the men resumed crawling after the main group. Ikolivsaak was again able to get very near to a seal that was sleeping more soundly than the others, and which ignored him even after awaking briefly. He killed this seal by slamming it in the head with his rifle butt. Then two more seals were shot and killed before they could escape into the water.

Usually nowadays the men crawl to within rifle range, each picks out a seal, and then all shoot at once. In this way every man is likely to get a seal. The rest move so quickly that it is not possible to get off another round before they reach the water. In this kind of hunting it is probably best to aim for the head or neck, as is done in sleeping seal hunting. Men who go spotted seal hunting during the fall probably rely mostly on shooting seals in the water from boats, and hunt seals on the sandbars if an opportunity arises. On one hunting trip during the fall of 1964, two men shot and retrieved twenty-four harbor seals near Avak Inlet. About ten more were shot but were lost owing to sinking. A catch this size is considered very large.

Netting

Although all the old men in Wainwright seem to have netted seals in the past, it is almost never done nowadays. Kaviḳ made a net for harbor seals several years ago and still owned it during the summer of 1966. He spoke several times of his desire to go to Avaḳ and do some netting in the fall, but could not do so because of a part-time job in the village. A few years ago he had netted thirteen seals, which was considered quite a good catch.

No seal netting was done in Wainwright during this study, so we will not attempt to describe it fully here. A process as complex as this must be learned by actual practice before it can be fully and properly documented. We might make a few brief comments about it before moving on.

The best places for seal netting are narrow parts of a river frequented by seals. In such places the net stretches from one side almost to the other. Seals moving up or down the river through these narrows are likely to hit the net, because there is little room to swim around it. About 8 miles inside the Avaḳ River there is such a place, noted as the best netting spot in the region.

At a similar narrows in the Tunalik River, which branches off the east side of Avaḳ Inlet, some Eskimos found excellent netting one autumn about sixty years ago. They were able to catch four to six seals a day with a net made of sealskin thong. By the time they finished netting they had caught about sixty seals in this one place, netting for only part of the day, then leaving the net out to dry for a time before starting again. Rather than attempt to haul all these seals to the village, they went to the coast and brought logs back to build a winter house right where their catch was stored. Then they moved back to Wainwright in the spring.

This points out some of the great changes which have occurred because of larger dog teams and motorized boats. In aboriginal times there were only a few dogs in a team, so it was difficult to transport game from one place to another. This situation made it inconvenient for Eskimos to settle in permanent villages which would require bringing in game from long distances. So they lived in small, highly mobile groups scattered widely over the land. When the hunters made large catches of game, it was more practical to move their goods and families to the location of the meat than to attempt to haul the bulky cache to a distant village.

This situation was greatly altered during the twentieth century, when the people were attracted to large permanent settlements that developed along the coast. Because they now owned larger dog teams and (soon thereafter) motor-driven boats, it was possible to travel far from the village to kill game, and to transport the heavy loads back again. Had they been unable to do so, it would have been impossible to concentrate the population as they have and still maintain a hunting economy.

CHAPTER 13

Breathing Hole
Hunting

Ringed Seal *(Phoca hispida)*
Bearded Seal *(Erignathus barbata)*

Distribution of Ringed Seals

S EALS are probably the most widely distributed, abundant, and reliable food resource available to coastal Eskimo populations. Although some groups live mostly on caribou, fish, or walrus, only the seal is available to them all in fairly large numbers. Patterns of seal utilization have probably been disrupted less than any other, although methods of obtaining seals have been altered considerably, changing many aspects of the total ecology. Long- and short-term fluctuations in availability appear to be less marked in seals than in the other mammals of economic importance to Eskimos.

Along the northwest Alaskan coast there are four species of seals. One of these, the ribbon seal *(Phoca fasciata)*, is so rare that it will not be discussed here. The harbor seal *(Phoca vitulina)* is almost exclusively an open-water species, which is seasonally available and of minor significance to today's Eskimos. The bearded seal *(Erignathus barbata)* is found year round in this region, but is common only among the drifting floes of spring and summer. The ringed seal *(Phoca hispida)* is by far the most

228

important of the seals, occurring in abundance whenever and wherever there is sea ice. This is the species that the Eskimos depend on for winter sealing in north Alaska and throughout much of the Eskimo domain. In the discussions on seal hunting which follow, the ringed and bearded seal are usually considered together, because the habits of both species are very similar and, as a consequence, the methods of hunting the two are essentially identical.

The ringed seal or *netchik* not only is distributed throughout the circumpolar coasts, but may also be encountered far from any shore. Stefansson (1943, 1950) probably overstated his case when he hypothesized the presence of seals, in sufficient abundance to support human beings, anywhere on the ice-covered Arctic Ocean except in places where the ice never moves enough to create open water. Although seals may occasionally find their way to the central part of the Polar Sea, it probably happens only during the summer period of maximum open water, and even then it must be an uncommon occurrence. During the winter it seems unlikely that they are found more than 50 to 100 miles offshore, but the problem evidently still awaits study (see Davies 1958, and Sheffer 1958).

Stefansson did not believe the Eskimos who said that seals do not live far out from the coast, an idea which they still hold strongly today. Eskimos frequently state that seals remain near to the land because the water is too deep beyond 30 to 50 miles. However, depth actually seems to make little difference, because ringed seals do not have to reach bottom to feed. The organisms on which they live are, in fact, found clear to the pole.

In Stefansson's large work, *The Friendly Arctic* (1921), he throws doubt upon his own statements regarding the availability of seals far from shore. As he and his men moved back toward the land, after traveling hundreds of miles out on the ocean ice, they ran desperately short of supplies. When they stopped at leads to hunt for seals, they always saw nothing. Yet Stefansson refused to believe that seals were truly absent. He mentioned that every day or so he saw at least one breathing hole scar, made by a seal breaking through newly formed ice to breathe. This demonstrated to his satisfaction that seals were there the previous fall, and if they were there in September or October, he felt that they must still be around in April (Stefansson 1921, p. 172).

Several pages earlier, however, Stefansson has told how fresh-water ice, formed near the Mackenzie River, was moved 100 miles out to sea by the pressures of wind and current. But he implied that in the same period of time the ice which was scarred by a seal had not moved at all. Indeed, these marks could have been made but 10 feet from shore; or if they were in fact made farther out to sea, the seals could have moved into areas of thinner ice and greater ice movement for the winter period.

Stefansson and his companions spotted their first seal on May 7, when the thaw had progressed so far that they were worried about being able to make it to shore without waiting for the autumn freeze-up. This was far offshore in the vicinity of Banks Island. After May 15, they saw seals in abundance, when they were 75 to 100 miles from shore, in water over 700 meters deep. This disproves the Eskimos' theory that seals shun deep water, but does not help us to learn if they range far out to sea, especially during the wintertime. By the time Stefansson found seals there was no longer much formation of young ice, and open water had spread everywhere among the floes. His conclusion that he had proved the existence of seals throughout the ice-covered Arctic Ocean is open to question.

My own information on this question is anecdotal, to be sure, but it may offer some further hint regarding the occurrence of seals far from the coast in winter. Although they were not par-ticularly concerned with watching for seals, some men who worked on the Ice Island stations maintained by the Arctic Re-search Laboratory reported that they almost never saw seals. This was true in spite of the fact that open water is very often present at all seasons around the edges of the Ice Island, caused by its moving at a different rate from that of the surrounding floes. Seals are attracted by open water, and are easily seen and identified when they appear at its surface, so we can perhaps accept the fact that seals occur only rarely in the areas which the Ice Islands have covered. Since they have moved through great areas of the ocean, this includes a sizeable territory. Also, the fact that polar bears are very rarely seen may reflect absence of food in the central parts of this region.

Another piece of information, drawn from only a single locality, comes from one of the Eskimos who worked during the winter at a temporary sea-ice station some 100 miles offshore from Point Barrow. Although the ice was admittedly flat and fairly undisturbed, this man saw only two seals in seven weeks, despite the fact that he spent considerable time searching for them. An excellent seal hunter, he was raised in northeast Alaska, where most sealing was done at breathing holes. He was able to find only a few breathing holes during this time. Although this refers only to a single ice area, the findings of this Eskimo are of interest.

It is impossible to draw any conclusion from this scattering of information without thoroughly searching the literature and perhaps awaiting further research. It seems safe, however, to assume that ringed seals are likely to occur in abundance only fairly near to the coast. During the winter especially, they probably move in toward shore and away from the regions far out in the sea.

The local distribution of seals is of far greater concern here than their occurrence beyond the Eskimos' hunting range. It appears from the comments of Eskimos that seals are most abundant where there is a strong current, although this conclusion may relate more to hunting methods than to actual numbers of animals. Ringed seals are found, and hunted extensively (formerly at least), in the great unmoved ice plains of central Canada. Closer to the region being studied here, areas of undisturbed ice, such as Peard Bay and the area north of Icy Cape, are "covered" with seals basking on the surface in late spring. Perhaps they move into these areas at this time because it is safer to sun on flat ice, where they are most difficult to approach; however, there are many seal holes in these regions all winter.

Location and Characteristics of Breathing Holes

Seals start to make their breathing holes (*allu*) when the ice is just forming and is so weak that they can break through it with their heads, leaving an open round hole with a few small chunks of ice around it. As the ice thickens beyond about 4 inches they can no longer do this, so they open and maintain holes by gnawing and scratching through the ice. In thick ice these holes have a small opening only about an inch in diameter at the surface. The old head-holes that are left to freeze over will remain as "scars" on the winter ice, little circles of ice chunks on an otherwise smooth surface.

As the ice thickens around an active breathing hole, seals must maintain it continuously, keeping the opening large enough inside to get their heads up into the small ice "igloo" which forms over it. This characteristic dome-shaped or conical formation is created by water sloshing out onto the ice surface each time a seal enters from below. This eventually builds up around the hole and closes over as an ice dome, with a small opening in its top. If a man peeks in through the opening, he sees a large circular hole, filled to the top with water. If the hole has not been used within a few hours, the water will be frozen over. Beneath this surface structure the hole widens into a tunnel through the ice, large enough to accommodate the seal's body as it comes up inside. If the ice is only a foot thick, this is not noticeable, but in 5-foot ice there is a cigar-shaped passage leading upward. Breathing holes of *uguruk*, the bearded seal, are quite large and have a tall ice "igloo" outside.

A single breathing hole, or *allu*, is often used by several seals. Thus if a seal is killed at an *allu*, the hunter can return to it a few days later and hunt again. It is simple to tell whether a hole is being used. Active holes have open water or thin ice inside, either of which looks quite black. Unused holes are gray inside, showing that they are solidly frozen over. If it is difficult to see inside clearly, a small hole can be chipped in the ice to get a good look. It must be carefully closed again with a small piece of ice or snow, so the seal cannot detect any change. Hunters sometimes cannot get a clear shot at the opening, so they shoot right through the ice "igloo" to hit a seal that rises inside. Another way to tell if an *allu* is in use, in late winter or spring, is to smell it. If a male seal (*tigak*) visits the hole, there is a strong musky odor. The female (*aġnasalluk*) leaves no detectable odor, however.

Seal holes may be easy or difficult to find. On flat young ice a recently formed hole shows as an elevated circular platform, obviously caused by water pouring out over the ice and freezing, with a small open hole in the center. If it is a bit older, it is built upward to form the usual irregular dome shape. These domes are easily visible from 10 to 20 yards away, and cannot be mistaken for anything else. In winter ice this type of *allu* is found wherever a crack or lead has been closed with young ice. If the ice becomes rafted, the holes must be abandoned.

In areas of rougher ice, where young ice has been "wrinkled" or "buckled," or along the juncture between winter ice and thin young ice, where there is an abrupt wall above the thin ice surface, seal holes are much harder to find. Sometimes they are absolutely invisible and can only be found by breaking the ice open or using a dog to smell them out. But they may be betrayed by the characteristic buildup of ice outside, caused by water flowing and spraying out when a seal arises inside. If breathing holes become snow covered, they cannot be found without the help of a dog. In areas where the ice moves a lot, this is not necessary, because holes can always be found in young ice without snow cover. In northeast Alaska and central Canada the holes are snow covered all winter, so the people rely heavily on dogs to locate them.

According to Stefansson (1943) each seal has six to twelve holes. He also states that holes which do not become snow covered are abandoned, because they freeze over too fast. This apparently is true in the flat ice plains of the Canadian Archipelago, but does not hold for northwest Alaska. Ice conditions in the two regions are sufficiently dissimilar to explain this difference in behavior.

Traditional Method of Breathing Hole Hunting

Breathing hole hunting is not done anymore in north Alaska except by older men at Point Barrow and perhaps occasionally at Point Hope. It requires a long and very cold wait, with a maximum yield of two or three seals in a hard day's waiting. The modern method of rifle hunting at open water is so much more efficient and comfortable that the young men cannot be persuaded to undertake breathing hole hunting. Old men point out that at an *allu* retrieval is assured once the animal is killed, without the need for a boat or snagging hook. This may be the best hunting method for drift-ice survival in winter, but it requires no small amount of skill, great endurance, and considerable resistance to cold.

Perhaps the most complete description of the prerifle method of breathing hole hunting is that of Boas (1964, pp. 63–74) on the Central Eskimo of Canada: the equipment includes a harpoon, snow knife, piece of fur for a footrest, piece of ice for a seat, two notched sticks for a harpoon rest, and a leather thong to tie the hunter's legs together to prevent them from getting tired on long waits.

The harpoon is a wooden shaft with an iron rod at one end and a stout iron point at the other. A toggling harpoon head is fitted on the end of the iron rod. A line attached to the head is fastened to the harpoon shaft with a slip-hitch, so that it will be held in position until the seal is struck. The stout iron point is used for chopping rough ice and making holes. When the harpoon head is not in place, the iron rod is used to test snow depth and ice strength. The harpoon is set onto the two notched rests, which are stuck in the snow alongside the Eskimo as he waits.

The hunter goes out by dog team to the sealing area, where he takes one dog from the team to find a seal hole. Once a fresh hole is found the dog is returned to the sled. A small peep hole is made to check whether the *allu* is fresh, and is then filled again with snow, with a mark left to indicate its center. Hairs from the man's clothing must not fall into the opening lest the seal smell them and be frightened away. If the snow covering is thick, it is shaved down with the knife. Then it is re-covered with loose snow, heaped around the end of the harpoon, which leaves a mark over the hole when it is removed.

If the seal is expected to return soon (Boas does not explain how this is judged), the hunter stands on a small piece of skin and waits. When the seal comes, he drives the harpoon heavily into the hole, striking the animal in its head or neck. He immediately plays out the line, playing the seal like a hooked fish. The harpoon shaft may disengage from the line and fall onto the snow, or it may be pulled down through the hole and help to impede the seal's struggles. The hole is enlarged so that when the seal comes back up in the hole it is easily killed. Then the hunter pulls it out onto the ice.

If the Eskimo expects to wait all day or even longer, he will build a snowblock windbreak. In its lee, and alongside the hole, he places a block for a seat, and a small piece of skin for a footrest. His knees are held together by a thong. A snow knife lies at his right and the harpoon, on the two rests, at his left, while the line is coiled in his lap. The hunter pulls his left arm out of its sleeve. When a seal is heard breathing, the arm is carefully slipped back again, the coil and harpoon are lifted, and the seal is struck. One or two seals are usually killed in a day.

Modern (Rifle) Method of Breathing Hole Hunting

The contemporary Eskimos of northern Alaska no longer use harpoons for breathing hole hunting. Instead, they have devised a method of hunting with the rifle. This may or may not be more efficient. The principal disadvantage of shooting seals at their *allu* is that no line is attached automatically, so the killed animal may sink or drift away with the current. The advantage is a sure kill, without the risk of having the line break or the harpoon head slip out. As we noted above, few Eskimos do any breathing hole hunting nowadays, but most of the men over fifty years old have done it and know a great deal about the technique. The information below was gathered by hunting at breathing holes with an old Barrow man, who had used the method all his life.

Hunting at seal holes can be done at any season, but is most common in late fall and winter, when there is no open lead nearby and before seals have started sleeping atop the ice. It is possible to hunt seals this way when there is a lead nearby, but most men would rather hunt along the open water than sit for hours at a breathing hole. If a man has no means of retrieving a seal shot in the water, he can probably find an *allu* nearby. Seals always maintain these holes, because they will need them when the lead closes. Because this type of hunting demands a long quiet wait during the coldest parts of the year, the hunter must be dressed for maximum warmth. This means the best skin clothing, preferably caribou parka and pants, with fur boot liners and warm gloves. Down clothing could be used instead, but it is not preferred. The Eskimos say that after a long cold wait caribou-fur clothing is easier to rewarm.

The equipment required is not elaborate. The rifle should be fairly heavy—30.06, .264, .243, or a similar caliber—but if these are not available a .22 caliber rifle or a pistol would probably suffice. In addition to the weapon, the hunter wears his white cloth parka-cover so that the seal is less likely to see him beside its hole, an *unaak* to hook the seal and to chop the ice (a metal hook will suffice if it has a handle at least 1 foot long), a knife, and a rifle case. The rifle is usually carried in a homemade canvas or sealskin case, which is slung on a strap that passes across the upper chest and allows the rifle to hang horizontally across the small of the back. The case may have loops on it, through which the *unaak* can be slung. Many hunters carry their *unaaks* behind them by simply draping their arms across them to hold them against their backs. These methods of horizontal carriage and straps across the upper chest are much preferred by the Eskimos, because they are comfortable and are easily used with bulky clothing.

The breathing hole hunter arises early in the morning, usually before sunrise, and walks or rides his dog sled out onto the ice. The only advantage of using a dog team is that he travels faster and can bring game home more easily. But dogs must be put 100 yards or more from the seal hole, lest their noise frighten the animals away.

Arriving at an area where he knows the location of seal holes, or where he will probably find some, the hunter leaves his dogs and locates a hole that is being used and that he feels would be a good one at which to hunt. This done, he checks first to see where the seal will rise in the *allu*. This can be discerned by look-ing at the ice "igloo" to see if it is narrower at one end than at the other, and if the small opening to the outside is a bit off center. The narrow end, or the area nearest the opening, is where the seal's nose will be. A seal hole seldom tunnels vertically through the ice, so its angle may also be noted. In this way, when the Eskimo shoots, he will aim for the seal's brain and angle his rifle a bit to correspond with the angle of its body. In actual practice it is very difficult to miss as long as the rifle is held straight over the hole or the ice "igloo," so this trick is less important than some of the others. It is important, however, never to touch the hole while examining it. This would leave a scent that seals can detect immediately.

Next, the hunter checks the ice surrounding the hole. If it is snow covered there is little problem, and he can stand directly on the snow if he wishes. But if there is little or no snow on the ice, the seal can detect the dark shadow of his feet from beneath and will not rise in its hole. In this case the hunter must sit or stand on ice blocks, snowblocks, or a little wooden stool. These stools are only about 8 to 10 inches high, with three tapered legs, and have a triangular seat not over 10 inches across. If he stands, he will face the hole, holding his rifle in his hands. If he decides to sit, the hole will be at his side and his feet will be propped off the ice on a block of ice or snow. In this way he is seated with his legs straight out, supported above the ice by two blocks or one block and the stool, with the rifle laid across his legs.

The *unaaḳ* is stuck in the snow or laid on a small ice block, within reach of the hunter. If it is laid directly on thin ice, its shadow can also be seen from below.

These preparations are made quickly. The actions are almost automatic, because the hunter knows what he must do, and the more quickly he finishes, the better his chance of being quiet by the time a seal approaches the hole. Three factors determine where the hunter sits relative to the hole: (1) if the sun is shining, his shadow must not fall across the opening; (2) he must not sit upwind of the *allu*, but should be at a right angle, or better yet, downwind of it—he also tries to avoid facing the wind; (3) he should try to sit in a position so that the seal will not see him through the small outside opening. This factor is less important than the other two, and if the opening is larger than a twenty-five-cent piece, a small chip of ice or snow may be placed alongside it (with a gloved hand) to block the seal's view. This is probably more important if the hunter is standing up while he waits.

If ice blocks or snowblocks are to be used, they should be at least 6 to 8 inches thick. Once these blocks (or the wooden stool) are in position, the hunter seats himself. He covers the seat and footrest with pieces of fur or cloth (e.g., his gun case) to prevent heat loss and moistening the clothing. The rifle is laid across his legs, on the upper part of his boots, where it is less likely to compress the clothing and cause chilling. The muzzle faces toward the hole, but must not hang over where the seal might see it. And a bullet is in the chamber, with the safety off. He has placed himself so that he is close enough to reach out over the hole easily, but not so close that he will be seen. Now he will wait.

The greatest difficulty of the wait is not boredom or cold, but being unable to move for hours at a time. In some ways it may be easier to stand, because then the legs are not held straight out in front. This sitting position stretches the leg muscles and makes the seat seem unbearably hard after an hour or so. Alaskan Eskimos very often sit this way, however, so they are accustomed to it. The Canadian method of sitting with legs bent would appear to be the more comfortable. During the wait a man should move only his arms and head. A Barrow man smoked continuously during a four-hour sitting. But no move can be made that could transmit sound to the ice below. With this in mind the seat blocks or stool must be set very firmly onto the surface so that no movement or rocking is possible.

In the silence of the sea ice, and after the boredom of waiting, the arrival of a seal is startling and exciting. It may come as little as fifteen minutes after the hunter begins, but normally it will take an hour, and often several hours. Canadian Eskimos have been known to sit by an *allu* for twenty-four hours, if they are very low on food. The first sign of a seal's approach is pulsation of the water in the hole, and then some water flows or sprays out through the opening. This is caused by the seal's rising in the narrow tunnel below, forcing some water up ahead of it. The seal may also scratch and clean the hole briefly. During this time the Eskimo is perfectly still.

Shortly thereafter the seal takes a short breath. It is only smelling the air and checking for any sign of danger. The hunter does not move a muscle. He knows that this will be followed by another brief silence, but that the next breath will be a deep one.

The first deep breath, the third part of the seal's appearance, differs from the short scenting breath. It is deeper and longer. The hissing sound is loud enough to drown out other noises. Now the hunter must move. If he is standing, he spreads his arms enough so that his clothing will not scrape noisily and moves the rifle over the hole. If he is seated, he also spreads his arms and moves them to the rifle, being careful not to turn his parka ruff into the wind if it is strong enough to hiss through the fur. When the first breath stops, the hunter freezes.

On the second breath, if the hunter is standing, he holds his rifle over the hole and shoots. If he is seated, he may also move his rifle to the hole and shoot, but he probably will only raise it to a vertical position, holding the thumb of his upper hand on the trigger. On the third breath he quietly moves the muzzle over the hole and shoots. Breathing holes are sometimes beneath ice overhangs, inside a "roof" of upward-buckled young ice, or in other hard-to-reach places. In such cases it may be necessary to fire with the rifle held at an angle, or to shoot through the ice itself. Usually the overlying ice is too thick, so a shooting hole is made with the *unaak* and concealed with a thin sliver of ice. As long as the rifle is of a fairly large caliber, it can be shot directly through the thin ice of the "igloo."

When a seal is shot in the head, it does not go limp immediately. It usually quivers and shakes briefly before relaxing. The Eskimo therefore tries to enlarge the hole quickly and hook the seal with his *unaak;* then he holds it until all movement stops. It is then pulled up into the opening so that a slit can be made through its lip and a line attached to it. The line is held beneath one foot while the hole is enlarged enough to withdraw the seal. If the ice is thin, the carcass may be carried away immediately by the current, so it must be hooked very quickly. In thick ice the seal is held inside the vertical tunnel by its own buoyancy, preventing its being swept away. Only a few seals will sink during the winter.

In actual practice the northwest Alaskan Eskimos rarely hunt a seal hole alone, preferring to use a partner. One man sits and watches the hole, while the other walks around him in a large circle, 50 to 200 yards away, to frighten the seals away from their other holes. In this way the maximum wait should be an hour, and if a seal does not show up by then, they look for another hole to hunt. If a man is alone, he can also go around and either touch all other holes he finds or urinate on them. This frightens the animals away, forcing them, he hopes, to use the *allu* he has chosen to hunt. This probably is done only on smooth young ice, where there is a chance of locating most of the holes.

The Eskimos say that it is best of all to get a group of three to eight men, and find a breathing hole for each of them to watch. In this way a hunter can be stationed at each of the holes in a given area, minimizing the seals' chances for escape. This technique has been used in recent years only when there is no open lead. It enables each of the men to get a seal during the day's hunting. The same method is known in Canada, where even the women and children may wait at holes just to scare away the seals that come up, forcing them eventually to a hole where there is an armed hunter. Techniques such as these are most effective on very flat ice during the spring thaw, when every *allu* can be found.

Calving Den Hunting

During the winter some breathing holes are deeply covered by snowdrifts. In such places ringed seals may enlarge their breathing holes and excavate a hollow beneath the snow large enough to crawl out of the water and rest inside. In northwest Alaska, seals also open holes into hollow places beneath warped or piled ice, and use these for dens. Seal dens may be 7 or 8 feet long. They are often used by more than one seal, perhaps up to six or eight.

Both kinds of den serve as a shelter for the birth and early rearing of seal pups. The silvery-furred babies must be born on top of the ice, and are unable to swim for some time afterward. So they must be kept in a place safe from predators. Foxes and bears can locate snowbank dens by scent, and will break into them to get the baby seal. Eskimos in the eastern Arctic are able to find the dens, and they take the young and often the female as well. In northwest Alaska most dens are in rough ice and cannot be found.

Adult female seals were seldom shot in open leads during the winter of this study. The Eskimos attributed this to the fact that females tend to stay beneath the ice more, and inside dens in heavy ice farther out beyond the leads. The young are not born until April, so this does not explain females' using dens as early as January. Seals are rarely seen at all in open water from March until the end of May, because they stay beneath the ice and shun the leads. After this time they appear both in the water and on top of the ice.

In former times Alaskan Eskimos used dogs to help locate seal dens. When the dog began to smell around a drift or other likely spot, it had probably found a den. The hunter would then make a little peep hole through the snow, so that he could look inside and watch the open hole, by which the seal would enter. When the water in this hole began to shake and pulsate, the hunter knew that a seal was about to rise. As soon as its head came up inside, it was shot through the hole made in the outside wall. The old man who described this technique had taken ringed seals this way in his youth. No mention was ever made of the breeding habits of or use of dens by bearded seals.

Eskimos in central Canada take their dog teams out over the snow-covered sea ice and ride the sled while their dogs smell out the cavities below. When the dogs find a den and stop, the Eskimo runs quickly from the sled and jumps on the snow, bursting through the roof. He hopes to cut the seal off from its retreat into the water. The female often escapes, but the pup is slow and may not even be old enough to swim. He pulls it out by a hook on a wooden shaft and kills it by stepping on its head or kicking it in the head. The pup might also be tied to a thong and dropped into the water, with the hope of attracting the female so the Eskimo can harpoon it (Boas 1964, p. 74).

Summer Breathing Hole Hunting

During the spring and summer, breathing holes are enlarged by melting and by the seals themselves, so that they can climb out onto the ice to sleep and bask in the sunshine. By June these round tunnels through the ice are encountered frequently. They seem to become larger in diameter as the thaw progresses.

Summer breathing hole hunting can be done by methods similar to those used in the winter. On Baffin Island the Eskimos use a harpoon, which consists of a long steel shaft (shoulder high), rounded at one end, and wound with sealskin line at the other end to form a handle. A toggling harpoon head is socketed onto the rounded end, with a sealskin line attached to it. In order to hold the head in place, the line is wedged into a metal loop on the harpoon shaft. When an animal is struck, a tug on the line releases it, freeing the toggle-head.

The man sits near the hole and waits for a seal to appear. He lays the harpoon shaft across his knees, with the head facing toward the left (for a right-handed man), holding the line in his hand. He must keep his feet flat and still on the ice, lest the seal hear a noise and be frightened away. If the hunter stays about 2 feet from the opening, the seal will not see him when it rises in the hole. He rests as he waits, putting his elbows on his knees, watching the water in the opening. When the surface starts to rise or pulsate, he raises the harpoon, so that he can plunge it into the seal's neck as it breaks water (Wilkinson 1955, p. 90).

This is done on occasion by the Wainwright Eskimos. Seals are quite often seen during travel over the sea ice, their heads seeming to appear out of the solid ice 50 to 200 yards away. If the hunter moves very fast, he might get a shot at them, but usually they dive too quickly. There is no point in waiting for them to return unless he has plenty of time, because they will not reappear in the same hole for quite a while.

If a man decides to wait at an *allu*, he follows the same method as that described above for harpooning. It is best to sit or stand just a few feet away, so that the surface of the water can be watched. When it begins to pulsate, the seal is rising in its tunnel; so the hunter raises his rifle and aims where the seal will come up. As soon as its head breaks the surface, he shoots. Then he hooks the dead seal with his *unaak* or pulls it out by hand.

Another method of rifle hunting is described for the eastern Arctic: A hunter stations himself near a series of breathing holes, sitting on the ice with his rifle and harpoon. When a seal surfaces in a nearby hole, it becomes curious about the man sitting on the ice nearby, and rises higher and higher in the hole, trying to get a better look. When the seal shows itself most clearly, the hunter shoots it in the head or neck. Then he must jump to his feet quickly, dropping his rifle and grabbing his harpoon. The seal begins to sink through the hole and down into the sea immediately after it is shot, so he must reach it as fast as possible. He runs for the hole, harpoon poised and ready to throw as soon as he gets within range (Wilkinson 1955, p. 86).

An old man who moved to Wainwright in 1966 from the village of Point Lay is said to use a method of snaring seals in their *allu* during the early summer. This method was never described accurately, but involves the use of a fairly small (index finger-length) barbed iron hook attached to a strong line. The hook is fastened loosely to a kind of crosspiece which is imbedded into the ice walls of the tunnel. The hook protrudes into the passageway, so that when the seal backs down from the hole, it will catch in its flesh. The seal sets this hook as it struggles to get free, and the barbs will not tear loose from its tough skin. The line must be attached firmly to the ice at the surface, but the method of doing this was not described. This man was said to have used the technique with success during the early summer of 1966.

About twenty years ago, Eskimos from Dolphin and Union Straits in the central Canadian Arctic started using three-pronged barbed hooks for catching seals at their breathing holes in wintertime. The hooks are made from 6-inch spikes or quarter-inch iron rods, the last 2 inches or so bent around and barbed. Three of these hooks are bound together to form a grapnel, and 2 or 3 feet of line or chain is attached with a swivel hook. A piece of stout wood is fastened to the other end of the line to act as a toggle or anchor.

> With six or a dozen of these hooks the Eskimo is ready to go winter sealing. Taking his best sealing dog on the end of a long line he sets out from camp. In fifteen or twenty minutes the dog will have smelt out the first seal hole. The Eskimo, by cutting away the snow covering the hole, finally exposes a small opening an inch or two in diameter. This opening is enlarged enough to drop the hook through into the water. The hook is then set by letting it hang to the extent of its chain, the wooden toggle across the top of the hole acting as anchor. The hole is then covered with snow and a snow block marker erected near it [Joss 1950, pp. 43–45].

Any disturbance of the toggle reveals to the returning Eskimo that a seal is hooked. In midwinter, hunters average two seals per day by this method. When the days lengthen, up to twenty hooks may be used, with a daily catch of ten or twelve seals. Two or even three seals may be impaled on a single grapnel, one on each hook (Joss 1950, p. 45).

Seal Netting

Seal netting is seldom practiced today at Wainwright. The older men have all netted seals on the winter ice. They often say that they would like to teach it to the younger hunters, but this is apparently never done. Netting requires physical hardship and danger. Though it can yield productive results there is little incentive to face these discomforts. It demands, first, that the men go out on the ice during the darkest nights of winter, with no more than the light of the moon's last quarter. The darkness greatly increases the danger of being unknowingly rafted away from land on an ice floe. And second, it requires that men stay outside watching and working the nets in frigid cold, without a chance to sleep or warm up.

Seal netting was supposedly introduced to these northern people by other Eskimos long ago; before this, all sealing was done with harpoons. By the time Murdoch visited Barrow, in 1881, seal netting was an important activity (Murdoch 1892, p. 252). There are two basic methods of netting, vertical net and horizontal net. The horizontal type is probably the easier to learn and to set up.

A vertical seal net (*kuvraḳ*) resembles a fish net hung beneath the ice. Each mesh is measured to be the circumference of a man's head. Three holes are chopped through the ice, one at each end of the net and one in the middle. The net lines are run down through these holes. Nets described by Wainwright Eskimos are not long, up to perhaps 20 feet for a large one. Weights are hung along the bottom edge of a net, one at each end and one in the middle for a long net, at the ends only for a short net. If there is no open lead offshore, the nets are set beneath smooth ice surrounded by hummocks, which shield the net from current. Perhaps this is done because seals feed on organisms that congregrate in places with little current, or it may be simply to assure that the net hangs straight down in the water.

Murdoch (1892) describes a method in which the net is set parallel to a lead, about 100 yards from its edge. The netters attract seals by scratching the ice, walking around, or thumping the ice with a heavy stick similar to the methods used today for open lead sealing. Seals moving back and forth from the lead will blunder into the net and become entangled. Wainwright Eskimos say that up to forty seals can be taken in a night with vertical nets, but half that number would be considered an excellent take. Around Bering Strait nets are placed close to shore where seals pass around the ends of points or headlands (Nelson 1899, p. 126). Similar nets are used by Greenland Eskimos.

The horizontal net (*igalik*) is used when there is no open lead nearby. It capitalizes on the seals' use of breathing holes. During the day a hunter finds breathing holes and remembers their location. Then in the dark of night he returns to an *allu* and chops four holes in the form of a square around the hole. With a long pole and line, the four corners of the net are attached through these holes and pulled up to the ice, leaving a gentle sag in the middle over the entrance to the breathing hole. The seal swims to the hole close to the surface and does not hit the net, but in diving it goes straight down, becomes tangled, and drowns. If a seal is caught and pulled out by enlarging the breathing hole itself, the opening can be covered with snow, with a small hole in the center. Other seals will return to it after this is done. Netting at breathing holes can be carried on well into the spring and early summer.

There is a traditional belief that in the blackness of night a strange creature with the head and face of a human may become entangled in a seal net. Old-timers advise that a netter should feel the head of his catch, and if it has long hair, he knows it is a "merman." Should this happen the hunter must lick his palm and then touch the creature with that hand. If this is done properly, he may catch many seals that night. A man at Icy Cape is said to have caught one and released it as he was told to do, but he did not do the necessary palm licking. A short while later he looked into his net and saw human hair in it. Reaching down to investigate, he was nearly pulled into the water by the angered creature, because he had not done what was required. (For another version of the "merman" see Spencer 1959, pp. 261–62.)

CHAPTER 14

Ice Edge Sealing

Ringed Seal *(Phoca hispida)*
Bearded Seal *(Erignathus barbata)*

Occurrence of Ringed and Bearded Seals

IN THIS CHAPTER we will discuss one of the most important subsistence activities of northwest Alaskan Eskimos. Ice edge sealing occupies a substantial part of the Eskimo year, from November until July or August at Wainwright. It is a very productive activity. At Point Hope a single man may kill two hundred ringed seals and a few bearded seals in one winter. A crew of hunters at Wainwright can sometimes take twenty seals in a summer's day. Ice edge sealing comprises a highly complex technological and behavioral system. It was brought to florescence by the introduction of firearms. This, in turn, caused a series of changes in aboriginal technology and in the patterns of human ecology in northwest Alaska. The importance and complexity of this activity is reflected in the volume of material which must be presented in this chapter.

Ringed and bearded seals are found in north Alaskan waters throughout the year. The ringed seal or *netchik* is a truly Arctic species, found throughout the domain of coastal Eskimos. It remains common as long as sea ice is in the vicinity. The bearded seal, or *uguruk*, winters in the north to some extent, but is much more common during the warm months. Both species undergo marked seasonal fluctuations in numbers and in patterns of availability.

When the sea ice begins to fragment and open in late spring and summer, ringed and bearded seals increase in number. Although it is difficult to evaluate the magnitude of fluctuations in the population of ringed seals, it is certain that the number of bearded seals increases manyfold. In fact, both species undertake a migratory movement of impressive magnitude, usually during the month of July. Although much ice edge sealing takes place in the midwinter months, the period of maximum productivity derived from this method occurs during the migration. For the sake of later reference, therefore, let us briefly consider these movements as they took place in the summer of 1966.

Ice edge sealing is seldom done by Wainwright Eskimos during the month of June, because seals spend so much time sleeping on the ice that they are not often seen in open water. By middle or late June, the Eskimos begin to anticipate the seal migration and the great abundance of ringed and bearded seals that can occur during their seasonal northward passage. The migration is said to occur predictably around the first week in July. Because it passes quickly, hunters must be lucky to be on hand at the right time to take advantage of it. One man spoke of shooting thirty-five seals on a single day during the migration, far beyond the number which can be killed at any other time of year. Another man said that he and several others had gotten about one hundred in a day during a migratory movement. Sea-ice conditions at these times have a great effect on the ability of Eskimos to hunt the seals effectively.

If the sea ice breaks up early, and the floes are widely scattered when the migration passes, hunting will be relatively poor. If there is a wide lead offshore, it will not be as good as when the lead is very narrow. The best hunting conditions occur when the seals are forced into small areas where Eskimos can get good shots at them. Ideally, there are a few scattered openings, so the seals are forced to move from one to the next as they swim northward. Fortunately for the hunters, seals migrate when there is a strong south or southwest current helping them along. The same current pushes the ice ashore at Wainwright. Thus it is quite likely that the seals will find only a narrow lead or a series of openings, perhaps only a shore lead, as they pass along this coast.

Migrating ringed and bearded seals, especially the young ones (*ḳairalairaḳ*), prefer to move in close to the beach and follow the shore lead. If the landfast ice is still extensive and solid, they usually can reach the shore lead by swimming landward through the open water created by strong currents flowing out of the Kuk River. From there they move northward past Wainwright, following close to the beach. This makes them quite vulnerable to the Eskimos, who watch the open water constantly during early July for signs of the migration.

During the summer of 1966, conditions were ideal for hunting when the migratory seals arrived. On July 2, a lead began to open offshore, but current flow was so strong from the north that none of the people felt that seals could move northward against it. During the next few days the ice opened and began to break up, and a wide shore lead was formed. During the "night" of July 8–9, an increasing number of ringed seals, all moving northward, were noticed by hunters 20 miles south of Wainwright. The next day they steadily increased in number, moving consistently toward the north. Forerunners of the migration reached Wainwright that evening.

The behavior of these animals was very different from that of nonmigrating seals. If the hunter's position was stationary (i.e., on grounded ice or on land), he saw each seal come up only once in the same place; then it would reappear a short distance to the north before moving out of sight on succeeding appearances. At other times, when seals were not migrating, they seldom showed this consistent movement, and would rarely swim along on the surface as the migrants did. In fact, during this period, nearly every seal that was seen had its nose pointed northward, and continued moving in that direction even while it surfaced.

During 1966, the heaviest migration took place on July 9 and 10. On the evening of July 10 a breeze arose from the north and the seals appeared to have stopped temporarily. The next day a somewhat smaller number of seals were moving along in the open water (during these days there was little open water except for the shore lead), stopping again when a northerly breeze blew in the evening. From this date through about July 20 there was a slowly diminishing movement from the south, varying according to the current and time of day. Little movement took place as long as there was a north or northeast wind, perhaps because this slowed the prevailing south current. It was also stated that seals move at "night" more than during the day, because they prefer to stop and bask in the sun while it is warmest.

Most of the comments above refer to the ringed seal, because there seemed to be a much less distinct movement of bearded seals at this time; but during early July bearded seals quite suddenly became common, whereas few had been seen previously. Apparently, they usually move north rather slowly, following along as the ice breaks apart and drifts with the current. During this year the movement took place offshore and was not seen from the shore as the ringed seal migration had been. The Eskimos state that bearded seals usually move north along with ringed seals in early July, but this would not involve such a large number of animals, and most likely would take place well offshore.

Both species of seals are quite dependent upon the presence of sea ice. When the ice recedes to the north, they follow it. Once the ocean is completely free of ice, maritime hunting activities almost cease. Once in a great while, seals are sighted in the Kuk River, where a small number remain through the summer. But during this study, not one seal was seen in the ocean after the sea ice was gone. During the fall, seals move southward again with the expanding ice pack. At this time of year there is no impressive concentrated movement, however. By the time the Eskimos begin ice edge hunting in late fall or early winter, the seal population has apparently reached a level that will remain more or less constant until the following spring.

Winter Hunting Apparel

Ice edge sealing goes on during the coldest winter months, when the thermometer may stand at 30° to 50° below zero for weeks on end. During these clear and cold days of midwinter light easterly winds hold the lead open offshore, aided by the abiding current. It is at this time that intensive hunting for seals is done along the edge of the open lead. Since seal hunting requires that the men remain out for three to eight hours at a time, or more when the days grow longer, they must wear some of their warmest clothing.

In most cases this means that fur clothing is used. Dress for these activities most closely approaches the traditional types, but a completely native outfit is never worn today, and there is considerable variation in the degree to which it is approached. As winter fades into spring, fur clothing is replaced by cloth articles purchased from "outside."

Perhaps the most important element of the hunting outfit is footgear, and in this the Eskimos are closest to maintaining the aboriginal pattern. During the cold months, and until the time when the ice and snow are melting, essentially one type of boot is used for all sea-ice activity. This boot, called *ugurulik* in Eskimo, is made of caribou and bearded sealskin. The most important part of the *ugurulik* is its sole, which is made from tough, waterproof bearded seal hide with the hair removed.

The soles are prepared by first cutting two oblong sections from a skin. The hair is removed with scrapers. After softening them in water, the soles are crimped with flat-nosed pliers around the toe and heel, so they can be bent up to meet the caribou-skin uppers. If the skin has been allowed to rot outside during the summer, the hair can be pulled off by hand, and the sole will be dirty white in color. If prepared by scraping, it will be black. Light-colored soles are preferred, probably because they are easier to make. Skin soles are occasionally equipped with a simple tread, made from a strip of bearded sealskin about ½ inch wide and 3 inches long, sewed across the toe and heel of each boot.

The boot uppers are made from the skin of caribou legs, one boot requiring the skin from all four legs of an adult caribou, preferably killed in the fall when the fur is in prime condition. When legs are skinned for boot construction, care must be taken to cut the skin as far down around the hoofs as possible, and to slit the skin down the front of the forelegs and down the back of the hind legs. The pieces are then laid out in the snow to freeze flat and are taken home to dry inside the house. In two or three days they are dry, and are ready to be scraped on the inside until they are soft and pliable.

The four legs are then sewed together, with the two foreleg skins forming the boot sides, one hind leg forming the rear, and the other hind leg extending down the front and over the instep. The boot upper, which reaches to just below the knee, is then sewed onto the boot sole, with a strip of ringed sealskin between. Most sewing is now done with nylon dental floss, which is waxed and very strong. Braided sinew was formerly used, and is still seen in the better-made boots, especially when waterproof seams are desired.

Uguruliks are quite warm because of their caribou skin uppers, and are preferred for sea-ice hunting because the soles are waterproof. Sea ice, especially young ice of several days to two weeks' formation, is always wet on the surface. This moisture would spoil caribou-skin soles, to say nothing of the fact that moisture soaking through the boots causes discomfort and possible freezing of the feet. In former years skin of the white whale was used for boot soles. It is said to be tough and waterproof, much the same as bearded seal. Around the boot top there is a thin strip of cloth, through which a drawstring is usually threaded. With this the boot can be closed tightly around the top, preventing snow from getting inside and sealing out water should the wearer fall through the ice.

Boot soles are liable to be the first part to wear through, especially if the wearer is forced to walk many miles over the ice, as he would be if he should drift away on the pack. In this case there are ways of providing emergency repair. Eskimos frequently mention that pieces of sealskin or bearskin can be tied or simply frozen around the outside of the boot sole, giving extra warmth and protection. In former years, bearskin with the fur turned outside was tied to the bottom of the boots for silent stalking of game. Sealskin is used with the fur inside for emergency boot soles.

Inside the *ugurulik* there is always an insole. In modern times this is often a felt insole bought from the native store; but some men prefer to make their own from caribou skin, which is probably much warmer. In order to prevent these fur insoles from sliding out of place, they are made with the toe end turned up and over and sewed along the sides. If fur insoles are used, the man will probably wear cloth socks. Usually several pairs of wool socks and perhaps a pair of felt "booties" are worn inside the *ugurulik*.

In cold weather, however, hunters prefer to wear caribou skin "socks," called *aleksi*. These are boot liners made entirely of caribou skin with the fur inside, unlike boots, which have the fur outside. Caribou socks are made in two lengths. The usual length reaches 6 or 7 inches above the ankle, but some extend to the top of the boot. These are exceedingly warm and comfortable, and offer several advantages over cloth socks. Should body or outside moisture soak cloth socks, they will freeze into the boot and be difficult to remove for drying. Caribou will not freeze into the boots, and is warmer than cloth when it is damp.

Several writers have noted that Eskimo boots sometimes appear to be very tight fitting. For example, Thornton (1931, p. 35) says that some young men are ". . . very particular about the fit of their clothes, especially as to the smallness and snugness of their boots; consequently it is to be feared that they sometimes suffer from cold feet." It is more probable, however, not that the boots themselves are tight but that the ankles are small. There is a tendency to taper the boots at the ankle so they will hold more tightly to the foot. This makes them rather difficult to pull on, but there is always ample room once the feet are inside. The Eskimos state emphatically that footgear must not fit tightly, and that room must be allowed for several pairs of heavy socks or for caribouskin boot liners.

Uguruliks, with their sealskin soles, are not nearly as warm as the other important kind of boot, which has caribou-skin soles. These boots are called *tuttulik*, a word derived from *tuttu*, which means caribou, just as *ugurulik* derives from *uguruk*, the word for bearded seal. The tops of both kinds of boots are made the same way, and, in fact, a given pair of uppers may be switched from one type of sole to the other. *Tuttulik* soles are made from the toughest skin of the caribou, which is dried and scraped, but has the hair left intact. They are cut so that they wrap around the foot, with the hair inside, and join the boot upper, which has the hair outside. There is no need for insoles with *tuttulik* boots, since thick fur already lines the bottom. Cloth socks are all that is usually worn inside, since they are far warmer than the *ugurulik*.

Ringed sealskin is sometimes sewed over the soles of these boots, also with the hair turned inside. This not only makes them usable on the wet sea ice, but also adds to the warmth and durability of the soles.

Tuttuliks are normally saved for use on inland hunting and trapping excursions and for ice fishing, where maximum warmth is required and where the boots will not get wet. Very rarely a pair of *tuttuliks* with sealskin covers sewed onto them will be seen in use on the ice. Since most winter ice hunting lasts only a single day, Eskimos feel that *uguruliks* are warm enough. Caribou-sole boots are also seldom used for walking around in the village, because they wear through more readily than bearded seal.

Both types of boots have the soles treated with seal oil, particularly those which are used for sea-ice hunting. The oil protects them from moisture and apparently helps to prolong the life of the sole. The only other important boot care is drying, a very essential factor in maintenance of all skin clothing. Care is taken each night to hang up the boots, socks, and other damp clothing, often on lines strung from the ceiling of the house. This is something that nonnatives tend to neglect, whereas the Eskimos are aware of the additional safety and comfort of dry clothing, as well as that skin clothing rots quickly if it is not kept dry. Caribou fur sheds easily and must therefore be treated with care. If gloves or socks become very damp while a person is traveling, they can be dried by tucking them inside the belt or shirt to dry against his own warm skin.

Next in importance to footgear is the parka (*atigi*). During the winter months the traditional caribou-fur parka is used by the great majority of sea-ice hunters. There are only a small number of men who use fur parkas of mouton or badger skin bought from fur dealers in the lower "forty-eight." Fur parkas are always worn with the hair inside and the skin side out. Trim around the hood is generally wolverine (*Gulo luscus*), which sheds frost easily and does not fill with snow when it is windy. Caribou fur is occasionally used for the trim, and is said to have the same qualities as wolverine except that the hair sheds more readily.

The fur parka is never worn without a cloth cover (called *atigiluk* or *ḳategani*) over it. This cover is usually made from a single layer of cloth and is intended to protect the skin and seams. It is usually white, so it also serves as camouflage against the background of snow and ice. Little extra warmth could be derived from it. Occasionally the hood of a parka cover is made so that it can be drawn over the wolverine-fur trim, protecting the man's face from blowing snow or concealing the dark fur from game during a stalk.

Caribou-hide parkas are exceptionally warm and light, and do not require a lot of clothing underneath them. Typically the Eskimo hunter prefers several light layers of clothing to a single heavy one, and therefore several cloth shirts are usually worn. Some men wear a light nylon jacket or down-filled vest beneath the parka. The hood is always made to fit rather tightly around the face so that wind cannot blow into it; even so, a hat is usually worn inside any parka.

A knit stocking cap is preferred by some Eskimos, while others prefer hats with visors in front. Some of the knit caps are of a type that can be drawn down over the face, with openings for the eyes, nose, and mouth. A few men use knit ear bands rather than caps. The main interest appears to be protection for the forehead, which is not covered by the hood, and the ears, which are sometimes chilled by wind entering the hood.

Traditional Eskimo clothing, especially that worn by groups in the eastern Arctic, included the use of both an inside and an outside parka. Rudiments of this are still seen at Wainwright, where several men use caribou-hide parkas with the hair turned outside, worn over the inside fur parka. This double parka is actually too warm for most outdoor activities which are undertaken nowadays, so it is used only in severe weather or for fishing during periods of intense cold.

In earlier times there were more activities that required a long patient wait, and generally more activity outside during cold weather. Notable among these were hunting at breathing holes, seal netting, and whaling. For these pursuits it was quite essential to use the warmest clothing. Wainwright Eskimos also mentioned the former use of "undershirts" made from fawnskins, as well as pants with the fur turned inside. These are no longer made here.

Some men own manufactured down parkas today, but they

wear them usually in warmer weather when fur clothing would cause overheating. For warm temperatures it is also an advantage to have a zipper in the front to facilitate cooling. In the spring-time men begin using cloth and down clothing as soon as the temperatures are in the 10° to 30° above zero range. There is also some use of muskrat, fox, badger, or caribou-skin parkas with the fur outside, a cloth lining inside, and a zipper in front. These are considered to be fancy parkas, intended mostly for sale to visitors, though they are occasionally worn for hunting.

Birdskin parkas were formerly made by northwest Alaskan Eskimos, but are no longer existent today. The older men re-member having used them and sometimes talk about having one made because they are so warm. In the region south of Point Hope, cormorants (*Phalacrocorax*) were killed and skinned in order to make long bulky parkas, which could be used with the feathers turned outside. Loon-skin parkas are also described, made entirely from the neck skin and feathers of (probably) the com-mon loon (*Gavia immer*). They were said to be waterproof and very warm. Some birdskin parkas were undoubtedly made to be worn with the feathers turned inside and with another parka out-side, as was done among other Eskimo groups.

Outside the parka, especially if a wind is blowing, a rope or cloth belt (*tafsi*) is sometimes worn. This belt prevents wind from blowing up under the parka and holds the man's warmth inside. It also affords a place to carry a hunting knife. The belt is some-times trimmed with a tail of wolverine fur and is called *pamiuktak*, derived from the word for tail. Belts were apparently used more in the past than in modern times. Nowadays they are much more in evidence at Point Hope, where they are sewed into the cloth parka cover, than at Wainwright.

Men occasionally use chin protectors, made from the tail of a red fox (*Vulpes fulva*) or Arctic fox (*Alopex lagopus*), or from folded strips of caribou hide. This piece of fur is provided with strings at each end, and is tied outside the parka hood and around in front of the chin and mouth. It becomes frosted quite rapidly in very cold weather, so it is rotated periodically, bringing dry fur to the front. Once the entire piece is covered with frost it must be thawed and dried or else removed and replaced by a fresh one.

The only face protection besides this and the use of knit stocking caps that pull down around the face is that provided by growing a mustache. As fall and winter approached in 1964 many of the men began to grow mustaches, which they kept at least until the spring warming trend. This is done for two reasons. First, moisture from the breath collects in the mustache hairs, which prevents it from contacting the skin of the upper lip. It is more comfortable during extremely cold weather to have the mustache collecting frost than to have the exposed flesh chilled constantly. Second, according to the Eskimos, fresh ice which forms on the mustache can be used for water, especially in an emergency situation. Indeed, while they are hunting or traveling, they often lick off the small beads of ice at the corners of the mustache.

Whether it is inherited or acquired, Eskimos show a hardy resistance to cold. It seems at first that their resistance is much greater than one's own, but the difference becomes significantly less as time passes. One of the most convincing evidences that Eskimos are fairly insensitive to cold is that they seldom wear anything more than cloth "work" gloves, even in midwinter. To be sure, they often clap their hands together or slap them against their sides to keep warm, but they will nonetheless stay out in minus 35° weather all day with only these light gloves on.

In cold weather such as this, and up to around zero, most of the Wainwright hunters wear two pairs of gloves. Rather than have a tight fit by placing two identical pairs together, they will either mix sizes, placing the larger on the outside, or turn the outer pair inside out, which increases its internal dimensions. Thus two pairs of gloves can be worn without the discomfort caused by a tight fit.

However, certain individuals prefer some heavier type of glove or mitten. When it is very cold or they are on the trail, many hunters use more than just cotton gloves. Some men are able to obtain leather gloves with wool inserts, but these are not in common use because they wear out too quickly and do not offer sufficient advantage over cloth gloves. At least one man has five-fingered gloves made from summer-killed caribou, which has very short but warm hair. These appear to be very useful and warm but few people own them, probably because they are so difficult to make.

Mittens (*aaḳadik*) are made from animal hide, and are of several types. The first is a typical mitten design with a thumb and no fingers. These are easily made, even by men, but are not popular because they must be removed in order to shoot. Caribou mittens with the fur inside are usually so warm that gloves are not worn inside them. Thus, removing the mittens to shoot is out of the question in cold weather, since the hands are moist and the flesh would instantly freeze to the trigger. The second type of caribou mittens is called *tikelak*, derived from the word *tikiḳ*, which means index finger. These mittens have a thumb and index finger, with the other three fingers together in one space. They are made from summer skins, and are excellent for hunting, since it is possible to shoot without removing them.

Fur mittens are sometimes made with the hair turned outside, but this is not common. They are made from caribou, seal, dog, wolf, or bear skin, and are designed with only a thumb and a hand space. Included with these we should mention army surplus mittens which are available from mail-order dealers. Although these types are occasionally carried, they are infrequently used, since cloth gloves are usually sufficient.

If gloves are worn inside, one would expect that mittens could be removed in order to shoot; but it is less advisable to remove the mittens than simply to go without them. The hands and gloves become warm and moist inside the mittens, and if suddenly exposed to the outside cold for several minutes, the hands become very cold and even numbed to the point of uselessness. It is therefore wiser to wear gloves or mittens with fingers so that the hands are adjusted to the temperature at which they will be used.

Each type of fur has qualities that lend themselves to particular uses. This is taken into account whenever mittens are made. For example, sealskin and polar bear skin are waterproof, and make the best mittens for use on the sea ice; however, no polar bear mittens and very few sealskin mittens are used today at Wainwright. Hunters will occasionally make mittens of dog skin, which is preferred to caribou because it is resistant to moisture and wears very well.

Mittens with very long fur outside are sometimes used for fox trapping, because they are the best for brushing snow over the trap set to conceal it. One such pair was made by Titaliḳ from the skin of grizzly bear (*Ursus arctos*) one day while he was in his trapping camp. These mittens appeared very large due to the long fur outside, and were, in fact, fairly large inside; so cloth gloves were normally worn with them. The fur was turned inside around the wrist.

Fur mittens not only are used when smoothing snow over fox traps, but they also have several uses beyond keeping the hands warm. Most fur mittens are hung around the neck by a harness so they can be removed without danger of losing them. They are kept available by leaving them hung on the harness and twisting them together behind the back to keep them out of the way. In the case of Titaliḳ's bearskin mitts the harness was made long enough so that they could be placed on the ground under the wearer for a seat. This could be especially useful on the young sea ice, where seal hunters must often sit on the wet surface to shoot.

In addition these mittens could be used as improvised boots in case of emergency, such as drifting out on the sea ice and subsequently wearing holes in one's boots. The wrist flap is simply turned out so that the mittens become quite long. Then they fit over the feet with caribou "socks" on. Besides emergency uses the mittens can also be used as boots for stalking caribou or polar bear when the snow makes noise underfoot. Titaliḳ also uses these mittens to warm his face during cold weather.

The junction between the top of any kind of mitten or glove and the sleeve of the parka is often loose enough to expose a man's wrists to the cold air, especially when he is driving a dog team. Frostbite on the wrists is almost as common as on the face. In order to prevent this, wristlets are made from fox, caribou, or other types of fur. They consist of a piece of skin folded in the middle so that the fur is outside on the top and bottom, and then sewed together at the ends to form a bracelet of fur. Wristlets are used only in very cold or stormy weather.

Just as aboriginal fur mittens have largely been abandoned in favor of cloth, so have fur pants given way to heavy cloth pants of various types. During precontact times seal, bear, or caribou-skin pants were worn, sometimes with a caribou-fur liner inside. The use of fur pants, and other fur clothing as well, has diminished in spite of the great advantage of wearing it. Perhaps most important is the fact that fur clothing, especially caribou, is much warmer than any manufactured type available to the Eskimo. This is particularly true in emergencies, such as when lost or drifting out on the sea ice, where clothing may be the only heat source for many days. It is still the practice of some older men to carry extra fur clothing out on the sea ice in case they drift away.

Fur parkas are usually designed so that the wearer can pull his arms inside and then turn the sleeves inside out or plug them with mittens. The neck and waist of the parka can be tied closed with rope to further prevent heat loss. Caribou parkas and pants are also invaluable for use on sea ice because of the buoyancy of caribou hide, which acts as a life preserver should the wearer fall through the ice. Caribou skins being carried on the dog sled or in a boat have also been used for this purpose. Fur clothing is also more waterproof than cloth, and water is more easily removed in case of an emergency. This is especially true of sealskin sewed with sinew, which is impervious to water.

In spite of these advantages, caribou-skin pants are worn only in the coldest weather and sealskin pants are used, by the few men who own them, only in late spring or summer on wet ice. The most popular types of heavy pants in Wainwright are various kinds of army surplus pants with wool liners, Air Force flight pants, and down "insulated underwear" pants with cloth overalls outside. Again the preference is for several layers of clothing under the heavy cloth pants. When fur pants are worn, however, only underwear or a pair of light cloth pants is worn underneath.

I owned a pair of heavy caribou pants while staying in Wainwright, but only wore them once before reverting to heavy cloth pants. There are two reasons for this: the caribou pants proved to be too warm even for use in minus 30° weather, and the leather restricts movement to a much greater degree than heavier cloth pants. In fact, it is apparent that the Eskimo habit of bending over stiff legged, which is still present today, probably came about as a result of the confining skin pants.

The warmest type of cloth pants besides down are the blue flight pants. Many individuals in Wainwright own these, but often prefer other types because the flight pants are quite heavy and usually have a zipper down each leg, which admits the cold.

Those without zippers are coveted and frequently used, especially on the sea ice where it is damp, because they are fairly waterproof. Sealskin and bearskin pants, as well as other items of clothing, will be dealt with in a later chapter.

Preparations for the Daily Hunt

The Eskimo hunter always takes note of the weather and ice conditions the night before he goes seal hunting. During the winter and early spring months he is especially concerned with the presence of an open lead offshore. If he feels that there is a good possibility for open water the next morning and that the weather conditions will probably be favorable, he will plan to arise before dawn the next morning. In December this means that he can sleep until around 9:00 A.M., while in late March or early April he must be up by 3:00 or 4:00 A.M. Through the spring and summer months it is always light, so he can go out whenever he feels like it. Somewhat regular hours are always kept, however, so he is likely to wake up between 5:00 and 9:00 A.M. On awakening, he listens for the wind. If it is rattling the chimney and buffeting the wall, he probably will not even get out of bed; otherwise he checks the smoke from the chimneys and the other indicators of wind speed and direction to see if the ice will be favorable. He also looks over the ocean ice to see if there is an open lead, easily visible even before dawn if there is a steam fog or water sky. Temperature alone is rather insignificant, except that he might use it to help predict the weather. Only if it is 45° below or colder, or if there is a chilling wind with temperatures less than minus 30°, will he be deterred.

Once he is awake the hunter's primary concern is to reach the lead edge before the other men. If he eats, he does so hurriedly. He, or his wife, makes tea, and some of it may be poured into a thermos bottle to be carried along. When he goes outside into the stinging cold, it is probably still dark. He pushes his sled into position beside his dogs, staked on individual chains. If he owns a small retrieving boat, he lays a caribou skin on the sled, then lashes the boat securely on top. To do this he strings a rope back and forth across the boat and through a series of rope loops along the sides of the sled. The ropes are pulled very tight. Inside the *umiahalurak* ("little umiak") or kayak, whichever he owns, he places his rifles, *manak* (snag hook), and other equipment.

Men who do not own boats place a caribou skin on their sleds, and on top of this they lash one or two rifles (inside cases) and an *unaak*, or ice testing rod. Other gear is carried inside a cloth sled bag that hangs from the upstanders. For all seal hunters this includes ammunition, a large knife, a seal-pulling harness or *uniutak*, and some extra gloves. He may decide to stiffen the line of his snagging hook by dropping the float in his sled bag and unwinding the line as he travels, dragging it along on the ice. He may also put in a pair of binoculars or a telescope. Men who do not carry a boat seldom carry a stove. They take a thermos bottle full of tea, or just a cup from which to drink tea brewed by another hunter. Everyone usually takes some food along, such as pilot bread, pancakes, or a can of sardines. Those who carry a boat generally have a camp stove and a "grub box" with bread, pilot bread, seal oil, and other food inside. These men are also likely to carry extra equipment which they probably will not need—extra clothing, an axe, an extra rifle, and so on—because these things might come in handy and are easily put into the boat.

In the late spring and early summer, when men still travel out to the open lead, they are less apt to carry food with them. At most, they take a thermos of hot tea and a few pieces of pilot bread. In summertime rifles cannot safely be tied on the sled itself, because they are likely to become soaked while crossing puddles. If a boat is taken, they can be put inside, usually atop a piece of skin or cloth for padding. Otherwise, the hunter carries his rifle slung across his shoulders, inside a case to protect it from moisture.

Once he has loaded his sled, which he does in only five or ten minutes, he brings the dog harnesses and lines from the hallway. The harness line is attached to the sled with a shackle. A two-pronged (one-pronged in the case of Point Hope) snow hook is also attached and plunged firmly into the hard snow to anchor the sled. The dogs begin to bark and howl with excitement while he lays out the line and untangles the harnesses. The Eskimo silences them as much as possible, lest their noise give haste to other hunters making the same preparation.

An exception to this rule of competitiveness is the hunting partnership, in which two men habitually go out hunting together. This may be a stable partnership, where the men almost always hunt together; or it may be a day-to-day arrangement, in which the pairing changes for the individual each time he goes out, but includes a small number of usual partners. Certain individuals generally go with one of their partners whenever they hunt, while others will go out alone but join up with someone when they reach the lead edge. Men who decide the day before that they will go hunting together usually leave the village at the same time, one having gone to wake the other and tell him that he is preparing to leave. Occasionally two men will travel on the same sled, sharing equipment and dogs. This is not favored, however, because the dogs run slowly with the load, and the men are forced to hunt too close together.

Once an Eskimo has his dogs in harness, he waits for nobody. As soon as the dogs feel the sled jump forward when the snow hook is lifted, they run eagerly for the trail and out onto the ice. This is where the man with fast dogs has the greatest advantage, because he will probably be first to reach the lead. Since the behavior of seals is such that they are most abundant in the dawn hours, and diminish quickly once the shooting starts, the "early bird," indeed, gets the "worm."

Winter ice edge sealing consists of traveling out to the edge of the flaw ice and waiting near the open water for seals to appear close enough to shoot. During early summer this kind of open lead sealing lasts only until the landfast ice is broken up and rotten, and the pack ice is so scattered that there is no longer a single open lead. After this, ice edge sealing continues, but hunting places must be reached by boat rather than with dog teams.

During late spring, before the landfast ice breaks up, seal hunters reduce their teams to five or seven dogs when they travel out to the lead. Not as many dogs are needed to move over the slick wet ice or snow, and fewer dogs are easier to handle. A little retrieval boat is usually taken along at this time, both for retrieving seals and as a safety precaution in case the weakening ice breaks away.

Some of the hunters, especially when the ice becomes quite rotten, prefer to walk out on foot to hunt along leads or cracks.

They may push a dog sled along in order to minimize the labor of hauling killed seals back to the village. Retrieval boats are not usually taken out this way, however, so these men prefer to find narrow cracks or open holes. In such places there is a better chance of getting close shots so that killed seals can be retrieved with snag hooks.

At this time of year, after whaling is finished and before the ice breaks up, there is actually not much open lead sealing. Eskimos prefer to hunt for seals sleeping atop the ice instead. There are not many seals in open water until the ice breaks up into drifting floes, so it is not considered worth the effort to go to the lead.

After the landfast ice becomes rotten or is gone, there is no longer any open lead sealing as such, because Eskimos now concentrate on hunting with boats. Some of this is done directly from the boat, which we have called *umiak* hunting. But during the course of *umiak* hunting, the crews often land on the ice and shoot seals that surface near the edge. This is almost exactly the same as open lead sealing, except that a boat is used to reach the hunting place and a crew of five to seven men all hunt close together. Because there are many seals (especially during and after the migration), this ice edge hunting is much more successful than winter or early summer open lead sealing.

Movements of the Eskimo hunters involved in summer ice edge sealing are very different from those which are observed during wintertime. In the first place, the entire attitude of the men is less hurried and businesslike, because they need not worry about the onset of darkness or about chilling due to excessive cold. There is also no need to arise early and work doggedly to reach the open water ahead of the others. Time for hunting in the winter is always limited, as is the amount of ice edge available. By contrast, there is more open water during the summer, and hunters have the time to scatter widely over many miles of ice edge. There is no need to compete vigorously for chances at seals.

When the ice breaks up so that seals are hunted by *umiak*, the amount of hunting space is limitless. Competition among *umiak* crews for walrus and bearded seals certainly occurs, but there is no need to compete for ringed seals. Crews do tend to remain well apart from one another, but this is intended to maximize everyone's chances for good hunting. Nobody seems to care very much if one crew reaches a particular hunting place first, because the others can always go somewhere else.

Use of Dog Teams

Before we discuss the techniques of ice edge sealing, we should briefly consider some aspects of the use of dog teams for hunting on the winter ice, since they have become an essential tool of the modern Eskimo seal hunter. On the northwest Alaskan coast, dog teams range in size from three to sixteen dogs, with a good-sized team considered to be nine to eleven. This differs sharply from the situation sixty years ago and earlier, when, as a rough estimate, the average was closer to four or five. The increase is facilitated by a more affluent economy in recent years, in which less of the game (and perhaps as much game is taken per individual as in the past) is used by humans, so more can be diverted to use for dog food. Men therefore accumulate larger numbers of dogs for prestige, increased mobility, and in recent years for racing. Whereas the optimum number of dogs, for mobility per amount of food consumed, might be set at seven (G. Ray Bane, personal communication), many individuals own and use twice that number.

Thus the individual hunter who is able to outdistance his fellows in what is now competitive seal hunting can shoot more seals, transport the load home quickly, and regain safe ice more rapidly if danger should arise. He also ranges farther in all hunting activities, and is able to use some hunting methods, such as chasing caribou herds, to greatest advantage. Dog teams which can cover 30 miles in two and one-half hours (in dog races at Wainwright), or travel 100 miles to Barrow in twenty-four hours, are much more efficient than the old-time teams that plodded along behind a woman who led them.

Changes have also occurred in the types of sleds being used and the methods of construction. At Point Hope the light "basket sled" is used on the ice, a type which can be pulled very fast and adds little weight to already heavy loads. The more bulky flat sled or "scow" sled is used at Wainwright and Barrow for ice

Several typical buildings at Wainwright, Alaska. Large drifts behind the dog sleds were formed by winter storms blowing through the village. The chain in the foreground is used as a line along which the dogs are tied.

The *umiak* is the main vehicle for summer travel and hunting. In winter it is stored on a wood rack near the owner's house.

An Eskimo hunting seals at an open crack. Several seals have been sleeping on the ice bordering the crack, as is shown by the markings in the snow.

An aerial photograph of a lead as it is beginning to open, near Barrow, Alaska. This type of fracturing is apparently more common in this region than the simple fracture.

Several hunters have followed this newly frozen crack through the rough ice in the background. Areas like this often have many breathing holes of ringed seals.

The edges of floes are eroded by wave action in summer, causing dangerous overhangs like the one pictured here.

The sea ice in late June: slush and water fill every hollow. In the distance a water sky darkens the overcast, clearly revealing the trend of an open lead.

Brash ice forms owing to grinding along the edges of leads and floes. It appears deceptively safe, but many disintegrate when stepped on.

An irregularly shaped and topheavy floeberg such as this is dangerous, because it may fragment, disintegrate, or roll over at any time.

A weathered floeberg grounded offshore from Wainwright in July, 1966. Large solid formations such as this are fairly reliable stopping or camping places.

An *umiak* outfitted for walrus and seal hunting. Note the harpoon,
rifle, and binoculars held in thongs along the gunwale, ready for use by
the bow man. Gear and clothing are under the canvas, and two bearded
seals are lying crosswise in the middle of the boat.

During cold and stormy weather, a hunter's face and his parka ruff are liable to become frosted by condensed breath and windblown snow.

An *allu*, breathing hole, with characteristic buildup of the ice surrounding the opening.

A ringed seal *(Phoca hispida)* in an open lead presents a small, moving target.

A seal hunter awaiting his prey at the edge of a lead far offshore from Wainwright. Note the sharp contrast between safe gray ice and unsafe black ice along the ice apron.

The *azigaun*, seal lure, is made from seal claws fitted on a wooden handle. Nowadays a large knife is usually substituted as an effective lure for seal hunting.

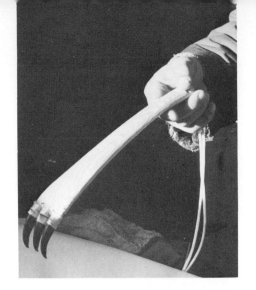

Two Eskimos covering an *umi-ahalurak̦* with a new bearded seal skin.

The *unaak*, ice tester, can be placed on thin ice at the edge of an ice apron while the *manak* is tossed to retrieve a seal. The dark streaks indicate places where seals have been pulled out of the water.

Returning to the ice apron after retrieving a seal with an *umiahalurak*. The man at the left spreads his legs wide to prevent his breaking through the thin ice. He will use the hook of his *unaak* to draw the boat up onto the ice.

The *umiaḥaluraḳ*, open retrieval boat, lashed to a sled to be carried to an open lead.

During midwinter's intense cold, hunters sometimes put up a tent for a tea break, warming it inside with a portable stove. In this instance, frozen seals and a sled are used to secure the tent ropes. The sled at the left carries an *umiaḥaluraḳ*.

An *umiak* being used for whaling at Point Hope.

After the shooting ends, unharmed walruses may be reluctant to leave the area. Eskimos seldom shoot these animals unless they become very aggressive.

A hunter standing atop heavily piled polar ice,
scanning with binoculars in search of polar bears.

After all wounded animals are killed, the hunters sharpen their butchering tools. Lines tied to the walrus in the foreground prevent it from slipping into the water.

Large knives, *ulus*, and sharp axes are used for butchering walrus.
Two or three men usually work together on each animal.

hunting. This type consists of two heavy wood runners 8 to 12 feet long, made from 2 × 8 lumber. The bed is 24 to 36 inches wide, made of 1 × 4 planks. These sleds are sturdier on the rough sea ice, but are also heavier. Both types use iron-shod runners, which slide fairly easily over the sticky salt ice. Hardwood runners are used for travel inland during the cold months, but steel is used on land in the spring and fall. In the rear of the flat sled, or *ḳamo-tigiluuraḳ*, there are two upright stanchions which the driver stands behind and holds. This kind of sled was introduced in fairly recent times, evidently by Rasmussen and his Greenlander companions on their great trek across the Arctic.

Sleds used in Barrow during the latter nineteenth century were much shorter on the average, running up to 8 or 9 feet long (Murdock 1892, p. 357). They apparently were seldom taken onto the ice. These sleds had runners of ice-coated mud, whale bone, or ivory. The latter was considered best for sea ice use (Brower 1963, p. 46). The entire complex of dog technology deserves a thorough study while it is still actively carried on, both as to historical changes and as to the economic and cultural influences of recent changes.

Locating Open Water

We mentioned earlier that before a man prepares to go out on the ice for ice edge sealing, he checks over the ice for signs of open water. He must know not only whether or not an open lead is present, but how far offshore it is, what size it is, and in what direction it trends. Using several indicators of open water, he can guide himself to the best hunting places as he travels toward the lead, before the water itself is visible to him.

During the clear cold months of winter the best sign of open water is the heavy "steam fog," or *puġuroaḳ*, which forms due to contact of salt water with air that is over 14°C below the water temperature. In midwinter the difference in temperature can reach as much as 40°C (Zubov n.d., p. 33), causing a thick bank of fog to hang over the surface of a lead. Streamers of *puġuroaḳ* may also rise from small open cracks or holes.

Steam fog can occur only when the intensely cold surface air is overlaid by warmer air (temperature inversion), which limits convection. The surface of winter sea ice acts like the land, causing intense back radiation of heat, thereby lowering the temperature of the air stratum near the surface so that it is colder than the air above. The inversion layer is sometimes shown in cold, calm weather by the leveling off of smoke from the chimneys of Eskimo houses at a point 50 to 100 feet above the roofs. Under these conditions, evaporation from open water causes supersaturation of the air; i.e., fog is produced. This can occur not only over open leads and cracks, but over newly formed ice as well (Zubov n.d., p. 33).

Steam fog usually reveals itself as a very dark haze right along the horizon and not extending far above it. At times it resembles a prairie fire along the distant horizon, with a curtain of black smoke instead of white. Hovering above the steam fog there is always a "steam cloud," stretching out over the lead for miles. The cloud probably forms along the conjunction of cold surface air and the warmer air overlying it. The steam cloud is usually all that is visible when a lead is in the far distance, perhaps 10 to 20 miles away. On clear days it is obvious to the Eskimo that there will be no clouds in the sky except over a lead. Then a long stretched-out cloud or series of clouds hovering just above the horizon certainly means open water.

Steam fog also rises from small holes or cracks, but is much harder to detect from a distance than fog rising from a wide lead. A series of thin streamers rising out over the ice, usually disjointed but obviously in a line of some sort, means that a narrow lead or crack has opened. Widely spaced steam clouds or plumes of fog may simply indicate holes which have opened or have not closed over completely when the ice comes in to cover a lead. These phenomena are very difficult to describe, unless they are demonstrated right on the ocean ice. To some extent this kind of knowledge must come from experience; it eludes description because it almost amounts to a "feeling" that is slowly acquired. But a typical steam fog is immediately apparent to anyone who sees it after it has been described to him. It is easy to mistake a rather dark haze, which always occurs on the horizon of the sea ice in winter, for steam fog. The error will be made as long as one does not carefully watch for the ever-present steam clouds hanging above the low-lying fog. In fact, the cloud is sometimes seen when no fog is visible at all, usually on clear days with a near-zero temperature.

Puġuroak̦ is visible in varying degrees according to the light. Fortunately, it is visible as long as some light is available, either sunlight or moonlight. Steam clouds cannot be seen at night, but the fog shows as a deep black separating the gray ice horizon from the dark-blue sky. Sometimes it is easier to see steam fog at night than during the day, depending upon the relative position of the observer, the sun, and the fog. When a man travels from Wainwright out to a lead paralleling the shore, the morning sun shines from behind him and onto the bank of fog to the north and west, revealing it as a black cloud of steam. Toward the south and the southwest, however, the fog appears as faint white steam, because the sun is shining more or less through it. From a position between the sun and the fog it is therefore much easier to discern the steam fog than from a position where the fog is between the observer and the sun. When one attempts to sight the trend of a lead or the position of open water, it is much simpler and more reliable, then, to do so in directions facing away from the sun than in those facing toward it.

This bears on one of the very important uses of steam fog by sea ice hunters. When the sky is clear, the only warning of ice breaking away between the hunter and the shore is usually the appearance of steam fog. At times of potential danger he watches carefully toward the shore again and again to assure that he is not caught on the far side of a widening crack. If the sun shines from behind the resultant steam fog, it might be difficult to detect the crack, so the danger of being set adrift is greater. Steam fog can also be a guide for crossing a lead, since areas where it is not rising are indicators of solid ice. It also serves as a guide to the hunter before he goes out onto the ice and as he approaches the lead edge, because from it he can trace the position and outline of cracks, leads, and openings.

However, *puġuroak̦* can be a hindrance because it cuts down visibility at the lead edge, affecting the ability to see game and to reconnoiter the size and trend of a lead. The Eskimos say that drift-ice survivors have great difficulty because of the darkness if they drift away during midwinter. The far (seaward) side of a lead is usually its downwind side, so the thick steam fog drifts out over the pack, darkening the sky both "day" and night.

Steam fog is present throughout the winter months, so it is an important factor in sea-ice activity during this season. When the temperature is 30° or 40° below zero, there may be only 20 to 30 yards visibility out over the lead. This makes it difficult to spot seals until they are very close to the edge. In addition, the visibility is further reduced whenever the hunters start their camp stove to make tea, because the breeze carries the heat out over the water, which for some reason increases the fog. The same thing is caused by the heat of a rifle when it is shot; a man who shoots downwind at a seal may not know for fifteen seconds if he killed the animal because it is hidden in a thick line of steam. This effect even carries over to the smoke or heat of a village, such that steam fog downwind from the village rises more heavily than anywhere else along a lead.

Clouds are another important factor in locating open water and navigating on the sea ice. During the dark winter months they are a deterrent to navigation, because they reduce the already dim light even further. Equally important is the fact that the uniform white of the ice, snow, and sky blends into a confusing nothingness when the light is diffused by clouds. This condition, sometimes called a "whiteout," eliminates all shadows so there are no ways of discerning relief on the ground. On such days or nights a man's eyes must strain in order to walk or pick a trail for the dogs, much less hunt for animals. Cloudy skies which occur increasingly often after March or April create conditions for snow blindness and necessitate the use of sunglasses.

But in spite of the fact that clouds often create difficulties for the sea-ice hunter, they can also be of service to him. When skies are overcast, a "sky map" is often present. The sky map is a reflection in the clouds of the color of the surface beneath it. On overcast nights a sort of sky map hangs over a city, caused by its lights reflecting in the clouds. From this, highway travelers can tell the location of a city even though it may be out of sight over the horizon. For the Eskimo hunter, patterns of sea ice, land, and open water are revealed by different-colored reflections in low uniform clouds.

For instance, during the winter sea ice reflects as dull white and the snow-covered land as a brilliant white. A traveler can trace the trend of the coastline far ahead of his position by reading the sky map. If he is out on the ice, he can tell from it which way he should go to reach the land. The most pronounced type of sky map, however, is the water sky, a dark streak in the clouds reflecting an open lead below. If the clouds are high, a larger area is reflected in the sky map, and more information regarding the position of cracks, trend of a lead edge, and distance across open leads can be discerned. If the water sky is overhead, open water is very close by, and if it is lower toward the horizon the water is some distance away.

The Wainwright people watch for a water sky, which they call *kissuk*, after each strong offshore wind. Before the blowing snow has cleared, they can see how high the dark reflection appears overhead and know how far out the open lead will be. They always hope that the *kissuk* will show its dark hue almost over the village, indicating that the lead may be less than a mile offshore.

For the practiced eye it is possible to read much from a sky map regarding the ice and leads. Stefansson was able to tell smooth ice from rough ice surfaces by the colors of a sky map, although the Eskimos do not mention this skill. Smooth ice is said to be reflected as a uniform white color, while hummocky areas give a mottled effect. Freshly frozen leads reflect as black ribbons across the sky, nearly the same as open water. If they become covered with new snow, they reflect as unusually bright pathways in the clouds.

The water sky is of value to the Eskimos in planning their hunting activities. It is used, whenever present, to tell if there is any lead near the village. This is especially important when a lead first opens or if it is closing, because the hunter can decide if it is worthwhile to go out and in what direction he should travel for the best hunting places. A water sky may show that the lead is very far offshore in one direction but close to shore in another. If the lead is closing, this is revealed by narrowing of the dark band in the sky. The widest parts of the *kissuk* indicate where it is likely to close last or where open spots remain.

As a hunter approaches the lead he watches the sky map to see where there are points and bays along the edge, so that he can decide which area might be the best hunting spot and the safest ice. If he goes too far out or by some misfortune gets caught on the far side of an opening lead, the first warning may be a dark streak across the sky between his position and the land. The sky map can also show in which direction to travel to find the narrowest part of a widening lead, and may even reveal ice bridges that still remain across the water.

In late summer, after the pack ice is carried out to sea, Eskimos watch for a bright whitish reflection near the horizon. This is "ice blink," the reflection of sea ice which is out of sight beyond the horizon. Thus, the sky map occurs as an aid to navigation, irrespective of temperature, throughout the year. All that is needed are low clouds in the sky overhead. The sky map is an important aid to sea-ice travelers and hunters whenever it is present, because it enables them to see what is beyond the horizon. It lessens the difficulty of all kinds of sea ice travel, because it partially alleviates the trial and error factor in navigation.

There is one more phenomenon that Eskimo hunters use as an aid to finding open water and navigation on the sea ice. This is *iññipkak̦*, the peculiar refraction or "looming" that is usually present along the ice horizon on clear days during the warm season. Its appearance is difficult to describe, although it is so unique that it is easily recognized. It consists of a white refraction that bulges or hangs above the horizon like a curtain of brilliant white fog, slowly changing in size and shape throughout the day. It resembles the white reflection that shimmers along the surface of a highway on a hot afternoon. When it is very warm and sunny, *iññipkak̦* appears to be close to the point of observation, so that one cannot see clearly for over a mile out on the ice. On cooler days it is far in the distance.

Iññipkak̦ can be used in navigation, because it makes things visible which are over the horizon. Thus distant open leads, which are always difficult to see, even from the tops of the highest ice piles, show clearly as dark streaks in the refraction. A man who becomes stranded on the pack may be able to see the brown color of tundra refracted into sight by the *iññipkak̦*. Eskimos can even pick out somewhat distorted but clearly visible tents along the beach far down the coast, looming above the horizon on a warm summer day. *Iññipkak̦* is not often very useful, however, because it usually reveals landmarks that are very far in the distance, while it distorts those close by.

Locating Seals along an Ice Edge

One might expect that in a uniform environment such as a length of regular coastline the day-to-day distribution of seals would remain fairly constant, and that they would be more or less evenly scattered throughout a given area. This is far from being true. For reasons that seem largely unfathomable, they are always congregating and moving from place to place. Therefore, Eskimo hunters are much concerned with predicting the occurrence of seals on particular days or in certain places. In all hunting there is an element of luck or randomness involved in finding game. The Eskimos try to minimize this random factor by applying their collective knowledge of animal behavior and by exchange of information on the movements of the game.

Information from hunters who report what they have seen during their activities on the same (or preceding) day is quite important to the seal hunters. In fact, one of the first things they do before going hunting is to find others who have recently returned and talk to them about the location and movements of game animals. For example, during the summer congregations of seals around the mouth of the Kuk River occur quite unpredictably. If a hunting crew returns to the village reporting many seals in that area, other groups of men will hurry there to partake of the abundance while it lasts. Sometimes it is possible to hear the shooting from the village. If many shots are fired, this is enough to inform the men that hunting is good.

There are other ways that Eskimos can make general predictions as to the probable abundance or scarcity of seals along the ice edge even before they leave the village or before they reach the open lead. Certain general factors of weather, ice, or time of the year influence the availability of seals in the lead or amid the drifting pack, although none of these is so definite that deviations can be called uncommon. The seasonal movements of seals were mentioned earlier. Hunters put in their maximum winter sealing effort from December through March, because they know that by late March the seals begin to disappear from open leads. From this time until June or July they will see few seals in open water. Their sealing reaches a frenzied peak for a few summer weeks, before the ice and seals disappear until the fall.

The occurrence of seals near the edge of the landfast ice is influenced by the wind. When there is a strong wind blowing, ringed and bearded seals seek out smooth water along the upwind edge of the lead. This means that they crowd in along the landfast ice during any wind that opens or widens a lead. Hunters seldom travel out on the ice when the wind exceeds 20 or 25 m.p.h., because of the danger and because seals are hard to shoot and retrieve in water that is not fairly smooth. But the seal hunters awaken early every winter morning when they expect that the wind may have subsided, because immediately following a storm seals are still abundant along the edge.

They also say that there are usually few seals in a lead which has opened within the past four to twelve hours. Thus, if a lead is wide and has remained open for several days, it is better for sealing. However, the occurrence of seals is influenced by other behavioral idiosyncrasies as well. Variations in the abundance of seals, in general areas or around particular ice formations, are sometimes understood by the Eskimo to the point where he can predict them. At other times they remain a mystery even to these people who continually observe them and must know how they behave in order to hunt them.

When a man reaches the lead before dawn, he stands peering into the deep blackness of the water, hoping to glimpse the shadowy motion of seals swimming near the edge. More often he will hear the loud splash of a seal which has surfaced nearby and, after watching curiously for a moment, has become alarmed and submerged with a quick sidelong dive. The hunter knows that seals do this when they are not moving in any particular direction, and that the inquisitive animals will usually reappear shortly after such a violent dive. If it is too dark to shoot he will wait quietly, perhaps joined by other hunters, for the earliest gray light. Those who have telescopic sights on their rifles are more fortunate, because with a scope it is possible to see better in the dark, and therefore to start shooting earlier. Sometimes a man will overestimate his ability at this and annoy other hunters by shooting before it is light enough for him to hit the seal's small, dark head. This only frightens the animals away.

If he arrives after some of the others, the Eskimo is likely to find that they have been shooting and have frightened away the seals in the spots closest to the village. He will have to try to catch up with them. He first notes the current direction and then will probably travel along the lead up-current, knowing that seals usually move with the current. He tries to catch or pass the other hunters in order to reach places where the game is not yet "spooked." Seals tend to be found up-current, but this is by no means always the case. They might turn up almost anywhere, up-current or down-current. If there are few seals to be seen, hunters will most likely move along the lead against the current, searching for areas where seals have congregated. If the current is not running parallel to the lead edge or if it is flowing very slowly, the men will go in either direction, depending on their whim or on their knowledge of the bays and points along the edge.

Sealing is said to be best when there is a strong current, evidently because the animals keep moving along with it. Thus by sitting in one place the hunter can wait for them to come by. At other times he must move around to find groups of seals or scattered individuals that are not moving in any particular direction. During the summer the best chance of finding seals in open water is when the current flows strongly from the south. And if it is from the north, especially during the migratory period in early July, chances of finding seals seem to be reduced.

The weather also influences seal behavior throughout the year. For example, immediately before a summer windstorm seals seem to disappear from the open leads. Those which do surface will stay up only briefly and then be gone. On warm, sunny days in June the Eskimos are not likely to try ice edge sealing, because most of the seals are basking atop the ice. When the weather is like this, they will hunt sleeping seals during the day. If it cools off at "night," especially if clouds reduce the brightness, they will look for seals in the water again.

Ringed seals do not occur evenly along an open lead, but tend to congregate, so that when several are seen there are liable to be more in the immediate vicinity. These groups are localized, however, so that in one spot the hunters may see many seals, while a few hundred yards away there might be none at all. This is true for all seals except the young males, which are said to be "loners."

One man told of a day during late winter when many hunters went out to a lead, but there were almost no seals. He went far to the north by dog team, and in one small area he found seals in great abundance. He shot and retrieved eight, while the other hunters went home almost empty-handed. Wilkinson (1955, p. 155) saw a similar phenomenon on Baffin Island. He was waiting for narwhals (*Monodon monoceros*) near a large open hole when seals began to surface in it. In a span of fifteen minutes the first ones were joined by more and more until there were over thirty seals swimming around and intermittently surfacing in the pool. After half an hour he shot one and the rest apparently disappeared. There is a goodly amount of luck in finding such a concentration of seals.

The Eskimos usually say that seals group together where they find a concentration of food. There are places along leads, for example, where seals tend to occur with great regularity. In midwinter at Wainwright a lead remained open near a huge ice pile for about two weeks. Every day, even if there were none anywhere else, there were seals near this hummock. And during mid-July there was a large grounded floeberg near the village. Men would take their skin boats to that floeberg to hunt, feeling that seals would stay near it. The Eskimos explain that fish or little "shrimp" on which seals feed are usually abundant around such large hummocks, where they can find places to get out of the current. Seals would naturally be attracted to such spots.

There are other ice formations that are considered good places for seal hunting. Eskimos seldom wait for seals along straight, featureless ice edges. Rather, they follow along the ice apron (in winter) until they find some sort of irregularity such as a point (*nuwuk*) or bay (*kaŋełłuk*). In such places seals are more often spotted as they rise close to the edge of the ice. This is partly due to the fact that, especially with a strong current, they surface to breathe on the up-current side of a point, then swim under it and bob up near the edge on the opposite side. As for bays and other irregularities of the ice edge, seals prefer to stay in these places for some unknown reason.

Seals also move out around the ends of points to pass by them. Thus, hunters will station themselves at the ends and await their game. Or if a point juts out from the opposite side of a narrow lead, hunters wait just across from it, because seals are guided closer to the landfast side of the water by it. An ideal spot is where there are two points across from one another which overlap in their projection. Seals will tend to rise between these two points. If the down-current point is on the landfast ice, the hunter can shoot seals and let them drift in to him. This seldom happens along a straight edge, because if the current flows onshore, the lead will close over with ice before much hunting can be done. Basically, then, Eskimos hunt near irregularities in the ice edge, the more sharply defined the better.

We noted above that in winter hunters usually stop in one place for a while and then move along the lead, traveling along the ice apron. How do they decide when it is time to move and how far to move, and under what conditions do they "stay put?" In the first place, there is no clear-cut basis for the decision. They usually decide to move when the seals have been frightened away from an area and are not moving enough to keep appearing at one place. In this case the hunters have to look for them. As they ride their sleds along the lead margin, they watch the water closely until they spot a seal, and there they usually stop to try for it. They might also see a promising point or bay ahead and move there. If few seals are sighted, the men move frequently. If seals are abundant, especially if they are swimming with the current, it is best to remain stationary. It is especially preferable to stay in one place for long periods, an hour or more, if there are many hunters along the lead edge.

During a winter's day an Eskimo will travel 3 to 10 miles or more along the lead. By midafternoon he begins traveling back along the edge toward the village, stopping to hunt as he goes. In the evening hunters often congregate to talk and wait. They say that seals come in toward the landfast ice around dusk, when the winter sun silhouettes them and makes very easy shooting. At times there are groups of five to fifteen men standing around watching half-heartedly for the occasional seal, finally breaking up to go home.

The occurrence of seals follows somewhat different patterns during the summer, when Eskimos hunt them from the edges of drifting ice floes. During June and July the hunters must always be alert and ready to shoot quickly, because they can never tell when a young seal will bob up right along the edge of the ice close by. These small seals are said to stay under the ice most of the time "because their mothers teach them to stay away from open water," but when they do appear, they are quite fearless and curious. One of these unpredictable animals may surface at any time even when there are no other seals around.

When ringed and bearded seals are migrating north, it is very simple to predict where they will surface most frequently. As we have mentioned, points that intersect their line of travel, where they must swim beneath the ice, are good places to hunt. During this period, long straight edges which parallel the coast, such as the margins of a wide shore lead or the edge of a huge floe, may be excellent hunting places.

Seals will surface south of the hunter's position, so he keeps watching in that direction so he will see them before they reach him. Once they are 50 to 200 yards away he scratches the ice with a knife or rifle butt, which attracts the curious animals. There is a very high probability that in a minute or so the seal will bob up (*puizoak*) very close to him. Each seal will surface nearby once or twice before moving on to the north, so the hunter must shoot quickly and accurately. When seals are on the move, there are few second chances.

If the Eskimo is waiting on an ice floe with its edges at right angles to the animals' direction of movement, he can expect them to show up suddenly and without warning, especially if he is stationed along the north edge. This is because seals swim along beneath the ice and surface here to breathe, as we noted above. If the floe is very large, acres in size, it is better to wait along an edge that parallels their movement, because they prefer to swim around rather than under such extensive ice fields. The northern end of such an edge is best, because then a hunter can see the seals once or twice when they surface to the south. On small floes or pans (50 to 100 yards across) edges running at right angles to the seals' movement are better, because they swim under these obstructions rather than around their edges. Generally speaking, bearded seals behave less predictably in these situations than ringed seals.

Some general areas along the coast are for some reason particularly attractive to seals. We mentioned that the waters outside the Kuk River outlet are often quite good for sealing. Also, some places where the current runs swiftly near the shore, such as Atanik̦, north of Wainwright, are generally good at any season. To the south, where vast expanses of ice lie unmoved and unbroken all winter, sleeping seal hunting is good, but leads seldom open close to the land. There is a place called Ķipoholak̦, just south of the Kuk River, where sealing is usually excellent during the migration (at least when the pack is held tightly up to the shore). For some reason the seals pass by this place within a few yards of the beach when conditions are right, and the water is so shallow that killed seals are easily retrieved with a snag hook if they sink.

Attracting Seals

The behavior of ringed and bearded seals toward man changes markedly according to what the seals are doing when they detect his presence. They are frightened immediately by the sight or sound of man when they are basking atop the ice or using a breathing hole. But in open water, including leads, cracks, or large pools, seals are curiously fascinated by the sound and even the sight of man. Whereas a breathing hole hunter must be perfectly silent, an open lead hunter intentionally makes noise to bring the seals toward him. A seal that has been sleeping on the ice dives into the water the moment it sees a man, but this same animal a few minutes later would (presumably) be little afraid of a man it saw while swimming in open water (Degerbøl and Freuchen 1935, pp. 203–5).

Eskimos capitalize on the peculiaries of seal behavior when they hunt from the ice edge. It is largely because of these predictable traits that this is such a productive hunting method. A man who did not use some method of attracting seals would never be very successful. Ringed and bearded seals are irresistibly drawn toward almost any kind of sound, especially mechanical noises such as scratching and pounding. The best way to attract seals if none are seen, or to draw those that are sighted within range, is by scratching the ice. The traditional implement is the *azigaun*, a wooden handle with two to four bearded seal (preferably) claws attached to it. Although this makes the loudest scratching sound, it has largely disappeared today. An ordinary hunting knife works almost as well, and the point of an *unaak* or the butt of a rifle will also suffice. The Eskimo simply scratches the ice near the water's edge with rather firm and slow rhythmical strokes. He pauses occasionally for a moment, but continues scratching until the seal has been drawn as close to the edge as possible.

Other methods include chopping the ice with an *unaak*, making a raspy "Donald Duck" sound in the throat, beating the side of a sled or skin boat with a stick, operating a camp stove, whistling, humming, stamping or scraping the ice with one's boots, driving a dog team along the ice apron, or just talking loudly. Whistling is rarely used except after a seal has been sighted near enough for a good shot but is not exposing much of its head. A little whistle will often turn its attention toward the hunter, and it will stretch as high as possible to see what is going on, making an easy target.

But as much as seals are attracted by noises, they are sometimes frightened by sudden movement, especially if it is close by. For this reason the Eskimo hunter sits on the ice or on his sled while he waits so that he does not have to move around to shoot. If he is standing when a seal appears nearby, he crouches over, grabs his rifle, and sits or lies prone to shoot. One of the greatest assets of the Eskimo as a hunter is his alertness. Whether he is brewing tea, driving his dog team, or talking to another man, his eyes are constantly flashing over the water. When a seal bobs up, he has his gun in an instant and fires.

During the summer migration, men who scratch the ice more or less continuously will get the most shots. The best time to make noise is when seals have been seen within the past few minutes, because they seem to pass by in bunches. Typically, two to five animals will appear within a space of five or ten minutes, and then none are seen for the next fifteen minutes to a half hour. Occasional loners appear, but generally after one is seen others will pass within a few minutes. If a man is using some sort of scratcher, he gets the closest shots. Seals will suddenly break the surface very near the source of the noise (10 to 30 feet from the edge), staring inquisitively in its direction.

During a migration seals will rarely swim across or against the (north-flowing) current to investigate a sound. They are so intent on moving that they are only distracted for a moment at best, and then they continue on their way. At other times they can be attracted from any direction. The effectiveness of noise-making varies according to many factors. When seals come up too close, as they so often do, it is hard to raise one's rifle without scaring them away. But when they submerge, especially if they do a splashing sidelong dive, they will almost invariably poke their heads up again in thirty seconds to two minutes—this time a little farther out. So the hunter aims his rifle near where the animal will be and waits for it, while he continues to scratch the ice with one hand.

Kaviḳ said that if a canvas screen or block of snow is used so that they cannot see the hunter, he will get very close shots. Eskimos rarely do this today, nor do they use natural obstructions (ice piles). It is probably an old method that is no longer bothered with by the less particular hunters of the present generation. During the peak of the migration seals sometimes do not reappear again close by, but continue moving northward (where another man is probably waiting). For this reason each hunter tries to aim and shoot fast, before the seal dives and moves off. Hurried shots tend to be less accurate, however.

The bearded seal and *ḳairalayraḳ* (young ringed seal) are the easiest to attract. They are also the most likely to appear very suddenly and unexpectedly right near a group of men. Eskimos say that bearded seals like to look at people and see what they are doing; and indeed they must. They often will come swimming along the surface, with frequent hesitation, straight toward a crew that is sealing or butchering walrus on an ice pan. The ringed seal does not seem to share this interest in the sight of man, which has cost many a bearded seal its life. Neither the bearded seal nor the young ringed seal is easily frightened by being shot at. Sometimes they just duck under and then reappear after a moment; occasionally they just look to see what made the noise without even going under. Seals sometimes appear to be attracted to an area by the sound of shooting, although the opposite effect is far more usual.

Nearly all the hunters agree that for open lead sealing it is best not to wear a white parka cover (*kategani*), because it makes the seals afraid, thinking they have seen a polar bear. But this is one of the more obvious instances when the actual practice differs from the ideal: during the winter (at Wainwright) at least 75 per cent of the men who were seen hunting seals wore white parka covers, and about 50 per cent did so in the spring. In fact, men were heard saying that white should not be worn for this kind of hunting, while they themselves were sealing and were wearing white. On the other hand, the Eskimos strongly and consciously avoid wearing red during any hunting. "It will scare some animals like seals away and make other animals, like bears and walruses, more dangerous."

Shooting Seals

One of the older hunters said that young men of today are not as good at seal hunting as their elders, for two reasons: First, they do not shoot as accurately, and second, they do not wait for the best and closest shot. Anyone who hunts seals with the Eskimos will soon learn how to aim and shoot quickly. This is especially true when groups of men hunt close together, such as the members of an *umiak* crew hunting from an ice pan. The Eskimo prefers to miss a quick shot rather than get no shot at all. So if a seal rises fairly close to a man and he does not expect it to stay nearby after it dives, he will aim and shoot as fast as possible. The underlying philosophy is that expressed in the familiar proverb: "He who hesitates is lost."

Also, when a man is hunting with others, he cannot wait for

the best shot, because if he waits too long, another man will shoot first. If they are spread out along the ice edge, seals that rise in front of a man are in his "territory." Breaches of this vaguely defined territory by individuals who are farther away are met with tacit disapproval; but serious comment is rarely made to the offender unless he does it consistently. If a seal rises equidistant between two men, or far enough from the edge to be anybody's game, anarchy prevails. There is never any "gentlemen's agreement" to wait and try to bring the seal in and allow the closest man to have a clear, careful shot. There is no question that this lack of organization results in less total productivity.

Sometimes they are willing to let a particular man shoot first, depending on a variety of conditions. If one man has shot fewer seals than the others, he is usually allowed the first shot (especially true among the members of an *umiak* crew). If he misses, especially if he has been shooting poorly all day, someone else is apt to take the second shot. Occasionally they agree that one man will shoot alone, usually because he saw the seal first, or because he was the one who scratched the ice to attract it.

When seal hunters are widely spaced, each individual is able to wait patiently until the animals are attracted as close as they will come, or until they rise high in the water for the best possible target. As a result they kill a higher percentage of the seals they see. A man will wait too long on occasion, thinking he can bring the seal just a bit closer, only to have it tire of the game and disappear. One Eskimo told of waiting until two seals had lined themselves up perfectly and then shooting both of them at once.

When many hunters are close together, they take longer shots and aim hastily, resulting in lower success. During such times hunting may not be taken very seriously and some men will not even bother to sit or kneel while shooting. Some men have "bad days," when they shoot very inaccurately. Their problems result from poorly sighted weapons as often as from bad shooting.

Most Eskimos are not reluctant to use a few bullets for sighting their rifles, feeling that in the long run they will waste less ammunition. Cardboard targets are set up on the beach or sea ice, at a distance of 25 to 35 yards for ice edge sealing. A seal in the water, with only its small moving head visible, is not an easy target. Misses are very frequent. One of the most commonly asked questions besides "How many seals did you get?" is "How many shots did you take?" Occasionally a man will shoot fifteen times or more without a hit, but one hit in three or four shots is probably closer to the average.

Where the ice along a lead is flat, the Eskimo shoots from a sitting position, suppporting his arms on his knees. Occasionally he kneels, sits on a sled, or braces the rifle on a sled to shoot. In rough ice he lies prone with the gun supported on a piece of ice. In former times a notched bone or stick was used as a rifle support. This is not done today. During the warm months a man is careful not to sit or lie directly on wet ice. In fact, at any season it is the practice to put a piece of fur or cloth underneath to keep moisture off the clothing.

Hitting any part of the seal's head is usually enough to kill the animal or knock it unconscious. During the summer most seals will sink after they are shot, unless they are only wounded. For this reason hunters sometimes aim for the snout only. Seals are so high-strung that a hit on the nose or lower jaw (or even a crease on the skull) usually knocks them out. When this happens, they float until they die or regain consciousness. This is done especially with bearded seals, because they sink more readily and are highly valued. For all seals, neck shots are avoided during the spring and summer, because they are most likely to cause sinking.

Some Eskimos use .22 caliber rifles at this time to increase the chance of wounding seals rather than killing them. A gun this small is rarely used in wintertime, because it lacks power and is only advantageous when a weak hit is desired. Bearded seals can be killed with a .22, but this is rarely attempted except when a wounded one is harpooned and must be dispatched.

In 1965 the Wainwright Eskimos owned eighty-four high-powered rifles, an average of two per household, and fifty .22 caliber rifles, an average of 1.7 per household. In addition, there were fifty-seven shotguns, with only four households owning none, and twelve pistols. Thirty out of forty-four households owned at least one rifle with a telescopic sight (G. Ray Bane, personal communication). Many hunters use scope sights for ice edge sealing. They are especially useful during the winter, when the light is usually rather dim.

Most of the high-powered rifles, which are the types used for seal hunting, are .220, .222, .264, .270, .308, or 30.06 caliber. The smaller calibers, with high velocity, are perhaps the most accurate, and make a smaller hole in the skin. There are some days in mid-winter when almost every man is shooting inaccurately, and the weapons must be resighted. This is supposed to be caused by changes in the velocity of bullets as a result of fluctuations in temperature. Some Eskimos suggest that carrying the shells inside a mitten or in a pocket will help to maintain accuracy, but they never seem to do this. Rifles must have all lubricants removed from them so they will not freeze up. Hunters store their weapons in a cold place, such as the hallway of the house, to prevent condensation of moisture that would result from bringing them into a warm place.

Retrieving Seals in Open Water

In aboriginal times the harpoon was used for immobilizing or killing seals and for their retrieval. Once the animal had been struck, a line was automatically attached to it, so its recovery was more or less assured. But when a seal was shot from the lead edge, it still had to be retrieved. The solution to this problem brought about some important changes in the marine hunting technology of northwest Alaskan Eskimos. In the early days following the introduction of firearms, each hunter carried a harpoon for retrieval. After he shot a seal in the water, he hurled the harpoon into the floating carcass so it could be pulled in with the attached line. If the dead seal was too far from the ice edge, a cake of ice might be used as a raft to float to within harpoon range. This technique persisted until at least 1915 at Wainwright (Van Valin 1944, p. 204).

Sometimes it was (and still is) possible to retrieve the seal without any tool at all, or at most the hook on one end of the *unaak*. The *unaak* itself has evolved from the aboriginal harpoon, leaving the ice-testing pick at one end (ivory picks were attached to the butt of harpoons) and replacing the foreshaft and point with a sharpened metal hook. In fact, the word *unaak* means harpoon. If the current flows toward the ice edge, or parallel to it and at right angles to a point, a killed seal will float toward the ice until it can be hooked with an *unaak*. If the current is just slightly onshore, the hunter may try for the closest possible shot by waiting 30 yards or so from the edge and attracting seals as close to the ice as he can. This way the seal will drift in to the ice. Sometimes a floating carcass cannot be retrieved because it is out of range. If it is in a closed bay or hole where it cannot drift away, the hunter can return the next day hoping to find it frozen into ice solid enough for him to walk to it and chop it out.

Soon after the beginning of rifle hunting the floating retrieval hook or *manak* was developed. In the early days both the retrieving harpoon and *manak* were carried by seal hunters. The superiority of the latter for retrieval from the ice edge became evident soon after its introduction, however, and the harpoon was no longer used for this purpose. Floating retrieval hooks were known to the Cape Prince of Wales Eskimos as early as 1891 (Thornton 1931, p. 185). Saint Lawrence Islanders also use this device, which they say was introduced to them by the Siberian Eskimos (Hughes 1960, p. 109). The *manak* is used today throughout northwest Alaska during the period when seals will float (roughly fall, winter, and spring), whenever a boat is not available or necessary for retrieval.

The *manak* is a long cord or line, perhaps 50 to 70 yards in length, with a three- or four-pronged snag hook tied to one end. Attached to the end of the hook is a pear-shaped, egg-shaped, or oblong wood float (*igithak*). The *manak* hook may consist of an ivory shank with metal barbs put through it, or it may be a manufactured triple hook. There may also be three or four sharpened nails protruding from the circumference of the float, bent forward to serve as hooks. One or both kinds of hooks may be used on a single *manak*.

There is considerable variation in their design. Some men prefer oblong floats longer than the usual 5 to 7 inches. A few Wainwright men use a piece of 2 × 4 with bent-nail hooks on the flat sides. They feel that this design is most certain to get its hooks into floating game. One kind of *manak* has a special float, with a cylindrical end and rodlike "handle" and three hooks on the circumference of the end. This type is used for thin-ice retrieval, evidently because it breaks the new ice and is less likely to get caught and be lost.

At Point Hope the retrieving hook and its coiled line are fastened under the bottom of a small sealing stool, such as is used for breathing hole hunting. This may be done in order to keep the line straight. These stools are perhaps carried along for use in sitting on the ice apron, or perhaps they are taken in case the man drifts away and must hunt at breathing holes to survive. They are never used at Wainwright today.

Seal hunters may carry their *manak* lines coiled up, hanging on the upstanders of their sleds or inside their hunting bags, or they may drag them along on the ice behind them. This is done to moisten and stiffen them so they do not tangle as easily when used. The last 3 to 4 feet of line above the float or hook is either braided cord or, preferably, bearded seal-hide thong. This part of the line must be very strong because of the tension put on it when the float is whirled around preparatory to throwing. At the end of this extra-strong line there is a wood, bone, or ivory toggle which the man grasps when he tosses the *manak*.

There are three ways to swing a *manak* preparatory to tossing it. Close targets can be reached by giving the line a couple of underhand swings and then releasing it. For longer throws a circular vertical swing can be used, whirling it around several times with a wrist motion, arm bent slightly so that the hand is even with and slightly behind the shoulder. With a quick overhand flip of the arm, the line is released. The longest tosses are made by swinging the float or weight horizontally over the head, also rotating mostly by wrist action. This is followed by a tricky overhand release, which makes the method most difficult to master.

Once the hunter lets the line fly it can be guided so that it falls directly over the game and not off to the side. If the line is coiled before the toss, which is usually not done, the coil is held in the left hand. One hand is always used as a guide, while the line slips through it. More often the line is laid on the ice loosely coiled so that it cannot foul as it flys out. The thrower runs to one side or the other as the line hurtles out, trying to make the cord land right over the animal when the toss is completed.

If he misses, there is not a moment lost. He bends over and reels back the line as rapidly as possible, tossing it loosely onto the ice. Then he can take a second or third try. When a good throw is made, the line is slowly pulled in until the *manak* hooks touch the dead seal's skin. Then a sharp tug sinks them into its hide. Once it is hooked, it is pulled in very gently. If the current parallels the lead, a hunter may snag the seal and just hold the line, allowing the current to bring it in to the ice, but he must be careful not to let it drift beneath the ice and come unhooked. It may be possible to drag the seal up on the ice with the *manak* line. It is usually necessary, however, to hook it with the *unaak*. When this is done, the seal should be hooked only in the head, because it can slip off too easily if it is hooked in the body. Usually hooking is done through the nose, upper lip, or lower jaw. If there is a large bullet hole, this may be used.

The Point Hope Eskimos are considered to be the best *manak* tossers. This was especially true in the past, when they depended entirely upon this method of retrieval. Some men are considered experts today, and they seldom miss even the longest tosses. Traditionally, a young hunter would practice throwing his line over targets set on the ground so that in hunting he would not lose game that he had killed. Retrieval hooks are used for snagging belugas, walruses, and waterfowl, in addition to seals.

When a man uses a *manak*, he is always limited by the distance and accuracy that he is able to achieve. Although some men can fling a *manak* 50 yards or more, they usually do not shoot a seal farther out than 20 or 30 yards. This is done because of the current, which can carry a seal away from the edge very rapidly. Also, a man who has only a *manak* available is usually hunting alone and can therefore hold his fire until the seal comes within close range. An Eskimo will sit and watch a seal for half an hour before shooting if it is out of range and would probably drift away before he could snag it.

The *manak* is not as efficient as a boat for retrieval. For example, an Eskimo was once seen attempting to snag a seal floating 30 or 40 yards from the ice edge. Again and again he threw the hook out, but each time it fell short or to the side. Fortunately, the current paralleled the ice edge, so after innumerable misses he was finally able to hook his seal. Often the current flows away from the edge, carrying the animal beyond reach after only three or four tries. A group of hunters once reported shooting fourteen seals in an afternoon and losing half of them because they drifted too far out.

For this reason, men always try to carry a retrieval boat on the dog sled. With a boat it is easier and quicker to fetch killed seals, and there is no chance of loss as long as they do not sink. With a boat there is also no need to wait for the closest shots, since there is no limit to how far out a man can go to get his killed game. In northwest Alaska it was rifle hunting which gave the impetus for development of the small skin boats which are now used almost solely for retrieving seals killed from the ice edge. There are two types, the *kayak* and the *umiahalurak*. The former is older but is now almost obsolete, and the latter is more recent and has become very popular. Some details of the history of these boats are given later in this chapter.

Not every hunter owns a boat. Because of this there are usually one to five, or even more, hunters following the man who is carrying one on his sled. Each man is allowed to borrow it to retrieve a seal that he has shot, provided he does most of the work himself. In former years the owner of the boat was given a small share of each seal retrieved with it, but this is no longer considered necessary. Some men who own boats complain that the other men are too lazy to build their own. Thus, men without boats always follow the boat owner around when he hunts. If he could hunt alone, the man having a boat would get more seals for himself. At Point Hope there are apparently more small boats per man, but this is only an impression resulting from the number of them seen around the village.

The man who shoots a seal unties the boat from the sled very quickly and pulls it to the edge of the safe ice. Usually another man helps him carry it, so that it does not have to be dragged. The *umiahalurak* is only 7 to 10 feet long, and 36 to 40 inches wide, so it is not very heavy. The *kayak* is 9 to 12 feet long, 24 to 30 inches wide, and is much lighter in weight. Rough estimates of the weights would be 40 to 60 pounds for the open skin boat or *umiahalurak*, 35 to 40 for the *kayak*.

If he is using an open boat, the hunter pushes it onto the thin ice at the edge of the ice apron (in winter). To do this he stands at the back with his legs spread wide to prevent breakage of the ice. When the boat breaks through the thin ice, he enters it from the rear and sits on the bottom, facing the stern. With the two short oars, which are fastened to the gunwales with lashings, he breaks the ice and forces the boat into open water. He may also use a stick or a *niksigaurak* (gaff hook) to pull or push the boat through the remaining young ice. When a *kayak* is used, the Eskimo straddles the cockpit as he pushes it out, and when the ice begins to break or bend, he slips into the boat. The 8-foot long double-bladed paddle is braced across the foredeck and onto the ice for stability during entry. Then it is used to force the boat through the ice and into open water.

Dead seals float very low in the black water and are not easily spotted, especially from the *umiahalurak*, in which the man does not face the direction he is going. Whenever it is very cold, there are certain dangers involved with paddling out into a steaming lead. If the seal is hard to locate, and if it has drifted 80 to 100 yards out, the oars or paddle become encased with a bulky coating of ice. The ice gets very heavy and reduces the efficiency of the blades. At the same time the man's hands get colder and colder from gripping the handles so tightly. They will grow numb and eventually freeze if retrieval takes too long. For this reason heavy mittens may be carried inside the boat. The current and wind can also impede progress, especially when a seal is being towed. Finally, it is easy to become trapped in young ice which is too thick and firm to paddle a boat through, but not safe to walk on. The gaff hooks can be used in such an emergency to pull the boat through the mat of ice, or an *unaak* may be carried for the same purpose. A combination of these difficulties could prevent a man's return to the landfast ice, and he would be carried away in the ice.

Once a seal is reached it is hooked in the head with a *niksigaurak*. This is a metal rod attached to a wooden handle, with 6 feet of heavy cord strung onto it. The rod is bent to form a sharpened, barbed hook which can be stuck through a seal's hide with a quick stab. Once the seal is hooked in this way the Eskimo holds the cord in his teeth as he paddles back to the ice, dragging the seal along in the water. Two hooks are usually carried so that one can be used for each of two seals. If more are shot at one time, the line is threaded through the skin of each. When a man finds that there are many seals at one place, and if the current is sluggish, he will shoot up to five before going to retrieve them.

After a seal is shot the current begins to carry it away. Thus, if the hunter cannot retrieve it immediately, he stands a good chance of losing it. The location of a seal can be marked by throwing chunks of ice into the water at intervals of several minutes. The chunks drift out in line with the seal and can be followed until the seal is reached. One man who cannot use a *kayak* said that he did this when he hunted with his father. The father would retrieve with the boat while the son shot. The son would throw out pieces of ice, remembering the number he had tossed. He would then tell his father, for example, that after he passed the seventh piece he would reach the seal. This must be done because the steam fog along a lead often reduces the visibility considerably. But men are usually able to reach their seals well before they vanish from sight.

Seals are dragged with the cord held in the man's teeth, never tied on the boat, because of the danger of a walrus's coming up and pulling the animal away. Once the hunter has paddled back to the ice edge, he is pulled up in the same spot where he broke the ice to go out. His partner hauls the boat up with the hook of his *unaak*. If there is no partner, he ties a line to his sled anchor (a heavy iron hook) and sets the hook into the ice, so he can pull himself up when he returns. This is seldom necessary. The boat must be pulled up far enough onto the safe ice so that he can get out. Then the seal is also dragged up onto the ice by the partner, who hooks it with the *unaak* or pulls it with the gaff hook line.

Back on the ice the boat is turned upside down and the heavy ice which has formed on the bottom is removed by beating it with slender sticks carried for the purpose. The encrusting ice on the paddle blades is scraped off with a large knife. Seals are often attracted by these noises.

Retrieval boats are used in essentially the same way during the warm spring and summer months, except that there is less danger involved and there is no ice apron to contend with. Thus, rather than launching from a bending skin of young ice which lies right at water level, one must step down into the boat from thick solid ice that stands well above water level. After the boat has been slid into the water, one oar is laid across the solid ice and held there firmly to keep the boat from tipping. In a *kayak*, the paddle is placed across the foredeck and held on the ice in a similar manner, to act as a sort of "outrigger." Some men show great confidence and skill in their use of retrieval boats, while others are not at all adept.

One further difference in summer retrieval with small boats is the occasional replacement of the gaff hook by a small retrieval harpoon (*unaavirak*). Some seals are lost in summer because they sink before they can be hooked securely. A small harpoon about 4 feet long can be tossed or jabbed more quickly than a gaff hook. The most important use of a harpoon for retrieval is seen during *umiak* hunting, or ice edge sealing where the large *umiak* is used for retrieval.

Throughout much of the summer, as we have stated, the large skin boat is used for transporting hunters to the edge of an off-shore floe, where they can conduct ice edge sealing. In this case small retrieval boats are not carried along, because the *umiak* serves fairly well for this purpose. The boat is always pulled fully onto the ice, bow first, in a place that is low enough to allow easy landing and launching. Two or more men stay close to it during the hunt, so they can launch it immediately when someone shoots a seal. As one man jumps to the stern of the boat the others push it out. At the last minute one of them hops into the bow, where the harpoon rests in position. By this time the stern man has the engine started.

While they are speeding toward the floating carcass, the bow man picks up the harpoon and stands poised, holding the line in his left hand. As the right side of the bow passes the seal, his arm flashes down, the harpoon head plunges deep beneath the seal's skin and holds fast. When he feels the strike, the harpooner pulls with his left hand, freeing the line from the harpoon shaft so that the head stays in the animal, now affixed only to the line (*naulik*). A ring on the shaft, through which the line passes, keeps the shaft from floating loose. Without stopping the boat is turned back toward the ice edge, the seal dragging along in the water. The boat is returned to position, and the seal is pulled up on the ice so that the harpoon head can be cut out and put back on the shaft, ready for use again.

This whole operation is very fast. It takes only thirty to sixty seconds to reach the seal. However, it often is not fast enough. After he shoots a seal, the Eskimo watches closely. He can usually tell by the dull thud of the striking bullet that he has hit the animal, but he watches for its floating body to appear. The water around it is almost instantly covered by an expanding oil slick, which smooths the surface ripples. Some seals will sink (*kivi*) immediately, but most rise to the surface, their rounded backs riding low on the water.

There is no assurance, however, that they will remain afloat, so the hunters wait forty-five seconds to a minute before launching the boat. If bubbles appear around the head region, the seal will sink in five to ten seconds. This can happen at any time, but if it does not start almost immediately, there is a good chance that the boat will reach it. Not infrequently, however, the carcass disappears at the last moment, and the harpooner can see nothing but a widening cloud of blood. When this happens, the seal is probably lost for good. Retrieval by *umiak* is used far more frequently in the summertime than the other methods discussed above, because most ice edge sealing is done out on the drifting floes which cannot be reached by foot or by dog team.

When a seal sinks to the bottom, it can be retrieved only with a weighted snag hook or *niksik*. The *niksik* is designed essentially the same as the floating hook (*manak*). The line is somewhat longer, about 60 to 70 yards in length (35 fathoms, measured by outstretched arms, is recommended), and instead of a float at the end there is a lead sinker. The hook, fastened between the line and the sinker, consists of an oblong piece of brass or iron with two holes drilled through it at right angles. Iron spikes or pieces of metal rod are put through the holes, bent, and sharpened to make four hooks.

The weight is usually made from lead shot, bought at the native store and melted to the desired size and shape. It is oblong and usually somewhat flattened, so that it drags along the bottom without constantly rolling over. It weighs 1 to 1½ pounds. A toggle is tied into the line about 3 feet above the hook.

There are several ways of judging where to aim with the *niksik*. If the water is shallow and clear, the upturned bellies of dead seals are easily visible against the dark sea bottom. In these cases the hook is dropped down over the side of the boat and is dragged over the seal's body. An Eskimo told of hooking twenty-four seals this way without firing a shot. They had been killed on a previous day by other men, when the water was too murky to see them. By cruising around in a boat watching the bottom, he spotted and hooked their catch.

Another way to locate a dead seal is to mark the spot with a float. This is usually done only for bearded seals that are shot near the ice edge. The marking device consists of a weight (about 5 pounds) affixed to a long line with a float at the other end. The line is shortened so the weight can just reach bottom, keeping the float right over the kill. Then they drop the weight from a boat in the spot where the animal sank. If this spot is reached within a few minutes, it will be marked by a patch of crimson blood. Sometimes the line is adjusted for the proper water depth while the men are hunting, so that no time is wasted in marking a kill. After the float is in place, men on the ice begin tossing their snag hooks, aiming about 10 to 15 yards beyond it. When they use a marker, they seldom fail to retrieve the seal.

The least effective way to retrieve with a *niksik* is to try to remember where the seal went down. Marking devices can only be used from nonmoving ice (i.e., grounded or landfast). Sometimes it is possible to line up the spot where the animal sank with features of the sea ice or land in the distance, though again, one must be positive that the landmarks are not moving. Once this is done the Eskimo begins to toss his hook, starting to one side of where the seal should be and working gradually toward the other side.

Before he uses a *niksik*, the Eskimo carries its coiled line some distance back from the water. Then he stretches the line across the ice as he walks back to the spot from which he will throw. It is rewound into a very neat coil for the first shot, having had all tangles and kinks removed. Men are extremely particular about keeping the line as perfect as possible, to avoid snarling. With the coil held loosely in his left hand, he grasps the toggle between the index and middle fingers of his right hand, and swings the weight back and forth in a broad underhand arc. When the aim seems correct, he takes one longer swing and hurls the weight in a low trajectory far out over the water. An effort is usually made to throw the weight well beyond the distance where the animal should be.

This done, the line is very slowly and gently pulled inward, moving each hand about 1 foot ahead of the other, holding it with bare fingers to maximize sensitivity of touch. The hunter always waits until the sinker hits bottom before he starts pulling. If the hook seems to catch on something, gentle tugs are given on the line. If the line pulls itself back—if it has snagged something with a lot of give and resilience—it is probably touching the soft and moveable body of the seal. If it does not pull back when he releases the line, it has probably hooked a stone or bottom irregularity. As he pulls the line in, he drops it into a neat, loose pile in front, at the sides, and between his feet.

This is done so the line can be flung out again without having to coil it. On these later tosses at least 30 feet of line should be stretched out on the ice away from the edge, so if all of the line is used on a toss (or if a tangle goes out with the line), it can be grabbed or stepped on before it is all pulled away and lost. Thus a careful watch is kept on the line as the *niksik* flies out, so that there is no chance of losing it.

If the hook touches a seal's body, the Eskimo grasps the line firmly and gives it a strong tug. This will bury the sharp barbed hooks into its tough skin. Sometimes the hooks do not set, and it is necessary to start all over again. When they catch properly, the added weight on the line shows that the animal has been hooked. Then it is pulled in with a steady pressure, so that it cannot slip off. The carcass is lifted onto the ice by hand or dragged up with the hook of an *unaak*.

This method is not highly successful without a marker to show where the animal sank. Sometimes a man tries for one or two hours without success. But this sort of perseverance is necessary with such a hit-or-miss technique. By keeping a rifle nearby he can still hunt while he uses his *niksik*. This is actually a good way to relieve boredom while sealing. Using a *niksik* is much like fishing. Every toss may be the one that gets a "bite." The Eskimos appear to share this attitude.

The number of seals that are lost by sinking varies greatly with the seasons. During the winter, nearly all seals float after they are killed, but a small percentage (5 percent to 10 percent) will sink and be lost. Rarely, a seal will sink several feet below the surface and then go no deeper. Seals begin to sink in the month of May, and by June almost every one shot will eventually sink. Around the end of August or in early September they begin to float again.

A tally for one hunter during the summer of 1966 showed twelve seals retrieved successfully out of twenty-two killed. The average seems to be even lower. For example, in early June one man shot six seals and retrieved four, while another shot two and lost both. In mid-July a crew killed twenty-eight seals and were able to retrieve only eight. Another crew shot seven and retrieved one. During two days at the peak of the July seal migration, ninety-one seals were brought home by five crews, and the number which sank and were lost must have equalled this figure.

In spite of this tremendous loss there seems to be no method which could permit more effective retrieval and still allow equally large kills. Certainly the Eskimos put every possible effort into retrieving the animals they kill. If there were a better way, they would undoubtedly use it. Harpooning is not practical for open lead sealing, because of its short effective range.

Open Crack Hunting

During the summer months, Eskimos occasionally hunt at openings that are considerably smaller than leads. When temperatures are at winter levels, cracks and ponds freeze over so quickly that there is seldom much chance to hunt at them. These small places are not regularly hunted at any season, because of the preference for hunting at wide leads or for sleeping seal hunting. However, if an Eskimo sees seals in such a place while he is traveling on the ice, he is likely to stop to hunt there for a while.

The method of hunting is essentially the same as for open lead sealing. The Eskimo positions himself 25 to 40 yards back from the crack, if it is narrow, or right near the edge, if it is wide. He may scratch the ice to attract seals, but they generally appear to be less curious when the open water is so confined. Seals that come up in cracks usually will not reappear after they have gone under. If he shoots a seal in a small opening, the hunter jumps up and runs to it quickly, hoping to hook it with his *unaaḳ* before it sinks. In wider cracks a retrieval hook can be used. An Eskimo told of once shooting sixteen seals on each of three consecutive days in June along some narrow (3 to 4 feet wide) cracks outside the Kuk Inlet, but this kind of success is unusual.

Kaviḳ had seen excellent conditions for bearded seal hunting when he was at Point Hope about forty years ago. During the spring migration one man could take ten to fifteen per day, and as many as fifty to eighty in a season. Each hunter would station himself at an open pond, which remained his territory for as long as he stayed. There he would remain, hunting seals for days on end. When he became tired, he slept right there, and his wife brought food out to him. After killing and retrieving a seal, the hunter would drag it to the beach, and from there the women (with help from children and dogs) took it home. Sometimes they made long slippery trails with the blubber laid along the ground, making it easier to drag the bulky seals. So many were taken that there was not time to butcher them fully. The skin and blubber were removed, and the carcass then cut into three large sections and thrown into cold storage places. Some of the meat was eaten raw and frozen (*ḳwaḳ*) during the winter, and some of it was prepared by drying (*paniktaḳ*).

Hunting at small ponds and cracks is usually coincidental with other activities. For example, seals might bob up in a small pond where a man is waiting for seafowl to fly over. More commonly, they are seen in a nearby crack by a man who is traveling along on his dog sled. Sometimes it is possible to stop and shoot before the seals take fright and disappear. Sleeping seals that flop into the water as a man approaches will frequently reappear briefly, staring curiously at the intruder; but once they dive they are usually gone for good. There are too many other open places for the seals to go, so they do not come back if frightened. Eskimos feel that it is more productive to hunt sleeping seals or find the edge of a lead than to waste time waiting at cracks.

Shore Lead Hunting

Hunting in the lane of open water that forms between the beach and the sea ice usually begins in late June or early July. It continues for as long as the pack ice is present, whenever an on-shore wind brings the ice ashore and leaves open water between the land and the tightly packed ice that grounds 100 or 200 yards offshore.

Whenever the shore lead (*killigisiñek*) is present and there is little open water farther out, seals will follow close to the land as they move northward (which they do for quite a long period in summer). It is apparently easier for them to follow this open strip than try to swim from hole to hole farther offshore. This is especially true of young seals, while older ones may prefer the deeper and safer areas out at sea. During early summer, while the ice is solid and unbroken, the situation is reversed; older seals are found nearest to land and young seals stay well offshore. Young ringed seals are easy to hunt, because they are unafraid of man, and they float more often than older seals after they are shot.

All this makes for rather good hunting, without having to travel far from the village. In the latter part of June there may be many young ringed seals (and some bearded seals) in the open water outside the mouth of the Kuk River. Some men camp on the beach there to take advantage of the good hunting. Seals may be shot right from the beach, or from ice which extends only a short distance out from the beach. Occasionally, someone will shoot a seal from the beach at Wainwright, but the seals are usually frightened away from there by the noise and movement. Beach hunting is said to be a major activity at Point Hope in June.

When seals are shot from the land, they are recovered with snag hooks or retrieval boats. When a boat is available, the Eskimos usually prefer to go across the shore lead to the opposite side. Chances are better there because the seals tend to stay out from the shallows as far as possible. A hunter will paddle his little retrieval boat across the water to a place a few hundred yards to half a mile north or south of the village. He carries a rifle, snag hook, *unaak*, gaff hook (*niksigaurak*), and sometimes a harpoon. He may also carry a piece of canvas or skin to sit on.

When he reaches the far side, he picks a good spot, such as a bay or point, where he has seen seals before or expects them to appear. It is best to get well away from the village, so there is little danger of hitting people. In fact, many shots are passed up to avoid shooting toward the village. Once he finds a good place, the Eskimo pulls his boat onto the ice. Some men sit right inside their boats on the ice, using them as comfortable seats and blinds; others prefer to walk around or sit on the ice. Those who are hunting birds at the same time prefer to stay in the concealing boat.

The method of hunting is the same as we have described for open lead sealing. Not many seals are shot and retrieved success-fully by this small-boat technique, because when there are lots of seals around the men prefer to travel away from the village with a large *umiak*. Only five or six men at Wainwright carry on shore lead hunting regularly, which is few compared to the number who could profitably do so. Older men who have an open skin boat (*umiahalurak*) available to them, and one or two men who are employed in the village during the day, are the most frequent shore lead hunters. This is one of the few chances these people have to hunt at all. When seals are abundant, crews of hunters take motorized *umiaks* to good hunting spots in the shore lead, such as near the Kuk outlet. This kind of hunting is the same as summer ice edge sealing.

Transporting Killed Seals

In winter and spring, killed seals are hauled to the village by dog team or by pulling them along on foot. After seals are hauled up on the ice, they are usually left close to where they were caught, to be picked up by the hunter when he passes by on his way home. When it is cold, they are left lying on their backs so they freeze flat and load easily onto the sled. If the hunter is not carrying a boat, he ties the seals in the middle of the sled with

THE BIOLOGICAL ENVIRONMENT ·

their heads facing forward. When he is carrying a boat it is not so easy, because the seals must be lashed alongside. If there are one or two, they are placed on their sides right against the stern of the boat. Additional seals are lashed along the bow; and if there are more than four, the boat is put on top of them. Seven or eight seals are a very bulky load for any sled, piled in two or three levels, with no room for a boat.

Hunters favor large sleds, 11 to 13 feet long and about 30 inches wide, for sea-ice use. This makes it easier to ride through rough places and to carry heavy loads without too much danger of breakage. The stanchions take a severe beating and are broken several times each season. At Point Hope, where basket sleds made of hardwood are used, the sleds are frequently broken and have a rather short life expectancy.

The Eskimo who goes sealing on foot is faced with the problem of getting his game home. If there are no dog teams around, he will shoot no more than one or two seals. If he kills and retrieves one, and decides to try for another, the first is buried in a snowbank to prevent it from freezing hard. Then when it is pulled its head turns up "like the bow of a sled" and it rides easily over irregularities.

The seal-pulling harness, or *uniutak*, consists of a rope or bearded seal-hide thong that forms a loop large enough to be used as a strap across a man's chest. A line about 4 or 5 feet long, with a small double loop at the end, is attached to the strip. One end of the loop is tied to the harness line. The other is put through a slit cut inside the lower mandible and looped over the animal's snout. In this way it is easy to fasten it on a seal without tying any knots, and it is equally simple to remove the line.

Nowadays men pull their own seals home, sliding them laboriously through even the roughest ice. But their wiser predecessors had two kinds of draught animals to pull the game home for them. The first was a dog, which could be sent ahead of them with a seal; and the second was their wives, who were instructed as to the whereabouts of the ringed or even a large bearded seal, and gamely went out and pulled it home. This was not considered unjust, since the men might have waited a full twenty-four hours for the seal.

A seal can be lightened by cutting it open and removing the

blubber from the ventral half of its body. The blubber is left on the ice, and the seal's skin is sewed back together with cord. An old-timer told of shooting two large bearded seals when the snow was gone from the ice in the spring. At this time the Eskimos say the pulling a seal over the ice is like dragging it on sand, because the bare ice offers so much resistance to the sealskin. This man was on foot, and could not leave the seals until the next day because of the ice conditions. So he cut one up, removing the skin and taking the meat from the bones. He partially butchered the second, leaving the skin, backbone, head, and some other bones, and discarding the ribs. Then he put the remains of one inside the other, sewed it together, and began dragging. The load was very heavy, and he pulled "all day and half the night" to reach the shore. This, he said, was one of his most tiring experiences. But now, at over sixty years old, he still walks out on the ice, pulls his own load, and scorns the laziness of youths, who insist on riding everywhere.

To avoid the difficulty of hauling seals across the bare summer ice, hunters who go out on foot feel that it is worth the extra effort to push or pull a small dog sled with them, and use it to carry the game back. A fairly long sled (8 to 10 feet long) is also useful for crossing deep rivulets or as a safety device on weak ice. An Eskimo said he once brought seven or eight ringed seals home by pushing a sled. In former years it was common to use a small sled that was pulled with a line and harness. This sled measured only 2 or 3 feet long. Its runners were sometimes made from walrus tusks cut in half. On Saint Lawrence Island today, and traditionally in other parts of Arctic Alaska, small baleen toboggans are used for seal hunting.

Uses of Seals

The various methods of ice edge sealing are the most effective means of hunting ringed seals. Many bearded seals are also taken this way. Ice edge sealing can provide a man with 1,000 pounds of game in a day, even more on occasion. A single bearded seal may weigh that much alone. A Wainwright man recalled taking thirty-five seals in a single day, and his son had once taken thirty. Almost every man has killed ten or fifteen seals in a day. Under normal conditions, however, during the winter the hunter brings home one to three seals each time he goes out, if he is proficient. In earlier times at Wainwright there were winters when a single hunter got over eighty seals by this method, and over one thousand were taken by the combined efforts of the hunters. But today only two or three hundred are killed in years when caribou are abundant, more when there is not enough of this preferred meat or when few walruses are taken.

During the summer, the number of seals killed by all crews must be very large indeed. On two days during the peak of the migration, between 125 and 150 seals were killed and retrieved by Wainwright hunters. This figure is over half the total number killed during eight months of winter sealing in 1964–65. Obviously, the summer kill of seals is rather important to the total economy of Wainwright.

At Point Hope the resources of caribou and walrus do not compare with those at Wainwright, but the sealing and whaling conditions are probably among the best in this part of the Arctic. Thus one hunter who put in a maximum effort got two hundred seals in the winter of 1964–65, equalling the number taken by all of Wainwright's hunters in the same period. Ringed seals are very abundant here all winter, but they are gone entirely after the ice leaves in June. Wainwright seems to have a more balanced and perhaps a more productive habitat, but the general impression is that not as much effort is put into exploiting its potential.

Seal meat is not important in the diet of the Wainwright Eskimos. Most of it seems to be used for dog food. During the summer, seal is eaten by campers outside the village, and occasionally for a meal at home. Seal blubber, used to make oil (*ohuzoḳ*), is much more important to these people. It is considered an essential part of almost every meal where meat is eaten. The meat, eaten raw and frozen, is considered an excellent emergency food for drift-ice survival. Under emergency conditions it is cut from the bones so that it can be carried in a light and compact load. Eskimos also eat the liver, intestines, and kidney of the seal, either frozen or cooked. Young seals are said to be the best eating. Wainwright

Eskimos usually cook seal by boiling it thoroughly and then eating it off the bones. Leg and shoulder joints, ribs and vertebrae are preferred. Seal meat is good for dog food, because less of it is required for feeding than most other kinds of meat. Many seals are probably used for dog food in the summer, while the blubber is used to help dogs stay warm during fierce winter gales.

The women usually butcher the seals their husbands or sons bring home. They first remove the skin. It is slit along the belly from the chin to the anus, and then it is quickly sliced away with the blubber attached. The skin is not removed from the fore flippers, and they are cut off after the skin is taken from the carcass. The blubber will be sliced and scraped from the hide later on. The thoracic cavity is opened by cutting out the sternum and cartilaginous portions of the adjacent ribs, and the flesh over the abdomen is cut away. The internal organs are then taken out. The rest of the meat is cut away by removing the fore and hind limbs, cutting the ribs out, sectioning the vertebrae, and butchering each portion into smaller pieces by cutting at the various joints. The Eskimo woman shows an extraordinary practical knowledge of anatomy as she cuts the entire animal into smaller and smaller sections without ever sawing or breaking a bone.

Ringed sealskins can be scraped and dried with the hair left on. They are used for making boots and for sale to "outside" fur dealers. At Point Hope many people hunt seals and prepare the skins as a major source of income. The skin of summer-caught seals is not worth much to the Eskimos nowadays. They cannot sell it because the fur sheds too easily (sometimes the skins are practically bald). They usually want the fur intact for their own use as well. Some skins are made into *naloak*, which involves removing the hair and bleaching the hide by hanging it outside in the cold and wind. Such skins are now used for making thongs for boots and gear; and they were formerly prepared for tent covers, kayak covers, and other waterproof purposes. During the early summer the Eskimos discard the skins of the seals they feed to their dogs in camp.

The Wainwright people store seals by putting them into underground ice cellars during the summer. These cellars keep the meat frozen solidly and prevent spoilage. Seals are not skinned before they are put inside. In winter they can be left on meat caches outside, as long as they are out of the dogs' reach. During summer camping trips they may be placed temporarily in cold puddles on the sea ice to prevent spoilage.

It is interesting to note, on the subject of food, that among at least three Eskimo groups the most preferred food is the one that is the most available. The Wainwright people shoot a great number of caribou, the volume of which considerably exceeds that of seals. They often say: "You never get tired of caribou, even though you easily tire of all other kinds of meat." The Saint Lawrence Islanders, who apparently shoot a greater volume of walrus than anything else, say that you never get tired of walrus (Hughes 1960). The North Greenland Eskimos depend heavily on seals, and are quoted as saying "One may get tired of all other kinds of meats, but never of seal meat" (Vibe 1950, p. 76). The Wainwright people are traditionally inland Eskimos, and certainly their predecessors ate more caribou than anything else. Similar statements probably hold with reference to walrus for the Saint Lawrence Islanders and seals for the North Greenlanders. These Eskimo groups appear to have adapted their attitudes to their particular food supply, preferring the common foods over all else.

Ice Edge Hunting and Culture Change

When firearms were introduced, they were substituted for the harpoon in each of the methods of hunting seals, but the techniques remained basically the same. Only in the method of open lead hunting was it necessary to evolve extensively different or new technological equipment. Although the material changes were rather important, the effects upon the economy, the kind of activities pursued, and the ecological patterning were extensive and profound. Firearms made available to the Eskimo a resource which he was never before able to utilize with any degree of proficiency: marine mammals in open leads and near the ice edge.

The aboriginal Eskimos put some effort into hunting at the water's edge. During the spring migration, seals tend to move along very near to the ice edge. At this season they also have a habit of "sleeping" in the water for several minutes at a time with their heads laid back and noses pointed skyward. Each of these behavior patterns was important for ice edge sealing with the harpoon.

When the seals were "sleeping" it was sometimes possible to sneak close enough to the edge to harpoon them. More often, the Eskimo would construct a blind of ice or snow right at the water's edge. He sat in the blind watching through cracks between the blocks for an unwary seal to come close by or to start sleeping within a few yards of the blind. When this happened, the hunter would rise and harpoon the animal, then run back from the edge with the line in hand. The seal would struggle to dive or to swim away, but eventually would have to surface for air. As it did, the line would slacken and the hunter would pull it toward him, drawing the animal inward. Thus it would break the surface right next to the edge of the ice, where it would be killed with a club made from a heavy round rock on a wooden handle.

Such a method, limited to open-water periods, mostly done in the springtime, and probably not more productive than breathing hole or sleeping seal hunting, would not be a particularly favored one. This was especially true since during most of the open lead hunting season seal netting was also going on. One old man, for example, said that he had successfully harpooned seals in open leads only twice in his entire life. Therefore the Eskimo's only attraction to open water would be for spring whaling. The general situation would compare to that described by Boas, who worked in the central Arctic during the 1880's:

> The immense land floe of Davis Strait is not so valuable a hunting ground for the Eskimo as Cumberland Sound, the ice being very rough a few miles from the coast and at some places even close inshore. When the sea begins to freeze in the fall, the newly formed ice is broken up by severe gales and by the currents and is piled up into high hummocks before it consolidates. The sealing on rough ice during the winter is very difficult and unsuccessful, as it is hard to find the breathing holes and the travelling is very laborious. It is only in the northern parts of Home Bay and in the large fjords that smooth ice is formed... In every place where smooth ice is formed we find

that natives either are settled or have been settled. . . . On the long shores between them [the bays], which are unsheltered from winds and currents, the ice is always very hummocky, and, therefore, the natives do not settle upon them in the winter [Boas 1964, pp. 52–53].

Farther on he writes specifically with reference to the use of open water. Note that he definitely states that seals are hunted on the solid ice near the open water, but does not make any reference to actual open-water hunting:

There are only a few districts where the proximity of open water favors walrus hunting during the winter, and all of these have neighboring floes on which seals may be hunted with the harpoon. . . . As to the remainder the Eskimo live altogether independent of the open water during the winter [Boas 1964, p. 53].

A later reference to open-water sealing is of particular interest:

Whenever water holes are found they are frequently visited during the winter by the Eskimo, *especially by those who have firearms.* They lie in wait at the lower side of the hole, i.e., the side to which the tide sets, and when the seal blows they shoot him, securing him with the harpoon after he has drifted to the edge of the ice [Boas 1964, p. 74; italics mine].

The same method is described for the Barrow natives by Murdoch (1892), and a brief description of harpooning seals at leads is given by E. W. Nelson (1899, p. 138) for the Bering Strait region. In this case Nelson simply states that if a man harpoons a seal from the ice edge and for some reason cannot hold it, he lets go, with the linestand for a drag at the end of the line, and chases it with his *kayak*.

It seems possible, in view of a brief survey of the literature, that a situation similar to that described by Boas for the late nineteenth-century central Arctic might have been present in northwest Alaska before the introduction of firearms. It may be, and perhaps archeological surveys will some day offer evidence, that formerly there were settlements all along this coast and the area to the south, without the preference for points and headlands that is seen in the modern settlement pattern. In this case sites of inhabitation would be scatttered everywhere during the winter, within the protected bays as well as on the exposed coasts

—in areas of flat unmoved ice (e.g., the site of the modern village of Kotzebue) as well as in areas where the ice is continually in motion. Larger settlements would be present at localities such as Point Hope and Point Barrow, because of an abundance of seals, available by various harpooning methods, but more so because of the excellent whaling which provided a resource beyond that available to the more protected settlements. The settlements in exposed places would see a temporary expansion of population in the whaling season due to an influx of people from inland and protected coastal areas.

The introduction of firearms altered this pattern by making ice edge hunting a focus of interest rather than a minor activity. As the availability of rifles increased and knowledge of this new hunting technique expanded, there may have been a tendency for people to move to exposed localities for the midwinter months, in order to take advantage of the increased availability of seals. Since that time this pattern has become increasingly prevalent, with people eventually giving up living inland and at protected coastal localities. Of course these movements were influenced and catalyzed by the decline of the caribou, introduction of disease, and attraction to centers of white influence. In the latter instance, establishment of schools and trading stores, usually in exposed coastal places, was particularly important. As the method of open lead hunting took hold, the other methods such as breathing hole hunting were abandoned. All this took place in a span of one hundred years.

We can speak with greater certainty about the technological changes that resulted from the introduction of firearms. In the first place, certain hunting implements were rendered obsolete by the use of rifles. The harpoon and a series of devices associated with its use (lines, line stands, floats, etc.) nearly became obsolete. A simple harpoon is used today for some kinds of retrieval. Other items such as seal nets and sealing stools have been lost, along with a considerable body of knowledge and techniques. The loss and atrophy of technological devices and techniques are balanced against a series of changes and new developments of other items, some previously in existence and some entirely new. Some of these were already discussed with reference to dog teams and modes of transportation. Of particular interest, however, is the development of retrieval devices.

As we mentioned earlier, in the days when seals were harpooned there was no retrieval problem. The head of the harpoon was attached to a line, which automatically took care of the problem once an animal was struck and immobilized. And so, first of all, the *manak* and *niksik* snagging hooks either were invented or were modified from a previously used implement. But retrieval hooks are inefficient because of their short effective range. This is why the kayak was adopted very early for retrieval purposes.

In many parts of the Eskimo domain, kayaks have come to be used for retrieval since firearms were introduced. They were used for this purpose at Cape Prince of Wales, Alaska, by 1891 (Thornton 1944, p. 185). In the eastern Canadian Arctic, Eskimos take their long (about 18 feet) kayaks over the flat ice to wide cracks during early summer. After a seal is shot, a man who has been sitting in his kayak ready to go paddles out and harpoons it (Wilkinson 1955, pp. 85–86). Almost the same technique is used by the North Greenlanders, who apparently do not use retrieval hooks (Vibe 1950, p. 74).

In northwest Alaska the aboriginal kayak was a sleek boat, very long and narrow, similar in design to the Caribou Eskimo kayak or Central Eskimo kayak. During Murdoch's stay at Barrow (1881–83), the kayaks were similar to the "old-time" boats described by elderly informants. They measured 17 to 19 feet long and a little over 20 inches wide, with a U-shaped cross section. They were used mostly for hunting caribou as they swam across inland lakes and rivers, much as was done by inland Eskimos of Canada. They were also used to some extent for short trips between camps, for setting nets, for hunting flightless moulting waterfowl, and (sometimes) for harpooning seals in the open ocean. Their usage, as one would expect from their design, was strongly inland-oriented. None of the early works on this region mention short boats of any type, open or decked.

The aboriginal kayak was designed for speed and for use on relatively calm water. It was used primarily for chasing caribou that were driven into inland lakes and rivers. After rifles became available, this technique of caribou hunting died out, and the kayak did not fit into the new methods that developed. It was no longer necessary to approach the animals to within a harpoon's throw or an arrow shot. And unlike the motorized *umiak* and larger dog teams, kayaks were ineffectual for transportation of game. The inland uses of kayaks must have disappeared soon after white contact. The only uses that remained were those related to exploitation of marine resources. However, there was very little emphasis on use of kayaks in the sea during aboriginal times.

Kayaks would, therefore, have disappeared entirely at this time were it not for the new demand for an effective means of retrieving seals shot in open water. But certain modifications would be necessary in order to make the kayak fit for use on the sea ice. In the first place, the kayak must be transported from the shore to the edge of open water, which always involves traversing rough ice. Unlike the places mentioned above, in northwest Alaska a long and lightly built kayak being carried across the ice on a sled would be pounded to bits in a short time. What was needed was a kayak that would be short enough to fit onto a dog sled without extending beyond the sled itself, so it could be protected from continual banging and scraping against jumbled blocks of ice.

Further, to compensate for its shortness, the kayak was widened to make a stout and stable little craft suitable only for the one purpose of game retrieval. The impetus for other uses having been lost during the same period, it was no sacrifice to alter the design in this extreme manner. Thus the native kayak was modified to form what is known today as the *kayapaurak* ("little kayak") or *kayapak* ("fat kayak").

Ikolivsaak, an old Wainwright man, said that by the 1920's the old kayaks were gone, but the new type had become very popular. Nearly every man owned one of these little seal hunting boats. There was a fair amount of variation in length and width, depending on individual preference. They ranged from 9 to 12 feet in length and 2 to 3 feet wide. Basic design, with an up-turned foredeck, slanted cockpit rim, flat rear deck, and rounded U-shaped cross section, was retained. The details of construction were also little changed, except that some men used resilient baleen withes for ribs, to reduce the chance of breakage. Associated with the evolution of short boats, which could be transported on dog sleds or hand sleds, was the use of the gaff hook for pulling seals to the ice edge. The kayaks were also used for retrieving waterfowl and setting nets, but these were purely secondary functions, not responsible for the decrease in length of the boat. For a brief period of fifty years the *kayapaurak* was used in the villages from Barter Island to Barrow and south beyond Point Hope, where it now survives as a remnant in every village except Point Hope.

There were only three functional kayaks and one uncovered kayak frame in Wainwright during 1964–65. This is a considerable decrease from the time when "every" man owned a retrieval kayak. There are two reasons for this change. First, there has been a decrease in seal hunting activity in recent years, and those who hunt today do not equip themselves completely but depend on sharing with others instead. Second, a new type of skin-covered retrieval boat was introduced from the south and has rapidly replaced the kayak in this area in recent years.

The new retrieval boat, which we described earlier in this chapter, is called *umiahalurak*, or "small umiak," which accurately describes its appearance. Like the little kayak it is quite short, measuring between 7 and 10 feet in length. It is, however, much wider at the beam (3 to 4 feet), and the sides are 20 to 30 inches high. The design is quite stubby and makes it very stable in the water. The frame is very simply constructed with a series of widely spaced ribs.

The *umiahalurak* apparently spread into northwest Alaska from the south during this century. The first to reach Wainwright was brought by Kavik, a man from Teller, around 1920. He suggested that they may have been used originally for setting nets in open water, implying that their function changed following the acquisition of firearms. But there is an equally good chance that these retrieval boats developed by a process of evolution analogous to that which produced the little kayak in more northern areas, only without the simultaneous loss of the original larger prototype.

The open retrieval boats are very popular today at Point Hope, Wainwright, and Barrow, and will replace the little kayaks in the near future. There are several reasons for the change: according to the Wainwright Eskimos the *umiahalurak* is easier to enter and leave, is less likely to be caught in young ice, can be used to rescue several men or a man and some of his dogs from drifting ice, is easier to build, and is not as tippy as the kayak. The last reason is the really important one. The northwest Alaskan Eskimos nurture an almost pathological fear of the kayak. This may be simply a rationalization that justifies their loss most easily, covers up for the fact that kayaks are just too difficult to build compared to the open boat, or has arisen for some other reason. The *kayapaurak* is actually one of the most stable kayak designs used by any Eskimo group, and for the learner it is at least as easy to master as the *umiahalurak*.

A check of the literature reveals that there is a historical basis for this fear of kayaks, related to the fact that even in aboriginal times these people were not highly skilled in their use. In the late nineteenth century, Murdoch made the following observation on the Point Barrow Eskimos:

> Although nearly every male above the age of boyhood owns and can manage one of these canoes [long-type kayak], they are much less generally employed than by any other Eskimo whose habits have been described, except the "Arctic Highlanders" [North Greenlanders] who have no boats, and perhaps those of Siberia and their Chukchee companions. The kaiak is used only during the season of open water, and then but little in the sea in the neighborhood of the villages [Murdoch 1892, p. 328].

He further notes that although they were "skillful and confident" in the kayak, they did not go out in rough seas. They were also unable to right them should they upset, unlike most maritime Eskimo groups. In the light of this historical situation, it is not difficult to understand why kayaks are totally absent in Point Hope today (where the aboriginal kayak would have been particularly useless because of the marine location), and entering the throes of extinction in Wainwright and Barrow. Young men at Wainwright, and many of the middle-aged hunters, generally do not know how to use kayaks and are afraid of them. There is no future for the kayak in this region, and the few which are now in existence will not be covered with new skins many more times. The *umiahalurak* is still growing in popularity and will probably remain in use until the men no longer hunt.

CHAPTER 15

Sleeping Seal Hunting

Ringed Seal *(Phoca hispida)*
Bearded Seal *(Erignathus barbata)*

Summer Camping

JUNE IS THE MONTH when groups of men, or men and their families, pack up bulky loads of gear and move along the coast by dog sled or skin boat to establish summer camps on the beach north or south of the village. Besides being an escape from the village with its mud and crowding, these camps are used as bases for sleeping seal and waterfowl hunting. Other less permanent camps are used in conjunction with hunting trips, when hunters decide to set up an overnight camp.

Whenever Eskimos go hunting for sleeping seals or when they travel down the coast by boat, they carry camping gear with them. It is always difficult to anticipate how far it will be necessary to travel in search of game or whether it might be found in abundance. Camping equipment is most likely to be carried when boats are used, because the weight and bulk of camping gear is less significant in a boat than on a dog sled. But temporary and "permanent" camps are an essential part of many hunting trips for sleeping seals, so we will discuss them here.

The basic and essential item for summer camping is a tent.

During the time when dog sledding is still going on, a tent is wrapped over the gear which is carried on the sled. After the sled is unloaded at a camping place, the tent is set up. In an *umiak* tents may also be used as a load cover, or they may be folded up and a tarp used to cover the gear.

Tents are not really essential as protection from the cold temperatures during the summer, although this is part of the reason they are used. Rain is probably the primary reason for having a tent, and the discomfort caused by wind is another factor. Because the sun remains above the horizon for nearly the entire summer, tents serve as a place of relative darkness, which adds to their convenience as a sleeping place. Finally, there is that notorious pest of the summer, the mosquito (*kittoġiak*), which may swarm along the coast in calm and warm weather. A tightly-closed tent, kept very warm inside by a camp stove, seems to be one of the best escapes from mosquitos. When the tent heats up inside, mosquitos alight on the walls and roof, where they may be killed easily. Mosquitos are rarely seen over the sea ice or ocean beyond a few hundred yards from shore.

Summer and winter tents are of basically similar design, but there are some differences worth noting. Both are made from white canvas that can be purchased at the native store. Some of the tents are commercially manufactured, but many are sewn by the Eskimo women. The typical winter tent has a floor space measuring about 7 feet square. There are low walls around the sides, with a low-peaked roof about 4 feet high in the center. Summer tents are nearly always larger, with a floor space from 7 × 7 feet up to 10 × 12 feet or more. The largest tents are usually reserved for whaling camps or summer beach camping, where a whole crew of men or a family plus a considerable amount of equipment must be accommodated. The walls are usually higher and the roof rises to a steep peak 5 or 6 feet high. There is little need to conserve heat or minimize the amount of heat-collecting space in the roof at this time of year.

Summer tents can accommodate six men or more, if they are tightly crowded. The usual number is three or four, however. The tent is supported by a ridgepole and two vertical end poles, like the winter tents. There is no built-in floor, but the lower edges of the walls are quite long, so they can be folded inside beneath the canvas, caribou skins, and gear to hold them securely. Sometimes sand is piled on these flaps to anchor them. Staking the lower edge of a tent is much less effective than this Eskimo method for keeping out wind and rain.

The best way to erect one of these tents, and the only way if there is a heavy wind, is to lay the tent out flat on the ground with the poles inside. At each corner a stake is driven into the ground, and the corner rope is secured to it. Two men crawl underneath and lift the roof, socketing the end poles into place by fitting them into holes carved in the roof beam. This way the walls are secured against the wind, and the structure is solid as soon as the poles are in place. Then the remaining side ropes are secured to stakes or to equipment, such as gas cans or sleds. There are no end ropes at all, although the corner lines are set out in the direction that the corner points, i.e., not at a right angle to the side.

The placement of the door relative to the wind direction is important. When there is any appreciable wind blowing, the tent is oriented so the door faces directly downwind. Rain must be kept from blowing in the door (so it does not face upwind), and it also should not beat against the sloping roof (so it is not placed at a right angle to the wind). Thus a wind-driven rain always strikes the back wall of the tent. When it rains, an extra tarp is usually laid over the back wall for added protection. The placement of shelter openings is different in winter, when the door should be at a right angle to the wind to prevent snow from blowing into the opening or drifting over it and covering it.

Eskimo tents are not treated with any waterproofing, because it causes stiffness and cracking in cold weather. This is why a hard rain will soak through the sloping roof if it beats directly onto it, and why extra tarps are laid over the tent when it rains. Care must be taken not to touch the tent roof during a rain, because it often leaks if this is done. On one occasion, a severe gale and driving rain struck an Eskimo beach camp. The tents were oriented so that their side walls faced the wind, and they began to leak. At the height of the storm, the tents were taken down and set up again in the right direction. The men were completely soaked, but they chose immediate discomfort over the protracted misery of sitting all day and night in leaky tents.

If a camp is to be used for a week or more, windbreaks may be set up around the tent, especially outside the door, so that it is not necessary to move the tent whenever the wind shifts. Windbreaks are made from pieces of canvas, supported by frameworks made from driftwood sticks. Sometimes they are set up along the windward wall. More frequently they form an L-shaped wall around the tent door, with the open side facing downwind.

Pressure-gas stoves are used to warm the tents. If no sleeping bags are available, which is sometimes the case in summer overnight camping, the stove burns all night. This provides enough heat to allow the men to sleep. Heat from the stove can be important at times like this, especially if it is windy and cold outside. Wet clothing can be hung along the ridge pole through the night if the stove is kept burning. It dries very quickly in the top of the tent where the heat is more intense.

Hunting crews often do not bother to carry sleeping bags, and are consequently forced to use other means (in addition to the stove) of staying warm when they sleep. When men travel with their own dog teams, they carry sleeping bags; but they apparently do not consider it worthwhile to load five or six bulky sleeping bags in an *umiak*, with the constant possibility that they will be soaked. Only when they definitely plan to be out for several days do they carry sleeping bags.

If they have no sleeping bags, the men lie very close together to maximize heat conservation. They prefer not to wear their parkas, but use them as blankets, especially to cover the legs and feet. They seem more concerned with covering their lower extremities than with their upper bodies. Some men also remove their boots, or at least loosen them as much as possible. This is one way to camp, but it is definitely not the warmest way to do so. Most nights spent under these conditions are visibly uncomfortable for all concerned, although they are not considered a real hardship by the Eskimos.

Much of the time, especially before the sea ice breaks up, campers have their sleeping bags available. These are almost always down-filled mummy bags. A single bag is used, summer or winter. During the summer the zipper is frequently left open to avoid excessive warmth. Some insulating material, such as caribou skin or heavy clothing, is laid between the bag and the canvas floor. On wet ground or ice caribou skins are seldom used, because the hide can be spoiled by absorbing too much moisture. Some men own and use air mattresses, which are greatly preferred but have a high mortality rate from puncturing. In more permanent camps a small commercially made mattress or pad may be used, but they are rather cumbersome to haul around.

Food is a very important part of all camping. This is particularly so because the Eskimos believe that good food is essential if they are to work to full capacity and keep themselves fortified against the cold. During the summer they seldom mention the value of food for keeping warm, but the frequency of breaks for hot tea and bread during cold weather demonstrates that warmth is probably the underlying motivation.

Favorite wintertime foods, such as frozen caribou or fish, are not commonly eaten during summer. Of course it is impossible to keep meat frozen during hunting trips, because the temperature stays above freezing. But even at home, where frozen meat is easily available from the ice cellars, other foods are preferred. "Soup" made from duck, goose, or caribou meat boiled with rice, flour, pepper, and onion is one of the most common dishes. Less elaborate meals consist of plain boiled meat (usually caribou or seal) dried meat (caribou or seal), or whale meat prepared by cooking or by fermenting in a closed barrel. The seasonal change from predominantly frozen raw meat to cooked meat may also relate to the kinds of animals that are available. For example, waterfowl is a popular food at this time, because this is when birds are available. They are normally prepared as soup, and apparently are never eaten raw. Seal oil is not used as frequently during the summer either, although it is usually provided when boiled meat is being eaten. Each person cuts pieces of cooked meat from the bone and dips them in seal oil before eating them. Some Eskimos like to use salt on raw and cooked meat.

At home the women prepare most of the meals, but during traveling and hunting the men have to cook for themselves. If two or more men of approximately equal age and skill are traveling together, they either prepare the meals together or play a game of cards to decide who will do the work. If there is a younger man in the group, especially if he could be called an apprentice hunter, he will be required to do the cooking and other menial tasks. In some instances certain older individuals do most of the cooking. These men seem to be the least proficient hunters—men who provide the least game and occupy the lowest status within the particular group. In *umiak* crews there are usually one or two persons who attend to these menial tasks. Because four to eight men regularly travel together in each boat, there is considerable group unity and an opportunity for a pattern of internal organization to emerge.

In camp, a morning meal is usually prepared before leaving. It is not very substantial, however, typically consisting of several cups of hot coffee with some bread or biscuits. Some men enjoy cereal or leftover meat at breakfast. From breakfast until supper there are no set meal times, but food and drink are prepared intermittently. These meals include hot tea, bread, and perhaps some leftover meat. The frequency of meals depends on the people and their activities. During long days of confinement by foul weather, meals may be almost continuous. On the other hand, when men are active meals are infrequent but more substantial.

The big meal of the day is "dinner," which comes sometime in late afternoon or "night," depending on the men's activities. This meal is often prepared by more than one person. During the summer, it consists of a main course, usually boiled meat or soup, which is eaten first. While the meat is being eaten, water is heated so that tea and bread can follow.

During early summer camping the dogs are fed each day, but amounts are small. Seal meat, cut from fresh kills, is the most important food. Birds are occasionally used, but this is uncommon because most of the available birds are types that are valued as food for people. On one occasion a dead walrus was lying on the beach where it had washed ashore the previous fall. The hunters camped here so they could cut away the decomposed remnants of its hide to feed their dogs.

An Eskimo said that when dogs are fed seal meat on the beach, where they ingest considerable amounts of sand with their food, they will become constipated. Indeed, some dogs have considerable difficulty and pain during elimination after a few days of this sort of feeding. To avoid this, the Eskimos throw the meat to each dog so it can be caught in midair, lessening the amount of sand that covers the food. Blubber should be fed to dogs once in a while, they say, to loosen their bowels. People also suffer from constipation while camping. Not infrequently the men joke about their condition and the number of days that have passed without relief.

Hours of activity vary greatly during the summer months, because they are not determined by the rising and setting of the sun. The sun dips lower toward the horizon around midnight, and the temperature may fall somewhat, but there is nothing to prevent the Eskimos from hunting around the clock. During hunting activities there is some tendency to start out late in the morning and to quit between 11:00 P.M. and 2:00 A.M. (roughly). In camps, however, men sometimes follow very unusual hours and get little sleep. Sometimes they play cards and talk inside the tent until perhaps 5:00 A.M., and then sleep late the following day. At times this late sleeping prevents them from doing much hunting the next day.

We mentioned earlier that protection from rain is one of the most important functions of shelters during the summer. As one would expect, rain is almost unheard of at these latitudes during the winter months. By March, however, it is possible to have wet fog, drizzle, or rain associated with weather systems from the south. By May, rain is common, and these late spring rains help to thaw the snow quickly.

At any time of the year Eskimos will carry on as usual if a light rain starts falling when they are out hunting. But their reactions vary when it starts falling harder. In March of 1965, for example, there was a soaking rain for several hours while many seal hunters were out on the ice near Wainwright. There were few seals, so about twenty men gathered to drink tea and talk while watching along the edge. The rain fell harder and harder, but the men stayed as though it were just an unseasonably warm day, ignoring the fact that their clothes were completely soaked. Had they been required to stay out overnight they would undoubtedly have done everything possible to avoid getting wet, but they were all returning home where they could change into dry clothing.

This same rain was followed by sub-zero weather, which froze the wetness into a heavy ice crust over the snow everywhere. For several weeks the crust remained in many places that were swept clean of snow. The crust was so thick that the dogs and sleds did not break through, and it was so slippery that the dogs literally fell down while pulling. At the same time, ice covered the steep sides of snowbanks and drifts, rendering it nearly impossible to walk over their slick surfaces. In fact, even under normal winter conditions it is difficult to walk over the steep hard drifts, especially so because Eskimo skin boots have such smooth soles.

During the summer months Eskimos try to avoid going on hunting excursions when it is raining, even if the rain is light. It is surprising, therefore, that when they are caught out in the rain they seldom change their course or even comment on the situation. If it rains while the men are at home or in camp, they spend their time loafing around, or find something with which to occupy themselves indoors until the weather improves. Sometimes they will pass up good seal or walrus hunting to avoid traveling in the rain. It should be said, however, that if animals are reported in abundance near the village or camp, no amount of rain, or any other condition that is not dangerous, will prevent Eskimo hunters from going out.

There are some other responses to rain as well. In one instance a crew was traveling by *umiak* about 20 miles from Wainwright. The day had been intermittently rainy. As another fairly heavy shower approached, the crew went quickly ashore and pitched a tent. All gear was unloaded and put inside, followed by the men, who drank tea while they weathered the storm. When the rain passed, they reloaded the boat and returned to the floes to hunt seals.

In another incident, which we mentioned earlier, a storm-driven rain started leaking through the tents at an encampment. The men and their gear became thoroughly soaked while they moved the tents to stop the leaking. They actually became quite angry about the weather. This is most contrary to the usual

Eskimo attitude toward unfavorable conditions, although this situation could have developed into quite a dangerous one. The Eskimos usually laugh in earnest at such misfortunes, even when they are happening. Those who do not do so are gently chastised for their unhealthy attitude. Such an approach is genuinely adaptive here, where so many things can go wrong, and where discomfort is a part of everyday life.

Wilkinson (1955, p. 70) describes an occurrence similar to this one. He and an Eskimo were camped on Baffin Island during the summer when a long, soaking rain began to fall. Their tent started to leak, and soon their gear was wet and their sleeping bags were soaked through. Rather than sit it out they broke camp, rolling everything inside a bearskin, and began traveling. Their clothing became completely saturated, but they preferred to be active since they had to be wet anyway. This is probably the wisest procedure under such conditions.

Before discussing the techniques of sleeping seal hunting we should briefly consider the kind of footgear that is used during this and other summer activities. Footgear is certainly one of the most essential items of clothing in the Arctic. One of the most marked differences between winter and summer clothing is the type of boots that are worn. The *ugurulik*, which has caribou skin uppers and bearded sealskin soles, is unfit for use on the wet snow and standing water of summer sea ice. They would leak badly and be ruined quickly under these conditions, so people do not use them outside the village at this time. Some Eskimos prefer to use a type of *ugurulik* around the village as long as the ground is not wet and muddy. These are shorter than winter boots, with uppers reaching 5 or 6 inches above the ankle. They are also made from summer skins, which are light and comfortable. Such boots are considered dressy.

Sealskin boots are the only skin footgear used for traveling and hunting on the sea ice in the summertime. These boots have been described many times in the literature and are found throughout much of the Eskimo domain. The soles are made from bearded seal hide, and the rest is made of ringed sealskin with the fur turned inside and dark leather outside. The seams are all sewed with sinew, which makes the boots quite waterproof once they have been moistened to swell the thread. Thin straps of sealskin are used to tie the boot securely. Wool socks and felt liners are usually worn inside.

Few Wainwright men wear sealskin boots nowadays. They are apparently quite difficult to make, and not many women are willing or able to sew a pair even for their husbands. Sealskin boots are admired because of their lightness, warmth, and comfort, and because they are impervious to water, if they are properly made. One drawback is that they should be cared for after each use. This means that they must be dried, if they become wet, and softened by working before they are worn again. Occasionally they should be greased with seal oil to maintain their waterproofing and to prevent rotting. Wilkinson (1955, p. 88) reports that on Baffin Island the work of drying and softening boots was so great that if a woman had more than three children, she could not keep up with the demand for dry boots.

Sealskin boots will soak up water slowly until they dampen the wearer's socks. They also become quite cold on the bottom, where they are always in contact with the subsurface. Although rubber footgear gets damp inside from perspiration, it is still warmer than skin, until the cool fall weather sets in (Wilkinson 1955, p. 88). Stefansson (1950, p. 267) agrees that no boots can keep the feet completely dry on the wet summer ice, but apparently prefers sealskin boots over any alternative.

Among the Wainwright Eskimos today, various types of manufactured rubber boots are by far the most popular summer footgear. These boots vary considerably, but are usually about 12 inches high and are closed with laces. Some men use "insulated" types, which are warmer but heavier. Many Eskimos prefer slip-on boots that reach just below the knee. These are sometimes fashioned from old hipboots with the tops cut off at knee level. One or several pairs of socks, usually made of wool, are worn inside rubber boots. Leather boots, commonly used for outdoor activities in the "States," are seldom used here, probably because they are more expensive and less adequate than rubber boots.

Rubber hipboots are the most common footgear in summer. Although they are quite expensive and can be heavy and clumsy for walking, hipboots are often essential for travel over spring and summer sea ice. Especially during the month of June, the sea ice is covered with an interlacing network of puddles and rivulets so complex that it prevents effective travel without frequent wading. Similar conditions prevail on the tundra at this time. Although much of the water drains off the ice by July, there are still many puddles and a sort of all-pervading wetness on the summer floes.

There are other advantages to using hipboots. First, they are quite warm as long as two or three pairs of socks are worn inside. In addition, the entire leg is protected by them from wind and water. This is important not only for wading in water and slushy snow, but also for protection from wind, rain, and sea spray while traveling by boat in rough seas. These boots also offer protection from moisture and abrasion when hunters must crawl over the ice stalking sleeping seals. Finally, hipboots are convenient when walruses are being butchered, because they prevent the legs from getting soaked with blood and oil.

Whenever they do not need to protect their upper legs, Eskimos fold their hipboots down so they reach just below the knee. They prefer to wear them this way to minimize perspiration, especially while they are walking or exercising strenuously. Hipboots, or any other type of rubber boots, are dried as often as possible. If a man falls through the ice when wearing hipboots he may be in real trouble, because the air trapped inside them holds his legs on the surface, forcing his head down. He cannot regain proper equilibrium until the allows the boots to fill with water. Only then can he hope to get back onto the ice.

Sealskin "hipboots" were formerly used in this region. They were probably light and very serviceable, if a bit difficult to dry and care for. In the years before rifles were available, they were probably especially useful for stalking sleeping seals on the wet spring ice.

Before leaving the subject of footgear and camping, we should mention camp shoes. Eskimo hunters often use some sort of warm and comfortable boots or slippers in and around the tent when they are camping. These may be hand-sewn boot liners or slippers made of caribou or other soft fur. Often they are manufactured slippers or comforters. Some men just use a pair of light leather boots or the short-topped *uguruliks* described above. When he has something else to wear, the Eskimo can dry his hunting boots immediately upon arrival in camp. Less snow or loose dirt is carried into the tent, also, because they can be slipped off and cleaned before stepping inside. The additional warmth and comfort of changing into something soft and dry after a day's travel is probably sufficient reason for carrying this extra footgear along.

Behavior and Occurrence of Sleeping Seals

During the spring and summer ringed and bearded seals crawl up through enlarged breathing holes or cracks to lie atop the ice. They do this especially when the weather is warm, so they can nap and bask comfortably for many hours. But it is not only during the warm seasons that this kind of behavior occurs. In Hudson's Bay, sleeping seals are seen at any time of year, though only on the warmest days. In North Greenland they come up on the ice until October and November (Degerbøl and Freuchen 1935, p. 198).

The situation in northwest Alaska is similar to that in North Greenland. Sleeping seals are not found during the depths of winter, but they appear as early as February (Point Hope) or March (Wainwright) when the weather is unusually warm, i.e., 10° to 20° above zero. Bearded seals are especially likely to appear atop the ice during these late winter warm spells.

It is not until May or June that sleeping seals become common around Wainwright—common enough that a real effort goes into hunting them. Around the end of May and beginning of June standing water covers wide areas of the ice surface, preventing the seals from coming up in large numbers. But drain holes form soon afterward and the surface is "dry" again. At this time, while many large areas of flat ice are still intact and the weather is balmy (by Arctic standards) seals are scattered on the ice everywhere. Bearded seals seem to prefer areas far offshore. Not many are seen until the *umiak* hunting begins, when they are found sleeping on drifting ice pans.

Seals usually crawl up on the ice during the part of the day

THE BIOLOGICAL ENVIRONMENT

when the sun is highest in the sky, when the temperature reaches its peak. At "night" they go back into the water, perhaps to feed, unless the weather is especially warm. A seal will sometimes lie on the ice for twenty-four hours at a time. During the cooler spring and summer days few seals are up, and those that are do not sleep soundly or for a very long time. The Eskimos do not bother to hunt them at such times. The few seals that are seen will be hard to stalk, because they sleep so little and will flop back into the water at the slightest disturbance. Seals apparently stay off the ice entirely when it rains.

In early summer, before the breakup, seals do not come up on the ice when it is in motion. The obvious reason for this is the danger of having the crack or hole close, preventing the seals from returning to the water. Later on, when the floes are broken and scattered (during *umiak* hunting), ringed seals are found only on the largest ice floes, which rarely fracture or pile even though they are drifting slowly with the pack.

In the Wainwright region there are certain areas where sleeping seals are predictably common. These are the large expanses of flat or little-broken ice which are found south of the village, from the abandoned site of Ḳiḷḷamittaġvik all the way to Icy Cape, and in Peard Bay to the north. During the period of optimum conditions for sleeping seal hunting the Eskimos set up camps along the beach, from which they travel onto the ice to hunt. Once they have killed enough seals (and waterfowl) for a sled load, or less if they are not lucky, they haul them back to Wainwright. They usually return to the camp almost immediately, carrying fresh supplies with them.

Sleeping seals are also hunted on daily trips out from the village. The area near Wainwright is not very productive, because the ice is often quite rough and most of the seals have been killed or frightened away by the concentrated hunting activities of winter and spring. So it is best to take a dog team and go north or south of the village, or to travel far offshore when a west wind causes safe ice conditions.

It has been noted above that seals prefer to come up on the ice in areas where it is seldom moved and piled. In these flat expanses the seals face a minimum of danger from polar bears or

Eskimo hunters, because they can see anything that approaches while it is still far off. According to Freuchen and Solomonsen (1958, p. 178), seals in the eastern Arctic will not lie atop the ice unless it is absolutely flat all around them. Thus the Eskimos can avoid rough ice when they travel, because there will be no game in such areas. This statement certainly does not apply in northwest Alaska.

Along the coast from Point Hope to Barrow there are few areas where the ice is as flat as the vast unmoved sea ice plains of the Canadian Arctic or the fjords of Greenland. If seals were to require such conditions here, they would rarely find an area where they could come on top of the ice. So they are forced to climb up onto smaller flat areas which are surrounded by ridges and hummocks. They definitely tend to seek the largest and flattest areas in the immediate vicinity, however. There may even be a general movement to areas such as the protected bight north of Icy Cape, where there are extensive fields of flat ice. Eskimos say that seals also avoid the land when they sleep on the ice, especially when an offshore breeze carries the tundra smell out over the ice.

Knowing these things, the Eskimos have a good idea of what kind of areas to look for sleeping seals. As they travel over the ice from place to place they can accomplish the double objective of reaching their destination and hunting seals at the same time. Yet the most productive sleeping seal hunting is done when the man goes out with this specific purpose in mind. In any case, frequent stops are made to scan from the top of high ice piles. Binoculars are very important for this, because there are always many dark spots or irregularities on the ice that look like seals. The hunter must often watch each one for a few minutes to see if there is any movement. Seals lift their heads to look around at frequent intervals, so they are fairly easy to identify in this way.

When he stops to scan, the hunter checks the largest flat places (*kaiaksuakpak*) first, because these are the most likely areas for seals to occur. Then he looks at the smaller flats, hoping to spot a seal lying close enough to rough ice so that it could be shot by sneaking up behind this cover. Before going out onto flat places, the Eskimo usually stops his team to look around for seals. Bearded seals are especially careless about sleeping near rough ice. When a man is walking, he stops to look around before showing himself even on quite small flat places, hoping to see a bearded seal basking nearby.

Stalking Sleeping Seals

The Wainwright Eskimos seldom bother to stalk seals in the large flats, even though they may be there in abundance. Instead, they leave these seals and move through the rough ice, waiting for the easier and closer shots. In the long run, a hunter gets more shots if he does not attempt difficult and time-consuming stalks. Once in a while a man will take a long pot shot at a seal in a big ice flat, hoping for a lucky hit but not wasting much time at it.

Occasionally, a lone seal becomes overwhelmed with curiosity when a dog team is driven straight toward it. The hunter may be able to stop his sled and take a shot at it before it scrambles into the water, but this rarely happens. If there is a group of seals along a crack, they usually frighten easily when a dog team appears.

Baffin Islanders have a more effective method for hunting lone seals on flat ice: When the ice becomes very noisy underfoot in spring (e.g., when cold night air makes the surface crunchy), it is very hard to stalk seals without alerting them by the sound of one's footsteps. These Canadian Eskimos just drive their teams at full speed toward the seal. It may see the sled coming and dive into the water, but sometimes it is curious and stays up to watch. In the latter case, the hunters give "a long steady drawn out *Ooooooh*, as loud as they can." The seal becomes more curious, rolling around and stretching upward to get a better view. At about 150 yards a man who is riding as a passenger jumps off the sled, runs doubled over until he has a clear shot, drops to one knee, and fires. If the seal is unusually curious, the hunter can sit down and aim carefully (Wilkinson 1955, p. 88).

A hunter usually spots a sleeping seal through binoculars from some distance away, and then drives toward it with his dog team. Somewhere nearby, say 50 to 200 yards away, he anchors the sled securely and walks toward the place where the seal is lying. Sometimes there is an ice pile within shooting range of the animal, so that almost no stalking is necessary, but this is rare. More often, there are some flat areas that must be crossed in order to get within shooting range. In these cases, the hunter must know about the behavior of sleeping seals in general; and he must take some time to study the idiosyncrasies of the particular animal that he is about to stalk. He also looks over the ice in the area so that he can take advantage of every irregularity in the surface as he approaches his prey.

This reconnaissance is done from the concealment of the closest ice pile, which is reached by walking quietly and keeping out of sight. From here the hunter watches his seal to see what its pattern of alternate sleeping and awakening is. Some seals sleep for only ten or twenty seconds and then raise their heads to look around; others will sleep for up to a minute or more and then glance up briefly before napping again. On warm days they sleep most soundly. If it is very bright and hot, however, they must keep turning over to cool off, making their sleep periods as short as they are on cold, windy days (Degerbøl and Freuchen 1935, p. 199). Some seals do not want to be bothered at all. It seems to take a supreme effort on their part just to lift their heads for a moment before dropping them back to the ice. Others are nervous and wary, so they spend almost as much time looking around as they do sleeping.

As the hunter watches and analyzes the particular seal that he will stalk, he takes note of the surrounding conditions. As much as possible, he will try to keep some little irregularity of the ice between himself and the seal, so that by crouching or crawling he can stay out of sight. At the same time he must not get upwind or the seal will smell him. It is also necessary to be fairly quiet. This may be difficult when the ice surface is crunchy or when there are water puddles to wade across. Because he is almost certain to be in plain sight some of the time, the hunter wears a parka cover of white cloth (*kategeni*), which resembles the color of the surrounding ice.

It is best to approach from the rear of the seal, if possible. This is not hard to do if there is only one seal, but if there are two or more, they usually face in different directions. If one of the seals takes fright and dives into the water, there is a very good chance that those nearby will follow suit. Those farther away may be put on alert. Thus, groups of seals are very hard to approach, and Eskimos much prefer to stalk a lone seal. A seal that senses danger will sleep only in brief snatches, raising its head often—almost always looking straight at the hunter, if he has been detected. A seal that has been alerted is quite difficult to stalk; and the hunter must be very still for a long time until the animal resumes its normal sleeping.

Whenever a hunter is close to a seal (within 50 to 100 yards), he is very slow and cautious about every move he makes. When the seal's head is up, he stops dead in his tracks and does not move until the animal sleeps again. It is important to stay in a position where the seal can be seen at all times, in order to avoid making a noise while it is awake. The Eskimos says that it is not a good idea to stare at the seal while its head is up, however. It is better to glance at it briefly so that it does not become frightened. They also advise against wearing sunglasses, because of their dark color and reflective surface. Sometimes a seal (especially a bearded seal) that becomes suspicious will not even lift its head when it looks around. Hunters must have keen vision to see when it opens its eyes, or to see a shadow on the ice when its head is lifted just a few inches off the ice.

Seal hunters often carry a knife, or ice-scratcher (*azigaun*) made from seal claws, which they use to scratch the ice. They sometimes scratch the ice while stalking a sleeping seal, especially if it becomes alarmed and keeps watching. When the seal lays its head down, scratching is stopped; and it is started again when the animal awakens. It is best to start scratching softly and then increase until a fairly loud sound is produced. The seal will probably look around for a while and finally sleep again, but now more soundly than before. Seals often scratch the ice themselves, which perhaps explains why the sound makes them less afraid.

There are a few behavioral traits specific to the *uguruk*, or bearded seal, that make stalking this species different from stalking the ringed seal. In the first place, the bearded seal is much easier to approach. It can be hunted even on very flat ice. According to the literature, bearded seals have very keen vision. But they sleep more soundly, awake less frequently, change position less often, and generally care less about what is going on around them. They will also lie on the ice close to hummocks, allowing easy approach to within shooting range.

Because bearded seals will crawl up onto small pans of drifting ice, they are sometimes shot from a boat or are approached by getting out onto the ice cake. For example, an *uguruk* was once found asleep on an ice pan about 50 yards in diameter. Although the animal was not disturbed by the sound of the outboard engine of another *umiak* that was nearby, the men who approached it stopped their engine and paddled quietly up to the ice pan. Then one of them stepped out onto the ice, crawled a few yards, and took careful aim before shooting from a prone position. After the seal was shot and its head dropped limply to the ice, the men started their engine and sped around to the other side of the pan, where the animal was lying very close to the edge.

It is very difficult to watch men stalking sleeping seals, because this type of hunting is highly individualistic. In open lead sealing, for instance, there is some individualism, but there is considerable social activity as well. This is partly because the hunters are concentrated along the limited space at the margins of open water. They also tend to band together in groups of two to five, for mutual assistance and expediency. The only time this occurs among sleeping seal hunters is when two men go together and one watches the dogs while the other goes after a seal. They must stalk the animals alone, however. It is also difficult to make contact with other hunters, because they are scattered widely over many square miles of ice surface.

In spite of the fact that sleeping seals are fairly alert, it is not difficult to hunt them by the modern technique. If he understands certain basic characteristics of seal behavior and knows something about the stalking technique, a man with common sense and some hunting ability can easily achieve success with the method. It is easy to understand why this is one of the first methods that boys learn, and one of the last to be given up by old men.

The basic principles of modern sleeping seal hunting are intimately bound to the peculiarities of seal behavior. These same
principles were used in the prerifle days, when it was necessary
to creep to within a harpoon's throw, and sometimes even closer.
They have been carried over into the new method essentially
unchanged, except that less skill is required of today's hunters.
The older hunters' ability to stalk seals is illustrated by two old
men from Wainwright, Igruk and Paniktak, who have gotten
so close to seals that they killed them with a knife. Kavik has
twice grabbed seals with his bare hands. These were all young
seals, which are the easiest to approach.

Another method of stalking seals, which is no longer used
today, is "playing seal." This method is similar to the one described
above except that the hunter wears dark-colored clothing so that
he will look like his prey. Instead of trying to sneak up to it unde-
tected, he wants the seal to see him. When he gets to within a
few hundred yards of the animal, the Eskimo begins to play
seal. He imitates the movements of a seal whenever it is awake,
and crawls straight toward it while it sleeps. He must always stay
in plain sight and never deviate from a particular line of approach,
because to do otherwise would frighten the prey.

As soon as the seal begins to watch the hunter, he makes the
movements of a seal, flapping his arms like flippers and lifting his
head periodically, never crawling forward until it sleeps again.
The Alaskan Eskimo also scratches the ice to perfect the mimic.
If the hunter does these things each time his prey looks up, the
animal will eventually disdain watching the man any longer,
and will only look in the other direction, secure in the belief that
another seal is near. Eventually the hunter crawls to within
shooting range.

The use of white shooting screens is a method fully described
for Greenlanders and Canadian Eskimos, but less well known
among the north Alaskans. A shooting screen is simply a white
cloth "sail" held on a wood frame. It may vary in size from only
1 or 2 feet in height to several feet wide and up to 4 or 5 feet high.
A common type described in the literature is small and fits onto
a very little sled. The hunter crawls behind this rig, with his
rifle pointed through a hole in the screen. This type was described

by Eskimos from Kotzebue, Point Hope, and Wainwright, and was said to have been used only by "old timers." Another kind of screen described was triangular and was carried by hand.

Shooting screens are very effective and their use requires less skill and practice than any other method of hunting sleeping seals. The hunter crawls or walks behind the screen, stopping each time the seal looks up. He is careful to step quietly and not to get upwind. He also keeps the sun more or less in front of him so the screen looks like a piece of ice and does not catch his shadow. If possible, some rough ice or snow-covered land should form the hunter's backdrop. Making a low humming sound has been suggested for a cover-up, if the ice crunches loudly underfoot (Wilkinson 1955, p. 88). Scratching the ice might also be used. Northwest Alaskan Eskimos do not hunt this way today, probably because it takes more time than their method of stalking in rough ice areas.

Igruk described an unusual method of hunting sleeping seals in spring near the mouth of the Mackenzie River. When the river flows out over the sea ice in spring, coloring the ice dirty brown, the hunter walks out in search of sleeping seals. When he spots one, he walks straight toward it in plain sight, and eventually the animal flops into the water. He then goes to the hole and waits beside it with an iron hook or harpoon. Soon the water starts to pulsate, and the hunter knows his seal will rise in a moment. When it does, he harpoons it, or simply gaffs it with the hook and hauls it up on the ice where he kills it by hand. A similar technique is described for the Bering Strait region, where hunters cover the hole with an "arch of snow," so that the seal will not see the hunter and will poke its head up right next to him (Nelson 1899, pp. 128–29). Sometimes a seal will sleep so soundly on the ice that a hunter can walk right up to it and kill it (Boas 1964, p. 77).

Shooting Sleeping Seals

When seals lie atop the ice, they usually face toward the hole or crack from which they emerged, affording the quickest possible escape. Thus, if a sleeping seal is not killed or knocked totally unconscious when it is shot, it will no doubt flop into the water. In fact, the ice around the opening may be slippery enough that the impact of the bullet or a slight convulsion could cause the animal to slide into the water. The hunter must therefore know where and how to aim properly, if he is to be successful.

The best place to shoot a ringed seal is in the head, which will either kill it or knock it out cold. A neck shot, one that is sure to hit the vertebrae, requires surer aim but is just as deadly. If the bullet does not hit any bones, the seal will escape and die in the waters below. If the seal lies facing at an angle to the hunter, a head or neck shot will be fairly easy. A hit in the body from this angle will not stop the animal. If the seal faces directly toward him, the head and neck, as well as a direct shot through the chest and heart, are deadly hits.

Degerbøl and Freuchen (1935, p. 202) suggest that if a seal is facing away from the hunter, he will have to shoot through the back and shoulders to hit its head. But from this position, or whenever a seal is sleeping with its head on the ice, it is much better to make a noise so that the seal will look up to see what is going on. The Eskimos suggest whistling to get the animal's attention. Sometimes this sound is not loud enough, so other noises like loud scratching, clicking the rifle bolt, or shouting are necessary. There is no reason to hurry in this case, because any seal which is that lazy is not about to go anywhere. After a long and exhausting stalk, it is disconcerting, to say the least, if the seal refuses to wake up and look around when the hunter finally wants it to.

The bearded seal is not as easy to shoot, because if it is hit in the head its muscles contract spasmodically, then it begins to shake and convulse. This may be enough to cause the senseless body to slip down into the sea. It is best to hit the neck if possible, because this kills instantly without setting off convulsions. Also, a head-on shot in the mouth, chin, or just below the chin is very effective. It may be possible to hit the animal's neck while it sleeps, but if the neck is not clearly visible, it is better to make a noise and awaken it.

If the Eskimo shoots and misses, the animal may or may not dive to safety. If the bullet hits low, striking the ice somewhere nearby, the seal will dive instantly. If the shot goes over its head, the seal will look around anxiously, but usually will not dive. The loud report is not a completely foreign sound on the ocean ice, where violent cracking and thunderous piling are common occurrences. After missing his first shot, the hunter quietly prepares for another, aims a bit lower, and fires. For this reason it is always better to aim just a bit high, unless it is such a close shot that a good hit is certain.

Sled dogs have the unfortunate habit of becoming extremely excited when they hear a shot, after they have been left behind during the stalk. This is why one man is sometimes left to watch the dogs while the other hunts. In the Canadian Arctic, dogs are taught to lie down while the Eskimo goes after a seal, but at the crack of the gun, they race toward him. He may not have a chance for a second shot before the huskies come pounding into view and frighten the seal (Freuchen and Solomonsen 1958, p. 212). The Wainwright Eskimos anchor their teams with iron hooks, but the dogs sometimes jerk the hook loose in their excitement and run toward the noise. They are always punished for this, but nothing can stop it.

After a seal is shot, its head drops limply to the ice. If the bullet misses, the animal either flips into the water or snaps to startled attentiveness. Thus it is always easy to tell if the seal is hit. Because it might gradually slide toward the water, or might regain consciousness and escape, the Eskimo jumps up quickly and runs for it as fast as he can. If the carcass does slip into the water, it is probably lost. Sometimes it will float, however, so it is a good idea to check before giving up.

If the seal is unconscious but still alive, there are several ways to kill it. The most common method is to roll it over on its back and lift its head high, so the upper part of the body is off the ice. Then with the neck bent sharply toward its chest, the body is pressed down onto the ice slowly and firmly, until the bones of the upper neck snap loudly. Another method is to stamp on its neck, or step on the neck with one foot and stamp its head with the other. Old-time seal netters killed seals by slugging them in the ear. A stone-headed club was also used. Ringed seals (and presumably also bearded seals) are said never to bite or attack a man even when they are in grave danger. My own observations substantiate this, although Degerbøl and Freuchen (1935, pp. 202–3) write that ". . . when in danger it bites powerfully and bravely, and its bite is frightful."

It is sometimes possible to shoot more than one seal when several are grouped close together. If the first seal that is hit drops to the ice lifelessly, the others might not become alarmed. If it moves or dives, however, the rest will be gone in an instant. It is especially easy to shoot more than one bearded seal this way, because they are harder to frighten away. A hunter sometimes manages to line up two seals and shoot both with one shot. Needless to say, a man does this few times during his life. When a mother seal and her pup lie on top of the ice, which happens very infrequently, it is simple to get both seals. If the mother is hit first, the silver-haired pup will not leave, and can even be picked up unharmed.

Sleeping seal hunting lasts for only a few months of the year, but it is adaptable to several distinct methods of execution, requires little special equipment, can be carried on when there is no open water, and is not difficult where the ice is rough (as in this part of the Arctic). For these reasons, plus the fact that seals are abundant in certain areas during early summer, sleeping seal hunting is a highly productive method. During winter open lead sealing it is quite exceptional for a man to get more than five ringed seals in one day, and one or two is considered a normal catch. However, it is not unusual for a man to get five to ten seals in a single day (eight to ten hours) by the sleeping seal method. This might include a huge bearded seal as well.

CHAPTER 16

Umiak Hunting

Ringed Seal *(Phoca hispida)*
Bearded Seal *(Erignathus barbata)*

Preparation for the Hunt

UMIAK HUNTING begins during the spring whaling season, when crews patrol the open lead in skin boats, searching for seals and waterfowl. After whaling is over, and before the landfast ice breaks up, there is a lull in this kind of hunting. Occasionally a boat may be pulled out across the landfast floe and launched in the open water beyond, but this is probably done only when the breakup is late. *Umiak* hunting usually gets into full swing in late June or early July, when the boats have free passage through lanes in the grounded ice and out into the fragmenting pack ice beyond.

Of all the various summer activities, *umiak* hunting is probably the coldest. Long rides in open boats lend a biting chill to even the warmest Arctic weather. But temperatures at this time of year are seldom cold enough to warrant the use of traditional fur parkas. They might occasionally be worn for activities such as waterfowl hunting, where a hunter must sit quietly in a blind for hours on end. Caribou fur cannot be worn during the summer under any circumstances, because it must be protected from rain or excessive moisture. The main reason that fur parkas are used at all nowadays is probably because manufactured garments cannot compare with them for warmth. Fur clothing is also light and comfortable, but requires extensive care. Sealskin parkas, which probably were used for summer wear during aboriginal times, are not made in Wainwright today, except for sale to outsiders.

During the warm months Wainwright Eskimos find that cloth parkas are quite sufficient. By far the most popular type is made by the women from cloth they buy at the native store. They are very light, made with a blue, green, or black corduroy shell with a lining of quilted cloth. The design is similar to fur parkas, but there is a zipper in front. Wolverine or wolf fur trims the hood, and sometimes the cuffs and bottom edge as well. Typically, they are decorated with geometric cloth designs, some showing considerable skill and ingenuity. When they are new, these parkas are used only in the village and for social events, but as they become more worn, they are used for hunting.

This kind of parka is standard men's wear in summer, both around the village and for sea-ice hunting. Except in the balmiest weather, however, this alone is not enough for hunting. Several layers of additional clothing are usually worn underneath, including heavy shirts, sweaters, sweat shirts, insulated or thermal underwear, or another jacket. Typically, a man would wear a cotton T-shirt, one or two wool or flannel shirts, a nylon insulated underwear jacket, and his summer parka. This outfit will suffice for cool summer weather. Layers can be removed during strenuous activity or warm weather. Nylon insulated underwear is quite popular, as are the similar nylon jackets. Coats with zippers are handy because they can be opened easily to prevent overheating and perspiration, an everyday problem where alternations between protracted inactivity and bursts of strenuous exertion are common.

Heavier cloth parkas, either commercial (often down-filled) or surplus Air Force types, are used for the coldest summer activities. These warm parkas are reserved for certain occupations, notably traveling in the open skin boats, which require long periods of inactivity while exposed to the wind, rain, or ocean spray. It is always necessary to bundle up almost as if it were winter when traveling by boat, even when temperatures are high and winds are calm.

This chilling effect is compounded when it is necessary to travel against a wind, or when a constant soaking spray blows over the occupants of the boat. The Air Force parkas are more or less impervious to this spray, unless they are continuously exposed to it for an hour or more. Heavy parkas are worn only when they are needed. Thus, they are removed when the boat is drawn up onto the ice or when it is traveling with the wind on a warm day. The Eskimos are not disposed to overdress, even if it would not be particularly uncomfortable to do so. They would rather carry an extra parka along, using it only occasionally, than take the chance of wearing too much and becoming overheated or of carrying the extra weight on their shoulders.

Raincoats or rain parkas of assorted shapes and materials are used by some of the men for *umiaḳ* travel or for hunting during rainy weather. The most popular type is a hooded rain jacket, usually with a zipper in front. A light or moderate rain will not cause enough discomfort for the Eskimo so that he puts on a raincoat, although he might wear a heavy parka if one is at hand. A heavy or prolonged rainfall, or an especially heavy spray while riding in an *umiaḳ*, induces those who have raincoats to put them on. The ocean spray may cause considerably more soaking than the worst rainfall, especially for the men sitting near the stern and along the windward side of the boat. Generally speaking, raincoats are seldom used, although many hunters own them.

During the spring and summer, protection from brightness is almost as important as protection from cold. Hats with visors cut down some of the direct sunshine, but sunglasses are necessary to cope with the bright glare of snow, ice, and water. Aboriginal Eskimos used "sunglasses" which were made in two ways: one consisted of a narrow wooden piece that fitted over the eyes, with either one slit, two slits, or two holes carved in it; the other was made from two caribou hooves fastened together in the middle and tied around the head, again with slits to look through. These "sunglasses" cut down the brightness, and did not fog or frost as modern sunglasses do, but they also restricted the field of vision.

Sunglasses, which are now bought at the store, are used by most individuals by the middle of March. Early in spring the cold temperatures often render them useless owing to frost, and drizzle, or fog may do the same later on. They are probably most important during the spring and early summer, when the sun shines constantly and there is still plenty of snow to reflect its brightness. As summer moves along fewer men wear sunglasses. The tundra turns green or brown, and the sea ice breaks up into scattered pans and floes, with little or no snow remaining to brighten it. Not everyone is equally sensitive to brightness. Some men almost always wear sunglasses and others are never seen using them.

It is also necessary to protect the hands from the chill and wetness of summer ice hunting. Essentially the same kinds of cloth "work" gloves are worn year round, but only a single layer is required in summer. Gloves are constantly getting soaked during this season, either from the wet ice or snow, or from spray during *umiak* travel. Thus each man carries one or two extra pairs with him. Unless the weather is quite chilly, wet gloves are warm enough, but they eventually become uncomfortable and a change is made. Whenever they stop for a "coffee break" or make camp, the men dry their gloves by holding them over a gasoline stove or hanging them inside the tent. When Eskimo hunters work hard, as during hauling or butchering, or if the weather is warm, they usually wear no gloves.

In recent years cloth gloves with a rubberized outer coating have become available. Some of the better types are flexible enough to allow good dexterity, and are frequently used by Wainwright hunters. They are usually carried by some men in each *umiak* crew, especially for walrus hunting. They are good protection from the blood and grease that permeate everything when animals are butchered. Otherwise, the hands must be washed repeatedly with snow, slush, or water from puddles on top of the ice. Sea water is not good for washing, because it leaves a salt residue on the hands. Rubberized gloves are used for butchering all kinds of game in the summertime, but when temperatures drop to fall and winter levels, the rubber coating becomes stiff and they are no longer used. Their only other use is for protection from wetness during heavy rains, exposure to ocean spray, or for such things as crawling on wet ice while stalking sleeping seals.

The last item of clothing to be considered is pants. Here again there is almost no use of fur during the summer. During precontact times sealskin pants were worn, and they offered the advantage of warmth and waterproofing. They would be useful today for many summer activities, such as open lead sealing where it is necessary to sit or kneel on wet ice, or *umiak̦* hunting with its ever-present spray. But they must be treated with care, they are a bit too warm, and their stiffness impedes movement. There are some cold, wet summer days when sealskin pants would be very useful, but because of the infrequency of need and the disadvantages mentioned above, modern Eskimos prefer cloth pants.

Cotton or denim pants are purchased by mail or from the local store. Two or more pairs may be worn at once, often with a pair of long underwear. Nylon insulated underwear is frequently used. Heavy pants, usually some sort of Armed Forces surplus, are used during the coldest summer traveling or hunting. The most common of these are blue Air Force flight pants. Heavy pants are often carried along for *umiak̦* hunting, but they are seldom used. If the weather turns very cold and windy, or if rain or spray becomes a problem, they are worn. They can also be used as a sort of mattress by hunters who must camp without sleeping bags.

For wet conditions, or occasionally for butchering, some men wear rubber rain pants. These are not at all common, but the Eskimos admire them and often express their desire to have a pair. Rain pants are useful for the same conditions as hipboots or sealskin pants. The popularity of hipboots is probably one reason why few men buy rain pants, since both serve approximately the same purpose. Rain pants are never worn until conditions require them.

We have mentioned several times that Eskimos like to make frequent stops for food and drink while they hunt or travel. During boat travel tea breaks are usually elaborate, because traveling is very cold, because there are several men together in the crew, and because the break may amount to a major meal. Thus, when they prepare to go hunting, the *umiak̦* crew provides its "grub box" with tea, sugar, bread, butter, and other foods. The grub box, stove, gasoline, and food are usually furnished by the owner of the boat. Each man in the crew has to carry only his hunting equipment.

Umiak̦ hunting involves riding for hours at a time without much chance to move around and generate body heat. As a result, tea breaks are taken frequently, sometimes every hour or two, and are really intended as warming-up periods. Sometimes they take the place of a large meal, although the crew members can usually expect a good hot meal upon returning to the village or camp. The men always watch for seals as they prepare and eat their·food on the ice, so the tea break often adds another seal or two to the daily catch.

Two crews in Wainwright use motor launches for hunting. They are able to prepare meals while they travel, rather than stopping on ice pans to do so. As a result, these crews are probably better fed than their less affluent counterparts. This is one of the most common reasons for praising the value of these larger boats, in addition to their other comforts. Hunting for seals in the open water can be done effectively only from a skin *umiak*, however, so these larger boats are generally reserved for walrus hunting and for trips inland after caribou.

The Umiak̦

The *umiak̦*, or large skin boat, is distributed over the domain of coastal Eskimos from Siberia across North America to Greenland. In northwest Alaska the modern-day *umiak̦* is very similar to the aboriginal type, even though it is now propelled by an outboard engine. The frame is made of wooden stringers, nailed and lashed together. It is approximately 20 to 25 feet long, and about 5 feet wide at the gunwales. The sides slant inward to a narrow flat bottom, which is about 2 feet wide at the middle. This design gives the boat excellent stability and a large capacity. The bow is not as vertical in the north Alaskan *umiak̦* as it is in the boats of other Eskimo groups.

The greatest change in construction of the modern skin boat is the use of nails and bolts, and the addition of a small transom in the rear to accommodate the engine. There seems to be no tendency to abandon the use of skin as a cover, because it is much more durable than canvas. Six or seven skins of the bearded seal are used to cover one *umiak̦*. The skins are occasionally painted, especially if they are getting old and worn. After several years, darkening coloration and increasing numbers of brass or aluminum patches along the bottom show that the skins are rotten.

Making a new cover is a time-consuming proposition for the owner, so an effort is made to preserve it for as long as possible. While they are hunting, the men throw their used cartridges out of the boat so they will not become jammed between the frame and the skin. Care is also taken to remove sand and stones from inside the boat. If there is any blood in the bottom, it is washed out after beaching the *umiak*, because it is believed to rot the skin. In earlier times the skin was removed for the winter months and stored, to be put back on the frame in springtime. This practice is no longer followed.

In the *umiak* the Eskimos have found an almost perfect answer to the problem of traveling among the ice floes. It is light enough to haul over the ice, but so tough and resilient that it is almost indestructible. Yet it is large enough to carry very heavy loads in spite of its light weight. Because of these advantages, there has been little temptation to give it up in favor of various kinds of wooden boats, which have been available since the turn of the century. When wooden launches are used, a skin boat is always taken along and used in conjunction with them.

The first outboard engine in Wainwright was an eight-horsepower Evinrude bought by the native store in 1923. Since that time they have increased in number, and in recent years every boat owner has an outboard. The Eskimos do not use high-powered engines on skin boats because of the frame's strength limitations. Most boat owners prefer 15- to 18-horsepower engines, although they range as low as 10- or 12-horsepower. The more powerful their engine the better chance a crew has of reaching game (e.g. a herd of walrus) ahead of the others. For this reason a premium is placed on speed. Power is also essential for carrying heavy loads to shore as quickly as possible. In this land of great distances, fast travel is an important advantage for the Eskimo hunters.

Every boat still carries four to six paddles. They are used to move the boat out from shore before starting the engine and to approach walrus herds when silence is necessary. Engine trouble is also a frequent problem, so paddles are sometimes needed to get back home or to reach solid ice. The Eskimo is a fair mechanic, but he may be unable to make a temporary repair in case of a major breakdown. If the engine fails or runs out of gas, a sail may be improvised, fashioned after those which were used before motors were available. In one instance, *unaak* poles were used for a mast and yard, and a tent pole for a boom. A square sail was made from a canvas tarp and hung from the yard like a simple lateen rig, so that the boat could sail with the wind somewhat abeam.

In addition to the native skin boats, a few small wooden and aluminum boats are used for marine hunting. These small craft are quite effective for hunting seals, because they are faster and more maneuverable than the *umiak*. They can also range farther because of their higher speeds, as long as the sea is not rough. These boats are not popular, however, because of their small load capacity, their inability to withstand rugged use, and their relative unseaworthiness compared to the *umiak*. It is also difficult and expensive to get a boat shipped to Wainwright.

Ever since the days of the whalers, larger wooden lifeboats and launches have been available to the Wainwright people. These boats were actually the first motor-powered craft to be used in hunting. But they were very difficult to maintain, and they were so heavy that it was difficult to get them in and out of the ocean when the seasons change. Of the four launches that were being used in 1955 (Milan 1964, p. 47), none remained in service by 1964. However, during 1964–65 two new launches were acquired, one brought down from Barrow and another built from a kit.

Heavy launches offer several advantages to those who can afford to buy and operate them. They can weather rougher seas than the *umiak*, and they are able to carry heavier loads under any conditions. These boats are used mainly for travel from place to place, however, because only limited hunting can be done from them. This is why a smaller boat, either a manufactured type or an *umiak*, is towed along behind. By transferring into the *umiak*, men can effectively hunt seals in the open water or silently approach herds of walrus on ice pans. For this reason the following discussion of *umiak* hunting relates specifically to the use of smaller open boats.

While they travel among the ice floes, the hunters in an *umiak* (three to seven men) keep their rifles right in front of them, ready for use. The rifles range from a .22 caliber to .220, .264, .273, 30.06, and .30 caliber. Unless the sea is choppy, the rifle is uncased and lies crosswise in the bottom, leaning against a gunwale. The resultant exposure to salt spray does little to prolong the weapon's life, but it maximizes the hunter's readiness for the sudden appearance of game. Some men carry a shotgun as well, in case they encounter flocks of seabirds. The bow man, who does most of the shooting, is likely to have more weapons than the others.

Most of the hunters in a crew also carry a small hunting bag, mainly for ammunition and a few other items like matches, sharpening stone, large knife, and so on. They also like to carry some heavy clothing along. Communal gear includes a "grub box" with food and pots, a stove, assorted tools and knives, plenty of extra rope, tents and tarps, extra gas and oil, one or two harpoons, retrieval hooks, and an assortment of miscellaneous objects. A good crew is seldom caught without a piece of equipment it needs.

Wind has an important effect on *umiak* hunting, because it partially controls the movement of ice, and it can also discourage boat travel by creating rough water. When the Eskimos are hunting at sea with boats, however, there is usually enough ice present to dampen the waves. Sometimes *umiaks* travel far out among the floes in search of seals or walrus, and then an offshore wind arises. This may open a wide stretch of open water between the edge of the ice pack and the land, forcing the boats to weather rough seas in order to reach the coast. The problem is compounded by the fact that they are usually loaded heavily with walrus or seal as well. If it is not too rough, the crew heads for land immediately, possibly after throwing some of their load into the water. But they may be forced to stay within the safety of the ice floe and head toward the places where the pack usually remains closest to the land. From Wainwright this would probably mean traveling north toward Point Belcher and the Seahorse Islands, or perhaps south toward Icy Cape. They prefer to go north in this situation, because the current is usually from the south and consequently helps move them along faster.

Wind can also be an important factor during travel inland up the huge Kuk River. In the river there is always a choice of two shores, and therefore a greater chance of being able to travel on the calm side. But the Kuk is very wide (up to 5 miles near the mouth) and shallow, so treacherous waves build up in it. Hunting crews may be unable to go out from the village as a consequence, or they might become stranded on the shore, if a storm arises after they travel far from the village. When the wind blows off the ocean after the ice is gone, it is difficult to make the 3-mile trip from Wainwright to the mouth of the Kuk. Boats are usually left on the river beach after marine hunting ends, to avoid traveling on the ocean.

Locating and Shooting Seals

Eskimos look for the arrival of ringed seals, bearded seals, and walruses in abundance after the pack ice has been pushed far offshore by an easterly wind. They say that the pack should move clear out of sight over the horizon so the sea mammals will migrate northward in the ice-free waters. When the wind shifts so that the ice is carried back again toward the coast, it will bring the animals with it. Seals and walruses, concentrated along the margins of the pack, are available to the Eskimos who venture out with their boats. *Umiak* hunting remains a productive occupation as long as the sea ice stays in the area. After it is gone, there are said to be a few bearded seals and walruses far offshore in the open sea, but little or no effort is made to hunt them.

While the pack is still present, it usually lies some distance offshore from Wainwright. The only way to get to it is by boat. Once it is reached, the boats follow along parallel to its edge. The ice is usually scatttered more widely at the margins of the pack than it is farther in. The best areas for hunting have considerable ice, but less than a 50 per cent cover. This allows plenty of open spaces for sighting and following seals, and affords them less chance to escape amid a concentrated maze of pans and floebergs.

Umiak hunting is occasionally done in the Kuk River, which has a small population of ringed and bearded seals (as well as a few harbor seals) in the summertime, despite the fact that it is ice-free. Bearded seals are the most commonly sighted species. Eskimos who see these animals as they travel to and from caribou hunting places usually try to chase them down. Even though there is no ice to conceal their flight, they usually escape. Bearded seals remain in the lower part of the river, where it is briny and wide. Ringed seals and (especially) harbor seals go far up into the fresh narrow reaches of its tributaries.

Once out among the drifting pack, every man in an *umiak* crew scans the water constantly for the black head of a seal bobbing on the surface. The searching is more or less random, as the boat threads its way along. If a man spots something, he will not speak until he is sure that it is a seal and not a bird. To make the mistake of shouting "seal" when it is only a bird is the kind of behavior expected of white men and young boys, but not of good hunters. With a little experience, however, it is not difficult to tell the difference by the form and motion of the silhouette. In fact, it even becomes easy to differentiate between ringed and bearded seals from a distance.

There are several ways to distinguish these two species, by their appearance and behavior. The large *uguruk* is likely to remain quite still in the water when it is on the surface, while the ringed seal, or *netchik*, moves around almost continuously. Bearded seals also do not duck under and reappear in one spot as often as ringed seals. When an *uguruk* is resting on the surface, its long back will occasionally break the surface. It is quickly identified by its length, which greatly exceeds that of a ringed seal. In fact, the latter rarely shows its back out of the water except when diving. A bearded seal's head is also much larger, and it has a pushed-in "bulldog" face, unlike the pointed snout of a ringed seal. When they dive, both species usually roll their backs out of the water. However, the *uguruk* rolls more slowly and reveals its greater bulk as it does so.

When they are alarmed by an approaching boat, seals often dive vigorously, quite unlike the rolling dive just described. In ringed seals, this consists of splashing sidelong into the water with the head and upper body. When they do this, they usually reappear briefly. Bearded seals do a much more spectacular dive when alarmed. They take the same sidelong plunge, but throw their hind flippers clear out of the water and slap the surface, making a great splash. When an *uguruk* dives this way, it will remain submerged for a while. With their practiced eyes, the Eskimos can tell the direction of the dive and predict with some accuracy where the seal will reappear.

When a seal is spotted, the person who sees it (usually the bow man) signals its direction to the man who is running the outboard. He turns the boat straight toward it and throttles the engine to full speed (or nearly so, depending on how far away the seal is). The bow man raises his rifle and clicks the safety off as the boat rapidly bears down on the animal. Now, as the distance quickly narrows, the bow man must watch the seal through his sights (usually a scope), anticipating its actions. He must not wait too long or it will dive; but he also wants to get the closest possible shot.

Seals vary a great deal in their reactions to the boat. More than 50 per cent will dive soon after it turns toward them, and (especially ringed seals) will not be seen again. Probably over 75 per cent dive before they can be shot at. The remainder are curious and unafraid. They stare at the boat without moving, or watch it over their shoulders as they swim away on the surface. Some will swim along porpoise-fashion, undulating along alternately on the surface and just beneath it. Seals that behave in such a way can often be approached to within shooting range—25 to 50 yards. The easiest ones to shoot, however, are those which suddenly appear not far from the boat, attracted to the surface by the engine's sound. These seals usually do not move until someone shoots at them. The bow man must judge from these and other behavior patterns how close he can get before the animal will dive.

When a seal begins to swim away from the boat, it may roll and dive in the porpoise fashion mentioned above. If it does this, its back arches gently above the surface, showing that it will not dive deeply and will reappear after going 5 to 10 yards. When the seal arches its back sharply, however, it is gone for a while at least. Sometimes a seal will bob up and down in one place several times before it dives, drawn by its irresistible curiosity. When the hunter sees it dip slowly under this way, he knows that it will probably reappear momentarily. By watching the direction its snout faces, he can tell in which direction it will move as well. These behavior patterns occur in ringed, bearded, and harbor seals alike.

When a ringed seal dives, the Eskimos seldom wait around for it to come up again. In fact, they rarely even slow down or look back, especially if it looks like a deep dive. The longest they will ever wait is 5 or 10 minutes. They are usually more interested in looking for bearded seals, so whatever ringed seals they shoot are strictly coincidental to the main purpose of the hunt. Thus, they may chase after an *uguruk* for half an hour or more. If there are walruses in the area, on the other hand, they will overlook even the bearded seals.

Bearded seals are easier to approach closely than ringed seals, but they usually dive several times before they can be shot. Eskimos must be skilled in predicting their next appearance, and patient during the long waits. They are sometimes able to judge rather well where the seal will appear, but equally often they are incorrect. If there is little ice in the area, there is less chance for seals to escape, but among thick cakes and floes they easily disappear under or behind the ice. The *uguruk* is not a clever animal, however, and even after being shot at once or twice it is still unafraid. When it is surprised by the sudden appearance of the boat, it may even become "paralyzed" and rigid in the water, so it can be shot from very close range (Degerbøl and Freuchen 1935, p. 226).

The *uguruk* feeds along the bottom in shallow coastal waters. It prefers gastropods, such as *Buccinum*, but also eats shrimps (*Spirontocaris, Sabinea*), small fish (e.g. cottids), worms, and sea cucumbers (*Cucumbaria*). In deeper waters it feeds on fish, such as the polar cod (Vibe 1950, p. 57; Freuchen and Solomonsen 1958, pp. 274–75). It is the habit of this species to remain more or less in one area while feeding. Thus, the Eskimos sometimes wait in the same area where the seal went down in order to be ready for its reappearance. They say that the *uguruk* makes noises while it feeds, and by putting a paddle into the water and holding it next to his ear, a man can hear these sounds.

On one occasion a bearded seal surfaced some distance from an *umiak*, in such a position that the boat was hidden from it by the sun's glare. The bow man quickly picked up a .22 rifle and shot close to it, frightening it under before it could see what was approaching. Then the seal, which was feeding, came up several minutes later in the same area, very close to the boat. It showed very little fear until the bow man shot at it again and missed. Bearded seals sometimes swim along the surface directly toward an oncoming boat, until they are only 15 to 20 yards away. A seal may also lie still in the water and dive leisurely while it is still outside shooting range. If the crew stops where it went down, there is a good chance that it will reappear close by.

When a bearded seal is seen by ice edge hunters, they prefer to launch their *umiak* and chase it. This affords a better chance to harpoon and secure the animal, which usually sinks like a stone when killed. But it is much easier to hit a seal's head from solid ice than from the bow of a speeding boat, so there are times when just the opposite procedure is followed. In one case a crew set out after an *uguruk* that they had seen from the ice edge. This seal, a young adult, was intensely curious and playful. It would swim well ahead of the boat, surface, and then dive with a great splash. Once it jumped completely clear of the water ahead of the boat, like a frolicking porpoise, looking back over its shoulder, as if to see if the boat was following. It was futile to chase this playful animal, so the crew "beached" on an ice floe and scratched the ice until it bobbed up nearby. They shot it easily.

Another method of shortening the chase is to shoot at the seal whenever its head appears, and in this way prevent it from breathing. If it does not escape under the ice, it may not be able to remain submerged for over a minute. In this condition it is easy to approach and kill. A similar thing happens when a ringed or bearded seal has been shot and only wounded. Especially in the latter species, even a slight wound makes them unable to remain under water. Sometimes their movements become erratic and disoriented, and they evidence little fear.

Bearded seals must be shot with heavy caliber rifles, while the smaller ringed seal can be hit with shotguns or .22 rifles with the intention of wounding. From the *umiak*, a shotgun blast will often blind or disable any kind of seal so it can be harpooned or killed with a heavy gun. A blinded seal will usually just swim

along on the surface, making no attempt to escape unless a harpoon is thrown into it. If a bearded seal is knocked unconscious,
it is harpooned first and then killed by shooting it in the neck, ear,
or top of the head with a .22 rifle. This usually requires two or
three shots from point blank range. As we noted for summer ice
edge hunting, wounding is preferred when the animal cannot be
harpooned within a few seconds, because it prevents sinking.

During *umiak* hunting, seals are sometimes found asleep on
small ice pans. These seals, called *tuwakisak*, can often be approached very closely and shot before they take fright. It is easy
to paddle a boat up to a bearded seal while it sleeps, because it
fells very secure on a drifting island of ice (Degerbøl and Freuchen 1935, p. 226). In fact, it may remain even though it sees
the boat approaching to within rifle range.

Harpoon Retrieval

This brings us to the techniques of using a harpoon for retrieval, an essential part of *umiak* hunting. The harpoon is 6 or 7
feet long, with a shaft made from wood. At one end is a piece of
dense bone about a foot long, which curves to a blunt point. This
bone piece is mainly for balance. At the other end is a similar
bone foreshaft which is swollen toward the front and has a flattened face. Projecting from this face is a short (*ca.* 3 inches) metal
spike, if a toggling head (*tukkak*) is used; or there may just be a
small hole for a detachable head (*kukigak*). The two end pieces
are fitted into wedge-shaped openings cut in the shaft, and around
the joint tight bindings of sealskin thong are wound.

A few inches to the rear of the balance point there is a small
bone or antler finger rest. The harpooner grasps the shaft so that
his index finger curls behind this rest, giving added leverage for
thrusting. On the opposite side of the shaft, about 1½ to 2 feet
above the head, there is a short (*ca.* ⅛ inch) iron peg. Affixed to
the bindings that hold the foreshaft is a loop made from hide or
iron (about 1 inch in diameter). The harpoon line (*alik*, *naulik*),
which is attached to the head, passes through this loop, so that the
shaft is always held to the line. In order to hold the head firmly in

place until an animal is struck, a piece of heavy cord is tied to the harpoon line and is pulled tight and fastened onto the little peg above the foreshaft.

The harpoon line is made from bearded seal or baby walrus hide, and is 10 to 30 or more yards long. A loop of nylon rope 6 to 12 inches long passes through the head, and the hide line is attached to this loop. When the harpoon head is to be put back onto the end of the harpoon, the light cord (which is tied to the nylon loop or hide line) is looped over the peg, and then with a little stretching the head can be fitted into its socket. When a toggling head is used, its prong side must be faced away from the side where the line fastens onto the shaft. This keeps the prongs from becoming entangled in the line, which could prevent it from toggling.

All modern harpoon heads are made from metal. The *tuḳḳaḳ*, or toggle head, is cut and filed from brass. Fitted into a slot in front is an iron blade, held in place by a metal peg. The hole in the back end of the *tuḳḳaḳ* must be exactly the right size, so that it fits loosely enough on the shaft to detach easily, but tightly enough so that it will not wobble around. The *kukigaḳ*, or detachable head, is cut from heavy iron. Both types closely resemble their aboriginal counterparts, which were carved from bone or ivory.

Both are used in Wainwright today. Some crews carry two harpoons, each having a different kind of head. The toggle head supposedly holds better, but it is more difficult to thrust deeply enough into the animal so that it catches. The detachable head always catches, even when the animal is struck lightly, but it is more likely to pull loose if great strain is placed on it. The detachable head is said to be better for killing an animal that is only wounded. The fact that both types are used in equal proportions probably demonstrates that neither is superior to the other.

We noted above that a seal is shot when it is only 25 to 50 yards ahead of the speeding boat. The bow man must be an excellent shot, but even after he hits the seal, he does not have it "in the bag." Immediately after shooting, he grabs the harpoon, which is always held in the thongs along the right gunwale. Simultaneously, the motor has been slowed and the boat steered so that the floating carcass passes along the right side of the bow.

At this moment, only a few seconds after shooting, he raises his arm and plunges the harpoon straight downward into the animal's neck or upper body (if he is a good aim). He is holding the line in his left hand, and now he pulls it tight so that the little cord releases from its peg and loosens the head from the shaft. The shaft falls free, trailing along in the water fastened to the line. He pays the line out somewhat and holds tightly as the boat stops in the water. If the animal is a ringed seal, it is lifted into the boat by one or two men, but if it is a big *uguruk*, this cannot be done.

In the latter case the harpoon line is tied securely to the bow of the boat, with the seal pulled up close alongside. A rope may also be tied around one flipper and onto the gunwale, but this usually is not necessary since the harpoon head is capable of holding a great amount of weight. The seal is dragged to the nearest ice pan, where the animal and the boat are hauled up. Ropes are tied to both front flippers, or a rope may be threaded through an incision cut under the skin of the cheek from the bottom of the eye to the inside of the upper lip. The men grab these ropes and the hind flippers, while the boat is tipped on its side so that the seal can be hauled inside. Bearded seals are usually placed crosswise in the boat, with their hind flippers hanging over one gunwale and their heads against the other. If the boat is overloaded, one or two seals may be dragged in the water.

The harpoon head must be replaced before resuming the hunt. The wound is enlarged with a sharp knife so the head can be withdrawn easily. With a toggling head it is necessary to probe inside with a finger to release it and pull it out. Sometimes a chunk of skin and flesh is cut out, with the head imbedded in it, to save time in removal. Eskimos are always careful to wash the blood from the line before replacing the head, because they say that blood causes rotting.

Many seals are lost in *umiak* hunting because they sink before they can be harpooned. If the animal is shot directly ahead of the boat, it is almost always retrieved, because it takes only a few seconds to reach it. The only loss in these cases occurs when the harpoon misses or the harpoon head pulls out. But if the bow man shoots to the side while the boat is circling or moving slowly, the carcass may be gone before it can be reached. As a rough estimate, 25 to 50 per cent of the seals killed are lost.

In spite of this loss, sealing from the *umiak* is a very productive method. Nearly all bearded seals are taken in this way, which alone compensates for the time and expenditure that go into it. The numbers taken vary according to the year and the sea-ice conditions. Usually two or three bearded seals or seven to ten ringed seals are considered a very good daily catch. During the summer of 1965, one man shot over thirty bearded seals himself. In 1966, good bow men got only six to twelve, because of the short season.

The meat of bearded seals is divided equally among the members of an *umiak* crew. The skin, plus an extra share of meat, goes to the owner of the boat. If the motor is borrowed, its owner gets a share of the meat. Ringed seals go to the men who shoot them, without any shares for the boat owner, except those which he shoots himself. The same system of division is used by the North Greenland Eskimos (Vibe 1950, p. 76).

Bearded seals are butchered by the women after they have been brought home and dragged up from the beach to a grassy spot. The meat is seldom eaten, except for that which is dried (*paniktak*). According to Degerbøl and Freuchen (1935, p. 226), bearded seal "... must be counted as the poorest food in the Arctic." These authors state that some Eskimos will not eat it unless it is putrefied and frozen. The liver is said to be poisonous, much the same as that of the polar bear. The skin, which is used for boat covers and lines, is by far the most valuable part.

CHAPTER 17

Walrus Hunting

Occurrence

THE WALRUS, or *aiviḵ* (*Odobenus rosmarus*), occurs along the northwest Alaskan coast throughout the summer, as long as the pack ice remains nearby. In the fall and early winter, walruses are able to open holes by bursting through the ice from beneath each time they want to breathe. After the ice becomes 10 or 15 inches thick, however, they must move to places with open water or thin ice (Vibe 1950). Because of these limitations, walruses are only able to remain in the far north in areas where heavy current and tide rips maintain openings throughout the winter. In Alaska there are few such places, so they migrate southward with the ice in fall. In places such as Saint Lawrence Island, south of Bering Strait, walruses occur in abundance during the winter months. Here they are hunted at breathing holes and in open leads (Hughes 1960, pp. 102–3, 106), much the same as is done in North Greenland.

According to the Wainwright Eskimos, a few walruses will sometimes remain behind through the winter, breathing at holes which they break in the ice, at air pockets beneath ice piles, and at open leads or cracks. In early February, 1965, a series of holes believed to have been made by a walrus were found in young ice near Wainwright. An old Barrow hunter said that he had seen a walrus using breathing holes only once in his life, indicating how rarely they are found here in wintertime. These animals are accused of chasing the seals away, so if a hunter sees a walrus he will try to shoot it even if he cannot hope to retrieve it. It is always feared that walrus will come from beneath the ice and snatch away a seal that is being towed with a retrieval boat. This has actually happened once or twice at Barrow, but apparently not at Wainwright.

As spring approaches, open leads are more common and whaling begins. Wainwright Eskimos usually see a few walrus during May and June, probably early migrants that move north in the open leads. Lucky hunters may be able to shoot one or two of them, usually from the lead edge. Occasionally one is killed as it sleeps on the ice along a lead.

The season for walrus hunting really begins in July, after the landfast ice begins to break up and the pack becomes somewhat scattered. Their appearance is first reported from places down the coast by airplane passengers and boat crews, before they move north as far as Wainwright. Walrus herds probably hitch rides northward by lying atop the drifting floes and pans, rather than swimming north in the open water. Thus, the Eskimos watch for their first appearance after each period of rapid ice movement from the south.

The first herds to pass are composed largely of females and calves, and the bulls follow somewhat later. The same migratory sequence has been reported for North Greenland (Vibe 1950). Walruses remain in the area as long as there is pack ice, through the month of July and into August. The best hunting is said to be along the south margin of the pack as it passes by, because the heaviest concentrations of walruses are found along these trailing edges of scattered ice. The Eskimos always hope that the ice will pass along the coast a few miles offshore during the walrus season, so the animals can be reached along the fringes of the pack. If the ice jams too close to the beach, they move out into the dense floes, where boats cannot travel. If an offshore wind holds the pack far out at sea, it is impossible to reach the edge except by going far north of the village where the ice always stays close to the land.

In the month of August, if the pack has moved north beyond Wainwright, it can sometimes be reached by traveling to Point Belcher or the Seashore Islands. But this is not done unless the catch has been very poor. If the ice drifts back to Wainwright in

352

late August or early September, it brings plenty of walruses with it. More commonly, the pack is held far offshore by easterly winds, and the only walruses seen are those that migrate southward in the open water offshore. The Eskimos do not hunt them in open water, however, because they say it is too dangerous.

Sometimes, if there is no ice and the beach is snow covered, walruses will haul up on shore to rest. Eskimos walk up the beach from Wainwright early in the morning, hoping to find them. Because they sleep soundly and are little afraid, a man can walk within a few feet of them to shoot. This apparently contrasts with the walrus of the eastern Arctic, which must be stalked carefully and will take flight at the first sight of man. Wainwright people tell of an old man who once attempted to mount the back of a walrus on the beach and kill it with his knife. He was nearly dragged into deep water and drowned when the animal caught his legs with its flippers and slowly crawled into the sea. The man, frightened almost into insanity, was finally released.

Feeding

Walruses feed mostly on various kinds of sessile marine invertebrates which they apparently dig loose from the bottom with their large tusks. The principal food species in the Thule District of Greenland include *Cardium groenlandicum*, *C. ciliatum*, *Mya truncata*, and *Saxicava arctica*—all lamellibranchs (Vibe 1950, pp. 29–35). The Wainwright Eskimos state, perhaps more clearly, that the walrus in this area feeds mainly on "clams" found on the bottom.

In areas such as the Thule District, walruses are restricted to shallow "walrus banks." These are places where the water is less than 100 meters in depth, preferably between 40 and 80 meters. Along the Wainwright coast, water depths do not exceed 50 meters for at least 30 miles offshore (and probably considerably farther). Thus, the movements of walruses are not restricted, and they range far out to sea.

Several other kinds of animals are said to make up the diet of the walrus, some of which might seem unusual. Many Wain-

353

wright men say that they have found seabirds in walrus stomachs, including some ducks and especially murres (*Uria*). Sometimes only a single bird is found, but at least one man had seen a walrus stomach that was "full" of them.

Degerbøl and Freuchen (1935, p. 235) state that in Hudson Bay walruses eat many seals. Old males are especially prone to do so. The Eskimos in that region say that their tusks are yellowish, stained by the blood of seals, and their flesh has a bad taste because of their diet. At Pond's Inlet the Eskimos "fish" for walrus by dangling chunks of blubber on lines. A walrus swallows the blubber and is pulled to the ice edge, where it is harpooned. The walrus is said to be incapable of swallowing meat under water, so if a seal is suspended in the water, the walrus rises to the surface holding it between its fore-flippers, and then throws it on the ice. From this close range the walrus is harpooned (Degerbøl and Freuchen 1935, p. 244).

Kavik said that he once saw a walrus come up in open water with a bearded seal clasped between its front flippers. The seal was struggling to escape but was unable to do so. Finally the walrus stabbed it several times with its tusks. Old-timers say that walruses have "knives," because after they eat a seal they have little square pieces of skin in their stomachs that look as if they were cut with a knife.

Locating and Approaching

Walrus hunting is done in conjunction with *umiak* hunting, so the organization of the hunt and equipment carried are identical in both. But when the specific intent is to hunt walrus, interactions between different boat crews are not the same as for *umiak* sealing. In the first place, when walrus herds are known to be close to the village, hunting crews become quite competitive. Each tries to leave the village before the others and to reach the closest herds first. But aside from this kind of competitiveness there is a great deal of cooperation between crews that are traveling in the same area.

If several crews join to hunt a large herd, each benefits by the larger number of hunters and workers present. Only a fraction of a large herd can be taken if a crew hunts alone, because of the limited hauling capacity of a single *umiak*. With several boats and many men they have a greater total load capacity and more people to do the shooting. Equally important is the increased labor force, which makes the job of butchering somewhat less difficult. Also, the various crews can pool their food and share menial chores such as cooking. Whether or not the size of each man's share is increased by this procedure will depend on the number of men per boat and the size of the kill. Communal hunts maximize the net productivity for the village as a whole, however, because a greater portion of each herd can be taken.

When an *umiak* crew joins up with a launch, they will benefit greatly by the large capacity of the latter. The launch owner gets the same share for his boat as an *umiak* owner, even though he has a much greater investment. One further advantage of grouping together is the added safety of having extra boats available in case of emergency, such as damage to one *umiak* or failure of an engine.

At any time of the day or "night" someone is likely to be standing on the ocean bank or on a rooftop scanning the ocean with binoculars. Eskimos devote a great amount of time to looking around and scanning the sea ice, both at home and on hunting trips. Older men who no longer hunt are especially prone to spend hours each day watching over the sea. Thus, when walruses are abundant, they may be sighted from the village. Usually, however, it is necessary to go out to sea one or several miles and then search the scattered floes along the margins of the ice pack toward the south.

Hunting crews invariably head south to look for walrus, for a good reason. The ice is always being carried from the south toward the north by the current. After a few walruses are shot, it requires several hours' work to butcher them before heading back toward shore. During this time the ice is drifting toward Wainwright, shortening the trip home. Sometimes the current carries them north beyond the village, so they must travel south to get home. This is an inconvenience, because a loaded boat moves slowly against the current.

Walrus herds are usually found sleeping on ice pans far from shore. If an onshore wind blows the ice toward land, a herd will remain on its ice pan until it becomes grounded, but then they are almost certain to leave it. The Eskimos are not afraid to travel well offshore in their seaworthy boats as long as they can see the ice from land. The old-time Eskimos, before engines were available, warned that hunters should not try to reach ice that was over the horizon. They said that once a boat traveled over the "hump," it was hard to get back again, "because it was necessary to travel uphill."

Modern Eskimos frequently tell stories of traveling so far out after walrus that the high tower at the nearby Dew Line site could not be seen with binoculars. This is done especially when they use a launch. A crew that I traveled with once went out to a point where only the top of the tower was visible with binoculars. In this case it took the loaded boat, traveling against the wind, six hours to reach land.

Walrus herds are located in several ways. As we have noted, they may be sighted from the village. More often, herds are reported to one crew by another crew which has spotted them. The following field note entry is an example: "As we moved southward we passed Igruk's crew, just after they killed an *uguruk*. Igruk cupped his hand to his ear, bobbing up and down and smiling broadly as he pointed south. This indicated that he could hear walrus to the south. So we traveled down a mile or so and stopped to climb an ice pile to have a look around. We saw several herds of walrus not far away, with clear water between our position and theirs."

Without this kind of help, the crews search more or less randomly as they wind their way southward through the floes. At frequent intervals they pull the boat up on an ice pan with a high ice pile on it so they can *nesisaaktok*, or scan. Scanning is all important, so it is done slowly and carefully, always with binoculars. A walrus herd (*nunavak*) in the distance looks like a piece of dirty ice—a little dark smudge amid the maze of floes.

Visibility is therefore an important factor in walrus hunting. If it is not good, crews are very reluctant to go out, and quite unlikely to find game if they do. Sometimes the hunters travel around all day and "night" with no luck, though they are always able to shoot at least a few seals. When the visibility is bad, herds can be located by stopping frequently and listening for the unmistakable sound of walrus bellowing. This noise, even if one has never heard it before, could belong to no other animal in the Arctic. Each roar is a very deep, hollow, undulous belching or growling that lasts for fifteen to thirty seconds. By its magnitude it could only be made by a huge animal, and not by anything so small as a polar bear.

In the summertime, fog is the most common cause of reduced visibility. It is most likely to occur along the coastal strip, where land and sea winds meet. Nansen stated that fogs are most common during the summer out in the polar ice pack, especially in July (Stefansson 1950, p. 56). During the 1966 summer field study, fog occurred on about 30 per cent of the days, although only a few days were continuously foggy. Most often there was fog during the cool night hours, from about 11:00 P.M. until around 3:00 or 4:00 A.M. During the wintertime there is much less fog, except for steam fog over open leads and cracks.

The Eskimos usually are less concerned about getting lost in a fog than with avoiding the futility of groping around in the "soup" in search of game. Though they own compasses, they rely heavily on wind for navigation in fog, and are most fearful of becoming lost if the wind should happen to die. They sometimes tell stories of having been caught out at sea by calm weather and heavy fog, though they always seem to return without any problems. They can also navigate by watching the direction of swells, or noting the flight of birds that are probably flying back and forth from land. The Eskimos are also masters of "dead reckoning."

Once a walrus herd is located the men carefully scrutinize its position within the pack ice to decide whether it is possible or safe to move in among the floes. There must be plenty of open water between a herd's position and the edge of the pack, so that the crew will not be trapped by ice shifting and closing in around them. They are aware that although they might reach the herd easily at the present time, it will require several hours to butcher the kills; and the way must still be clear when the butchering is done and it is time to leave. Many herds that could be reached are passed by because of this danger. In spite of their caution, crews still have close calls on occasion. They sometimes have to track among close ice for several hours before they finally regain open water.

Kaviḳ related that he had been caught amid the ice many years ago. They had gone out in a launch, towing an *umiaḳ* behind. Despite the warnings of two older men, who said they should stay out of the pack, they went after a herd that was well into the ice. While they butchered, the ice closed around them and they could not escape. They tried to drag their *umiaḳ* to open water, using walrus blubber for skids, but the ice was too rough. For forty-eight hours they drifted northward, reaching a point 20 miles north of Wainwright, where the pack moves close to shore. Near the abandoned village of Ataniḳ they succeeded in pulling their boat into the lee of a big grounded ice pile (*kisissaḳ*), where they were no longer carried along with the pack. They waited there until a lane opened up and allowed them to escape.

Once the Eskimos have decided to go after a herd, they become very serious and speak in low tones. Walrus hunting, perhaps more than any activity except whaling, is considered to be a very dangerous business which must not be taken lightly. In this part of the Arctic, walruses are not frightened by man. We noted that it is possible to walk up to them as they sleep on the beach, and when they are on ice pans, they are completely unafraid of the *umiaḳ* as long as it approaches quietly.

According to some reports, walruses that come up onto the ice along a lead edge are very cautious, and they even post "sentries" to watch all sides, making approach by hunters very difficult (Degerbøl and Freuchen 1935, p. 247). A single gunshot is enough to frighten all the nearby animals into the water (Hughes 1960, p. 105). Perhaps walruses alter their behavior toward man in much the same way that seals do, depending upon what they are doing at the time. The fearless attitude of walrus lying on ice pans is even more surprising when a group of walrus 50 yards away are unaffected by several volleys of shots fired into a nearby herd.

When the *umiaḳ* comes within about a hundred yards of a basking herd, the outboard engine is slowed to its lowest speed.

Somewhat further on, it is stopped completely. Paddles are used so that a minimum of noise will be made. It is important not to go upwind of the animals with the engine running, because the smell of exhaust will always frighten them away. If a launch is being used, it is left about 200 yards from the animals, and an *umiak* is taken in for the actual shooting. As the boat moves toward the huge animals, each man dips his paddle as quietly as possible. The men speak in low murmuring tones, discussing the best shooting position and which side offers the best approach. They do not whisper, because they feel that it is more frightening to the walrus than low voices.

Shooting

From 25 to 50 yards away the hunters can see the ice pan and the animals clearly enough to plan their approach. Now they must note the size of the ice pan: if it is a high and narrow cake, it may turn over when the ponderous animals dive off. Sometimes the ice is held partially under water by their bulk, and it will always lift somewhat when they are gone. Around the pan's edges there is often a submerged ice shelf extending several feet to a few yards out. They must stay away from this, because when the shooting starts the walruses pile off the ice, and where there is an ice shelf, they might hit the boat before reaching deep water. If there is no shelf, they dive straight down and there is no danger of a collision.

The Eskimos prefer to hunt herds that are on larger ice pans. When many animals crowd onto a small area, the wounded ones are likely to slip into the water after they are shot. Larger pans are also less apt to be completely covered with animals. Thus it may be possible to pull the boat up onto some unoccupied ice, so that several men can get out and shoot from solid footing. This can also be done if empty ice cakes are drifting along next to the pan the herd is on. This offers not only a steadier place for aiming, but also greater safety from the huge beasts as they charge into the sea.

More often, however, it is necessary to paddle right up to them and shoot from the boat. In this case the hunters approach to within 5 feet of the animals before the shooting begins. All walrus shooting is done from this incredibly close range—so close that the hunters usually are lower than the animals and must aim upward to hit them in the head. When they have reached the place·from which they will shoot, paddling is stopped and the men carefully raise their rifles. Each one has now picked out the walrus he will shoot first, always a big "tusker."

For a few moments everything is quiet except for the breathing and grunting of the walruses. Some of them are lurching and moving about nervously, watching the intruders. Suddenly the air is split by the crack of the first rifle, followed an instant later by a volley from the others. Each man aims for the ear or eye region, hoping for an instant kill. If his aim is true, a massive head drops and the body is still. Another round is clicked immediately into the chamber.

Now the animals have taken fright, but, tightly packed and confused, they are slow to move off. Each man finds another big one in his sights and fires again. Wounded animals are shot as quickly as possible lest they struggle into the water and die in the sea below. Herds composed partly or entirely of females (in July at least) usually have a few small, dark pups crawling around on top of the adults. After the shooting begins some of the pups start bawling loudly. They must be shot immediately. Their bellowing will sometimes bring enraged adults to rescue them, which can mean danger for the hunters. After a few minutes of pandemonium the air stills, several limp carcasses lie on the ice, spilling streams of blood. The rest have escaped.

Sometimes the hunters do not shoot en masse, since this is actually less effective than using a limited number of shooters, while the rest of the men hold the boat ready to move onto the ice. If the boat points straight toward the animals, men in the stern may be blocked from firing by those sitting in front of them. In this case the two or three foremost men shoot. Sometimes one man shoots alone. Each time an animal looks up, he shoots it, being sure to kill it cleanly. Then everyone sits quietly until the herd settles down again, and he shoots another. When enough have been killed, the remainder are frightened off by firing over their heads, waving arms and shouting, or telling them to leave (since they are said to understand human speech). In spite of the fact that this method works very well, it is seldom used, probably because everybody likes to participate in the kill.

As soon as all the unharmed and slightly wounded animals are in the water, the boat is hauled up onto the ice. This is done as fast as possible, for two reasons. First, there may be some wounded walruses left on the ice that are limping or sliding toward the water. These are shot and killed. In spite of the fact that walrus hunters use heavy rifles, usually .273, 30.06, .308, or .30 caliber, it is not easy to kill these animals. Any walrus that is still twitching, convulsing, or contorting is shot in the neck. This is usually done from the top, near the occipital condyle—a spot which is marked by a vague cross formed by wrinkles. If the top is not visible, a shot in the side of the neck usually suffices, as long as it hits the spinal column. Each animal gives a bulky, convulsive lurch when it is shot. While the wounded ones are being dispatched, any carcasses that are in danger of slipping into the water are secured. They may be hauled up with ropes tied through slits cut in their flippers, or simply fastened to other carcasses farther back from the edge.

A second reason for getting onto the ice quickly is the danger of being attacked by the remainder of the herd. They are generally reluctant to leave the area, and are apparently motivated by animosity more than curiosity. Sometimes they try to help a wounded comrade floundering in the water nearby. A few men stand near the pan's edge with rifles ready, watching these animals as they surface in small groups, stare for a moment, then dive below. They are rarely shot, unless they rise so close that they could be retrieved by harpoon later. In one instance, several men shot at some walruses to frighten them away when they tried to help a mortally wounded animal escape. Females seem especially inclined to do this with their young.

If such groups of walrus do not leave soon, the Eskimos become concerned and begin speaking to them. Holding their hands up, they repeat *"tavzaaktugut, tavzaaktugut"* (we are finished) and tell them to go home. The mood at these times is very serious, almost melancholy, as if preeminent danger is present until they calm down. Unlike any other kind of hunting in which I have participated, walrus hunting is still interwoven with traditional beliefs (this may also be true of whaling).

Some of the wounded ones that manage to reach the water are secured with a harpoon before they are lost; others flounder and sink before this can be done. Those which are mortally wounded but are still able to swim will often try to climb on an ice pan to die. A walrus that is not badly wounded may be shot in the back so that it cannot stay down for long. Then a harpoon is tossed into it, and it is killed with a bullet in the head or neck.

Danger of Walrus

The excitement of the walrus hunt is tremendous. It seems to affect the Eskimos must the same as it does the outsider. But to the Eskimo, walrus hunting also means facing danger, and this is something that he views in a much different way. Danger is not "fun" to him, as it is to the westerner, for he encounters enough of it to drown his thirst for this kind of thrill. Walrus hunting is a necessary danger for making a living. The Eskimo knows what an animal of this size and temperament can do.

Before most walrus hunts begin, the men stop in their boats and one is called upon to pray. He mutters a Christian prayer, asking for protection and for a good hunt, while the others listen in silence. This is the only kind of hunting, with the possible exception of whaling, where prayer is an immediate part of the hunt. It replaces an earlier form of propitiation. Among the Wales Eskimos, Thornton (1931, p. 177) saw a shaman strip to the waist and recite an incantation before a group of men attacked some walruses with harpoons.

We have noted above that the walrus is able to "understand" human language, and a herd that refuses to go away after the shooting ends may be asked to leave. Similar abilities are attributed to some other animal species, but without the same attitude of respect. The walrus is regarded as being mysteriously intelligent and malevolent toward man.

With this in mind a man does not brag of his exploits with walruses, whether it be something he has done or something he plans to do in the near future. "Walruses are like people," the Eskimos say. "They hear you when you talk and if you brag they might get you for it. If you never hunted them before, I'll tell you something now. Remember when you hunt walrus you must not act like a man. Do not be arrogant; be humble. Always respect the walruses and watch them closely when you hunt them."

Once, while a group of hunters butchered two walruses close to an undisturbed herd, a young and impertinent Eskimo began to mimic the noise of the nearby animals, looking toward them as he did so. An older man silenced him immediately and warned him of the dangers of such mockery. Open chastisement is very unusual and reflects the seriousness of this situation.

It is said that an angry walrus might try to climb on an ice pan to attack a man, or that it might try to break the ice from beneath to do so. Hunters are warned not to stand too close to the edge of the ice in winter for the same reason. Walruses have undoubtedly tried to harm Eskimo hunters on numerous occasions. In at least one instance a middle-aged Wainwright hunter was chased up a steep ice pile by an enraged walrus.

Stories of walruses attacking kayaks or large *umiaks* are known from the literature. The Saint Lawrence Islanders warn that ". . . especially young animals two to four years old, can become enraged and will sometimes try to rip the skin boat with their tusks. Swimming underwater, they approach the boat on their backs and with their tusks rip open the bottom of boats made from the hide of their own species. In the spring of 1946, a boat was thus ripped open, but it was close enough to an ice floe that the crew could reach safety before the craft swamped." (Hughes 1960, p. 177). At Cape Prince of Wales Thornton was in a boat when a hole was punctured through the skin cover by a harpooned walrus (Thornton 1931, p. 177).

Kavik told of hunting walrus from a large wooden launch while traveling in open water. The boat was staved in by a wounded animal that thrust one of its tusks through the planking of the boat. By stuffing rags into the hole the leak was slowed, but a plank was torn loose for the entire length of the boat. Even though the crew bailed hard, the launch was low in the water by the time they reached land.

In another instance, a wounded walrus began thrashing wildly in the water, and eventually ripped a hole in the *umiak* with its tusk. One man held his foot over the tear, while the boat was driven onto a nearby ice pan. Here they sewed the opening with sinew. The man who told of this experience said that now he always carries a piece of plywood and some nails in the boat so that a quick repair can be effected even in open water. His boat was attacked another time, but in this case the damage was minor.

Another *umiak* in Wainwright had been badly damaged in the bow, but had been repaired. The frame was crushed by a walrus that climbed on the boat with one flipper. The boat struck the ice edge, and the animal's weight smashed the heavy wood of the bow. Rather than shoot the animal, they wisely hit it in the muzzle with a rifle butt so that it would climb off and escape. If it had been killed and had fallen limp on the boat, the danger and damage would have been greater. This is also done when a walrus hooks its tusks over the gunwale of an *umiak*, because if it were shot, its lifeless bulk would probably overturn the boat.

Retrieval

Walruses that are shot in wintertime will usually float, as will calves that are killed during the summer. But adults that are killed during summer hunting will usually sink, if they slide or are pushed into the water. In field notes from a walrus hunt in July were these comments:

> Many were shot from this group, which was basking atop a large, thick ice pan. In the scramble to get off, some dead or mortally wounded ones were shoved into the water, where they sank immediately. By the time all were off, two lay dead atop the ice, two large ones and a baby were in the water. The baby and one adult were alive, and one dead adult floated. Knowing that it would not sink, they shot the small one, and tossed a harpoon into the dead adult to secure it. The wounded adult was also harpooned from about 10 feet away, and when it turned its head to the side it was shot and killed.

After being harpooned the animal is hauled to the edge, and heavy ropes are tied through loops cut in its skin or hitched around its neck. Usually it will sink, and it takes considerable strength just to hold it on the surface. When there are only five or six men, an adult walrus usually cannot be pulled up onto the ice. (The Wainwrighters were never seen to use a block and tackle arrangement, such as has been described for the Thule Eskimos or Saint Lawrence Islanders). In such a situation the animal is either towed home or is butchered as it is gradually pulled out of the water.

In modern times a harpoon is not used until the walrus is thoroughly immobilized by shooting it. One seventy-year-old man told of seeing the aboriginal technique used once when he was very young, because two of his relatives decided to show him how it was formerly done. In this case both hunters used an *unaakpak* (large harpoon). Each man harpooned a walrus facing in an opposite direction. Then the two lines were quickly fastened together so that the animals would fight against one another until they became tired. Each was killed by lancing it through the ventral side of its neck.

Walruses were also harpooned from the *umiak*, using a heavy line made from baby walrus hide. This line would be at least 30 fathoms long (1 fathom equaling the distance between a man's outstretched arms), so that the animal had plenty of room to run. The crew members held the line while the boat was towed far and fast, until the walrus was exhausted enough to be lanced. When this technique was used, there could be no ice around, lest the boat be pulled into it.

A single walrus could be harpooned from an ice pan, and then secured by tying the line around a projecting chunk of ice. Among the Wales Eskimos the animal was then pulled forcibly to the edge and dispatched. When there was no ice around, they fastened sealskin floats to the line and allowed the walrus to "run" until it could be approached and killed (Thornton 1931, p. 177).

Butchering

After some walruses (or sometimes caribou) have been shot, one man usually begins to prepare tea and food while the others start butchering the kill. This tea break may amount to a fairly substantial meal, because in addition to tea and bread some meat is usually cooked from the walruses that were just killed. Pieces of meat, heart, and skin with blubber are usually boiled in a pot of fresh water. Caribou meat is sometimes carried along and is cooked instead of walrus or seal meat. It takes several hours to finish the butchering, if a fair number of walruses are killed, so there may be several breaks before the boat is loaded and the crew heads for home.

The method of butchering walrus will be described briefly here, although it may seem inconsistent since this has not been done for the other marine animals. But unlike the species previously discussed, walrus butchering is men's work. Seals are always left for the women. Second, after spending many tiresome hours laboring over huge walrus carcasses, one feels compelled to pass along the knowledge gained at such a price.

1. After several walruses have been killed, they are rolled or dragged to convenient positions on the ice. Double-bladed axes, long knives (*saviraaktuun*), and smaller hunting knives are sharpened with files and sharpening stones (*sillin*), in preparation for cutting the thick, tough skin. Ideally, the carcass is placed with its ventral side up, although cutting can also be started from the back or side. Using the axes, five or six slits are cut across the body of the animal, and then a single slit is made the length of the belly, crossing the previous cuts. This sections out long strips of skin and blubber (*kawk*) which can then be cut away from the body with long knives. A "handle" is cut into one end of each strip by making a slit through the hide.

By pulling the *kawk* away from the body with these handles, and cutting along the intersection of the blubber and muscles, these strips are cut clear down the flanks, laid on the ice and sliced free.

2. Then the animal is rolled over, and similar strips are cut from its back. When this is finished, all the skin has been removed except on the head and neck, front flippers, hind quarters, and rear flippers. Usually, the youngest men in the crew haul the *kawk* strips (which measure about 18 inches wide and 2 to 5 feet long) to the boat. An iron hook with a rope attached (*niksigak*)

is used for dragging the meat around, and for pulling it away from the body while another man cuts.

3. About this time, or while the skin is being taken off, the head is removed. This can be done with a large knife, after the skin is cut with an axe. The ventral side of the neck is cut first, severing the trachea and muscles, and cutting around until the head is severed through the cartilage around the occiptal condyle. By no means is this as easy as it sounds. The severed head is then placed on the ice, the tusks propping it up. The hide is removed from around the muzzle (i.e., the whiskers), and laid back as far as the eyes and the lips. The anterior part of the skull is then cut through with a dull axe, used only for chopping bones, removing a section of the skull with the tusks attached to it. The lower mandible and the parts from the eyes back are thrown into the water.

4. The shoulder girdle, including the front limbs and scapulae (*kyesik*), is removed after the *kawk* is off. One man pulls the flipper away from the body with a hook, while the other slices at the muscle with a knife. It comes away easily. The flipper is cut from this with an axe, and a slit is made in it for a handle. When load capacity is limited, the meat is cut away from the scapula and saved, while this bone, plus all of the limb except the flipper, is thrown away. The entire limb and shoulder are saved when there is plenty of room in the boat or when butchering is done in the village.

5. Now a cut is made along a cartilaginous area of the ventral portion of the rib cage, removing the sternum and attached ends of the ribs in one flat piece. Thus the chest cavity is exposed, and the abdominal muscles are cut away so that the internal organs can be reached. Before the viscera are removed, the remaining part of the ribs may be cut away by slicing along very close to the backbone. After the ribs are removed, they are divided into two or three sections by cutting the muscles that join them. If the boat is to be heavily loaded, all the ribs may be disposed of in the ocean; but when there is enough room, they are saved.

6. Either before or after the ribs are cut away, the internal organs are removed. This is done by hooking one of the iron meat hooks into the trachea and pulling it toward the rear while another

man cuts the viscera away from the dorsal area. As it is pulled back, the lungs are cut loose and the heart is removed and saved. The diaphragm must be cut when it is reached, and then the stomach, liver, and intestines are pulled away until the rectum is cut. The entire mass of organs is connected, and can be pulled to the edge of the ice and thrown into the sea. The kidneys are saved.

7. All that remains now is the backbone, pelvic girdle, and hind limbs. The vertebral column is cut away with an axe just forward of the pelvis. It is chopped into sections and saved when butchering is done in the village, but otherwise it is thrown into the sea. The skin around the hind flippers is cut with an axe, so that each limb can be removed by cutting around its condyle with a knife. The flippers are always saved, but the rest of the hind limbs is kept only if the boat is not overloaded. The pelvis is always thrown away when at sea.

If the boat is overloaded, the order in which portions will be discarded is approximately as follows: vertebral column, pelvis, scapula (after meat is removed), ribs, sternum, humerus (meat may be cut away), fore limb (except flipper). If the load is much too large, or in an emergency, the skin, flippers, and tusks are the last portions left behind. Whenever they are heavily overloaded, the Eskimos cut as much meat as possible from the bones and leave them behind.

Whenever parts of the walrus are discarded, it is customary to say "*ḳunnikun*" as they are thrown into the ocean. This word means "calm water," and is intended as a request for the little bottom creatures, who are being fed, to calm the seas, giving the hunters a safe trip home.

During one hunt in 1966, a crew of eleven men killed twenty-nine walruses, an exceptionally large number for a single hunt. They were able to do so because they used a launch and two skin boats to transport the catch. They were faced with the formidable job of butchering the kills. In eight hours they were able to do only eight carcasses fully and carefully. In addition several adult animals were cut into large sections and partially discarded, five calves were cut into two or three sections, and five adults were dragged in the water. It takes a long time to butcher each walrus.

Men usually work in pairs, and do a complete job in about an hour. When it is done in the village, four or five men can work together, which shortens the amount of time considerably.

Transporting Walruses

The number of walruses that can be killed is limited by the capacity of the boat. A Wainwright *umiak* can haul about three walruses inside and one or two more can be dragged in the water. As we have noted above, a launch will haul much more than this. The boats are usually loaded heavily when the Eskimos return from a hunt.

For example, on one hunt two walruses and two bearded seals were shot by a crew with an *umiak*. In order to load the walruses, everything was first removed from the boat. The skin (*kawk*) was thrown in the bottom, and all the meat, bones, and flippers were placed on top of it. The gear was piled above this, and the large seals were loaded into a section near the stern left open for the purpose. The boat rode low in the water, with only 3 or 4 inches of freeboard, causing some comment and joking by the men. The load was accommodated well, however, and the engine could be run at full speed. The boat bent and flexed noticeably as it rode through the moderate following sea, but it did not ship water.

We have mentioned that it is sometimes necessary to tow walruses back to the shore. This is no small task, because their weight and bulk creates considerable drag. In order to minimize this, the carcass may be inflated. The technique as observed at Wainwright was as follows. The animals were first dragged to a place where a long submerged ice shelf extended outward from the ice edge. They were anchored right next to the ice, where they would not hang straight down in the water and could be reached easily.

First, a small slit was cut through the skin, just deep enough to reach the junction of the blubber and underlying muscle. The slit was made on the ventral side near a front flipper. In the best tradition of acculturated peoples, a hand-operated tire pump supplied the air, its hose pushed into the finger-sized opening. After some pumping, the skin of the chest area would begin to puff out, until finally the whole carcass floated. When it floated fairly high, the hole (plus any bullet holes that were leaking air) was plugged with a rifle cartridge wrapped in cloth, or with a chunk of blubber. The hole was made larger on the inside than at the opening, so that the plug was held in place by air pressure, without being expelled.

To secure a walrus to a boat, a loop of heavy rope with a slip knot is put around its neck, with the line drawn out between the tusks. This allows very quick fastening, and it holds infallibly.

To secure a walrus to an *umiak*, its head (ventral side upward) is pulled up tightly against the gunwale near the bow, raising it clear of the water. The rope passes over the gunwale and is tied onto a longitudinal stringer inside. Sometimes a line is similarly tied to the rear flippers, but usually the carcass slips easily through the water without the extra support.

Productivity of Walrus Hunting

The Wainwright Eskimos are very sensitive about loss and waste in walrus hunting, and will take all practical measures to minimize it. They occasionally find rotting carcasses that have floated north on the ice—ones that have been killed and left after the tusks are removed—and they speak very disparagingly of the practice. Eminent danger occasionally forces them to leave a carcass on the ice. When this occurs, the hunters "forget" it, and never mention it to people in the village. This kind of loss is regarded with shame and embarrassment, unlike the similar losses which happen in seal hunting. No man is ashamed to say that he killed six seals and retrieved only two.

Of course there is an unfortunate loss by sinking of wounded or killed animals that reach the water, but everything is done to avoid it. Even some of these losses are recovered, when fall storms wash the carcasses ashore, or when they are discovered after they float to the ocean surface several days later. Those which are not recovered and become encased in the ice pack may be dug out and eaten by polar bears during the winter.

I have no reliable statistics on the number of walruses killed each year by the Wainwright people. The figure must vary a great deal. In 1965, about two hundred were taken, and many more could have been killed except that the men stopped hunting walrus. In spite of this excellent season, they were out of walrus for dog food by the following spring and early summer. In the summer of 1966, the walrus season lasted from July 13 to 31. During the first four days of hunting, eighty-four walruses were taken. After this, conditions were less favorable, and the total kill for the season was about 160. The Eskimos were concerned that they would run out of dog food early, and hoped for the ice to return.

We mentioned above that on one trip, twenty-nine walruses were taken by a launch and two *umiaks*. Kavik, a man in his sixties, said that this was the second highest figure that he could remember. Many years ago he accompanied a group of crews, including a launch and eight skin boats, when they took about thirty-four at one time. The usual kill for a single boat is one to four, although more will be taken if several boats hunt together.

While the walrus herds are in the area, men will hunt around the clock until they are too exhausted to continue. This keeps up as long as the people feel that they need more to fill their requirements for the coming year. Because the take is shared among all crew members, each crew usually hunts for more than a single family. The spoils are divided among the crew after they have been brought home. Separate piles containing *kawk* and meat are laid out, one for each crew member and one for the boat (this goes to its owner). A woman or child puts a slip of paper with a name on each pile, thus assuring fairness in the division. The tusks and baculum, which are sold to outside interests, always belong to the boat owner.

Ivory from the tusks can be used for tools and native equipment, but it is seldom kept for these purposes today. The dense white teeth are chipped out and carved into fishing hooks and sinkers. Pieces of heavy bone, such as the lower mandible, are used for making parts of harpoons. The hide of baby walrus is cut off in a large round section and then sliced spirally to make strong line. Membrane that surrounds the liver is used for the heads of native drums.

The Wainwright people do not eat much walrus at home,

although hunters usually boil some tidbits after making a kill. These favored parts include heart, liver, kidney, and skin with blubber attached. The flippers of walrus are allowed to "ripen" in warm places, and when they reach the proper stage of decomposition, they are eaten as a prized delicacy called *sitkok* or *ouzak*. The meat of baby walrus is also considered excellent eating.

Almost all of the walrus, however, especially the hide and blubber, is stored in ice cellars and cut up later for dog food. The dogs prefer it above all else and seem to thrive on it. It is also light and easy to carry on dog sleds. So long as there are dog teams in Wainwright, the people will depend on the walrus to maintain them.

CHAPTER 18

The Eskimo as a Hunter

THIS STUDY has largely been concerned with the knowledge, techniques and equipment which are used by the northwest Alaskan Eskimos in hunting and traveling on the sea ice. It deals with human behavior in the ethological sense, describing man as a predator, interacting closely with long- and short-term conditions within his environment. Because of this pragmatic orientation, little has been said about cultural factors, such as religion, folklore, social structure, and kinship, which bear an indirect relationship to the subject. In so doing, the importance of these practices is not being denied, but merely sacrificed for the sake of the particular orientation of this research.

There is one very important aspect of the Eskimo ecological adaptation which should be considered briefly, to draw attention to its presence and significance. The Eskimo hunter has certain mental attitudes which can be singled out as specifically adapted to exploitation of the Arctic environment. What follows is a brief discussion of these personality characteristics, derived quite subjectively from a year of extensive hunting and traveling with Eskimos.

In order to equal or approximate the success of his Eskimo companions, the outsider finds that he must go beyond simply learning the motor skills and obtaining a sufficient background of facts pertaining to the environment. He must add to these skills a mental framework or a group of attitudes which seem inbred into the Eskimo personality, but which can and should be mimicked. One of the most overwhelming and lasting impressions that one receives of the Eskimo hunter is that he is self-assured and competent above all. What are the qualities which give this impression of competence?

First, and most important, the Eskimo hunter is knowledgeable about every aspect of the environment which he exploits. This body of knowledge goes far beyond that which is essential for success in basic travel and subsistence activities, to include a large number of facts relating to unusual or rare occurrences, such as emergency conditions. Each Eskimo hunter is faced with an "emergency situation" of one sort or another during almost every season of every year, and he must draw upon this specialized factual background in order to make the correct responses. With this background, most of these situations are so aptly responded to that they can hardly be called actual emergencies; nor are they considered so by the hunter.

The Eskimos are traditionally concerned with knowing as much as possible, and individuals are given special respect and prestige if they are especially knowledgeable. Thus they are willing and anxious to learn from their fellows, both by watching them as they hunt and by listening as they recount their experiences or relate what they have heard from others. A great deal of time is spent discussing all aspects of the hunt, especially during the long idle nights of winter. In addition to watching and listening to others, the Eskimo hunter is highly observant of his surroundings and of his own experiences. These personal observations are always passed on to the others in later conversations, and thus the cumulative knowledge of the group is constantly being enlarged and improved.

Unlike the westerners with whom he has contact in modern times, the Eskimo seldom doubts what he has been told by others, especially if they are his elders. Thus, without previous actual experience in a given situation he will unquestioningly respond to it in the way that he has been told. The outsider, on the other hand, continually frustrates the Eskimos by doubting these instructions and attempting to formulate original solutions which he believes to be better. Those who live with Eskimos over a long enough period find themselves questioning less and less, and following whatever they are told to do by their more experienced native companions.

The Eskimo hunter is, therefore, uncommonly self-assured about his knowledge as well as his ability to cope with any situation. He is confident that whatever he has been told is true, and if he follows what he has learned, he is almost always doing the correct thing. It is my opinion that information given by Eskimos relating to successful hunting or survival techniques is nearly always correct and well founded, regardless of how difficult it may be to accept initially.

If the Eskimo is self-assured in his background of knowledge, he is equally confident of his physical competence and his ability to persevere in the completion of any task. This perseverance, both mental and physical, is a second important attitude which we should briefly consider.

The active Eskimo hunter is usually in excellent physical condition, as one would expect him to be. Thus he is able to perform difficult tasks over long periods of time with a minimum of discomfort. In addition to this physical stamina there is another quality which is as much mental as physical and which might be called "toughness." The Eskimo views prolonged exposure to cold, wetness, or extreme physical exertion with a different frame of mind than most non-Eskimos, and seems much less affected by it.

This ability to withstand physical discomfort often makes the Eskimo vastly superior to the white man in strenuous situations, because he is not so concerned with remaining perfectly comfortable at all times. He does not feel compelled to carry as much gear and clothing when he travels, which lightens the load and leaves more space for transportation of game. He carries whatever equipment he would require in an emergency, but bothers with few unnecessary items. This is especially true in the cold months of the year, and it is less closely followed during the relatively easy summer months.

The Eskimo also perseveres at almost any task until it is successfully completed. He is not likely to give up and become unhappy if conditions are difficult. Eskimos seldom turn back once they have set out, regardless of how tough the going may become. But they are wise and prudent enough not to begin traveling if there is much danger involved. They are seldom anything but thorough in the completion of a task, for they realize that if the job is not done fully, it may well cause more work in the long run.

For example, if the tide is rising and the boats should be pulled higher up the beach, they will be pulled to the very top of the beach where even the highest storm tide would not reach them. In no case will they be pulled only part way up, where they might be caught later if an unexpected gale begins to blow. If a man shoots a seal, he will sometimes stand for one or two hours attempting to snag it with a retrieval hook. Or if ten walrus are shot, then no less than ten walrus will be brought home, regardless of how much work and time must be expended, as long as there is not a great risk involved. In these and many other ways the Eskimo perseveres far beyond what would be expected of an outsider.

But although the Eskimo is perseverant in most tasks, he is also wise in the expenditure of energy, because energy is a valuable commodity here. In the completion of a task, whether or not it requires much strength, the best job is done with a minimum of unnecessary steps. Eskimos are experts at finding shortcuts in labor expenditure, as for example in moving through rough ice, where the best travelers stop and reconnoiter frequently in order to follow the smoothest trail. This always involves traversing a much greater distance, but in the long run much less energy is used by avoiding rough ice areas. Another example is seen in spring seal hunting, where the men go out on foot and push dog sleds ahead of them. They do this because they realize that killed seals are very difficult to drag on spring ice, and less energy is expended by pushing a sled both ways than by having an easy walk out but working much harder pulling the seal home.

This brings up another characteristic of Eskimo mental attitudes, that of foresight. Although foresight is not demonstrated in all realms and all activities, it is usually important in hunting and in any situation of immediate potential danger. Thus they will not travel out onto the sea ice in winter if there is any chance of being set adrift on a loose floe. They also pass by herds of walrus which are in thick pack ice, where the crew might be trapped after an hour or two of butchering, if the ice should close around them. And they will not take unnecessary chances or "fool around" under any circumstances, as exemplified by the fact that none has ever demonstrated to me the method of walking on thin ice, except on a completely safe surface. The Eskimos seem to have an unspoken concept of "percentage risk." Thus a certain activity might be done without danger eight out of ten times, but because of this 20 per cent risk the Eskimo seldom carries on the activity as long as it can be avoided. It seems that the western idea of doing things for the excitement of taking a chance rarely occurs here.

Although he seldom willingly faces danger, the Eskimo is extremely alert for unexpected situations, as well as for signs of game. Whenever he hunts or travels, he does not permit himself to become completely distracted by one activity, but is constantly on the watch for any change in his surroundings. Thus, no matter how intent he may be on stalking a seal lying on the ice, he still glances around the area in case a polar bear might be near, and he watches the surrounding ice lest it should begin to move and carry him away from the landfast ice. When crews of men are engaged in butchering walrus on an ice pan, they frequently look up and flash their eyes over the surrounding water in case a seal should surface nearby. And should they see one, they move with amazing speed to grab their rifles and shoot, knowing that the first chance is always best and often there is no second chance. Their secret is to avoid becoming too engrossed in what they are doing. One who hunts with them will find that for some time he will be too slow and deliberate, and hence will rarely get off a shot before the Eskimos do. Finally, some of the alertness and quickness is acquired, and it is a considerable advantage in getting along successfully. A measure of this sort of alertness could mean a life saved in an emergency as easily as in everyday life it means a seal brought home that might have gotten away.

Besides being constantly alert, the Eskimo hunter uses his abilities of imaginativeness and creativity to the utmost. Where there are no repair shops, specialists, or large general stores, it is frequently necessary to resort to improvisation in order to make or repair an item of equipment. Some of these improvisations are "standard" in the sense that they are done on repeated occasions when the same situation arises. In many instances, however, it is a unique problem and an entirely new solution must be devised. Having found it necessary to face these situations many times in their lives, the Eskimos are experienced and highly adept at this sort of creative thinking. Outsiders are seldom as quick and clever in devising solutions to these problems.

In situations where needed materials are not at hand, one must attempt to push his imagination beyond its usual limits. Outsiders often do not see an obvious solution as a feasible one, because they simply assume that it is impossible to deviate so far from convention with any hope of success; or they resign themselves that the situation is hopeless. An Eskimo will never do this. A familiar example from the literature is making an emergency sled from pieces of frozen meat. When the cross hairs of a telescopic sight are broken, they can be replaced on the spot with thin strands of dental floss (which is carried for sewing); or when a hole is torn in the skin cover of a boat, a small board can be quickly nailed over it as an effective repair. Nonessential pieces taken from other equipment are often used for improvisation. An iron rod from the grid of a camp stove can be removed and used to clear the barrel of a jammed rifle, or shaped into a serviceable gaff hook. One who has not grown up to think in this way will not equal the Eskimos, but it is easy to improve one's own ability markedly by forgetting about conventional solutions and allowing one's inventive imagination greater freedom.

Cooperativeness in hunting and traveling is an aspect of Eskimo life which has been discussed time and again. It has long been necessary for these people to work together and share the proceeds of their efforts, both large and small. Thus no man is ever left to retrieve a seal by himself when he is using a small retrieval boat. Someone will always come to assist him, whether or not he could do the job alone. For assistance rendered there is no expectation of immediate remuneration or expressed gratitude, but every man knows that someday in the future he will receive "payment" in kind.

Similarly, crews join together in groups to hunt walrus, so that the net kill is larger, the work proceeds faster, and equipment can be pooled. Then the spoils are divided among the crews so that all receive shares, even if they did not participate in the actual shooting. Sometimes a small group of men will encounter a localized concentration of game, such as a large herd of caribou or a school of belugas which has been trapped at an air hole by closing ice. When this happens, they may shoot a few animals, but then they will hurry to the village to get more hunters. Although several men could get more for themselves by remaining there and shooting alone, the total proceeds for the village are greater if they take the time to go after the others.

In the same way, emergency situations are always met with group effort. Certainly there would be no concept of "every man (or every crew) for himself." On one occasion a walrus hunting crew had outboard-motor failure and were loaned an engine by a passing crew that happened to have an extra. For the lending party there was no promise of immediate compensation for its assistance, but at some future date they might require some sort of aid and it would, of course, be returned. This kind of ability to cooperate is essential for life in this environment and could be especially important in emergency situations.

Sharing proceeds of the hunt or giving assistance is so much a part of this way of life that there is an entirely different notion of obligation and reciprocity. Whereas the non-Eskimo expects verbal thanks or material compensation when he has given something, the Eskimo has no such expectation. Misunderstandings between individuals of the two cultures are likely to arise because of this difference in custom. When the Eskimo expresses thanks for a gift, it is usually an affectation brought about by acculturation. If he feels gratitude in such a situation, it is usually not indicated by any overt expression. We mention this as an item of interest, not as an implication that such an attitude is necessarily adaptive.

The white man could learn a valuable lesson by observing the ways in which Eskimos avoid conflict in small groups with intense interpersonal contact. This sort of conflict is quick to arise in small groups, especially under dangerous conditions. Eskimos have learned not to disagree with one another openly or to issue orders to one another, qualities which are helpful in the avoidance of conflict. Whites, on the other hand, are notorious for becoming aggressive when small groups are confined for long periods.

We might illustrate this with a couple of examples. In the *umiak* crew, one experienced and active hunter usually takes charge of the boat. He decides where to go (with the aid of discussion among the others) and when to camp or return home. But regarding the actions and movements of other members of the crew, he has little to say. One man seldom tells another what to do. If a young hunter walks out onto the ice in summer without pushing a sled along, those who know better will probably let him shoot a seal and learn for himself how difficult it is to drag the seal home on the ice without a sled. Only in a dangerous situation will comments or hints be made, and even then they are often cryptic and indirect. Minding one's own business reaches extremes on occasion. I once saw two puppies pull an excellent caribou skin down from a cache and rip it to shreds, in full view of several Eskimos. It is better not to interfere in another man's affairs at all than to risk offending him, even in situations like this.

There is one other attitude of the Eskimo which seems to be adapted to his economic life. This is his ability to find genuine humor in misfortunes that befall him, or in his own errors. It is sometimes explicitly stated that a hunter should laugh when things go wrong, because anger never helps, while laughter makes him better able to overcome setbacks. In an environment where so much can go wrong, and it is so easy to lose something that has nearly been gained, such an attitude is almost a necessity. If a hunter has shot a bearded seal, and when the harpoon is tossed it glances off just as the animal sinks, this is an occasion for laughter, not for disgust. The old hunter, Kavik, never tired of telling stories of his exploits, and he would sometimes laugh until tears glistened in his eyes when he told of his greatest and most frustrating mistakes.

The following story is intended to illustrate some of the statements we have made above, especially those relating to the knowledge, ingenuity, and perseverance of the Eskimo. Titaliḳ, who told this story of his own experience, had a long trapline north of Wainwright. One day he came across the tracks of two wolverines that had investigated the bait near a trap but had stayed at a safe distance. The snow was fresh, and they left a clear trail off across the tundra. So Titaliḳ began following them with his dog team, knowing from the tracks that they could not be far ahead.

After a short time the dogs suddenly quickened their pace with excitement. Titaliḳ saw something black outlined against the snow, which he recognized as a wolverine. He took off his mittens and put on a pair of gloves so that he could shoot, but when he looked up again the animal had disappeared. He urged the dogs ahead, and suddenly they stopped, sniffing at a hole leading down into the snow.

After inspecting the hole he decided to try digging the animals out, using the shovel he often carried with him. After a while he dug down through the snow and struck the rock-hard tundra below. A large hole ran deep into the ground, its opening wide enough to admit his head. He could detect nothing inside. He needed a light and a long pole, but he had neither. At this point anyone but an Eskimo would have given up, because certainly there was no way to coax the animal out from its lair. But Titaliḳ was just getting started.

There was no brush or scrap wood around with which he might have probed the hole, but his sled was made from wood, and in his equipment bag he had a hammer. He removed two cross pieces from the upstanders and one long strip of wood from the top edge of the sled. All three were fastened together to make a pole about 15 feet long. He now had something with which to probe the hole.

He lay prone in the opening and slowly thrust the pole deep inside. After some moments it nudged a soft body. A low growl was heard and something snapped at the pole. He poked the animal repeatedly, trying to torment it until it would come out, but it did not move. Finally he went to his sled for his rifle. He had no way of seeing inside the hole, but he could aim along the pole for some indication of where to shoot. After many shots, he could hear the wolverine breathing heavily, and he knew that a bullet had struck it. He shot again, and finally as he lay prone in the opening, he felt the pole begin to push out toward him.

In a flash he jumped away and stood on a small ledge that he had shaped in the snow above the hole. After a few moments the dark head of a wolverine emerged beneath him. He killed it with a single shot. But he did not move yet, because he had an idea of what might happen next. After another wait the dead carcass began to move a bit, and alongside it a second wolverine stuck out its head. He shot this one also.

We have attempted in this chapter to show some of the ways in which Eskimo attitudes or personal qualities are adapted to their environment and economy. This is not meant to show that Eskimo personality is superior to others, except that it indicates better adaptation to particular situations with which others are seldom faced. Also, many examples could be given of deviations from these ideal modes of personality, for as in any culture, these frequently occur. We have discussed here some subjective evaluations of the ideal pattern, and the ways in which it is manifested in actual behavior.

It is felt that these patterns of personality, like many of the techniques and processes which we have described throughout this book, may have parallels in similar ecological situations elsewhere. All these aspects of the Eskimo sea-ice adaptation could be used by members of any culture who might face such conditions anywhere on the earth. After more than a century of "teaching" the Eskimo to live like ourselves, we should now turn about and ask what we may learn from him, as our culture spreads farther and farther over the domain of his ancestors.

CHAPTER 19

The Death of Hunting

T HE SKILLS and knowledge which had developed during the centuries before Eskimos were contacted by white men began to degenerate soon after the first whaling ships sailed these coasts. The processes of culture loss and acculturation which are involved in changes in this aspect of native life are too complex and interrelated to be understood without specific study. But it is undoubtedly true, in recent years at least, that the availability of food and material goods from "outside" is the most important factor.

Since the 1870's Alaskan Eskimos have been able to convert the proceeds of hunting into dollars. The heyday of baleen corset stays and buttons made rich men of many Eskimos until commercial whaling ended about 1915. With the demand for baleen and acceptance of more effective whaling equipment, whale hunting must have enjoyed a temporary florescence before settling into a slow phase of decline which continues today. With money from the sale of whalebone, Eskimos could purchase many of the white man's coveted goods from the traders, among them rifles, ammunition, whiskey, items of food, and other luxuries. Technological change must have proceeded rapidly in this period, but the position of hunting as the subsistence base remained unchanged. Following on the heels of the collapse of commercial whaling was a decade of wealth derived from trapping the Arctic fox. Affluence continued, some trappers bringing in pelts worth $3,000 to $4,000 each year (Chance 1966, p. 16).

Trapping diverted attention from the activities which formerly occupied the midwinter season, but during the first sixty years of contact most kinds of hunting activity continued at or above their aboriginal levels. The last twenty years, on the other hand, have seen a great decline in the importance of hunting. One reason is that after learning to want money, the Eskimos found that it could no longer be obtained through the sale of hunted produce. They were forced to accept wage employment, which partially or totally precluded hunting. With the rifle less effort was required to obtain the same amount of game. This left more time available for pursuit of the new cash economy. And there were some minor contributions to the trend, such as the missionaries' introduction of the Sunday hunting taboo, which is enthusiastically followed to this day. These changes partially explain why the Eskimos began to relax their formerly ambitious quest for game in favor of an increasingly lazy approach to the problem of acquiring their daily fare.

Although these processes started early, the older Eskimos of today still possess a great knowledge of traditional culture and were, in their prime, nearly as skillful as their parents. But their knowledge has been transmitted only in part to their children. There are several reasons for this. First, native social culture and tradition have been severely criticized by outsiders such as whalers, traders, missionaries, and teachers. This censure exterminated some of it and drove the rest underground. The effects of this loss of social culture, which augmented and supported the economic and material culture, were partly responsible. Second, the sons of men who are now old have become unwilling to put forth the effort required to derive complete support from hunting. At the same time they have not acquired all the skills and knowledge which their fathers consider necessary to an expert hunter.

These men, thirty to fifty years old, are content to be only semiproficient hunters, extracting their principal livelihood from hunting, but also requiring considerable cash to purchase canned foods and a wide range of manufactured goods. These "outside" products could easily be had without such extensive loss of native skills, a loss which has been especially heavy with regard to willingness to expend energy and time in hunting.

Although the adults of today are no longer the hunters that their fathers were, they are still proficient and knowledgeable enough to get along quite well in the environment. If it were necessary, they could derive their entire livelihood from hunting, although they would not like it. The greatest change and the heaviest loss of Eskimo culture is not occurring within this middle generation, but in the generation of their children, and to some extent their younger siblings. There are two factors operating in this younger generation that will all but destroy the native economy and will place these men and women in a state of cultural limbo. Most important of these is education. A second factor, child training practices, is closely connected or dependent upon the first.

The youngsters twenty-five years old and under have not had a chance to acquire more than a rudimentary knowledge of Eskimo economic culture. At five or six years of age they begin spending six hours each day in school, and the remainder of their waking hours are occupied by play activities with other children. There is very little communication between adults and children, which is partially a traditional holdover, and almost no opportunity for youngsters to accompany their elders for hunting activities even if the interest on either part were there. So the child spends eight or nine years in school within the village, during which time he acquires little more than a beginning knowledge, and even less interest, in traditional subsistence activities. When the Eskimos lived in mobile camps, children learned at an early age to accept responsibility—to ride the sled, hitch dogs, haul and carry equipment or game. They were able to watch their fathers as they hunted, and to mimic what they saw. Today, some of the young boys probably have not seen their first caribou by the time they become teenagers.

At fourteen to sixteen the Eskimo children finish school or leave the village for four years of high school. Individuals who show any promise leave the village at this time, either to return after four years without the least interest in being an Eskimo, or to find employment "outside." Those who do not go "out" to high school are youths with less intelligence and ability—young men with little or no promise as students and equally limited aptitude for hunting. So consider the eighteen-year-old who returns from the relatively cosmopolitan atmosphere at Mt. Edgecumbe High School in Sitka or Haskell Institute in Kansas. The village still attracts and holds him because it is the friendliest place he knows. But he will not learn to struggle in the cold of the Arctic just for the sake of seals and caribou. He has never acquired a system of values which would make him want or need to hunt, nor the intricate behavior that would enable him to hunt effectively. He is torn irrevocably between two sets of values. He is a cultural hybrid, half white and half Eskimo; but these two halves do not add up to a unified personality. The dilemma hangs over him; he should leave his home village, but he cannot live without it.

The few of them who are willing to put forth some effort to learn the Eskimo hunting ways are promptly set against it because of the sometimes harsh methods of training. Although in former years there was some verbal instruction of youths by older men, there seems to have been a greater emphasis upon practical "on the job" training. This sort of training still persists today. The young hunter accompanies older men on their hunting trips and learns by observing them. If he succeeds in duplicating their actions properly, he is rewarded by silent acceptance. If he should make an error, he is chastised and teased. This ridicule continues beyond that which takes place at the time. The other men are also told of his failings so that they can join in.

The system is very effective, and makes the youth even more determined to succeed under conditions of normal cultural stability. For example, any man who becomes lost or should happen to allow his dog team to run away from him is ridiculed and is considered something of a fool. The fear of such ridicule forces the Eskimo to learn his navigation skills well and to exercise caution whenever he travels. He consciously wishes to escape humiliation due to such errors, and thus, almost unconsciously, corrects his mistakes so that he probably will not face the grave dangers caused by them. Where the stakes are so high, a rigorous training system such as this is extremely effective and adaptive, and assures continuity of the group.

386

Today, the system is the same, but the response is different. In Wainwright there was only one man in this age group who was willing to learn the skills of hunting. There were many others who did not know these skills and were not willing to undergo the tribulations involved in learning them. This is partially due to the methods of training: the physical and psychological difficulties of learning to hunt. The young man must be willing to shrug off continual ridicule and teasing for his errors, and seldom is able to strike a counterblow. The would-be hunters of the past have been required to endure this "hazing" treatment because for them there was no alternative. Today, however, the youth who returns to the village after completing his formal education is, in the first place, not interested, and must, in addition, face the continual frustration of a learner, if he does attempt to hunt. In the past there was no alternative but to undergo the painful process, but today he can leave the village, find a job in the village, or live as an unproductive consumer.

The sadly beneficent government has made it easy for men to live without being self-sufficient. The Wainwright Eskimos are proud of being *Iñupait* ("Real People") but see no loss of pride in accepting monthly welfare checks. Therefore the government and the other villagers support various individuals who do not hunt. In fact, even the most active hunters accept this easy money. Welfare is another factor which is destroying the initiative of even the older hunters, and is aiding in the breakdown of incentive. It is obvious, therefore, that the native economy will die with the passing of the present adult generation.

And along with it the fascinating and impressive body of knowledge which has been developed over these hundreds of generations will be lost. It is fortunate that we realize ahead of time that there is considerable practical value, to say nothing of limitless intrinsic worth, in collecting and preserving this information. But in the next few years we must put forth a maximum effort to live with the people and learn from them whatever we still can, before it is lost forever in the icy graves of the old men.

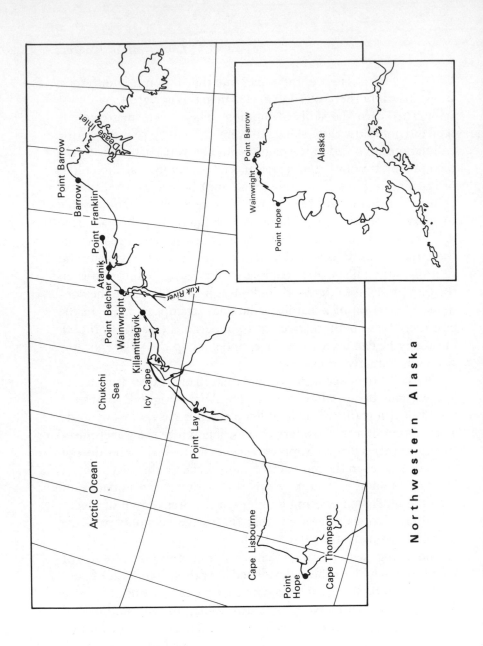

Northwestern Alaska

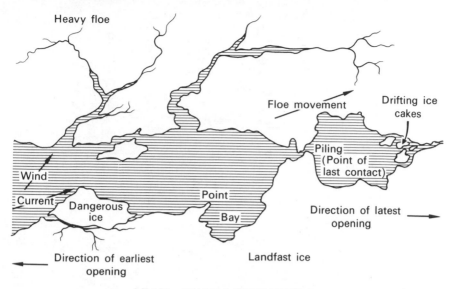

LEAD CHARACTERISTICS

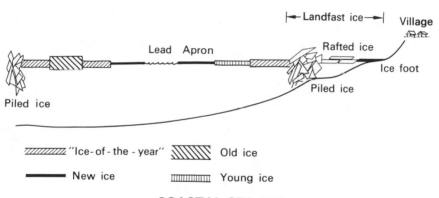

COASTAL SEA ICE

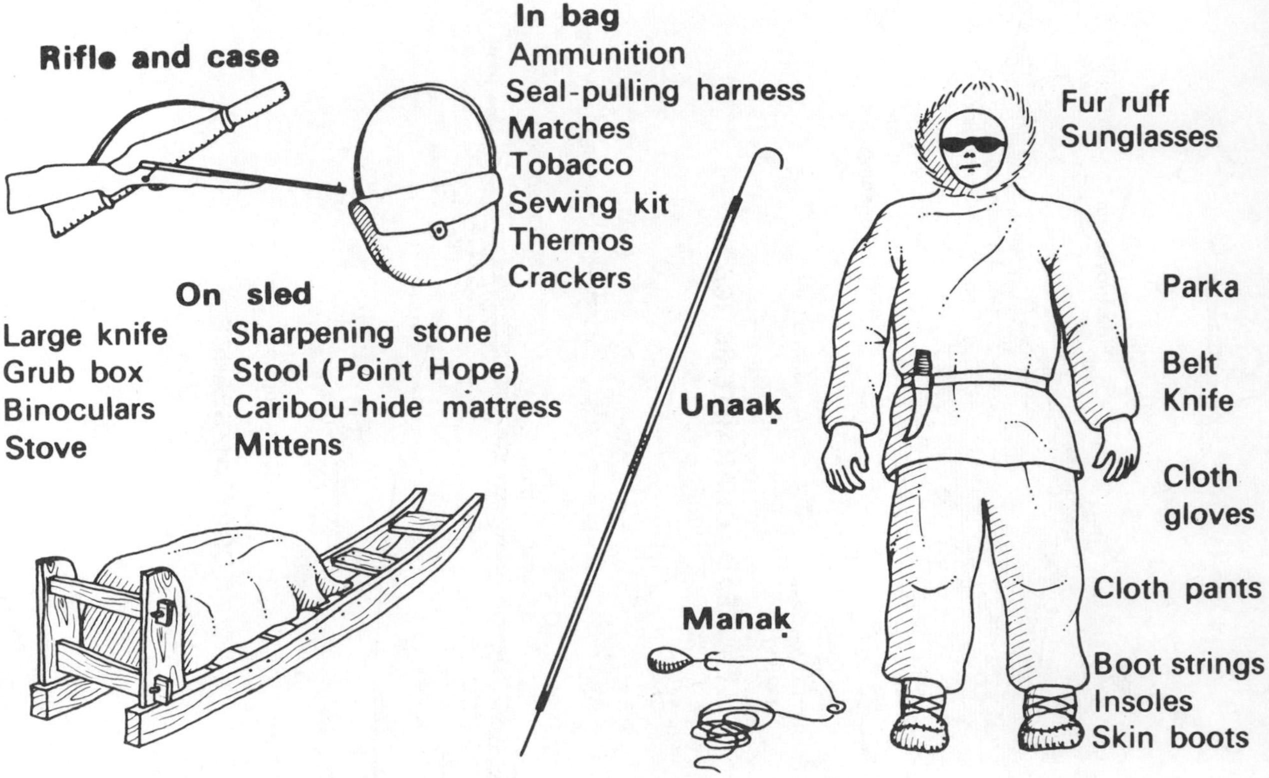

EQUIPMENT FOR SEA ICE HUNTING

Fur ruff
Sunglasses

Parka

Belt
Knife

Cloth
gloves

Cloth pants

Boot strings
Insoles
Skin boots

Unaak

Manak

In bag
Ammunition
Seal-pulling harness
Matches
Tobacco
Sewing kit
Thermos
Crackers

On sled
Sharpening stone
Stool (Point Hope)
Caribou-hide mattress
Mittens

Rifle and case

Large knife
Grub box
Binoculars
Stove

APPENDIX 1

Method of Study

The village of Wainwright, Alaska, was chosen as the principal site of this research for several reasons. First, a fair amount of background information on the region is available in the literature, including one study of Wainwright itself (Milan 1964). Second, sea-ice conditions in this area are excellent for this kind of study. They combine the characteristics of highly mobile coastal floes with those of relatively immobile ice plains found in protected areas and at great distances from the land. The sea ice also remains in this vicinity through much of the summer. And third, the Wainwright Eskimos still depend on proceeds of the hunt for their basic subsistence, and spend a great deal of their time hunting on the sea ice.

Before going into the field, during the summer of 1964, a survey was made of literature dealing with these topics. This provided background knowledge as an aid to fieldwork, and added to the information which was collected fom the Eskimos themselves. This study, entitled "Literature Review of Eskimo Knowledge of the Sea Ice Environment," was published in 1966 by the Arctic Aeromedical Laboratory.

The initial fieldwork was conducted at Wainwright from September, 1964, through April, 1965. Supplementary research was done during several brief periods at Point Barrow, and during the month of May, 1965, at Point Hope. A report on this field study was prepared during the two and one-half months immediately following return from the field. This report, entitled "Alaskan Eskimo Exploitation of the Sea Ice Environment," was also published by the Arctic Aeromedical Laboratory in 1966.

In order to complete the annual cycle, another field study was carried out from June through August, 1966, in Wainwright. A report entitled "Alaskan Eskimo Exploitation of the Summer Sea Ice Environment" was prepared immediately following the fieldwork. These three studies are combined in the present book.

It has been traditional in anthropology since the time of Malinowski (1932) to give an account of the methods used for collecting the information presented in an ethnography. Knowledge of these methods is important to anyone who might wish to assess the accuracy of the data. Because of the specialized nature of this study, certain specialized techniques were employed. These techniques are described in detail below.

In late August, 1964, I was flown into Wainwright. I was alone and knew no one in the village, but was identified in part by Dr. Frederick Milan, who had done ethnographic work there previously. The first problem was settling into the house provided by the Arctic Research Laboratory and, of course, getting acquainted with the villagers. As one would expect, their initial reaction was one of reserve, which gradually gave way to "acceptance" over the weeks and months of my residence. Newcomers and outsiders are regarded with reserve no matter what their business may be in the village, but certain factors can increase or diminish this reaction. School teachers, traders, and missionaries have been visiting North Alaskan villages for many years and have come to be regarded as something "normal." But the resident scientist appears much less frequently, and his motives are more difficult to fathom. Anyone who is continually asking questions appears to be greeted with somewhat more reticence than the "normal" visitor or temporary resident. This is especially true if the questions concern subjects which are considered unimportant or trivial, or are a part of the culture which has disappeared or gone underground. The ethnographer should avoid interrogation of any sort if he possibly can.

The most common questions asked of a newcomer are, "What are you here for?" and "When are you planning to leave?" The latter inquiry is a bit disconcerting at first, but no attempt to hasten the departure is intended. From the very first, I was quite candid and straightforward regarding my purpose in the village, especially since the nature of my interests was fairly easy to comprehend. The topics of this study comprise the Eskimos' proudest possessions, because they still represent his stronghold of superiority over outsiders. Eskimos never tire of talking on these subjects; one need only listen, not interview, in order to gather information. It was not necessary to risk becoming offensive by probing into matters which are regarded as taboo for discussion in the presence of nonnatives.

Language was only of peripheral concern to this research, so it was only possible to make an informal study of it. No concerted attempt was made to learn the Eskimo language conversationally, even if this were possible in such a short residence. The language is important, however, and a fluent understanding of it would greatly augment this or any study of a North Alaskan village. Essentially all the people speak good English and in only a few instances was an interpreter needed. Eskimo is the language used in normal conversation and a great deal of information could be picked up by a person who understands it. I found that an interest in the language, plus the ability to understand and speak certain simple constructions, was more an aid to establishing rapport than to gathering information.

This interest was of particular importance during the brief month of residence at Point Hope (May, 1965), since there was little time to become established there. I was impressed by the fact that a residence of at least several months would be necessary if any real study were to be conducted in a particular village. But several factors besides an elementary comprehension of the Eskimo language were helpful in making the stay at Point Hope a profitable one.

More important than the language was a knowledge of the "way of life." Knowing what to do in social situations and how to travel and hunt without depending upon others is almost an essential. In addition to this understanding of the Eskimo way of living, it was helpful to share mutual acquaintances with the Point Hope people, such as people at Wainwright or Point Barrow who had come from the Point Hope region or had relatives there.

In Point Hope, at times other than those spent out on the ice in whaling camps, the greater portion of effort was put into visiting a few households where the members were particularly friendly and knowledgeable. In this way it was possible to collect a sizeable body of data, since after a few visits there was very little shyness and reserve. For a brief stay such as this it would perhaps be profitable to use paid informants, although this arrangement was not used for any of the present research.

After spending a period of nine months in northwestern Alaska during the winter of 1964–65, I returned to Wainwright for three months during the summer of 1966. At this time I was accompanied by another anthropologist, Mr. G. Ray Bane, who did a parallel study of the exploitation of inland resources. The fact that both of us had spent time in the village previously was a great advantage. Our period of study was to be brief, so it was essential to begin investigations immediately upon arrival in the field. In fact, we were able to borrow a dog team to visit hunting encampments down the coast just one day after arriving. And we could begin our observations without delay, because the people were quite familiar with us and with our interests.

The primary method of data collection throughout this study is based on observation, but observation of a special nature. This is not "participant observation" in the sense that most anthropologists have used the term. It involves much more than living in a community and participating in its daily life only to the extent that one is always there to watch what is going on. This kind of observation without actually becoming involved as a part of the activity or interaction might be termed passive participation.

The present study utilizes a technique which I prefer to call "active" or "full" participation. This means that in order to document techniques of hunting and travel, the ethnographer attempts to learn and master them himself—to participate in them to the fullest possible extent.

When full participation is used to document a technique, such as a method of hunting, the ethnographer must learn to do it himself with at least the minimum proficiency necessary for success. In a sense, then, he observes others and learns from them, but he learns by observing himself as well. In order to carry out any technique of hunting or manufacturing, it is necessary to follow through a sequence of interlocking procedures, the one before usually an essential prerequisite for the one following. Often these procedures can be seen easily, but sometimes they cannot. Those which are "invisible" are likely to be as essential to successful implementation of the technique as are those which are highly visible. However, they can be documented only through the process of their internalization.

Some examples may help to make this clear. The literature on Eskimos is filled with accounts of various techniques of hunting, but rarely are these carried out in such detail that the techniques could be duplicated successfully by persons who had never observed them first-hand. This is because the documenter either has not learned them himself, or if he has, he does not record all the essential "tricks"—the invisible procedures—necessary for their use. Hunting for seals at breathing holes has been recorded in literally hundreds of sources, and to my knowledge not one description is complete enough to permit an inexperienced person to succeed with the technique. Anyone who learns to hunt this way discovers through his own failures and their correction by Eskimo companions what "invisible" procedures he needs to master. This is particularly important in a culture such as that of the Eskimo, where verbal instruction is less important than training by imitation.

What if an ethnographer who had never seen an automobile attempted to document techniques of driving? Certain things about driving a car would be immediately apparent to him: the steering wheel is turned toward the right to negotiate a right turn, the brake is pressed downward to slow the car, the clutch is depressed in order to shift gears. But would he then, after many observations of automobile drivers in action, be able to document the techniques accurately? Would he be able to drive himself? He would not know the subtleties of using the "friction point" of the clutch, or he might send his passenger through the windshield on his first stop.

Experienced automobile drivers know "intuitively" about "friction points," as practiced seal hunters know about the breathing patterns of seals. The difficulties involved in mastering techniques are lessened in our society by the tradition of receiving verbal instruction before first attempting them. This is not true in many cultures, where the learner (and the ethnographer) is normally expected to observe quietly and untutored, then attempt, and finally be corrected after he has made his mistakes. The only way to learn and document fully under these conditions is to learn and participate fully. The ethnographer must get himself "behind the wheel" if he possibly can.

There are other advantages to the method of full participation. While the anthropologist can never become a full-fledged member of a native community, he can do as much as possible to minimize his conspicuousness. This may be an important aid to establishing rapport and assuming a more normal role in the society. For example, how difficult it must be for some native peoples to understand why the anthropologist never "works." Where does he get his food and housing? Rarely, if ever, does he provide these for himself through the means which that society defines as normal. If the ethnographer wishes to participate, he should first of all be willing to do physical work. The Eskimos' evaluation of an outsider increases according to his willingness to live by and accept their pattern of life.

During this study as much time as possible was spent actually hunting and traveling with Eskimos. It was found that repeated experiences with the same techniques and activities were essential in order to approach as nearly as possible the total behavioral repertoire of both the hunter and the animals that he pursues. Many techniques could not be observed in only one or two hunting trips. It must be expected that certain special procedures will be called for only rarely or occasionally. Ideally, the investigator would be in residence for at least two full years, in order to observe each season twice.

Shortly after arriving in Wainwright I purchased a dog team, on the advice of Mr. G. Ray Bane, who had been the B.I.A. school teacher there for three years. It was possible, therefore, to gain a knowledge of dog-training practices and all aspects of dog team use. Without a team, it would be utterly impossible to participate actively in, or to observe, hunting practices on the sea ice during the winter, because this is largely an individual pursuit. It was also possible, by constructing a dog sled and various items such as lines and harnesses, to appreciate more fully the problems and methods involved. By using a dog team, each type of land and sea hunting could be learned, and observations of many individuals could be made during a single day.

In addition to constructing items for use for the dog team, I manufactured a full set of ice hunting gear, including a kayak. This was done with assistance from various individuals, in the house furnished by the Arctic Research Laboratory, which served well as a workshop. While I worked on such equipment, or assisted others on similar projects, considerable information was obtained not only regarding the construction of native implements, but also on a wide range of additional subjects. An overt attempt was made to be self-sufficient in all aspects of residence in the village, to live as close as possible to the local pattern. This involved hunting and traveling, constructing equipment, procuring food and water, learning skills of food preparation, wearing native clothing made by women in the village, visiting, and being visited.

Because these studies were based on first-hand observation and participation, there was little emphasis on interview. No use whatsoever was made of paid informants, because for the topics being investigated it was unnecessary and would probably have detracted from the other methods of study. Interviews, if they can be called that, consisted of informal conversations during visits to other households, while entertaining visitors, or while actually hunting or traveling. Living alone offered the advantage of being able to work and visit in uninterrupted sessions, and having privacy for note taking. Notes were written as soon as possible after hunting trips or fruitful conversations, and never while in the presence of informants.

During the summer I was a member of one of the regular hunting crews. This offered the advantage of being able to follow the normal Eskimo pattern in summer maritime hunting, of going along every time the crew hunted, and of learning exactly what was expected of a normal crew member as regards obligations and reciprocity within the group. There was a singular disadvantage in that I was exposed to a smaller sample of hunters than if I had skipped from one crew to another each day. This small sample could cause some bias due to individual idiosyncrasies. But the advantages in this case seemed clearly to outweigh the disadvantages. Contact with other crews was frequently possible during hunting activities, which helped to minimize this negative factor.

This brings up the problem of factional alignment. Standard anthropological dogma holds that the duty of the ethnographer is to remain strictly neutral in the community, to affiliate with no single faction within the village, but rather to move between and within them without commitment. The danger in affiliation is that it biases one's information, as we noted above, and it could also alienate some individuals of groups within the society.

There are two sides to every coin, however. Is it not possible that by remaining neutral and assuming a "wishy-washy" position the ethnographer substitutes superficial knowledge of the entire society for understanding in depth of a segment of the group? By spreading himself around without commitments, he does not "belong," in the normal sense, to any group. The ethnographer's choice between these two approaches depends on his own personality, the nature of his research, and his appraisal of which method would be most productive. The same is true of individual associations. Will he make two or three deep friendships or a hundred superficial ones? In the present fieldwork, affiliation was nearly always chosen, because I found it most satisfactory from both a personal and an ethnographic standpoint.

In spite of its advantages for a study of this type, the method of full participation is not an easy one to implement. The task of maintaining oneself by hunting, keeping up a household, and carrying on normal social activities is a full-time job, without having to conduct research in addition. When ethnography is a part of this routine, the task may become almost too much for a person working alone. At times, for example, data must be recorded after returning from several days of exhausting, sleepless travel and hunting at temperatures far below zero. During the summer study, when I shared a house with another anthropologist, Mr. Bane, the problems were decreased considerably by the sharing of household tasks.

Eskimo Sea-Ice Terminology

Because so many of their activities are carried out on the sea ice, Eskimos have elaborated their vocabulary relating to it. There are many separate terms dealing with the various types of ice and ice formations, some of which do not have equivalents in the English language. The writer is not a linguist, and does not speak the Eskimo language. This list is included for its general ethnographic value, though it may not meet the standards for accuracy and completeness set by linguists and ethnoscientists.

Ice Age or Thickness

Imak̲: water.

Taġeok: salt water.

Teshak: salt-water lagoon.

Uguruġiizak̲: grease ice; the earliest stage of freezing, causes wind ripples to disappear from patches of the water surface.

Mauɬlik: slush ice or ice rind; heavy development of grease ice, almost to the point of being nilas.

Isiġoaŋazuk̲: slush ice or ice rind; similar in meaning to the preceding term.

Pogazak: slush or mush ice formed by grinding along the edges of ice pans, floes, or cracks.

Mogazak: similar in meaning to the preceding term.

Iginik: similar in meaning to the preceding terms, except ice may be solidly frozen. Eskimos sometimes refer to this as "file ice," because it is formed by the ice "filing" itself.

Migalik: pancake ice; circular pieces of young ice, 1 to 6 feet in diameter, with raised rims; the shape and appearance result from rotation and collision with other cakes.

398

Puktełlhaḳ: similar in meaning to the preceding term.
Saloġoḳ: nilas, or black young ice; a thin flexible sheet of newly formed ice which will not support a man, is weak enough to enable seals to break through it with their heads to breathe, and breaks through with one firm thrust of the *unaaḳ*.
Sikuliwzaḳ: similiar in meaning to the preceding term.
Sikuliaḳ maptizoaḳ: gray young ice; young ice which rides high enough in the water to be grayish in color, and has become thick enough to support a man. Seals probably cannot break through ice of this thickness, but open breathing holes by scratching and gnawing. One firm thrust of the *unaaḳ*, or ice tester, will not break through ice of this thickness.
Sikuliaġezoaḳ: heavy or thick young ice; according to the Eskimo informant this is ice about 1 foot thick.
Sikuliaḳ: young ice; general term including all ice which is newly formed, from the time it becomes a cohesive mass until it has been modified by piling or rafting. This is a rather abstract term because it is used to refer to so wide a range of ice thickness.
Toḳaviñeḳ siku: winter ice; probably refers to ice which is about 5 feet thick, has not been modified by piling, and is still in its first season of growth.
Utoḳaġaviñeḳ siku: "old ice"; probably refers to polar ice; ice which has not melted during one or more summers and has become fresh. This type of ice differs from winter ice in its topography, its dark-blue coloration, its thickness and height above the sea surface, and its occurrence along the northwest Alaskan coast.
Paḳaliaḳ: polar ice; synonymous with the preceding term.
Aaḳaŋa siku: "mother ice"; heavy floe ice; probably a general term for the Arctic ice pack.
Ataŋan: synonymous with the preceding term.
Aumŋazuḳ: rotten ice.

Various Conditions and States of Ice Movement

Aulaalwichoḳ: literally, "no motion"; the sea ice is not moving.
Igiliktaḳ: the sea ice is moving.
Sunmuktuḳtuḳ: the ice is being carried away from the land.
Nunamuktuḳtuḳ: the ice is coming in toward the land.
Tuwagaatigut siku: the floe ice "comes ashore" and becomes attached to the landfast ice.
Tuwayagaatigut siku: the floe ice breaks away fom the landfast ice.

Siku sukumitkaksigaa: the sea ice is breaking up.

Eyecheḳtoḳ: opening crack.

Eyecheḳtaktoḳ: a crack which is pulsating or opening and closing.

Apuktaḳ: ice coming together or hitting together; probably refers to the convergence of large floes.

Kaloaġasitoḳ: the process of rafting, where one layer of ice is thrust over another, forming two thicknesses of ice.

Ivuzuḳ: the process of ice piling.

Ivoaḳsizuḳ: the condition of ice which is about to begin piling.

Ivaluḳtaktoḳ: the noise of piling ice.

Agiaktoḳ: shear or parallel crack movement, such as would commonly occur when an ice floe is drifting parallel to the edge of the landfast ice.

Ikolivsaaḳ: a floe or floeberg which is grounded firmly.

Sea-Ice Topography

Ḳupaḳ: a crack in sea ice.

Ḳupaġaluuzaḳ: a small crack in sea ice.

Ḳupaḳpak: a large crack in sea ice.

Ḳupasuguzuḳ: similar in meaning to the preceding term.

Ḳupaġazoak: similar in meaning to the preceding terms.

Nutaḳ ḳupaḳ: a newly formed crack.

Imaḳ ḳupaḳ: a crack with open water in it.

Sikuichaḳ ḳupaḳ: a crack without ice (with open water) in it.

Ḳupaḳ aputilik: a crack with snow blown over it.

Putu: a hole in the ice.

Imauraḳ: a small polynya or open spot in the sea ice.

Imaḳpak: a large polynya or open spot in the sea ice.

Ḳilligisiñeḳ: shore lead; open water along the coast between the beach and the ice offshore; formed in the spring and summer.

Imaḳtinik: a freshwater puddle on sea ice; formed during spring and summer.

Ivuuk: a pressure crack which has folded or "buckled" downward, the resultant basin having filled with water.

Uiñeḳ: and open lead; refers to a wide lane of open water, usually between the landfast ice and pack ice, from 50 yards to several miles wide.

Ḳaŋeĺĺuk: a bay or bight along the edge of a lead; also refers to the water on either side of a point along the lead edge.

Nuwuk: a point, either in the sea ice along a lead or on the land.

Tuwak: landfast ice; an expanse of ice which parallels the coast, extending outward for one-half mile to several miles, held stationary by large piles of ice within it which are grounded solidly on the bottom.

Kukuluginik: a crack or pressure area where the ice has buckled" upward to form a "roof" with open space beneath. The water underneath soon freezes, but such places are favored by seals for breathing holes, or if the formation is large, for dens where seals rest and give birth to young.

Tuhuzuginik: young ice which has been subjected to pressure and has "wrinkled" or formed undulations in its surface, leaving open spaces beneath. Also favored for seal breathing holes and dens.

Pikunik: similar in meaning to the preceding term.

Kaigechuk: rough ice.

Kayagalaak: rough ice; probably refers to large areas with rough ice caused by crushing of the edges of ice pans and floes.

Sikukazzaak: a piece or block of ice; probably refers to a large conspicuous piece.

Napaiuk: one large piece of ice which has been pushed up vertically to form a conspicuous landmark.

Ivunnik napaizoak: similar in meaning to the preceding term, but refers specifically to an unusually large vertical block, perhaps 20 to 30 feet high.

Napasalik: rough ice area which consists largely of pieces of ice which have been pushed into a vertical position.

Ivuunik: ice pile, ridge, or hummock.

Ivunnigich: rough ice; implies an area with many ice piles. Plural form of the preceding term.

Ivunikpak: a large ice pile or ridge.

Agayagnik: "file ice"; flat walls of ice, from 1 foot to 30 feet high, caused by ice piling followed by shear (parallel) movement along the ice pile. This creates a very steep vertical wall of ice which has been planed off by abrasion of ice surfaces. May indicate the edge of landfast ice, because such parallel movement often takes place there.

Agaipak: similar in meaning to the preceding term.

Agaiupak: similar in maning to the preceding terms.

Agaiupakpak: an unusually large "file ice" wall, 10 or more feet high.

Agaiupaurak: a small "file ice" wall, less than 2 feet high.

Kalagsinik: rafting of young ice which is too thin to support a man, but which becomes safe wherever it has rafted and doubled its thickness.

Ivuunik̦ k̦alligaich: areas where the ice has rafted; one layer of ice is thrust up over another.

K̦aiak̦suak: flat area in sea ice; may be surrounded by rough ice, forming an "island" of flat ice, or may be a huge flat expanse; general term.

K̦aiak̦suakpak: a very large area of flat ice.

K̦aiak̦suzak̦: a small area of flat ice.

K̦aimuguk̦: a flat "ice foot" along the beach, created by building up of ice from the splashing of storm waves. (Differs from the tidal ice foot which is formed along cliffs in the eastern Arctic.)

Ateg̊inèg̊ak̦: "ice apron" or fringe of young ice built out by freezing from the edge of open leads; important for travel while hunting because it is smooth.

Anag̊alu: an ice pile which has sand, stones, and other bottom debris incorporated into it, because it has been forced solidly into the bottom by ice piling and later being carried back to the surface.

Alliviñek̦: a piece of sea ice which rises to the ocean surface after having been buried and held in the bottom by earlier ice piling. This happens during the spring and summer.

Kisissak̦: a large grounded ice pile or floeberg; may become frozen into the new ice in the fall.

Aulaylik: a large floe or floeberg, of sufficient size that current prevails over wind in determining its direction of movement.

Puktaak̦: an ice pan or floe which is sufficiently small so that wind prevails over current in determining its direction of movement.

Kaŋattaak̦: a ledge of ice overhanging the edge of an open pond or lead; caused by undercutting by warm currents and waves during the summer.

Itcheak̦: a shelf of ice extending outward from the edge of an ice floe or pan beneath the water surface; probably caused by erosion of the ice above the water.

Phenomena Related to Sea Ice and Its Movement

Kissuk: water sky; reflection of the dark color of open water in the clouds.

Puguzoak̦: "steam fog"; steam which rises from the water surface of cracks and leads during cold weather.

Iññipk̦ak̦: a refraction phenomenon or mirage, which causes the ice, water or land surface that is over the horizon to "loom" above it; usually appears as a white curtain along the horizon, resembling low clouds or a fog bank.

Kanik: frost crystals which form on young ice as soon as it begins to develop. Scattered frost crystals become more and more dense as the ice thickens until, on gray young ice, they completely cover the surface.

Masaᴧhok̞: moisture on young ice, which causes slush to form in footprints or sled tracks.

Mafshaak̞: an open hole or crack which has been covered by storm-blown snow; open water lies beneath the snow, creating a dangerous condition for ice travelers.

Piḷag̣ag̣nik̞: a sinuous line of ripples or wavelets which forms on the ocean surface; probably caused by the meeting of two differently flowing currents.

Terms for Wind Directions

K̞ysenegek̞: south wind.
Uŋŋalak̞: southwest wind.
Kanagnak: west wind.
Ikagnak: north wind.
Nigik̞: northeast wind.
Nigik̞pak: similar in meaning to the preceding term.
Kiloag̣nak: east wind.

APPENDIX 3

Climatic Information

Temperature

The dominant feature of the Arctic environment is its climatic extremes, and the most important aspect of this climate is the temperature. The region with which we are concerned here, coastal settlements and the sea ice, is one of marked maritime influence. Temperatures are therefore warmer in the winter than are those characteristic of inland stations considerably farther south, but they are also much cooler during the summer.

The degree of maritime influence on the temperature regime varies considerably during the winter according to local sea-ice conditions. In areas of slight ice motion the climate is apparently more continental, with more intense cold than areas where the ice opens and moves frequently throughout the cold season.

> The vast ice layer covering the Arctic Ocean in wintertime has a pronounced effect on the climate of the Arctic Drainage Division [which includes northwest Alaska], particularly on that portion which lies north of the Brooks Range. After ice becomes fast to the shoreline and the open water virtually disappears for the winter season, the maritime influences are greatly diminished . . . some heat appears to escape through the ice covered surface to prevent low temperatures from reaching the extremely cold readings realized over the mainland of the Interior Basin [U.S., Department of Commerce 1959, p. 7].

The mean annual temperature at Wainwright is 11.7° F, which is comparable to the mean for the coldest month in Wisconsin. The highest recorded temperature at this station is 78°, and the lowest is −51°. During the winter of 1964–65 this temperature was equaled twice (unofficial), and during the preceding winter an unofficial low of −57° was recorded at Wainwright. These temperature statistics compare fairly closely with those for neighboring stations north and south along the Alaskan Arctic Coast. Annual mean temperatures are: Point Hope 18.7° F, Point Lay 13.3°, Point Barrow 10.1°, and Barter Island 10.6° (U.S., Department of Commerce 1963, pp. 26–27).

The following chart is intended to give an idea of the average and extreme temperatures at Wainwright. Temperatures listed are in degrees Farenheit (U.S., Department of Commerce 1964, pp. 27, 29).

TABLE 1

MEAN TEMPERATURES AT WAINWRIGHT

Month	Mean Temp.	Mean Min. Temp.	Mean Max. Temp.
January	−16.4	−22.3	−10.4
February	−17.9	−23.7	−12.2
March	−13.6	−20.0	− 7.2
April	1.7	− 5.7	9.1
May	20.5	15.4	25.6
June	36.2	31.1	41.3
July	43.6	37.2	50.0
August	42.0	36.9	47.0
September	31.9	28.1	35.7
October	20.1	15.6	24.5
November	3.8	1.5	9.1
December	−11.5	−17.1	− 5.9
Annual	11.7	6.2	17.2

During the winter of 1964–65 the temperatures at Wainwright were exceptionally cold, particularly during December, January, and February. Temperatures for these three months averaged 10° or more below the normal mean, which in some ways made conditions for this study more favorable. Owing to the cold temperatures, which held at −25° to −40° F for weeks at a time, there was more opportunity to observe cold-weather precautions and techniques. In addition there was a fairly high number of stormy days, when heavy winds increased the effects of cold temperatures and created other problems for outdoor activities.

We should mention here that the Arctic, though the temperatures do not reach extremes of cold, winds make the climate infinitely more severe than that of the calm inland regions. Thus temperature "equivalents," i.e., the temperature equivalent under calm conditions, reach the −90° to −120° range rather frequently (according to Air Force USARAL Chart 20–12, June 11, 1964, #4636–64). In these great flat expanses of tundra and ice the winds of the all too frequent storms blow unobstructed for hundreds of miles, but the Eskimos must travel and hunt in spite of them.

Summer temperatures are heavily affected by the maritime influence, which varies according to the distance inland from the coast. The Arctic Ocean does a great deal to cool the air along the coastal strip at this season, especially when the sea ice still remains. Temperatures are also influenced by the higher frequency of fog and clouds near the coast. The inland regions seem to be favored by clear skies and warm temperatures in the summer. This is especially true in areas 20 or more miles from the sea. The sky over the ocean is not nearly so clear, and it appears that the coastal strip, where inland and ocean air meet, is the most cloudy of all (Stefansson 1950, pp. 56–57). Thus Wainwright and the other coastal villages have a subdued daily and seasonal variation in their temperature regime. This is augmented by twenty-four-hour sunlight during most of the three summer months.

Wind

To the northwest Alaskan Eskimo, the weather is controlled by the winds. When he is forecasting the weather, he is forecasting the wind, not the precipitation, clouds, or temperatures. These are seen as secondary effects brought about by the wind. As we have seen, the wind also determines the ability of Eskimos to hunt and travel, it influences the movement of the ice pack, and it can regulate the habits and occurrence of game animals. The winds of the Arctic are both the friend and the enemy of the Eskimo, depending on their occurrence, direction, and strength.

At Barrow a maximum wind speed of 100 m.p.h. was recorded during the month of January. "Winds of 50 to 60 m.p.h. along this coastal area are not uncommon; and wind speeds of better than 70 m.p.h. have been experienced in February, March, and November at Barter Island with an extreme speed of 86 m.p.h. recorded in February" (U.S., Department of Commerce 1959, p. 12).

The following table illustrates the average wind speed and direction at Barrow, Alaska (U.S., Department of Commerce 1959, p. 12).

This table shows that winds in this region are brisk and constant. The most important winds, however, are the violent storms which periodically rake this coast. It is the storms, not the breezes, which affect the Eskimos most profoundly, because when high winds blow not only is it very cold, but the visibility is poor (in winter), the ice moves, the

TABLE 2

Wind Speed and Direction at
Point Barrow, Alaska

Month	Mean Hourly Speed	Direction
January	11.0	ESE
February	11.3	ENE
March	10.9	NE
April	11.5	E
May	11.8	NE
June	11.4	E
July	11.8	SW
August	12.7	E
September	13.7	ENE
October	14.0	NE
November	12.5	NE
December	10.9	ENE
Annual	12.0	NE

sea becomes rough, and game cannot be hunted. Storms have their greatest effect during the winter months when they cause blowing snow and dangerously cold temperatures. Thus it takes considerably less wind to cause discomfort and greatly alter activities at this time than during the summer. However, the most powerful storms usually occur in the wintertime.

From November, 1964, through March, 1965, there were 25 "storms" at Wainwright, Alaska; that is, 25 periods of one day or more with estimated winds of 20 m.p.h. or greater. At these times visibility was obstructed by blowing snow. Winter storms are often spaced through the month so there were several days or a week of good weather followed by a similar period of storminess. There were 3 storms of six days' duration and 10 storms of one day's duration. The rest lasted for intermediate lengths of time. During this five-month winter period there were 13 storms that attained estimated wind speeds of 25 m.p.h. or greater; and several of these reached velocities of 45 to 50 m.p.h.

During the summer of 1966 there were a total of 12 storms recorded, 6 of which lasted for only one day. The total number of days with storm winds during this two and one-half-month period was 25. The data are not complete, however, principally owing to the large amount of time spent away from the village on hunting trips. If they were complete, they would undoubtedly give a lower average number of storm days per month than the average of 11.6 during the winter of 1964–65. During the later period there was a maximum of 17 storm days in the months of January and March, and a minimum of 6 in February.

The following chart lists storm periods, as we have defined them, for the winter of 1964–65 and the summer of 1966. Limitations in the summer record, which were mentioned above, should be kept in mind for this storm table.

TABLE 3

STORM PERIODS AT WAINWRIGHT, ALASKA

Month	Date	Duration (Days)	Direction
November, 1964	12–17	6	E
	19	1	W
	23	1	W
December, 1964	14–16	3	NE
	18	1	NE
	20–21	2	SW
	23–24	2	W
	26	1	NE
	29	1	NE
January, 1965	1–6	6	NE
	9	1	NE
	18–23	6	NE
	25	1	E
	27	1	NE
	29–30	2	NE
February, 1965	1	1	NE
	3	1	NE
	11–12	2	NE
	15–16	2	W
March, 1965	4–7	4	NE
	9–10	2	S
	16–17	2	NE
	20–22	3	NE
	24–26	3	NE
	29–31	3	NE
June, 1966	10	1	NE
	23–25	3	SW
July, 1966	2–4	3	NE
	9	1	SW
	12	1	NE
	15–17	3	S
	21	1	SW
	25	1	NE
August, 1966	1	1	SW
	2–3	2	NE
	5–8	4	N
	10–13	4	NE

Precipitation

During the winter and spring months, when there is fairly solid sea-ice cover a high percentage of the days are clear. The percentage of clear days at Point Barrow runs from 51.1 per cent in March to 9.8 per cent in September, with an annual average of 29.8 per cent. The average percentage of partly cloudy days is 23.6 per cent and of cloudy days is 46.6 per cent. Summer and fall are the cloudiest times of the year in northwest Alaska. At Barrow (which is probably a cloudier station than Wainwright) the mean number of cloudy days is 19 in June, 21 in July, and 25 in August. This gives a total of 65 cloudy days during the ninety-two-day period, with an additional 16 partly cloudy days. This leaves only 11 clear days during the average summer (U.S., Department of Commerce 1959, p. 12). Notes from the summer sea-ice study reveal that similar cloud conditions prevail at Wainwright. From the general weather observations that were made, about 20 per cent of the days were mostly clear, and 30 per cent were completely overcast. The remaining 50 per cent were either partly cloudy all day or alternated between clear and cloudy skies. During some parts of the summer the sun was hidden by clouds or fog for many days in succession.

Although the tundra and sea ice are snow covered for about nine months of the year, the total amount of snowfall is actually quite small. Wainwright averages only 11.7 inches per year, while Barrow receives 26.1 inches annually. The average monthly snowfall at Wainwright during the winter months is slightly over 1 inch. Maximum monthly averages occur during October and November (6.2 and 2.0 inches, respectively), and the minimum snowfalls come during the summer months (0.1 inches in June and August). Although snow falls duing every month of the year, most summer snow is mixed with rain or sleet.

The annual snowfall in northwest Alaska is considerably less than many midwestern cities receive each year. The total annual precipitation is very slight, from 3 to 6 inches per year, which would give the area a distinctly Saharan climate if the temperatures and evaporation rates were higher. As one would expect, most of the rainfall (and a high percentage of the total precipitation) occurs during the summertime. Wainwright averages 0.15 inches in June, 0.82 inches in July, and 1.34 inches in August. There is considerable year-to-year variation (U.S., Department of Commerce 1963, pp. 24, 26).

Bibliography

Adney, Edwin T., and Chapelle, Howard I. 1964. *The bark canoes and skin boats of North America.* Washington, D.C.: Smithsonian Institution.

Bane, G. Ray, n.d. "Environmental exploitation by the Eskimos of Wainwright, Alaska." Unpublished manuscript.

Beechey, R. W. 1838. *Narrative of a voyage to the Pacific and Beering's Strait to cooperate with the polar expeditions performed in H.M.S. Blossom in the years 1825, 1826, 1827, and 1828.* Philadelphia.

Birket-Smith, Kaj. 1959. *The Eskimos.* London: Methuen and Co.

Boas, Franz. 1964. *The central Eskimo.* Lincoln: University of Nebraska Press. (Originally published in 1888.)

Brower, Charles D. 1963. *Fifty years below zero.* New York: Dodd, Mead and Co.

Burt, William H., and Grossenheider, Richard P. 1959. *A field guide to the mammals.* Boston: Houghton Mifflin Co.

Canadian Committee on Oceanography. n.d. "Proposed amendments to World Meteorological Organization (WMO) ice nomenclature."

Chance, Norman A. 1966. *The Eskimo of North Alaska.* New York: Holt, Rinehart and Winston.

Davies, J. L. 1958. "Pleistocene geography and the distribution of northern pinnipeds." *Ecology* 39 (1): 97–113.

Degerbøl, Magnus, and Freuchen, Peter. 1935. "Mammals." *Report of the Fifth Thule Expedition,* 1921–24, vol. 2, nos. 4 and 5.

Dunbar, Moira. 1960. "Thrust structures in young ice." *Journal of Glaciology,* vol. 3, no. 28.

Ekblaw, Walter E. 1926. "The material response of the polar Eskimo to their far Arctic environment." *Annals of the Association of American Geographers,* vol. 18, no. 4.

Elliot, Henry W. 1885. *Our Arctic province.* New York: Charles Scribners' Sons.

Foote, Don Charles. 1961. *A human geographical study in northwest Alaska.* Cambridge, Mass.: Atomic Energy Commission.

Freuchen, Peter, and Solomonsen, Finn. 1958. *The Arctic year.* New York: G. P. Putnam's Sons.

Howard, Richard A. n.d. *Down in the North*. Arctic, Desert, Tropic Information Center, Air University, Maxwell Air Force Base, Alabama.

Hughes, Charles C. 1960. *An Eskimo village in the modern world*. Ithaca, N.Y.: Cornell University Press.

Jenness, Diamond. 1944. "Grammatical notes on some western Eskimo dialects." *Report of the Canadian Arctic Expedition 1913–18*, vol. 15, part B.

———. 1961. *Dawn in Arctic Alaska*. Minneapolis: University of Minnesota Press.

Joss, William F. 1950. "Sealing—new style." In *The beaver*. Outfit 280, March, 1950.

Kane, Elisa K. 1856. *Arctic explorations*. Philadelphia: Childes and Peterson.

Kessell, B., and Cade T. 1958. "Birds of the Colville River, Northern Alaska." *Biological Papers of the University of Alaska*, no. 2.

Kumlien, L. 1879. "Contributions to the natural history of Arctic America." In *The Howgate Expedition, 1877–78*. Bulletin no. 15 of the United States National Museum.

Lantis, Margaret. 1954. "Problems in human ecology in the North American Arctic." *Arctic*, vol. 7, nos. 3 and 4.

———. 1962. "Present status of the Alaskan Eskimos." In *Science in Alaska*. The Arctic Institute of North America.

Larson, H., and Rainey, F. 1948. "Iputak and the Arctic whale hunting culture." *Anthropological Papers of the American Museum of Natural History*, vol. 42.

Laughlin, William S. 1963. "Eskimos and Aleuts: Their origins and evolution." *Science* 142: 633–45.

———. 1963. "Primitive theory of medicine: Empirical knowledge." In *Man's image in medicine and anthropology*, ed. Iago Gladstone. Institute of Social and Historic Medicine, New York Academy of Medicine, Monograph 4.

———. 1968. "Hunting: An integrating behavior system and its evolutionary importance." In *Man the hunter*, ed. Richard B. Lee and Irven De Vore, pp. 304–20. Chicago: Aldine Publishing Co.

Laughlin, William S., and Reeder, William G. 1961. "Rationale for the collaborative investigation of Aleut-Koniag prehistory and ecology." *Arctic Anthropology*, vol. 1, no. 1.

McLaren, I. A. 1958. *The economics of seals in the eastern Canadian Arctic*. Ottawa: Fisheries Research Board of Canada, Circular no. 1.

Malinowski, Bronislaw. 1932. *Argonauts of the Western Pacific*. London: George Routledge and Sons, Ltd.

Manville, R. H., and Young, S. P. 1965. *Distribution of Alaskan mammals*. Bureau of Fisheries and Wildlife, Circular 211. Washington, D.C.: Government Printing Office.

Milan, Fredrick A. 1964. "The acculturation of the contemporary Eskimo of Wainwright, Alaska." *Anthropological Papers of the University of Alaska*, vol. 11, no. 2.

Murdoch, John. 1885. "Natural history." In *Report of the International Polar Expedition to Point Barrow, Alaska*. Washington, D.C.

———. 1892. "Ethnological results of the Point Barrow Expedition." *Ninth Annual Report of the Bureau of American Ethnology*.

———. 1893. "Seal-catching at Point Barrow." *Smithsonian Miscellaneous Collections*, vol. 34.

———. 1898. "Animals known to the Eskimos of northwestern Alaska." *American Naturalist*, vol. 32.

Nelson, Edward W. 1899. "The Eskimo about Bering Strait." *Eighteenth Annual Report of the Bureau of American Ethnology*, part 1.

Nelson, Richard K. 1966a. *Literature review of Eskimo knowledge of the sea ice environment*. Arctic Aeromedical Laboratory, Aerospace Medical Division, Air Force Systems Command, Fort Wainwright, Alaska.

———. 1966b. *Alaskan Eskimo exploitation of the sea ice environment*. Arctic Aeromedical Laboratory, Fort Wainwright, Alaska.

———.n.d. "Alaskan Eskimo exploitation of the summer sea ice environment." Unpublished report submitted to the Arctic Aeromedical Laboratory.

Peterson, Roger Tory. 1961. *A field guide to the western birds*. Boston: Houghton Mifflin Co.

Rainey, Froelich G. 1947. "The whale hunters of Tigara." *Anthropological Papers of the American Museum of Natural History*, vol. 41, part 2.

Rasmussen, Knud. 1941. "Alaskan Eskimo words." *Report of the Fifth Thule Expedition 1921–24*, vol. 3, no. 4.

Ray, Patrick H. 1885. "Ethnographic sketches of the natives of Point Barrow." In *Report of the International Polar Expedition to Point Barrow, Alaska*. Washington, D.C.

Richards, Eva A. 1941. *Arctic mood*. Caldwell, Idaho: The Caxton Printers.

Rodahl, Kaare. 1963. *The last of the few*. New York: Harper and Row.

Scheffer, Victor B. 1958. *Seals, sea lions, and walruses, a review of the Pinnipedia*. Stanford: Stanford University Press.

Scott, R. F. 1951. "Wild-life in the economy of Alaskan natives." *Transactions of the North American Wildlife Conference*, vol. 16.

Simpson, John. 1875. "Observations on the western Eskimo and the country they inhabit. . . ." In *Arctic geography and ethnology*. London: Royal Geographic Society.

Sonnenfeld, J. 1960. "Changes in Eskimo hunting technology: An introduction to implement geography." *Annals of the Association of American Geographers*, vol. 50, no. 2.

Spencer, Robert F. 1959. *The north Alaskan Eskimo, a study in ecology and society*. U.S. Bureau of American Ethnology, Bulletin 171. Washington, D.C.: Government Printing Office.

Steensby, H. P. 1910. "Contributions to the ethnology and anthropogeography of the polar Eskimos." *Meddelelser om Grønland*, vol. 34, no. 7.

Stefansson, Vilhjalmur. 1921. *The friendly Arctic*. New York: Macmillan Co.

———. 1922. *Hunters of the great north*. New York: Harcourt, Brace and Co.

———. 1950. *Arctic manual*. New York: Macmillan Co.

Thornton, Harrison R. 1931. *Among the Eskimos of Wales, Alaska*. Baltimore: Johns Hopkins Press.

Todd, A. L. 1961. *Abandoned*. New York: McGraw-Hill Book Co.

U.S., Department of Agriculture. 1941. *Climate and man*. Year Book of Agriculture. Washington, D.C.: Government Printing Office.

U.S., Department of Commerce, Weather Bureau. 1959. *Climates of the states: Alaska*. Washington, D.C.

———. 1963. *Climatic summary of Alaska—Supplement for 1922 through 1952*.

U.S., Navy, Hydrographic office. 1946. *Ice atlas of the northern hemisphere*. Washington, D.C.

———. 1952. *A functional glossary of sea ice terminology*. Washington, D.C.

Van Stone, James W. 1962. *Point Hope—An Eskimo village in transition*. Seattle: University of Washington Press.

Van Valin, William B. 1944. *Eskimoland speaks*. Caldwell, Idaho: The Caxton Printers.

Vibe, Christian. 1950. "The marine mammals and the marine fauna in the Thule District." *Meddelelser om Grønland*, vol. 150, no. 6.

Weyer, Edward M. 1862. *The Eskimos*. Hamden, Conn.: Shoe String Press.

Weather Information Bureau. 1943. *Climatic atlas for Alaska*. Headquarters Army-Air Force.

Wilkinson, Doug. 1955. *Land of the long day*. Toronto: Clark, Irwin, and Co.

Zubov, Nikolai N. n.d. *Arctic ice*. U.S. Navy Hydrographic Office and American Meteorological Society, Translators. U.S. Navy Electronics Laboratory.

Index